RIVE
E

THE RIVER COTTAGE COOKBOOK

HUGH FEARNLEY-WHITTINGSTALL

PHOTOGRAPHY BY SIMON WHEELER

for Marie and Oscar,
my favorite recipe testers

with very special thanks to the River Cottage home team:
Frank, Maureen, and Richard E.

Ten Speed Press
PO Box 7123
Berkeley, California 94707
www.tenspeed.com

First published in Great Britain in 2001 by HarperCollins Illustrated, an imprint of HarperCollins Publishers.

Photography by Simon Wheeler

Library of Congress Cataloging-in-Publication Data

Fearnley-Whittingstall, Hugh.
The River Cottage cookbook / by Hugh Fearnley-Whittingstall; photography by Simon Wheeler.
p. cm.
Originally published: London: HarperCollins Illustrated, 2001.
Includes index.
Summary: "U.S. edition of the best-selling British cookbook featuring techniques and recipes for choosing, preparing, and storing food grown in the garden, butchered from prize animals, or foraged or caught locally, as well as opinions on supporting the environment, vibrant local economies, and resourceful use of plants and animals."—Provided by publisher.
ISBN 978-1-58008-909-8
1. Cookery (Natural foods) 2. Cookery, English. 3. River Cottage (Television program) I. Title.
TX741.F425 2008
641.5942—dc22
2007043795

Printed in Thailand
First printing in 2008

1 2 3 4 5 6 7 8 9 10 — 12 11 10 09 08

Hugh's acknowledgments

Huge thanks to the following for all their help and encouragement with River Cottage the book, River Cottage the television program, and River Cottage the life experience:

Simon Wheeler, Richard Atkinson, Clare Baggaley, Jane Middleton, Polly Powell, Matt Bourne, Antony Topping, Carol Heaton, Richard Ellingham, Andrew Palmer, Zammy Baring, Nick Powell, Ben Frow, Liz Warner, Karen Brown, Will Anderson, Alethea Palmer, Caroline Bottomley, Jane Stephenson, Hattie Ellis, Sue Dulay, Havana Marking, Richard Huddlestone, Joanna Nodwell, Sean Geraghty, Gary John Hughes, Billy Paulette, Melanie Jappy, Coll McDonnell, Geoff Craig, Rosie Taylor, Richard Hill, Godfrey Kirby, Patrick Acum, Portia Dean, Cherie Marshall, Dagmar Vesely, Frank, Nicola, Ginny, and Tom Greenway, Maureen and Phil Diplock, Antony and Sczerina Hichens, William, Penny, and Laura Knapman, Michael and Joy Michaud, Roy and Barbara Gunning, Peggy Darvill, Mike Bennet, Ray Smith, Victor Borg, Paddy Rudd, Maureen Rudd, John Aplin, Angus and Jane Carmichael, Washingpool Farm, Bridport Farmers' Market, Frampton & Sons, Snell's, Jack Woolmington, Andrew Wallace, Pots and Ivan Samarine, Charlie and Lucy Taylor, and Emily Hill.

BEAMINSTER SUMMER SHOW

15th August 1998

THIRD PRIZ

Six (6) Different Vegetables One Each

EXHIBITOR

contents

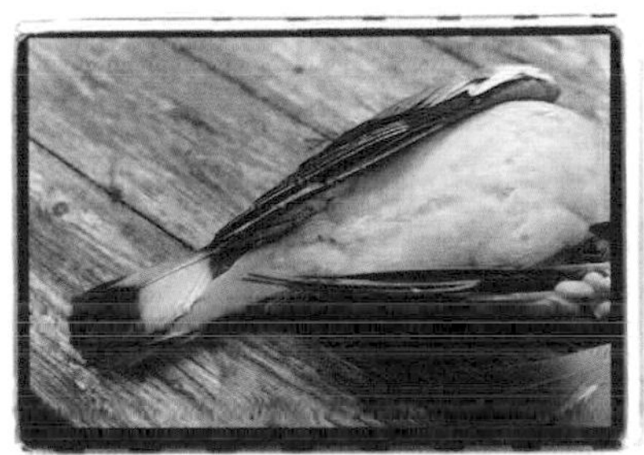

introduction

There are two reasons why you may want to buy this book. The first is more or less selfish, because the main aim here is simply to help you enjoy your life more – your life with food, that is. We all know that, on occasion, food can be the source of tremendous pleasure. My question is, why is it ever not? Since food is something that all of us have to deal with several times a day, it would be a shame to miss out on such regular opportunities to achieve, at least, satisfaction (the minimum aim of every mealtime), at most, outright joy. One of the most satisfying things about my life at River Cottage is that I've hardly ever had a bad meal here. Of course I've burned things, put too much salt in things, and otherwise messed up once in a while. But I never have that experience that used to seem all too common, where I find myself thinking, "Why am I eating this rubbish?"

I hope this book will help you to maximize the amount of pleasure you get from food and minimize, or even eliminate, the rubbish.

The second reason is more political. This book is written with a strong awareness that our current food production system leaves a great deal to be desired. Most of the meat we eat comes from industrially farmed animals that lead miserable lives and are fed on inappropriate diets. It is neither as tasty nor as healthy as it should be. Many of the fruits and vegetables we consume are the products of intensive agriculture that pollutes the land we live on and leaves unnecessary residues on and in the produce. I don't like that, and I know more and more people who feel the same way. This book is therefore also aimed at helping those who care about such issues make more informed choices. It's political, because if there are enough of us we can start to change the way things are done.

With that in mind, and before you start using this book as the practical guide it is intended to be, I want to encourage you to challenge the most basic assumptions about where your food comes from. I think it's fair to assume that most of the food most of us eat every day comes directly from, in the broadest sense, "the shops." Whether we are currently among the minority of conscientious consumers who have a favorite butcher, baker, grocer, deli, fishmonger, etc., and pick and choose our produce with a keen eye for quality and value, or whether, along with the majority, we simply wheel a shopping cart up and down the aisles of the nearest supermarket giant once or twice a week, heaving in whatever is convenient and familiar, we are all by and large dependent on third-party producers to grow and raise our food, and third-party retailers to sell it to us. It is the biggest of those retailers, the aforementioned supermarket giants, who make the biggest profit out of food, and who exercise the most power. By and large, they tell us what to eat, and they tell our farmers how they should be producing it. Is there anything we can do to change that? To have some things, at least, the way we want them, and not let them have everything their way? Amazingly, the answer is yes.

We can effect change because we still have a choice. And in truth that choice is far broader than most of us ever realize. Because, in fact, in terms of the way we purchase or acquire our food, each household or family unit operates somewhere on a "food acquisition continuum" (a phrase I've just invented) from, at one end (the far right if you like), total dependence on the industrial food retailers to, at the other (far left) end, total self-sufficiency. Incidentally, outside our own culture, in developing nations, there are still groups of people, aboriginals mostly, who operate even further left on the continuum – subsisting entirely on uncultivated wild food. That's not a serious option for us, but we do have opportunities to make wild food at least a small part of our diet.

Of course, the vast majority of Westerners occupy a place on the continuum very close to the far right. And probably only a handful of households in the entire country could claim to be truly self-sufficient. Nevertheless, that continuum really does exist, and all of us have the choice to move ourselves along it, in either direction. My contention is that any thoughtfully executed move from right to left, however small, is a move in the right direction. It will bring benefits to the individual, in body and soul, benefits to the community, in spirit and commerce, and benefits to the land and those who farm it, in a more direct and profitable relationship with the end consumer. In fact, the only people who may not benefit are the industrial food producers and retailers. But as far as I'm concerned, they've had it their way long enough.

So how do you move? Well, that's what the rest of this book is all about. It is deliberately structured to reflect the idea of the continuum, and to help readers find their place on it – both where they are now and where they'd like to be. The four sections represent the four major sources of food for me at River Cottage. Within each section there is advice on how to acquire your ingredients as close as possible to the source – either by producing them yourself or by going more directly to those who do the job in the way you would like it done (in the case of the Hedgerow section, that's Mother Nature). Overall, I will be encouraging you to be less dependent on industrially produced food; to support local small-scale producers of quality meat, fruit, and veggies; to support farmers' markets and other local food initiatives; to deal directly with farmers and growers. I will go on to suggest how you might find the time and space to produce some food of your own, both meat and vegetables. And finally, I will show you how you can take advantage, as often as it suits your lifestyle, of your country's fantastic wild-food pantry.

I am not calling for a mass boycott of supermarkets. I know that's not practical. Instead, I'll offer advice on how to get the best from the supermarkets, and keep the pressure on them to support small producers and independent, quality manufacturers. As a consumer, you have more power than you know.

This book is not meant to end up stopping doors, pressing flowers, or being used as a stepladder to reach the highest shelf. It is a manual, not a tome. I will therefore not attempt to provide a completely comprehensive guide to stock rearing, vegetable growing, or the identification of edible wild plants. Rather, I will try to kindle your enthusiasm for a number of possible projects and provide the essential information to help you get started. And where more detailed knowledge is required for long-term success, I will try to point you in the right direction.

How much of this book you incorporate into your life is up to you. But if all you do is grow a few herbs in a window box, start a compost heap, make nettle soup once a year, or try a free-range goose for Christmas instead of a frozen turkey, you will already, I hope, have gotten your money's worth.

Before I begin the practical part of the book, I think it's only fair to come clean about my own place on the continuum; to try to be honest about the extent to which I practice what I preach. My own life at River Cottage, both on screen and off, is not, as some have apparently taken it to be, a serious attempt at self-sufficiency. But it does represent a very big and very real change in lifestyle for me – a fairly radical shift toward the left of my continuum. And it has brought me much satisfaction and pleasure.

It is not true, as some critics have conjectured, that River Cottage is just a film set. I first rented the cottage, more or less with weekending in mind, two years before we began filming there, and right away I started making space in the garden for vegetables. But when Channel 4 agreed to let me make a series based at the cottage, I couldn't believe my luck. I would actually get to live there something close to full-time. I could keep chickens, raise pigs, and expand my vegetable plot. Before long, the phrase "it sure beats working for a living" sprang regularly to mind. After three series, and the best part of three years down here, I'm enjoying it more than ever. In the summer months, we grow all the vegetables we can eat, with some to spare. And thanks to the deep-freeze, the brine tub, and the smoker, I have enough home-reared meat to last all year round (I reckon that two pigs, two lambs, and a beef steer will put meat on the table about five times a week for a family of four). There's an abundance of wild greens in the spring and of wild fruits and nuts in the late summer and autumn. I can't remember the last time I went to a supermarket, but it was probably to buy diapers, toilet paper, and dishwashing soap.

I still spend time in London, and when I'm there I eat too many sandwiches and too much chocolate. The café near our production office does great bacon sandwiches, but I worry about the provenance of the pigs that provide the filling. On the other hand, I *never* go to McDonald's. But I do eat Walkers cheese and onion crisps several times a week. I think I should boycott Nestlé because of their powdered milk scam (a disgrace) in the developing world, but I can't resist a Toblerone. I'm in no doubt that I am inadvertently a hypocrite on a weekly if not daily basis. I feel guilty about that. But I forgive myself, as deep down I know I really care.

The honest truth is that total self-sufficiency is not a real ambition of mine. There are simply too many things, from oranges and bananas to chocolate and good claret, that I will always need to dip into my wallet to acquire. But true happiness and contentment around food and in the kitchen is a personal goal. I plan, before long, to move full-time to the country to help achieve that. Of course, I make my living not as a "real" small farmer, genuinely dependent on my acres, but as a writer and television presenter. I can afford a few luxuries. But since I moved to River Cottage, my idea of what true luxury is has changed: picking blackberries in the hedgerow in high summer, and trampling the wild garlic in early spring; buying a huge cod from Jack's boat in West Bay for just a few quid; netting eels in the River Brit; committing infanticide on my own baby fava beans; picking elderflowers; bartering eggs for cider – these are my new luxuries. They are luxuries that just about anyone can afford.

The best thing is that changing your ways with food – moving a little to the left, if you like – involves no sacrifice, no hardship or discomfort. Every step of the process should be a pleasure, with tangible rewards. Of course, to make a really big commitment, say, to growing your own vegetables or keeping livestock, one thing you will need to find is time. For many of you, that simply may not be possible. But for many others, it may turn out to be much easier than you think. For example, provided they have space, shade, and a warm bed, a pair of pigs need your attention for just a few minutes twice a day. That little bit of contact is invaluable quality time for the pigs, which will help to keep them happy and healthy. The curious and delightful thing is discovering just how much that time can do for you.

garden

I have been called, in various reviews and interviews, an "unreconstructed carnivore," an "enthusiastic muncher of small furry animals," and a "connoisseur of unmentionable body parts." It's a collection of epithets that might lead you to suppose my gastronomic life is devoted solely to the pleasures of the flesh; that vegetables, fruits, and herbs are an afterthought for me; that were they not useful fodder in the production, or flavoring, of animal protein for my pot, I would hold them in utter contempt.

Anyone who knows me or my work will already realize that this is simply not true. But just to be absolutely clear about this, let me say, right here at the beginning of the book, in capitals: I LOVE VEGETABLES. And I really want you to love them too. That's why the Garden is my section one.

When my family moved from London to a rented farmhouse in Gloucestershire in 1969, we inherited a wonderful vegetable garden in full swing. My first memory of the new house – I think it was the very day of our arrival – is sitting on the lawn eating raw carrots that my father had just pulled from the ground. It was a revelation to me to discover that anyone could grow their vegetables. That we might be able to do it ourselves seemed nothing short of extraordinary, and hugely exciting. Not that I became a seven-year-old expert gardener or anything. It was my father who was irreversibly infected by the vegetable-gardening bug, and his attempts to weave me into the fabric of his new hobby had only limited success. I would happily pick, and I would happily eat while I picked – especially the strawberries and the peas. But as for digging, sowing, weeding – no thanks. I was far too busy climbing trees and racing snails with our neighbors' children to find time for that kind of graft.

Our vegetable garden did, however, help me shrug off the usual childish antipathy to the very idea of vegetables for food. As a treat, a fresh pod of tiny peas, popped open and raked with my thumb straight into my mouth, was right up there with a sherbet Dip Dab. Still is. I enjoyed eating all the vegetables that my father grew and, I think, came to take quality and freshness almost for granted.

Nearly fifteen years later, when I was working as a sous-chef at the River Café in London, my appreciation of vegetables entered a new dimension. Here, the daily consignment of fresh vegetables, fruits, and herbs – for the most part grown by specialists known personally to the chefs – was inspected with as much critical vigor as the meat and fish. And they were prepared and cooked with as much care and attention, too. The philosophy was to explore the infinite range of flavors, aromas, and textures that fresh garden vegetables have to offer. I learned to cook zucchini gently in olive oil to a luscious creamy pulp, which could be lifted to sensational heights with a few torn basil leaves and some Parmesan shavings. I learned to roast whole garlic bulbs and shallots so that their natural sugars were transformed to an almost toffeelike sweetness. And I learned how to mix simple salads of just-picked leaves that allowed the natural spiciness of arugula or the mild, metallic tang of baby spinach to speak for itself.

I soon came to realize that vegetables – and their vegetative relatives, herbs and fruits – are without a doubt the cook's greatest asset. And now I firmly believe that any cook who thinks that vegetables are the least interesting part of a meal, a bore to prepare, and a mere adjunct to meat or fish is missing the point. As far as I'm concerned, vegetables are staple, central, the main thing. Failure to realize this is the root cause of much dissatisfaction in the kitchen. And embracing the notion will do much to improve your life with food.

When I first arrived at River Cottage, my passion for vegetables was well entrenched, and although I was excited at the prospect of rearing livestock for meat (the River Café had also revealed to me the joys of meat raised by enthusiasts who really care), it was the creation of a kitchen garden that was my first priority.

I knew from my Gloucestershire days what good gardening looked like, but I had precious little idea how to go about it. I turned to my father for advice. "It's easy," he told me. "You plant stuff in the ground and it grows." I wanted a little more guidance than that. "Look after the soil," he said, "and the soil will look after the plants." That was pretty much all I got, along with some top tips on making a compost heap. Four summers later, as I look out on my little plot, I realize this was a very sound briefing. Despite a repeated lashing from the wind and rain, and some unseasonably cool weather for May, my seedlings have hung in there and are finally starting to respond to the long-overdue sunshine. I've just harvested my first radishes, and the early fava beans are not far behind.

The wisdom of Dad's pithy gardening course lies in the fact that the seeds you plant and the plants you put out really want to grow. You don't have to make them; you just have to let them. There can be setbacks, of course. Occasionally, you have to submit to the tyranny of the weather, and the determination of the natural competition for the edible goodies you are nurturing – particularly the slugs. Losing a whole row of tiny beet plants to a single mollusk can be the cause of a major foot-stomping session. But the chances are you'll get over it by suppertime – especially if the purple sprouting broccoli is still going strong.

I won't pretend you'll get away without having to do a bit of hard work once in a while: the unusually painful form of exercise called "digging" is pretty much a prerequisite for gardening success. But when that's done and the ground is ready for sowing, vegetable gardening becomes the very definition of a worthwhile project: something that matures slowly over time; whose progress is visible and tangible; and whose final rewards fulfill both a basic need – food – and one of life's finest luxuries – good food.

One of the main aims of this section, then, is to encourage those who think they don't have the time, space, or temperament to grow their own vegetables, herbs, and fruits to think again. I don't want to persuade you. I want to tempt you. But if somehow you can resist, or simply can't see a way through the practical obstacles your lifestyle presents, please don't give up on me. I'm writing for you, too. And I hope you will also be tempted, because vegetables acquired in the more conventional manner of the age – from retail merchants of one kind or another – can still bring you a huge amount of pleasure and satisfaction. Apply to your vegetable shopping and cooking just a fraction of the energy and commitment that you think a kitchen garden might demand, and you will reap the rewards.

When you get to the fleshy part of this book, you will find plenty of advice on how to acquire the best meat around, and a clutch of recipes designed to make every scrap of it a pleasure to consume (it so often isn't). But for now, I plan to show you that it is fresh vegetables, fruits, and herbs that hold the key to daily happiness in the kitchen and at the table – as the staple ingredients for family suppers, quick lunches, and even impromptu dinner parties. Keep your pantry constantly filled with a wide variety of them, and not only will you never get hungry, you'll also never get bored.

garden | vegetables

The produce of the kitchen garden is conventionally broken down into three categories: vegetables, fruits, and herbs. This seems natural enough and it will, I think, serve my purposes well in this section. But before I embrace it, I'd like to issue a gentle warning against being overemphatic about these distinctions. For a start, taxonomically they don't always hold water. Admittedly, the pedant who points out that the tomato is really a fruit may be a bit of a bore. But if, inadvertently, he encourages us to be more adventurous in the kitchen we may forgive him. Fruits do not necessarily spell dessert. Herbs do not always demand a savory application. And vegetables most particularly do not have to appear "on the side." Personally, I've never been convinced of the merits of the tomato sorbet. But a good pumpkin pie, on the other hand, . . .

From the cook's point of view, what's on offer in the garden is simply a range of tastes, textures, and aromatics, the potential combination of which is mathematically beyond limit. Once through the kitchen door, matters of classification are generally beside the point. That gooseberries should happen to make an excellent sauce for mackerel, mint a marvelously aromatic companion to strawberries, and apples a long-revered counterpoint to pork are some of the happy coincidences that have come to light over years of experimentation. There is no reason why any adventurous cook should not make new, equally thrilling discoveries.

But vegetables – the things we call vegetables – are different in one important way. I think of fruits and herbs as essential luxuries: joyous ingredients that I would never be without. Whereas vegetables are luxurious essentials: the primary building blocks for most well-constructed meals that I *could* not be without. When vegetables take center stage, even meat may become a spice.

Let me elaborate with some real kitchen examples. When I make a rich tomato sauce for pasta and decide to add some diced and fried smoked bacon (see page 102), it does not become a bacon sauce. It's a tomato sauce enhanced by the smoky flavor of bacon and given a more interesting texture by the little crispy pieces. The meat, as I said, becomes a spice. Even when I make a stew – a dish, you might think, that is practically defined by the central presence of meat – the end product is perhaps best thought of as a delicious sauce to accompany, say, a baked potato. If you think that's pushing it, imagine taking the pieces of cooked meat out of the finished stew, leaving just the gravy, or sauce, and vegetables in the pan. What would you rather have with your baked potato, the meat or the sauce? I would suggest that if the answer is the meat you probably haven't made a very good stew (try the Tagine of Mutton and Apricots on page 251). And what would you rather have on Christmas Day, the turkey or the trimmings? For me, there's no contest.

Luckily, one is not forced to make such agonizing choices. And the real joy of cooking is the alchemy of combining ingredients, be they animal or vegetable in origin, in dishes that become much more than the sum of their parts. But the bottom line is this: I frequently have vegetables without meat, whereas I almost never have meat without vegetables. So how could I possibly relegate vegetables to second place?

While I'm in the business of giving vegetables the hard sell, need I mention health? Everybody knows that vegetables are good for you. Less obvious, but worth thinking about, is my contention that the tastier they are, the better they are for you. It's a bit of a generalization but it is broadly true, in the sense that the cooking practices that retain the most flavor also tend to retain the most goodness. Much of this chapter is devoted to ensuring that the vegetables you eat will be varied, consistently delicious, and exciting. The benefits to your health will come without further discussion, and at no extra charge.

From the shopper's point of view, one of the best reasons for making vegetables the central focus of your culinary exploits is financial. Try going into a good produce market (or, if you must, a supermarket) and buying *only* seasonal fresh vegetables. Fill your basket to the brim, if you like – however much you manage to pile in, I guarantee you a pleasant surprise when you get to the checkout counter. In my experience, you can hardly spend £10 (about $20) on vegetables in season without having a bigger pile of shopping than you can easily carry. Spend £20 (about $40) and you'll need a forklift to get it home.

That vegetables are delicious, cheap, *and* healthy sounds almost too good to be true. Believe me, though, it is true. But this trinity of desirable qualities is fragile. To be upheld, it requires just a little commitment from you, the consumer – a commitment to look for quality, cook well, and eat sympathetically, with a readiness to appreciate subtle tastes and textures. Shop carelessly and boil to oblivion, and your vegetables will no longer be delicious or even healthy. The fact that they remain cheap will just provide an excuse to hold them in further disdain.

You'll never have this problem with vegetables you grow yourself. But before I consider the whole extra paradigm of joy that is available to the vegetable gardener, I have a bit to say about the most common modern method of acquiring vegetables: from retail outlets, in exchange for money.

buying vegetables

Compared to shopping for meat and fish, where quality is so variable and mistakes often so costly, shopping for vegetables is a doddle – provided you really care. Beyond caring, the only basic requirements are a sense of adventure and an eye for freshness. The latter requires no specialist knowledge or training; rather it is a matter of not being lazy. With close inspection, just about anyone can see whether a particular item is good and fresh or past its best. If the zucchini you had in mind turn out to have lost their luster, are a bit squashy at one end or rather bendy in the middle, forget them. Think again.

In other words, unless you have your sights on a particular recipe that binds you to choose certain vital vegetable ingredients, your trip around the produce market should be an open-minded hunt for whatever is best on the day. If the cabbages look better than the broccoli, take the cabbages. And if the January King looks dewier, greener, and crisper than the savoy cabbage you are used to, go for it, even if you've never cooked one before. (It won't bite; it's only a cabbage.)

In almost every case (carefully stored potatoes and carrots being a rare exception), you are simply looking for the specimens that have most recently left their growing site and been subject to the least abuse since then (in terms of exposure to heat, light, and handling). The key word is *vitality*. I prefer it to *freshness* because it expresses a more valid truth about produce: the nearer it is to being alive, the better it is to eat. This is why people who grow their own vegetables soon become expert vegetable shoppers to boot: they know what the things look like when they're still alive.

Indicators of vitality – or the lack of it – are largely common sense. Use your eyes first: in the case of green vegetables and salad leaves, crispness and depth of color are all. Look for browning and yellowing on outer leaves and the edges of leaves. Shun dullness, and avoid wilt like the plague.

Don't be afraid to touch (and if this basic right is denied you by the retailer, remonstrate; if he insists, shop elsewhere). In the case of tomatoes, zucchini, eggplant, peppers, chiles, etc., a bright color is again important, while smooth skin and firmness to the touch indicate a vegetable not long picked. And with all root vegetables, including potatoes, carrots, parsnips, beets, and rutabagas, a cold hardness, with no flabby wrinkles or rubbery bendiness, is what you are feeling for. Use (or excuse) fingers also to assess peas and beans in their pods, green and other pod beans: they, too, should feel cool, stiff, hard, and unwrinkled – almost pumped up (yes, vegetable shopping can be exciting).

Finally, with certain vegetables (as with many fruits), your nose comes into play. Tomatoes, fennel, celeriac, and, of course, most fresh herbs should all have a pleasing smell that forces you to anticipate their flavor. Where necessary (or if making an emergency decision about borderline produce), use your nose as a detector of negative indicators: cabbages shouldn't smell too cabbagey (ironically), and root vegetables should be free of the smell of must or mold. Basically, nice vegetables smell nice, and really nasty ones smell horrid.

These are the salient factors when choosing vegetables. Unfortunately, the powers-that-be would have us believe that other things, like size and shape, matter more. In the U.K., vegetables are marked with labels saying "class I" and "class II." But are these real indicators of quality? Do they imply a lack of chemical residues, a particularly tasty varietal strain, or an item harvested at the peak of its season? The answer is no. From the cook's point of view they are meaningless. They are indicators merely of conformity to certain European standards in size, weight, shape, and "acceptable blemish percentiles" (all right, I made that phrase up, but theirs is probably even worse). Forget about them.

So now that you know what you are looking (and feeling, and sniffing) for, where do you go to find it?

supermarkets

Vegetables are the one example of fresh produce where the range on offer in big supermarkets is often as wide, or even wider, than that generally available in specialized outlets. You might think that's good news, and if you're the kind of cook who enjoys experimenting with exotic fruits and vegetables from far-flung corners of the globe, then it probably is. To their credit, the supermarkets do generally complement their "global village" stocking strategy by providing information about the origins and possible culinary uses of the weird and wonderful vegetables they sell. The fact that these are clearly marketing ploys – nobody is going to buy a vegetable they have no idea how to cook – is no reason to disregard them. But personally I would be more ready to applaud their internationalism if they looked after their domestic suppliers better – and better served those customers who simply want the best of what is seasonal and local.

At a time when most Brits drive Continental cars, watch American programs on Asian-made televisions, and drink Eastern European beer while watching Premiership soccer teams with barely a pair of home-grown legs on the pitch, you might ask, "Does it really matter where our vegetables come from?" Well, it matters to me. Others may not always agree, but one thing I am convinced about is the reliably high quality of most home-produced vegetables – provided they are in season. This is not just patriotism. In Britain, we have a tradition of growing top-quality vegetables that goes back hundreds of years and still survives today. We have a superb soil and climate for growing a fantastic variety of vegetables, and we know how to make the most of it. From the huge market gardens of Kent or the Vale of Evesham, right down to the tiniest city allotment on which a pensioner is trying to grow a record-breaking squash, when it comes to growing vegetables, we British know our onions – and a lot more besides.

Apart from the fact that the British are simply good at growing vegetables, there is the travel factor: British fruit and vegetables destined for British shops do not have far to go. It should therefore be easy for retailers, including supermarkets, to find home-grown vegetables not long picked that have lost none of their goodness and flavor to the stresses of travel and the natural processes of aging.

If quality of produce and the interests of the consumer were their overriding concern, the supermarkets would be bending over backward to fill their aisles with the very best of what is seasonal and locally grown. Unfortunately, it is not, and they are not. Profit is their god, and the high priests of the temple are shelf life, consistency of supply, and uniformity of size and shape, all of which mean that the glasshouses of Holland and the temperate, unchanging climates of Israel, equatorial Africa, and South America tend to serve them better than the gumbooted, weather-wary vegetable farmers of good old Blighty.

The sad result of all this is that while the finest English asparagus may be hurtling skyward in some well-tended market garden on the peninsula of East Anglia in early May, the nearest supermarket could be selling Spanish asparagus cut five days earlier, whose natural sugars will have reverted to mealy, tasteless starch.

On top of that, the central warehousing policy of the supermarket chains means that even those vegetables that are bought from British producers are usually far from local. Or, if they are local, they may be so by virtue of an ironic accident that reroutes them via a warehouse 150 miles away and a forty-eight-hour round trip back to the supermarket that just happens to be a few miles from where they were grown.

The final insult is the way that supermarket buyers deal with their suppliers, both British and foreign. I was horrified to discover from a West Country soft fruit farmer just how pernicious is the system by which he does business with one of the big four supermarkets. When the weather is good and Wimbledon is on the telly, it will take just about all the strawberries he can produce – and pay pretty handsomely for them too. But as soon as the in-store demand wobbles, the supermarket reserves the right to shaft the farmer good and proper. So much so that an order received on a Tuesday can arrive at the warehouse precisely as arranged on a Thursday, only to be turned away. In these circumstances, there is no compensation paid either for the produce or for the travel costs. Even an accepted consignment may not make the profit the farmer was relying on. A price agreed on one day can be altered at will by the supermarkets the next.

The buying clout of the big supermarkets means they can afford to take liberties with their suppliers. But in the economic chain that brings in the megabucks there's one link they can't risk messing with – the consumer. And that brings me to my final thoughts on buying vegetables in the supermarket: if you have to do it (and I know it's ever so handy), then don't forget who's really boss – it's you. If you don't like the way a product is packaged or presented, don't buy it. If you share my enthusiasm for local vegetables, choose them in preference to imported. If you care about buying in season, let your shopping cart do the talking. And if you approve of a new initiative by the supermarket – for example, introducing organic produce – support it enthusiastically with your custom. Vote with your wallet. It's the only language these people understand.

local produce markets

Perhaps more than any other specialist mainstreet retailer, it is the local produce market or grocery store that has found it hardest to survive in the face of the choice and convenience offered by the supermarkets. This isn't a wholesale tragedy for the consumer. The realistic truth is that many "old-style" produce markets simply didn't cut it. They relied on a captive audience of local shoppers who were more willing than they should have been to put up with produce that was distinctly less vital than it should have been. No wonder they went to the wall.

The produce markets that survive today are consequently likely to be happier hunting grounds for the vegetable shopper than their predecessors. This is largely because their owners have realized the commercial potential of upholding precisely those values that the supermarkets have let slide: an understanding of basic seasonality, a commitment to local producers, and, most importantly, a willingness to engage in a dialogue with their regular customers. I am lucky enough to have just such a produce market in my local shopping town of Bridport. It's called Washingpool, it's a family-run concern, and most of the produce it sells is grown on the family's own farm, a few miles outside town. Much of the rest comes from other local growers.

To visit Washingpool on a busy Saturday morning reminds me of exactly what I imagine vegetable shopping used to be like. I see many regular shoppers on first-name terms with the proprietors, quick to offer comment – usually positive but occasionally negative – on the produce: "Any English asparagus in yet? I don't like that Spanish stuff . . ." ". . John says your purple sprouting's the best he's ever had . . ." ". . . These carrots are a bit bendy; anything fresher out the back?"

And it's two-way traffic, too, the knowledgeable staff ever mindful of their regulars' likes and dislikes: "Lovely savoy cabbages in today, Maureen. We picked them this morning . . ." "I'm afraid our leeks are getting a bit end-of-season woody in the middle. We'll have to get some Italian ones in next week . . ." "Those are the first sugar snaps from Michael's polytunnel."

To some that may sound like a bad episode of *The Archers*. But to me it is a reassuring reminder that shopping can still be a community affair, and that in some quarters vegetables are still grown by people with names, to sell to people with names.

food markets

There are few better places to buy decent fruits and vegetables than a good old-fashioned open-air fruit and veggie market. There are also few places more fun to shop. Competition can be literally between neighboring stalls, so that elegant displays of fresh produce piled high in neat rows or towering mounds compete spectacularly for your attention. The visual appeal is often backed up by a rowdy cacophony of vocal advertising, bringing to your attention the bargains of the day – and occasionally less relevant information, such as the fact that a rival stallholder is sporting a "syrup."

Such markets are the happiest of hunting grounds for vegetable enthusiasts: if you don't like the look or the price of the radishes on one stall, you can try another. And if you want to buy in bulk, then you can bargain for a deal on, say, a crate of oranges, a sack of potatoes, or a bag of onions. Sometimes, near-giveaway bargains can be had at the end of the day, while the traders are packing up.

In France, Italy, and Spain practically every provincial town still has its once, twice, or three-times weekly food market. In the U.K., we are not so lucky. With a few notable exceptions, our open-air markets tend to be confined to the major cities. And while the famous London markets of Portobello, Brewer Street, Brixton, and Chapel Market remain excellent places to go shopping for your vegetables (and much more besides), it is a sad fact that the old-fashioned open-air market is in decline.

That's the bad news. The good news is the emergence of a new kind of food market, smaller in scale than the provincial markets of former times, and less regular (often monthly or fortnightly), but nonetheless of considerable interest to those who like their produce fresh and locally grown. I'm talking about farmers' markets, of which more below.

farmers' markets

Farmers' markets are, in a pleasing sense, a revival of the oldest kind of market of all: a few local producers clubbing together to find a location where they can each set up a stall (often no more than a table) on which to sell whatever happens to be seasonal on their farm at the time.[1] For those who like to know where their food comes from, there is simply no better way to shop. Not all stallholders will be selling organic products, but what they are offering will have been raised and nurtured with their own hands. So just ask the man or woman behind the table and they'll tell you everything you could wish to know. And as for freshness – sorry, *vitality* – well, some of the vegetables will still have had their roots in the ground that very morning.

The farmers' market movement has really taken off in the last couple of years. Even so, an assured future for this excellent form of food retailing requires a strong show of support from a committed group of consumers. There is a curious tendency among some would-be shoppers to regard farmers' markets as somehow not serious, or not commercial. They turn up all right; then they wander about having a goo d chat with the

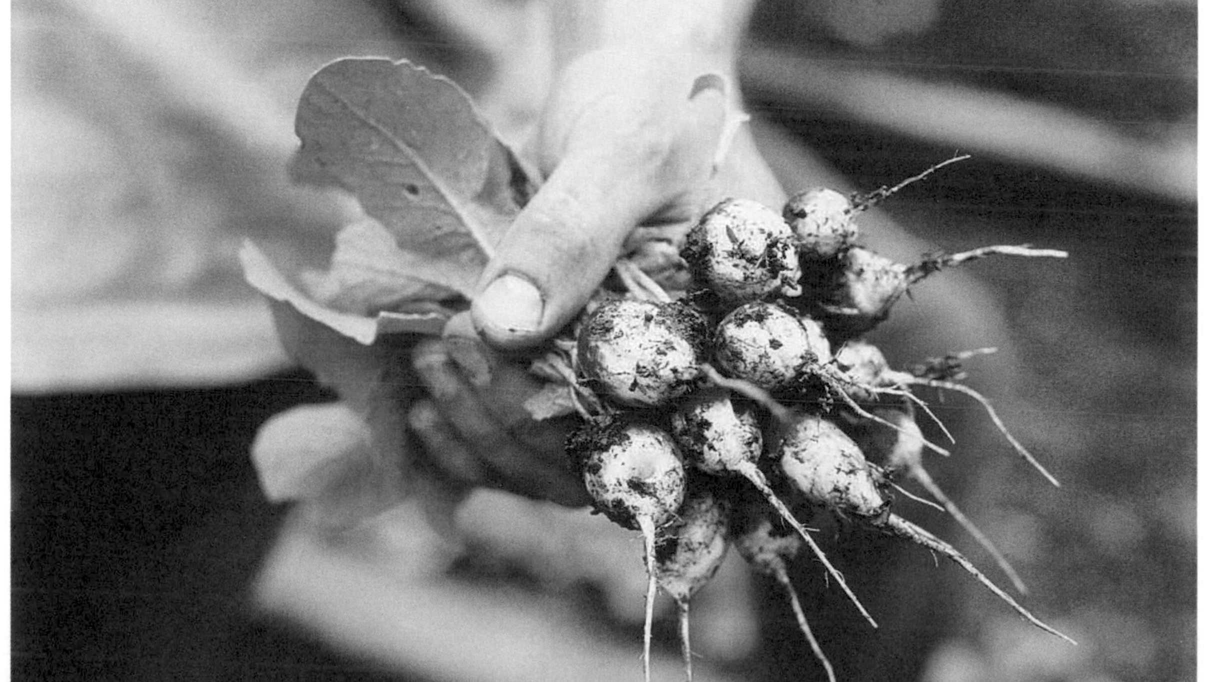

stallholders, sampling the taste-before-you-buy options (a strong feature of farmers' markets), then leave with half a pound of sausages and some basil in a pot.

Of course, every little bit of trade is prized by the stallholders. But really, fair-weather shoppers of this kind are squandering a golden opportunity. The combination of different farming trades – including vegetable growers, fruit farmers, meat producers, dairy farmers, as well as a smattering of purveyors of "processed" foods such as charcuterie, bread and cakes, jams and chutneys – means that a good farmers' market can just about cater for a proper "weekly" family shop. The honest truth is that if you want to enjoy farmers' markets for years to come, if you want to be part of the support network that means they can be weekly rather than monthly, then just showing up isn't enough. You've got to spend a bit of cash as well. Vegetables at farmers' markets tend not to be prohibitively expensive. Because the producers are selling direct to you, the consumer, they can afford to be very reasonable. For a start, there are no greedy supermarkets siphoning off a fat percentage.

other ways to buy vegetables directly

In reaction to the increasingly tight squeeze imposed by supermarket price fixers, many vegetable and fruit growers are finding ways of selling direct to the consumer. Organic farm deliveries (known in the U.S. as CSAs, for Community Supported Agriculture), mail-order services, and now the Internet are all playing their part. At their best, these offer a wide variety of locally grown, freshly harvested, seasonal vegetables. While some operate in summer only, reflecting the wealth of produce available at the height of the growing season, others are big enough to operate all year round. They can get a bit repetitive during the winter months (what, parsnips *again*?); on the other hand, your own imagination should prevent tedium from setting in: parsnip soup, parsnip crisps, parsnip gratin, creamed parsnips, curried parsnips, fried parsnip cakes, parsnip ice cream (?) . . .

Incidentally, although vegetable delivery services are generally run by the "good guys" – people who care about food and the way it is produced – your consumer rights should not be compromised in any way by that. Just because a cabbage is organic, it doesn't mean you should put up with it being yellow around the edges. If anything in your vegetable box slips below the standards you expect, let the suppliers know. If they really are good guys, they will do their best to make sure it never happens again.

organic vegetables (and genetic modification)

Although I have touched on organic vegetables in the section above, I wanted to save a more rounded debate on the whole organic issue until the end, as it cuts across all forms of vegetable retailing (at last).

I fully support the organic movement – which is, of course, committed to farming without the use of chemical pesticides and fertilizers. Its allegiance to sustainable systems and the environment is not the only plus. Organic certification is a strict affair, maintained by regular inspections. An organic label is therefore one of the few meaningful indications we can find on our food. It actually tells you something useful about how your food has been produced.

Just a few years ago, the word *organic* was practically a synonym for *cranky*. But such prejudices are rapidly dying out – today, consumer demand for organic produce has forced the supermarkets to offer organic alternatives in all their major lines of vegetables, fruits, cereals, dairy produce, and even meat. Organic vegetable delivery schemes are proving hugely popular in both Britain and the U.S., and organic producers in both countries are spearheading the burgeoning farmers' market movement.

Why is the organic alternative now so popular? I don't think it's because consumers suddenly believe that farming with chemicals is unequivocally destroying the environment. Nor is it because they are convinced beyond all doubt that the chemical residues in conventionally farmed produce are detrimental to their own and their children's health. It is because, quite simply, they are no longer sure. Health scares by the score in recent years – from mad cow disease, salmonella, and E. coli to residual chemicals in food and the whole GMO controversy – have heightened people's awareness of a simple truth: there is something seriously wrong with the way our food is being produced, and those who think they are on top of the situation (including the government) are deluding themselves.

I don't know for sure if there are any long-term risks associated with the chemical residues in, say, conventionally farmed carrots. There may be none. But for the moment there is nobody, in my view, whose word on the matter can be trusted. So if carrots that do not contain chemical residues can be produced (and, thanks to organic farming practices, they can), then I prefer to choose them.

I am not religious about this. I eat a fair amount of nonorganic vegetables – it's hard not to. My friends at Washingpool Farm, for example, are not organic. But they are at pains to minimize the use of chemical pesticides. They give the slugs a bit of a hammering in early spring and blitz the cabbage-loving caterpillars in high summer and that's about it. They still prefer a good load of well-rotted cow manure to a dose of pelleted chemical nitrates, and I applaud them for that.

But I am also aware of the environmental impact of chemical farming: I have seen it with my own eyes. The River Brit, which flows through my garden at River Cottage, is itself subject to the whims of farmers working upstream of my patch. Most of them use artificial nitrates to improve the productivity of their grazing pasture. The rain flushes these nitrates into the watercourse, and the river weeds get an unasked-for dose of fertilizer, choking the dwindling summer flow as they grow unchecked. Pesticides flushed into the river produce a soapy scum, which gathers like dirty bubble bath in the backwaters and eddies. Insects get caught up in it, like currants in a yeasty dough, and die. This is not the result of any illegal activity, the dumping of chemicals, or excessive use of fertilizers. This is normal farming practice. Indeed, I suspect that the farmers around me are, if anything, rather modest in their use of chemicals.

The wild brown trout in the Brit have not yet gone belly-up, and we still get an occasional glimpse of the kingfisher. The river system has not been destroyed by pollution – yet. But why should it be polluted at all? The fact is that all farming systems have an impact on the land. I prefer to support one whose impact is restricted to the land under cultivation, leaving neighboring land, the hedgerows, and watercourses unaffected. That is the organic system.

As for genetic modification of crops, the same argument applies. Am I convinced that it is a heinous evil that will make monsters of our children and spawn strains of hitherto unimagined superweeds? Not entirely. But previous experience (mad cow disease springs to mind) suggests that there is a Murphy's law about tampering with the natural order in the name of agricultural progress. If anything can go wrong when vegetables are genetically modified, then sooner or later it will – spectacularly. I sure as hell ain't volunteering myself or my family as guinea pigs in a bid to be part of the experiment.

For concerned consumers, the joy of organic produce is that it offers a peace of mind that is hard to find anywhere else in the food marketplace. Yes, I am looking for certain guarantees in the food I buy, beyond the simple matter of taste: guarantees of purity, sustainability, and transparency and openness on the part of the producer. When it comes to buying vegetables, fruits, and herbs, the organic label is currently the only thing that offers me those guarantees. It offers knowledge and understanding in place of ignorance and uncertainty. And that's worth a few extra pence.

growing vegetables

The way to know most about the vegetables you cook and eat is, of course, to grow them yourself. If you already do, then you may justifiably wonder what I have to teach you in this short section of the book. In all honesty, I am hardly a leading authority on the art of growing vegetables. Nevertheless, I am an unremitting, if recently converted, enthusiast. And by plundering the knowledge of others with far greater experience than myself (and reading the back of a few seed packets – see page 38), I have attained a level of competence that serves me well. Most of the time.

But really it is not my intention to teach gardening grannies to suck seeds. On the "how to" side of vegetable gardening, I'm still in the learning category. On the other hand, when it comes to the question, "why bother?" well, I think I've given that more thought than most. So if those to whom the open secret of the pleasures of vegetable gardening has already been revealed should find my suggestions tending toward the naive or inexperienced, all I can say is that they worked for me. And if, meanwhile, I can persuade a few vegetable-growing virgins to take up the spade and abandon themselves to the joys of homegrown greens, then I'll happily tolerate a few sneers from the experts.

Another mission of mine in this section is to persuade gardeners, new or old, to grow their vegetables organically – or as organically as possible. Why? Pretty much for the same reasons as I would advocate shopping organically (see above). It's true that a little bit of nitrate or pesticide on a small vegetable patch is not going to destroy the planet, but if we all fail to practice what we preach we could certainly wreak a fair amount of havoc. But, for me, the biggest reward for organic gardening is in the eating. The knowledge that something has been grown in harmony with nature and contains not the faintest trace of the artificial makes it taste all the sweeter.

I know what you want to know. Is organic gardening harder work? And is it less productive? I won't shrink from the truth: it is harder work, but only a bit. The extra labor really comes in only once or twice a year in the preparation of your soil beds – digging in plenty of good-quality organic manure or compost is certainly hard work. Plus a few nocturnal slug hunts. The good news is that if you look after your soil, there is no reason why your organic plot shouldn't be every bit as productive as any chemically enhanced vegetable garden.

why grow vegetables?

What can I say to the enthusiastic cook who is vaguely interested in the idea of growing his or her own vegetables but is still teetering on the brink of action? Realistically, for most of us these days there are no persuasive economic arguments for growing your own vegetables – at least, not if you cost out your time. (During summer gluts, my father used to pay me pocket money to pick and freeze peas, beans, and soft fruits from his vegetable garden. He once calculated that the resulting frozen produce cost him three or four times what it would in the supermarket. And that was without factoring in his own time.)

But there is still an important sense in which the vegetables you grow yourself really are free. When your time is given freely, what you make with it is free in the best sense of the word. When you buy your vegetables, you are a slave – to the car that takes you to the shops; to the methods, good or bad, by which the vegetables

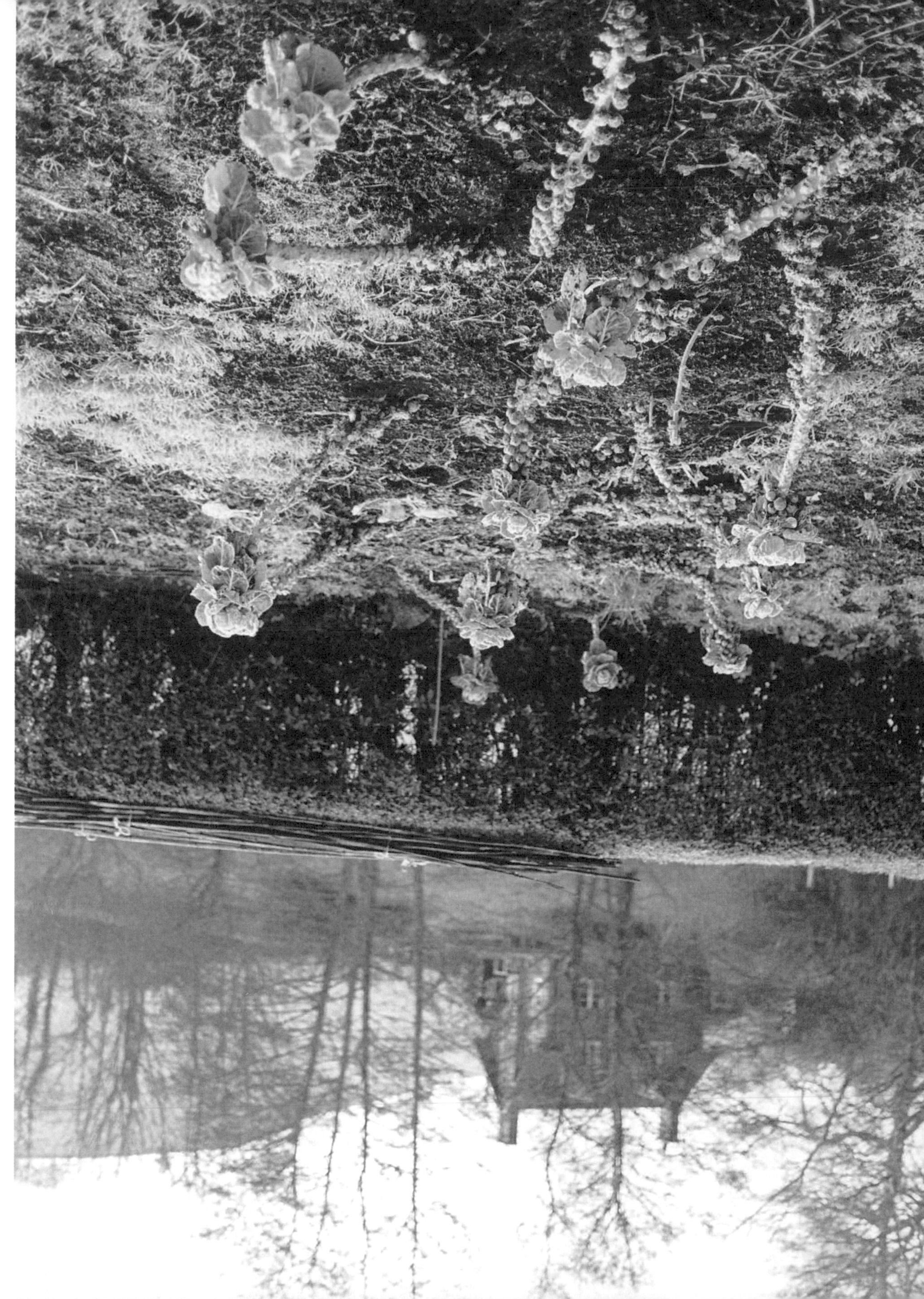

are produced; to the market forces, and the big bosses who fix the prices; to the shelf-stacking policies that determine the freshness, or otherwise, of the produce you buy. You have no say whatsoever in the means of production, no role in the quality of what becomes yours – only when you hand over the cash.

Grow your own vegetables and all that changes. Choose the seeds, the growing site, the time to plant, to weed, to water, to feed, to harvest. What you then take to the kitchen is not just a vegetable, it's a form of self-expression, an assertion of personal liberty. It's a kind of opting out of the world as you're told it must be in favor of the world as you'd like it to be. You may doubt the wisdom of loading something as ordinary as a carrot with such deep personal meaning. But try growing them yourself, and you will find that carrots are far from ordinary. They are sleek, pointed, orange miracles that come from nowhere to populate a bare patch of earth. And, almost astonishingly, you can eat them!

The fact is, those who already grow their own vegetables for the kitchen need no converting to the cause. I have yet to meet a vegetable gardener who complained that "It's hardly worth it, what with the choice available in the supermarket these days," or "It's too much time for too little reward," or "What's the point, you can hardly taste the difference anyway?" These quotations are the clichés of the uninitiated – those who do not yet know the prickly heat of a fat radish freshly drawn from the earth, washed with a quick wipe on a dewy tuft of grass, then eaten without further ado; those who have not tasted the extra sugar dose in a pile of self-podded peas thrown into boiling water within an hour of being picked; those who have not marveled at the unrepentant earthiness of freshly dug potatoes. . . .

If you are still wavering, let me offer you another, almost glib answer to the question, "Why grow vegetables?" Because you can. I mean, anyone can. As I said earlier, growing vegetables is easy. All you need is earth and seeds. Sunshine and water are important too, but in a reasonable year both should come in plentiful supply, courtesy of the man upstairs. A relaxed, laissez-faire attitude to growing vegetables will stand the beginner in good stead. While there is plenty of scope for fussing and fretting about your vegetable patch, you will probably find that obsessional attention to detail either does or doesn't evolve as the years go by, according to your personality. In other words, if you want to become the manic overseer of a manicured vegetable plot, you can; but it doesn't have to start off that way.

starting a vegetable garden

My experience at River Cottage has taught me that the hardest thing you will do all year as a vegetable debutante is clearing a patch of ground in the first place. And that's only hard in the sense of being a little bit exhausting for those not used to digging. Since it is the first thing you need to do in your bid to grow vegetables, it seems reasonable to hope that your enthusiasm for the project at the outset will carry you through the pain barrier for this initial physical labor. If you have your doubts about that, or if you are taking on a large plot with a view to getting stuck in big time, then you may want to rent a Rototiller. This petrol-powered machine is like a cross between a mower and a plow, and it does the digging for you. The first time you use one you'll find it slightly harder work than digging by hand. But, like an ox, once you've mastered the beast, you'll come to love it and rely on it. And if it ever breaks down on you, you'll probably burst into tears.

Some thought is required in choosing your patch of ground. All gardeners have to compromise, and while a south-facing, level piece of land, sheltered from the worst of the wind, with a rich, finely textured soil will get you off to a flying start, few of us are blessed with such perfect growing conditions. It's more a question of avoiding obvious negative factors. Light is vital, and a patch that is in near-permanent shade is simply not going to work. It's important, therefore, to be aware of the passage of the sun across your intended growing site from dawn till dusk. If the ground enjoys direct sunlight for more than half of daylight hours (that's about four in midwinter, eight on the longest day), you should be able to grow well on it. It's worth bearing in mind that you may be able to gain extra sunlight for your patch by cutting down an unfortunately located tree or two. This takes a bit of courage, and there's no point in breaking your heart by sacrificing a beloved feature of your garden for an extra row of peas. But trees are not sacred just because they are big. And of course there's the firewood bonus.

You can't make the sun shine where it has no plans to go, but questions of slope and shelter can be addressed – by hard labor. If the only plot available to you is on a steep slope, you may want to think about moving some earth to level the patch. I had to do this at River Cottage, and the resulting terraces, held in by hefty railroad ties, are actually an excellent feature to have in a vegetable garden. Soil moved in this way is inevitably extremely well worked: it drains well and makes a very good tilth (a nice technical term to acquaint yourself with; it means the topsoil, as worked by the gardener for cultivation). Terraces also lend themselves to features such as a strawberry cascade. Providing permanent shelter from crosswinds is well within the power of the (harder-working) gardener, too. If you plant hedges to delineate the borders of your vegetable garden, the effect can be decorative as well as protective. A lazy, temporary, but very effective alternative is to stake out some windbreak netting (a green polyethylene material).

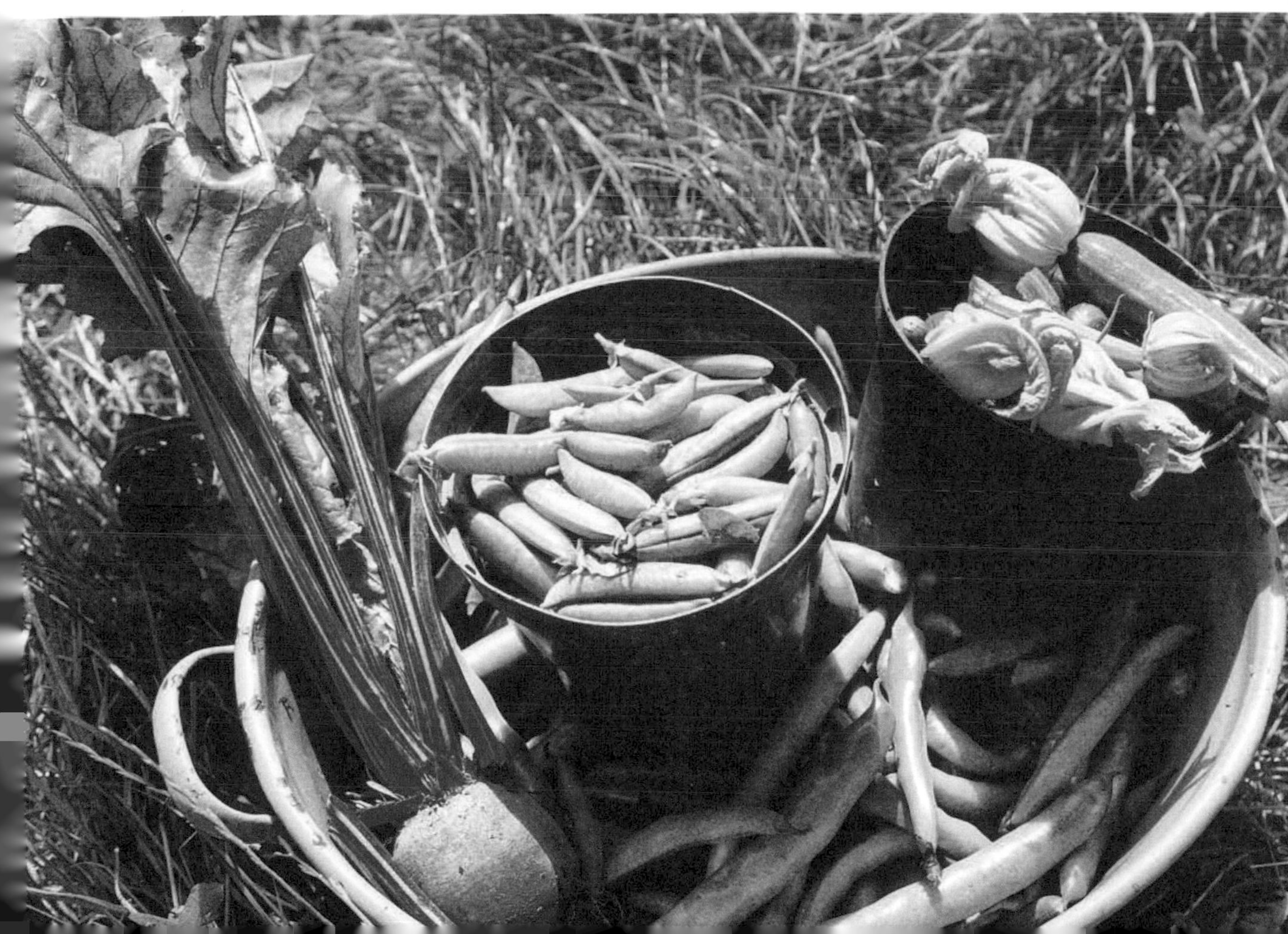

As far as the timing of your bed-creation scheme goes, you have two choices: late autumn for planting the following spring, or early spring for almost immediate planting. An autumn digging will give the soil a chance to settle and leaves time for existing green matter, such as grass tufts and the usual weeds, to rot down. The winter months ahead will allow this to happen without too many new weeds springing up. However, you will have to be on your toes come spring, as the weed seeds in the ground will leap at the first chance they get to germinate and take hold. Another good going over in early March will be essential if you don't want to be back to square one. If you're opting for a spring digging, you may as well wait until it's almost time to start planting: say, early April. Dig up your patch, removing all the grass and weeds you can, and simply work over your soil till it is nicely broken up and ready for planting.

How much work you have to do to get your patch ready for planting depends on what is there in the first place. An easy way to get started is simply to give over a patch of existing flower bed to the cultivation of vegetables. This is what I did at River Cottage to create the top beds of the vegetable patch, before digging out the terraces beneath. And I learned that if you take this route you have to be ruthless. Favorite shrubs can be relocated, but you will find it a bore to try to work around them in situ. The shadows they cast and the goodness they take from the soil will also hinder the progress of your vegetables. Best get them out, roots and all, and start with a clean slate. Converted flower beds may be nutrient depleted, and it will repay to work in plenty of organic matter, such as manure, leaf mulch, or vegetable compost (for more on compost and soil improvement, see pages 42–43).

A patch of ground currently under grass may look a bit daunting, but it's often the best place to start, as it involves less sacrifice of existing garden aesthetics and the soil beneath is usually free of large roots and rocks and rich in nutrients. The two strips of lawn I dug up to provide further growing space at River Cottage yielded the most fertile topsoil of all. Only after two seasons was it necessary to dig in some serious fertilizer.

A piece of pasture reclaimed from grazing can make an ideal growing site, as it will have enjoyed plenty of natural fertilizer from the animals that lived on it. Breaking up ground under grass is hard work, and again the Rototiller is a godsend (once you've got the hang of it). If you're working by hand, the best thing is to be an amateur turf cutter, using a spade to cut pieces of turf and removing them with the top few inches of soil, including all the roots of the grass. If you're working in the autumn, you can take deeper cuts and simply turn them upside down on top of your bed. The grass will rot down over the next few months and feed your bed the following spring. If, on the other hand, you're digging your patch in spring for more or less immediate planting, it's best to take your pieces of sod off site. Don't throw them away; use them, again upside down, to make the base of a compost heap or to fill in the bottom of large pots and tubs you're planning to grow in. Once you've skimmed the grassy top off your plot, simply dig up and break down the exposed soil, removing any large stones or roots that you turn up.

As for other patches of rough ground and waste ground, you'll just have to deal with them. The only way to find out what's happening underneath is to take a spade to them and dig down. Removing the three R's (rubble, rocks, and roots) can be hard work indeed, but if it lays the foundations for many happy years of vegetable growing and transforms dead ground to living, it's time well spent.

The worst thing that can happen when you set about making yourself a vegetable garden is that you discover you have near-unworkable soil – for example, a very heavy clay. If your vegetable-patch-to-be looks like a giant slab of wet Plasticine, do not despair, but do brace yourself for some very hard work: major soil improvement is going to be necessary. Late autumn is the right time to go to work on it, since there is little you will be able to do to address the problem in spring. Deep digging is the answer, and the incorporation of as much organic matter as you can lay your hands on – mushroom compost, leaf mulch, or, best of all, well-rotted horse or cow manure (all of which can be bought by the truckload relatively cheaply). Don't worry if at this stage the compost or manure refuses to mix in and you just seem to be stacking up great slabs of clay. The important thing is that you have opened up the soil and spread some fertilizer around. The winter frosts and early spring earthworms will do a surprising amount of work for you. Come March, the soil should dig or rototill much more easily.

If you're starting from scratch, any of the above routes to providing yourself with a virgin growing patch probably sounds like a daunting solo mission. So don't lose sight of one of the most valuable sources of gardening help: good neighbors. They may not come and dig your garden for you, but the world is awash with garden enthusiasts, most of whom are only too ready to give advice. An experienced local gardener will know more than I can ever guess about your local soil conditions and climate quirks, and will be full of solutions for problems I can't even anticipate. They may even be able to lend you the much-coveted Rototiller.

preparing for sowing

Let's assume that you've taken one of the routes outlined above and haven't done your back in. You've got yourself a patch of virgin soil, it's early April, and you're itching to get started. Impatience is inevitable at this stage in the proceedings – but there's one last bit of work that will make all the difference. We're talking tilth again. It's time to work your newly exposed earth to the perfect consistency for seed sowing. With the use of fork, hoe, and rake (in that order), you need to work over the soil, breaking up the larger lumps into smaller lumps, and raking the smaller lumps into yet smaller ones. Do it on a dry day, as wet soil will clog up your rake.

This business of final bed preparation definitely provides one of the first good opportunities for potential obsessives to start getting obsessed. I know gardeners who won't rest until their beds are like a vast expanse of instant coffee granules. There's no need to go this far. I go on breaking and raking until there are no lumps much bigger than a golf ball, and these I then tend to attack by hand, crumbling them through my fingers. When my patience starts to wear thin, I simply rake any remaining lumps right off the bed and shovel them into a wheelbarrow for the compost heap: a bit of soil is excellent for the texture of next year's compost.

A good way to test the readiness of your soil for seed planting is to see if you can easily draw a line in the soil with your finger: if you can, stop raking; if you can't, keep going!

what to grow

A trip to any decent garden center will whet your appetite for the extraordinary range of vegetables available to the home grower. It may also bring on a bad case of "options paralysis": there's just so much I *could* grow, but what *shall* I grow?

There is a golden rule that should govern your selection: don't grow anything that you are not genuinely enthusiastic about eating. That may seem obvious, but it is amazing how many vegetable growers end up with gluts of produce they don't really want. Cauliflowers spring to mind. On the other hand, if your tastes are as catholic as mine, this rule of thumb may not narrow the field down a great deal. So I apply a further, more rigorous principle: I tend to grow only vegetables that I believe will be significantly better – i.e., tastier – than the ones I can buy at the market.

I am the first to admit that this is entirely a matter of personal prejudice. My prejudices dictate, for example, that I don't grow much in the way of onions and cabbages. And although I do grow some interesting salad greens, I tend to steer clear of row upon row of "regular" lettuces. My rationale for these omissions is as follows. I don't grow onions because I use them all the time, and if I tried to grow as many as I use I would have to turn over the whole garden to them. Besides, onions in the shops are extremely cheap and keep well for months on end: I see no great excitement in a really "fresh" onion. I don't grow cabbages because they take up a lot of space, and I get excellent local varieties anyway, usually within a day or two of being picked. And I don't believe I can taste the difference between a cabbage picked two hours ago and one picked twenty-four hours ago (unlike peas, for example). I don't grow many lettuces because, again, what's available locally is excellent, and I prefer to devote the space to more unusual and distinctly flavored leafy greens, such as arugula, land cress, tatsoi, and others (for more of which, see page 55). On the other hand, although I continue to buy leeks and carrots throughout the summer (I use a lot of both), I also grow a few of my own. I like to pick the leeks younger than I can buy them in the stores and then grill them, to serve cold, dressed with olive oil. And my homegrown carrots tend to be eaten raw or lightly steamed, whereas the store-bought ones go into soups, stews, and stocks.

There is no reason whatever why you should share these prejudices. You may have a passion for onions that urges you to grow twenty different varieties on your plot and nothing else. Or you may have escaped the school-dinners exposure to cauliflower that has pretty much put me off it for life. Let your own prejudices and passions feed your choice of seeds.

So, here you are at the garden center, feasting your eyes on a wider selection of vegetable seed packets than you ever thought possible. Feast away. Anything that takes your fancy, pull off the shelf. Once you have made an initial selection (you may have five packets in your hand, you may have fifty), review it for a minute or two. If you have second thoughts about anything, put it back. If you're worried about limited space, try to cut back to the things you feel most enthused by. You may wish to think in terms of a balance of vegetable types: some peas and beans; some leafy greens; a selection of salad greens; a few reliable roots; some squashes or zucchini. Or you may have a highly personal, specialized, radical vegetable agenda: an out-and-out bean feast or a vertical tasting of beet varieties. Whatever finally fires your imagination, take them to the counter and cough up the cash.

I love heading home with a bunch of seed packets in my pocket. It's like being the god of a small planet: "And on the seventh day he created pumpkins. . . ." So what do you do when you get the seeds home? Does it sound awfully prosaic and dull to suggest that you read the instructions on the back of the packet? Now that's not quite so godlike.

seed-packet gardening

Seriously, that's exactly what I'd recommend. I am a self-confessed seed-packet gardener, and have no shame about that, since I have found, with very few exceptions, that most seed packets tell you pretty much all you need to know about growing the seeds inside. Take, for example, the packet of Chantenay Red-core carrots that I happen to have in front of me. I quote, verbatim:

When to sow: March to May.

Where to sow: Sow very thinly in drills 1.5cm deep with 25cm between the rows.

What to do next: Carrot fly is attracted by thinning, so try to avoid thinning at all. If you have to thin the seedlings, do so in the evening, water before thinning, and remove all debris from site.

Tip: Carrots prefer a well-worked, light-textured soil, free of stones, that has not recently been manured.

What else do you need to know? The two great bugbears of expert carrot growers up and down the land are carrot fly and root splitting. And all the wisdom those experts have accumulated over decades of growing and showing and arguing boils down to these essential tips: thin carefully, or ideally not at all, as the scent released by damaged plants attracts carrot fly. The soil should be well worked, more or less to the depth you intend to grow your carrots, and free of stones – if you care about having straight carrots, that is. Fresh manure is also best avoided, as the roots will tend to split in search of the goodness. Apart from a lot of entertaining hokum about soil sifting and drainpipes put about by vegetable showmen (a pursuit that I have myself indulged in, I confess) there's nothing else important to be said about growing carrots. In other words, if you've memorized the back of the packet, then congratulations: you are one of the world's leading authorities on carrot growing.

direct sowing versus seed trays and pots

Once the risk of frost is past (with any luck, by the end of April in most places) just about any seeds can be sown directly into the ground and expected to grow. But even the seed packet gardener will come across some alternative methods of propagation recommended on the back of their chosen packs: "sow under glass" is a phrase you will commonly encounter. The fact is that to encourage efficient germination and protect tiny seedlings in the first stages of growth from both harsh weather and hungry pests, many gardeners like to grow them in controlled conditions, in seed trays and small pots. This is most often done in a greenhouse or a cold frame (which is really a miniature greenhouse at ground level), but if you have a south-facing windowsill, you can do it on a small scale in the house.

I have adopted this technique, which is basically about improving the survival rate of your seedlings, in a big way. As an organic gardener, I find it particularly valuable in the battle against the all-consuming slug. With outside sowings, I have had whole rows of lettuce, frisée, and spinach seedlings decimated in a single night (I suspect by a single slug). Now, I tend to sow my salads and spinach in seed trays in a polytunnel, on a low table with metal legs that the slugs don't seem able to climb. I wait until I have a good few inches of strong leaf showing before transplanting them to the outdoor growing site. That doesn't mean my transplanted salads are suddenly impervious to slug assault: they're just bigger and more robust when the slugs get to them, so it takes a few more of the slimy mollusks to bring them down. Plus I can keep a few spares going in the polytunnel to replace the unfortunate victims.

Another reason for planting under glass is to get ahead of the season. If you sow seeds under glass in, say, mid-March, by the time the kinder weather arrives in late April, you will have sturdy seedlings, well on the way to productive growth, to transplant directly to the growing site. A second crop of the same vegetable can then be sown directly into the ground, and you can look forward to a properly spaced harvest about six weeks apart. I like to do this with peas and broad beans for the earliest possible harvest. I sow them in special seed trays made up of "plugs" – lots of little plastic pots, about 2 inches in diameter, joined together like ice cube trays. I plant one pea or bean per plug in early March, then transplant them to the growing site in early or mid-April, sowing another couple of rows directly at the same time. This usually gives me a first crop in late June, with a second crop following on in August.

Sowing under glass is more or less essential if you're growing zucchini, pumpkins, and other squashes. These are basically Mediterranean species that will not easily germinate until daytime temperatures are consistently above 60°F. This means they cannot be sown directly outside until late May at the earliest, and even then the young seedlings remain susceptible to harsh weather. In these circumstances there's barely enough summer left in Britain and other cold climates to bring the plants to maturity. They should therefore be planted under glass, one or two seeds in a 4-inch pot, sometime in April. By late May or early June, four or more good strong leaves should have appeared, and they will be ready for transplanting.

Incidentally, the best growing medium for sowing in seed trays and small pots is an all-around seedling/potting compost. You'll find dozens of brands in any garden center, but I'd urge you to choose something ecofriendly or, better still, organic – many of the products are peat based, and peat is not a sustainable commodity. The best alternatives are soil or coir (coconut fiber) based. A lot of serious gardeners have their own special recipes for seedling compost, mixing in perlite and vermiculite, and even varying the mix according to the type of seedlings they plan to grow. Personally, I plod on with a straightforward coir-based product and it does me fine. Compost for seedlings must not be overcompacted. Simply run the flat of your hand lightly over the surface to level off seed trays and pots – don't press down to cram it all in. Potting compost tends to dry out quickly, so seedlings should be watered at least every two days, if not daily.

All seedlings sown under glass need to be "hardened off" before transplanting: this means giving them a dose of the real weather outside their glass environment for a few days. Take them out of the greenhouse in the morning and put them back in before the temperature drops too radically in the evening. Do this for at least three days, ideally four or five, then give them a full forty-eight hours outside, day and night, before transplanting. They will appreciate your consideration.

Transplanting is easy and satisfying finger work, but a bit delicate with really tiny seedlings. The ground does not need to be as finely raked as for direct seed sowing. But you should loosen the earth immediately around each planting site with a trowel or hand fork, and ideally work in a little of the potting compost you have been using for the seedlings: it will help to cosset the roots and ease the transition. Make a hole a fair bit bigger than the root ball of the plant, then hold the plant gently in place with one hand, and bring in the loose soil/compost from around the edges to cover the roots. Be sure to bring the soil level up to the same point on the plant stem as the compost was in the pot – usually where white changes to green. Then firm the soil gently around the plant with your fingertips.

I find planting out seedlings one of the most exhilarating of all gardening jobs. The results are instantly visible, and you can fill up a whole bed with growing plants in just an hour or two.

Sowing under glass and transplanting is something to experiment with as you gain confidence in your vegetable growing, but don't worry; the basic instructions for this are usually given on the back of the seed packets. And if you don't have the space to grow under glass yourself, it's worth knowing that most larger garden centers grow a variety of vegetable plants suitable for transplanting directly into a growing site. My own local garden center, Groves of Bridport, is excellent in this regard, and I do a fair bit of "cheaty gardening" with their lettuces, corn, pumpkins, and leeks.

polytunnels and greenhouses

Once you start sowing under glass, you'll quickly realize what a reliable and satisfying technique it is, and pretty soon you'll want to get yourself a greenhouse. Or even a polytunnel. A polytunnel is of course nothing more than a giant greenhouse, the stretched clear polyethylene performing exactly the same heat-retaining, light-transmitting function as the greenhouse glass. But polytunnels are big and relatively cheap, and having one means that not only do you have plenty of space in which to get early outdoor crops ready by sowing seeds under glass (or under polyethylene), you also have room to cultivate whole extra crops from seed to harvest much earlier in the year than you would ever be able to achieve outside (I'm writing this on May 24 and I estimate that my polytunnel pea crop will be ready within a couple of weeks). That's not all; you can also grow exotic species from the Mediterranean, and beyond, that would barely survive outside in colder climates.

For me, the principal joy of greenhouses and polytunnels, besides the propagation of seedlings and a nice early crop of peas and zucchini, is growing tomatoes: in Britain, you simply can't buy tomatoes as tasty as the ones you can grow yourself under glass. A few peppers and chiles are fun as well. And it's nice to get some exotic winter salads in once the tomatoes have come out . . . the truth is, polytunnels are addictive, and addicts I know have successfully cultivated such exotics as sweet potatoes, ginger, and even pineapples. I haven't been tempted down that road yet, but I quite fancy a crack at some Charentais melons. . . .

I'm going to resist the temptation to expand this section into a "lovers' guide to polytunnel gardening." It's a fairly specialized (though not difficult) form of gardening and certainly involves a big commitment. Polytunnels are like pets: they need daily tending and cannot be abandoned for any length of time. But if the vegetable-growing bug is really starting to bite, and

you want to extend your seasons and edge a little nearer to the grail of vegetable self-sufficiency, let me assure you that a polytunnel is a great thing to have – undeniably ugly on the outside but, at harvest time especially, very beautiful and delicious on the inside. If you're thinking of taking the plunge, get yourself a copy of *Gardening Under Plastic* by Bernard Salt. It will tell you all you need to know.

compost

Once you've got the hang of seed-packet gardening, the only really essential information you need to know is how to keep your soil in tiptop condition, year after year. However good your soil, vegetables will take the best of the nutrients out of it on an annual basis – and on an annual basis it has to be put back in. How do you do that? For the organic gardener, who wants to avoid chemical fertilizers, there is a one-word answer to this question: compost.

Your garden and kitchen activities are sure to generate a considerable amount of vegetative waste. Your job is to make sure it isn't waste at all, but goes back to feed the plants that feed you. You can start a compost heap in any quiet but reasonably accessible corner of the garden (you'll need to be able to drive a wheelbarrow up to it), but it is a good idea to give it a little structure, rather than just make a big mound that slopes away at the edges. A three-sided structure, with "walls" of wood, corrugated iron, or straw bales, is simple to put together and will do very nicely. Don't make the base dimensions too huge or you'll never get any depth: about a yard square will do for an "average" household (as if there is such a thing!). A "floor," again of wood, or thick sheet plastic, will help retain moisture and heat. Moisture and heat, incidentally, are what composting is all about: any vegetable matter will eventually rot down into a form in which it will be welcomed back by the soil, but in a well-managed compost heap that stays warm and wet (but not too wet), the whole process can be speeded up considerably. Speed is important, because the faster you can make good compost, the more goodness you can put back into the soil at the end of the gardening year. If you generate enough waste and manage your heap well, a pile started in March can be dug back into the soil in November.

For this kind of efficiency, bulking out your heap with dry material is essential; it will also improve the texture of your finished compost. Straw is good for this, as are wood shavings, dry leaves, and even shredded newspaper (a particularly good way to incorporate newspaper into your compost heap is to mix it with grass cuttings, which anyway have a tendency to rot to an unpleasant slime if piled on undiluted). The bedding from your henhouse, be it straw or wood shavings, with its bonus of rich chicken dung, is an absolute must for the compost heap.

Just about anything of vegetable origin can go on a compost heap: the only thing to avoid is anything too coarse or woody that might lag behind the pace of decay of the rest of the material. Those with large vegetable gardens (who are forced to take their composting pretty seriously) sometimes address this problem with the aid of a powered compost shredder: it shreds coarser stalks down to a manageable size that will bring them in line with the rest of the pile.

Incidentally, one of the great dilemmas of the vegetable gardener who also keeps pigs is which vegetable leftovers to save as piggy treats and which to throw on the compost heap. Last year, I was so generous to the pigs that, while they thrived, my compost heap actually lost weight. This year, I am trying to be a bit more even-handed; leafy waste and peelings all go for compost, while thick cabbage and bean stalks, which are a bit coarse for quick composting but very nutritious, all go in the pig bucket, along with any starch and dairy leftovers.

An important aspect of making compost is knowing when to finish it. Keep piling on the waste until your heap is at least a yard high, ideally a bit more. Then stop. (Meanwhile, start a fresh heap somewhere else – right next door to the first one if you like.) You now need to turn the finished heap: use a fork or pitchfork to move as much material from the bottom of the pile to the top and vice versa: or at the very least, try to move the top layer to the middle by forking up the stuff at the bottom and piling it on top. Cover the turned heap completely with an old bit of carpet, plastic sheeting, or a thick layer of straw. Leave it for about a month, then turn it and cover it again. It will be ready about six months after that. I look on the end of August as a cutoff point: any heap finished before then should be ready for digging into the soil the following March/April. Heaps finished from September onward will need a good dose of spring sunshine the following year to complete the process, but can be used for top-dressing your soil or digging in with late plantings of zucchini, squashes, spinach, and salads. You can buy products, usually liquid, called compost accelerators, to speed the process even further. I've never tried them, though my dad swears by them.

Finished compost should be dark, rich, crumbly, and pleasant smelling – "like a good Christmas cake," my dad says, though I'm not sure I'd go that far.

soil improvement by winter digging

Late autumn or winter digging is the essential elbow work of your soil maintenance program; it's tough, though not quite as bad as starting all over again. It is also an opportunity to introduce some soil-improving material into the ground: your compost, for example, lovingly prepared according to the instructions above. But even this will not be sufficient to rejuvenate your soil, year in, year out. So once every two or three years you should take delivery of a trailer-load of good old horse or cow manure. Horse is reckoned to be the best of all, but cow will do very nicely. In either case, it should not be fresh, but well rotted: one whole summer sitting undisturbed will do the trick. You can tell when manure is properly rotted down because it is dark, almost black, does not smell too unpleasant, and always has a large number of earthworms in it. It is worth insisting to your manure supplier that you will only take delivery of well-rotted manure – and if he turns up with something too fresh, send it back. It's unpleasant to work with and won't do the job you require.

How deep you dig, and how thoroughly you work in the manure, is up to you, but the harder you work now, the easier things will be in the spring. The important thing is that you turn up any heavily compacted soil into large clods: the winter frost will then act to break these down. Rather than spreading an even layer of manure over the top (which can act to protect the soil from frost), I tend to heave shovelfuls into the gaps and ridges between the soil clods. As far as the overall quantity of manure is concerned, think in terms of an even layer, 3 to 4 inches deep, over the entire bed – or even more if you are aware that your soil is seriously depleted. But remember your carrots and leave a few manure-free patches, carefully marked out.

Early the following spring (early April at the latest), on as mild a day as possible (and obviously not when the ground is frozen), you should give your beds another going over with a fork or Rototiller. This is the time to distribute the manure as thoroughly and evenly through the soil as you can. If you have particularly rich soil of good friable texture, as I am lucky enough to have at River Cottage, you can get away without winter digging, although the bed preparation the following spring will be harder work, and you will need to start it well before the weeds get under way – about early to mid-March. You can dig or Rototiller in your compost or manure at this time and leave it for a few weeks to settle, before working over the beds again in preparation for planting.

controlling pests

Keeping your soil in peak condition is no problem for the organic gardener: natural fertilizers such as horse manure, cow manure, and mushroom compost are inexpensive and readily available by the truckload. There is no need to resort to chemicals when dealing with pests either. At River Cottage, the four creatures who make the most strenuous efforts to sabotage my attempts to grow vegetables are, in decreasing order of size and increasing order of threat, rabbits, birds, mice, and slugs. The tools I deploy to do battle with them are, respectively, a gun, some fishing line, some traps, and a flashlight.

Where rabbits are a problem, they can be a big problem. And, unlike birds, mice, or slugs, they have a tendency to decimate more mature plants that may be almost ready for harvest. But as they are very good eating, and very far from being an endangered species, the control of rabbits can be all to the gastronomic good. Shooting them is the most effective method, but you must know how to handle a gun and, of course, be licensed to do so. A shotgun and a .22 rifle are the only suitable arms for this job: an air rifle, however powerful, will wound far more rabbits than it kills and is not appropriate. Shooting at night, with a spotlight, from an off-road vehicle is a highly effective technique that can make a serious dent in a local population. But it has to be done by a competent shot in conjunction with a responsible driver. If you don't yet qualify, a local shooting school or a friendly gamekeeper will be able to show you the ropes. But if shooting's not for you, you will have to find a way of simply keeping the rabbits out of your garden. A low chicken-wire fence all around your vegetable patch,

pegged tightly to the ground to prevent them from crawling underneath, will be effective but unsightly. You may prefer just to put up with a few lost lettuces.

Birds, particularly pigeons and blackbirds, have a tendency to pull up young pea and bean shoots, which are packed with nutrition. Pigeons, being edible (indeed, delicious), can be tackled with a gun (see page 372). The edibility of blackbirds may be open to debate, but as it is illegal to shoot them the gun cannot come into play. However, a length of fine fishing wire, stretched a few inches above the ground between pegs or sticks in a tight zigzag pattern back and forth across your rows of peas and beans, will frustrate their attempts.

Mice have been a particular problem for me in the polytunnel. Their favorite trick is to dig up large seeds such as zucchinis, pumpkins, peas, and fava beans before they have even broken the soil. The telltale signs are a few measly crumbs scattered on the surface after the feast is finished. The only available remedies I would consider for mice in the garden are the same as in the house: cats and traps. I don't have a cat, but I do use the increasingly popular kind of box trap that catches mice alive. And then I relocate them – at least a mile away from the house. I have a sneaking suspicion, though, that they find their way home.

Problems associated with the above creatures are nothing compared to the slug. The mild winters and extremely wet springs we have had in recent years seem to have produced a plague of them, and for some commercial organic gardeners they are a real threat to business. The problem is that they like to attack the first and tiniest shoots: a single slug making its way slowly down a line of carrot or beet seedlings can wipe out the entire row in one night.

Michael Michaud, my local organic gardening guru, does constant battle with slugs, and told me that the most effective method of dealing with them is at night, with a flashlight. Slugs are on the feed after dark and can be gathered in huge numbers as they gorge themselves on your young plants. They are easy to spot in the beam of a powerful light – simply pick them up and put them in a jam jar for disposal at the end of the session. There are a number of methods of dispatch, to be selected according to personal sensitivity and squeamishness: salt, scissors, and the deep freeze are all effective. But my own preferred option is to feed them to my neighbor's ducks. They love them. So do hedgehogs (in the U.K.) and toads, which is a good reason to take care of them should they appear in your garden.

Slug hunts are quite fun once in a while, and when you have thirty or forty in a jar after half an hour of searching, you feel you must have saved a few plants. But in a really bad slug year, even nightly slug hunts fail to make much of an impression on the damage done. I must confess I have, after being deprived of two consecutive sowings of lettuce and beets, lost patience, and compromised my organic status by resorting to "wildlife-friendly" slug pellets. They kill slugs and snails by chemical means, and I dare say a few other little grubs may go with them. But the poison is impotent further up the food chain, and the impact on the soil is minimal. I use them reluctantly, and make only two or three applications in the first fortnight of any given crop's struggle to put out fresh leaves. Once plants are well on their way – say, 2 to 3 inches high, with a good crown of leaves – slugs may make holes in them but will rarely wipe them out.

There is one other means of controlling slugs that is organically approved: mail-order predators. The nematode is a microscopic parasitic worm that enters the gut of the slug and kills it. You can buy several million of them by mail, packed in a special medium that keeps them alive. I haven't tried it, but if next year is as bad as this, I think I'll give it a whirl. Incidentally, the nematode is just one of a number of predators available to organic farmers to help control various pests.

container vegetable gardening

If you are really limited in the time you can give to vegetable growing, or if the idea of creating and maintaining a dedicated vegetable garden from scratch seems just too daunting, you may nevertheless get some satisfaction, and some delicious meals, from what I call "container" vegetable gardening. The basic principle is to forget about preparing permanent beds and simply grow your vegetables in appropriate containers, which could be anything from large flowerpots, window boxes, and tubs bought at the local garden center, to old bathtubs, oil drums, and water tanks salvaged from a rubbish dump. Or you could use the most basic containers of all, good old grow bags. Container gardening is an excellent system and surprisingly versatile – you can grow whole trees if your containers are big enough.

The joy of containers is that anyone with even the tiniest bit of outdoor space, from a backyard, to a patio, roof garden, or even just a window box, can be a vegetable grower. And even if all you grow is a dozen carrots or a single zucchini plant, you can tap into that joyous feeling of creativity and independence. You may not quite be self-sufficient but neither are you 100 percent dependent on the industrial food machine. Believe me, the carrot you grow yourself will be the sweetest you taste all year.

The bare essentials of container gardening are to make sure that your chosen vessels are big enough to support the plants you grow in them, that they have decent drainage (i.e., holes in the bottom) to prevent waterlogging, and that you fill them with an appropriate growing medium. Most garden centers stock premixed growing composts that are suitable for containers, and the larger ones have organic options. Some of them even list the types of vegetables for which they are suited on the sides of the bags. But buying your growing medium can get very expensive if you're planning to fill several containers, so if you can find a patch of ground where you can dig up some good-quality topsoil you'll save a few dollars. Mix it roughly 2 to 1 with a branded compost. Move larger containers to their final position (chosen for maximum sunlight), *before* you fill them up: they may be far too heavy to move afterward.

Of course, the nutrients in your growing medium will be rapidly depleted by cultivation, but you can replenish containers on an annual basis by mixing in dry feeds such as blood and bone, calcified seaweed, potash, and chicken manure. Remember also that peas and beans fix nitrates in any growing medium, so containers in which they have been grown can be used immediately afterward for growing winter greens and brassicas (cabbages and broccoli).

So what can you grow in containers? Just about everything really, provided they are big enough. Once you have filled an old tin tub with soil and compost, to a depth of at least 20 inches, what you have is effectively a small vegetable patch, with all the versatility that implies. Again, the most important thing is to choose something you can really look forward to eating: you're not going to be able to grow vast quantities of anything, so make what you do grow a real treat. For me, the most satisfying things to grow in containers are zucchini, because they are so prolific and spill out all over the ground, and green pole beans, because of the vertical dimension. I happen to love eating both of them, too.

When calculating how many plants you can get into a container, the backs of your seed packets will again come in handy. Look at the final recommended spacing for a normal outdoor growing site and let that be your guide. So if zucchini should be grown 20 inches apart, then a single pot of a 20-inch diameter will do nicely for a single plant. One way to maximize the productivity of containers is to grow not in rows but in blocks: single beet, spinach, or chard seeds, for example, can be sown in shallow dimples made with your thumb, and spaced about

2 inches apart. Carrot seeds can be done the same way, about 3/4 inch apart. Wigwams of peas and pole beans should be grown in pots at least 20 inches in diameter, with plants spaced 6 inches apart, in a triangle, square, or circle. In all cases, you need a soil/compost depth of at least 20 inches.

The biggest threat to vegetable plants grown in containers is drying out. If, despite regular watering, your container plants do not seem to be thriving as you'd hoped, give them a good liquid feed: I particularly recommend the seaweed-based products.

choosing varieties for flavor

Having asked you to put your trust in the instructions on the backs of seed packets, I am aware that there is one thing they cannot do for you: tell you whether the seeds inside are the best ones to be growing for flavor. For any given vegetable, there are many different varieties, often dozens, which may have distinctly different eating qualities. While the seed companies are thoughtful and helpful to the vegetable gardener in many respects, they fall short of what might sometimes be a useful proviso on the packet: "Not recommended for eating."

To be fair, I don't know of any particular vegetable varieties that are unambiguously poor eating: it's pretty hard to imbue anything you've grown yourself with really negative qualities. But there are definitely some varieties that, over time, I have come to prefer for the table, and others that are perhaps more notable for productivity and shape. Again, this is largely a matter of personal prejudice, or at least personal taste. But since pretty much this whole book is about my personal tastes and prejudices, it is not my intention to leave you short of those commodities in the all-important vegetable chapter.

I am therefore going to end this section with a list of the vegetables I grow regularly at River Cottage, in each case including the names of the varieties I have come to prefer (or the U.S. equivalent). For what it's worth, I'll also throw in any useful information I can think of, above and beyond the undisputed wisdom of the seed packets I have such faith in.

PEAS I always grow peas and I never grow enough. Peas are frost resistant and can be sown directly into the ground as early as March. But the slugs like the small shoots and so do birds and even mice, so I still prefer to bring my first crop on in small pots under glass, planting them out when they are about 6 inches high in early/mid-April. I'll sow a second crop directly into the ground at the same time, for a second harvest. By the time these are up, the birds and mice are plentifully catered for elsewhere, though the slugs still need watching. You can start a polytunnel crop of peas as early as February and expect it to be ready by early June.

Hazel is the traditional wood for pea stakes in England; they should be at least 4 feet high. Chicken wire is less esthetic, but highly effective.

Recommended varieties Laxton's Progress (for early sowing); Sugar Snap (you can eat the whole pod, but they are fat, not flat like a snow pea); and Sugar Rae (a prolific dwarf variety of sugar snap).

FAVA BEANS My very favorite vegetable, fava beans have to be grown, not bought, as commercially they are always left to get too big. The bean seeds and young shoots are completely frost resistant and so can be planted directly into the ground in either autumn (November) or early spring, and simply come up when they feel ready. Autumn-planted beans are said to be more resistant to black fly, and it is certainly true that crops planted on the late side in spring (after the middle of May) seem to be susceptible to it. I tend to plant single beans in plugs or

small pots under glass in early March and plant them out in April for an early crop (ready mid- to late June), then do the same for a second crop starting two or three weeks later. Fava beans like free-draining ground that has been freshly dug and manured.
Recommended varieties Aquadulce for autumn sowing; Green Windsor and Bunyard's Exhibition for spring; and the Sutton, a prolific dwarf variety, for low maintenance (there's no need to tie them up).

GREEN POLE BEANS I love to grow green pole beans. Their triffid-like profusion and vertical takeoff are so satisfying to watch. And I love to eat them. I grow several varieties now, some suitable for eating whole when young, others that are podded for the beans inside when more mature. Some species are dual-purpose. In all cases, I get the plants started in small pots under glass: plant just one bean in each pot in March, then transplant when the risk of frost is past and the plant is at least 6 inches high.
Recommended varieties Blue Lake (the classic green pole bean, generally eaten as a whole pod when young and tender, though the mature pod, when tired and leathery at the end of the summer, can be harvested for the beans inside – these are what we call flageolet beans); Goldmarie (a lovely flat yellow variety; eat the whole pods when young); borlotti (these beautiful red-and-yellow-patterned shelling beans are grown to full maturity for the bean inside the pod, which is discarded; the beans can be eaten fresh, or dried for winter use).

BEETS I used to hate beets, which only ever seemed to be available pickled in vinegar. Now that I have tasted them fresh and grown them myself, they're a real favorite. My son, Oscar, loves them too, as you can tell from the picture on page 94. Beets are wonderfully easy to grow – a classic for the seed-packet gardener. When thinning beets, don't waste the leaves; eat them like spinach.
Recommended varieties Chiogga, Burpee's Golden, Detroit.

CHARD Related to the beet, but grown for its leaves and succulent stems, chard is an easy plant to grow, though it prefers ground that has been well manured and gets plenty of sun. Keep it watered in dry weather or it may bolt. Chard is a "cut-and-come-again" vegetable, and the same plants will give you several harvests from midsummer right through the winter to the following spring, when it will more than likely go to seed.
Recommended varieties As well as the traditional white-stemmed Swiss chard, there are some beautiful colored varieties, such as the deep-crimson ruby chard and multicolored ones with names like Rainbow Chard or Jacob's Coat. They are all good eating, but the colored varieties are rather less prolific.

SPINACH I don't grow "true" spinach, which has to be pulled up by the roots when harvested, but instead get great satisfaction from another kind of cut-and-come-again green Swiss chard, known as perpetual spinach. It can be slow to get under way, but a couple of rows planted in early April with, say, a dozen plants in each will provide you with a good pick at least once a week come June.

CARROTS See pages 38–39 for the essential wisdom! Plus one more tip for warding off carrot fly: grow garlic and chives (and, indeed, garlic chives) alongside your carrots. Carrot flies navigate by a sense of smell: they can apparently sniff out bruised carrot leaves from over half a mile away. When you thin your carrots – as you inevitably have to do if you are letting them grow to any size – pick a few chives before you start. The strong allium vapors may help to disorient the marauding carrot flies.

Recommended varieties Early Nantes and Chantenay (sow in spring for summer harvest; Early Nantes can be sown as early as February); Autumn King (sow June/July for autumn and winter pulling); James Scarlet Intermediate – a lovely, long, tapered carrot that is particularly good raw.

ARTICHOKES I finally got myself some globe artichokes, dug up from a friend's garden, this spring. They have done well. They are apparently easy to grow from seed (but must be started under glass), and I plan to do that next year. The fruits – i.e., edible flower heads – must be cut when still small the first year (they are still edible), and the plants should then be prolific for the next two to four years, after which they start to fade and need to be replaced. My wife Marie introduced me to the novel idea, apparently very popular in France, of eating really fresh young artichokes raw. They're lovely, but make your mouth turn purple.
Recommended varieties All of them!

ZUCCHINI Zucchini (which are related to vegetable marrows, which are thin-skinned, elongated squashes) are wonderfully easy to grow. If you don't have a greenhouse, seeds can be germinated, one per 4-inch pot, on a sunny windowsill from March onward. Then, providing you don't plant them out until the frost risk has passed, they will reward you with lots of fruit from late June until October. Like all squashes, zucchini love manure and compost, so dig lots in when you transplant. Don't miss the treat of deep-fried zucchini flowers in batter – best with a tiny baby zucchini attached.
Recommended varieties Aristocrat, Arlesa, Gold Rush (a beautiful yellow color, not so prolific as the green varieties, but just as tasty).

PUMPKINS and other SQUASHES Like zucchini, these are easy to grow if started under glass or on a windowsill, with the same proviso about frost. They need plenty of space and love manure so much that some people actually plant them on top of old compost heaps. I just dig plenty in when I transplant. Variety is everything with squashes and pumpkins: some (the Atlantic Giant pumpkin, for example) are bland and uninteresting, whereas others are sweet, creamy, and delicious.
Recommended varieties Hundredweight (traditional lantern pumpkin); Sweet Mama (lovely small squash); Baby Bear; and most varieties of acorn squash.

PURPLE SPROUTING BROCCOLI I don't grow a lot of brassicas, but purple sprouting broccoli is an absolute must. Once it has been cut, the sugars in the fleshy stem revert to starch within hours, so the broccoli you grow yourself and cook within an hour of harvest will far exceed anything you can buy in the shops. It also beautifully plugs that gap in the year after all the winter veggies have gone. This year I ate purple sprouting two or three times a week from the second week of March until early May and never got bored of it.

It's easy to grow from seed. Rather than planted under glass, it should be sown in a finely raked outdoor seed bed in April or early May for harvesting the following spring, then transplanted when easy to handle. It can replace an early pea crop, pulled out when finished sometime in June or early August, and will benefit from the nitrogen fixed by any legume (a posh word for members of the pea and bean family). In July and August, you can often buy small pots of growing purple sprouting in garden centers, ready for transplanting.
Recommended varieties Grow one crop of Late Purple Sprouting and one of Early, to maximize your season.

EXOTIC GREENS and SALADS I group a number of plants together here because, although they are not necessarily related, they are all cultivated – and eaten – in a similar way. All of them can be eaten raw, especially when young and tender, and most are also cooked when older. Some are popular imports from the Far East and are generally lumped together as "Asian greens," but there are distinctive varieties that deserve a little exposition here. I also include in the list below some lettuces, cresses, and leafy brassicas (of which arugula is an increasingly well-known example).

Arugula A delicious peppery salad leaf that is wonderfully easy to grow. Sow directly into the ground in March or April and start tucking into the first thinnings a couple of weeks later. A September sowing will give you a slow-growing but reliable winter crop too. A cut-and-come-again plant that just seems to keep on going, until it finally bolts and goes to seed.

Land cress Another zesty salad green, which is almost indistinguishable from its cousin, watercress. Easy to grow, exactly as for arugula.

Purslane A delicious curiosity, with rich, slightly soapy, spinachlike leaves. Again, easy to grow but horribly susceptible to slugs.

Mâche (lamb's lettuce) In some ways bland, but rather refreshing, as it is crisp and holds a lot of water. It grows like a true spinach, and the small plants are harvested whole, roots and all, when the clusters of half a dozen leaves are just a few inches high.

Tatsoi One of the increasingly popular Asian greens, this looks like a stubby version of chard, with dark green leaves spreading from thick white stems that form a lovely round bulb where they meet at the base. It has a mild, mustardy tang (it's sometimes called mustard greens) and is delicious raw in salads or cooked for a matter of seconds in a stir-fry.

Sorrel Broadleaf sorrel is a cultivated variety of the wild plant that is very productive and easy to grow as a cut-and-come-again plant, and it will keep you supplied from spring through to autumn. A few raw leaves add lemony bite to a salad, and a simple sorrel sauce is a delight with fish, or even just a poached egg – see page 424. See also page 307 for wild sorrel.

Valmaine lettuce I recently discovered this, and although the slugs nailed my first sowing, I persisted with excellent results. It's a deliciously sweet and crispy romaine-style lettuce (perfect for Caesar salads), but it grows in cut-and-come-again form. Very handy.

Mizuna Another Asian import, this one has spiky leaves and a lovely spicy taste. Like arugula and other hot and bitter leaves, mizuna seems to be slug resistant. I guess they haven't got the palate for it.

Frisée (or curly endive) Commonly thought of as a lettuce, frisée is actually a kind of chicory, and although it is usually grown as a salad leaf it can be cooked. Sown directly into the ground in June, it is really intended for winter harvest, and will be ready from early November onward. Like all chicories, frisée has a bitter taste but can be sweetened by blanching. To do this, all light is excluded from the plant for two to three weeks before harvest, either by placing an upturned flowerpot over the whole plant (put tape over the drainage hole to prevent light getting in) or by tying black polyethlene (a trash bag will do) around the base of the plant. A frisée and bacon salad, with soft-boiled fresh eggs and a few fried croutons, is one of the best simple suppers I know.

Radicchio Another member of the chicory family, radicchio has beautiful red leaves growing straight upward like rabbit's ears. Plant in June for an autumn/winter harvest. It is perfect for making the Radicchio and Chile Pasta Sauce on page 108.

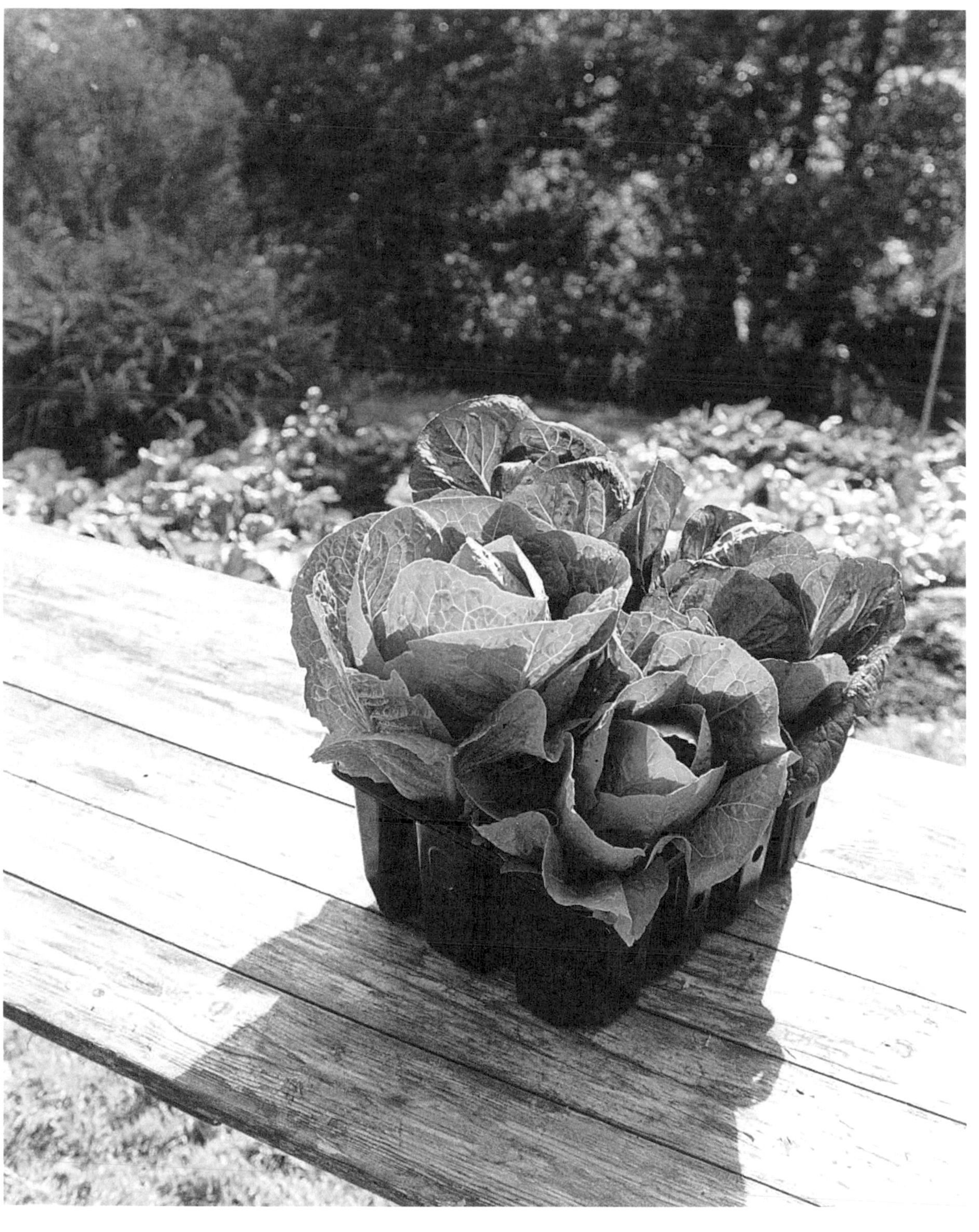

All of the above can be grown very successfully throughout the winter in a polytunnel. Plant them in September/October when the last of the tomatoes have been pulled out, and dig them up again in February to make way for early pea crops and general seed-sowing needs.

TOMATOES When I was a child, tomatoes were at the top of my list of "untouchable" foods (I was a fussy little so-and-so). What made this particularly odd was that I was addicted to ketchup, which had to go on everything, including my cheese sandwiches for school. I finally learned to love tomatoes – real ones – in my teens, when my father started growing them in his new greenhouse. He grew them in grow bags then, as he does now, and among them was a cherry-type of tomato called Gardener's Delight. He persuaded me to try one, promising a sweetness of which I was highly skeptical. But he was right. It was almost as good as ketchup.

Now, I love tomatoes – but only good varieties that have been allowed to ripen fully on the vine. Sour, unripe tomatoes, grown not for flavor but for their thick skins, which give them an interminable shelf life, still seem to pollute the supermarkets and produce markets, and I loathe them as much as I ever did.

Luckily, growing your own is easy – provided you have a greenhouse, conservatory, or polytunnel. (Certain species can do well outside in a very sunny, sheltered spot, but much depends on the right dose of sunshine at the right time. I stick to my polytunnel.) Growing tomatoes from seed under glass is not difficult, but buying small plants from the garden center is even easier. While the plants are still small – up until, say, mid-May – I tend to shuffle them around the polytunnel to wherever there is space. But once their roots are showing in the base of the pot, they need to be planted out to their final position, or at least transferred to a larger pot. A 10-inch pot filled to the brim with a premixed growing compost will take a tomato plant to harvest, but it will need a weekly feed once the first tiny green fruits appear.

All tomato plants will benefit from a liquid feed once the fruits start growing, and tomato enthusiasts have all sorts of special patented recipes for homemade feeds. There are hundreds of commercial varieties, too. The River Cottage recipe is to half-fill an old net onion bag with a few handfuls of dried sheep's droppings, a dozen nettle tops, and a handful of comfrey leaves, then suspend it from a stick in a ten-gallon water butt or rain barrel. Left in the sun for a few weeks, it eventually starts to smell pretty rank, but the tomatoes love it.

To help create strong, productive vines and avoid dissipating the plants' energy, certain side shoots need to be pinched out regularly. There are three types of side shoots growing out from the main stem: ones bearing flowers, and later fruit, which you leave; ones bearing leaves only, which you also leave; and ones that start to grow in the crux between the leaf-bearing stems and the main stem – those are the ones to remove.

Good strong tomato plants can go on producing fruit for over two months – well into October. As the weeks go by, start stripping back the tired leaves: this will improve ventilation and help the later fruit to ripen. Your last few vines of ripe fruit should be hanging on almost completely denuded plants.

Recommended varieties Small sweet tomatoes for salads and eating whole – Gardener's Delight, Sungold, Sweet 100; heavy-cropping large tomatoes for slicing and cooking – Early Girl, Alicante, Marmande, Big Boy.

POTATOES Growing potatoes is not as specialized or difficult as some gardeners would have you believe, but it does require a bit of space. If you've got that space, it is undeniably lovely to have your own spuds on tap, and the flavor of just-dug specimens is undoubtedly superior. There are also some interesting varieties that you can grow yourself that are expensive or hard to find in the supermarket or produce market. I like to concentrate on

the unusual waxy varieties, which are so different from the good old bakers and mashers you can find anywhere.

For successful propagation, all seed potatoes should be nicely "chitted" before planting. There is nothing mysterious about this: potatoes exposed to the light in early spring will develop nodulelike sprouts (everybody's seen them on potatoes forgotten for a week or two in the vegetable bin). These sprouts are the start of new growth, and are to be encouraged in your seed potatoes: I arrange them in egg cartons and leave them on a windowsill. *Chitting* is the process of removing all but a few of these sprouts in order to focus strong growth. I know some gardeners who leave three sprouts, others two, and a few who swear by one. They all get plenty of potatoes. Personally, for the record, I'm a two-sprout man.

One of the most sworn-by traditions of potato planting is the digging of trenches. This has always struck me as unnecessary labor, since each seed potato has to be planted a good 12 inches away from its neighbor. So why not just dig a good-sized hole for each potato? Acting on a tip from my father, I dig a hole about 8 inches deep and place one handful of wet shredded newspaper and another of good manure (well, probably a trowelful rather than a handful) in the bottom, then place my seed potato on top, sprouts pointing skyward. I cover it up with loose earth, which I compact lightly but firmly on top in a little mound so I know where to watch for the first shoots.

The next bit of strict potato-growing etiquette applies a few weeks after the plants have come up. Authorities insist on mounding up more earth around the base of the plants – and the trench fanatics do this with the entire trench. There is a good reason for this: to protect potatoes growing near the surface from exposure to light, which will make them turn green and spoil them for eating. But really, the lazy gardener, who is prepared to sacrifice the odd spud, needn't bother. I hear a murmur of disapproval gathering momentum over the potato patches of West Dorset and Idaho . . . .

Potatoes are ready for digging between three and four months after planting, but winter crops can be left in the ground after the plants have withered and rotted. If, however, your plants are struck by blight (which you will recognize by a yellow-browning and curling of the leaf edges), you should ruthlessly cut off any affected parts – remove the whole stem if any of its leaves are affected – and burn them. The potatoes beneath will more than likely stop growing, so you may as well start harvesting, however tiny they are. And if the blight comes back, dig up the whole crop at once, on a dry day, and store in a dark place covered in paper sacks, burlap, or newspaper, but not plastic, as they need to breathe.

Recommended varieties Pink Fir Apple, Rose Finn Apple, Yukon Gold.

freezing vegetables

Frozen vegetables will always be second choice to fresh, but even a small vegetable patch, when in full swing in the summer, is liable to produce more of something than you can easily consume. It would be a pity to waste it. I grew up in a house where freezing vegetables was close to a religion – my father always liked to have fava beans with the turkey on Christmas Day. But enthusiastic though he was, he knew very well that some vegetables freeze better than others, and some are a complete waste of time. He now believes – and I wholeheartedly agree – that the only vegetables that freeze really well whole, and remain worth serving as "fresh," are his beloved fava beans and green peas. In both cases, they should be shelled and frozen within an hour or two of picking. There is no need, as some authorities insist, to blanch them before freezing, but you should suck the air out of the freezer bags to create as near as possible to a vacuum, and reduce the formation of ice crystals. Never thaw, but cook from frozen in plenty of lightly salted boiling water. Keep an eye on them, as they only need a couple of minutes once they've come back to a boil.

Spinach and other leafy greens (including sorrel and young nettles) freeze reasonably well, but must be briefly wilted or steamed, then squeezed as dry as possible. When recooked from frozen, the results won't quite pass as fresh, but will be fine for such dishes as creamed spinach, sorrel sauce, nettle soup, and gnocchi.

Other vegetables that have a tendency to glut, such as tomatoes, zucchini, squashes, beets, carrots, celery root, and other roots, have too high a water content to freeze successfully. However, process them simply into soups, sauces, and purées, or other finished dishes, and then freeze them, and the defrosted, reheated versions will be almost as good as new. The Beet Soup with Feta on page 92, Zucchini Sauce for Pasta on page 99, Roast Tomato Sauce on page 102, and Celery Root and Chile Gratin on page 108 all freeze very well.

Pod beans such as green, borlotti, and runner beans are marginal freezers at the young stage – i.e., when you are eating them pod and all. When boiled after freezing, the flesh has a reasonably pleasant consistency, but the outer skin is always a bit slimy. However, all these varieties can be left on the plant to go "over the top" until the pod has withered to a leathery, semi-dried-out consistency. These are what Americans call shelling beans: they are shelled for the beans inside (flageolet, haricot, or borlotti, depending on the species). These can be eaten fresh (boiled until tender), frozen as for peas and fava beans, or, if you really have a glut, laid out on trays in a warm, airy place until completely hard and dry, then stored in jars for winter use. As with any dried beans, soak overnight, then boil hard (for at least ten minutes) until tender. These are the beans used for classic soups and stews such as the French *cassoulet* and the Italian *ribollita*.

garden herbs

When I arrived at River Cottage in the spring of 1997, the garden was looking pretty fine – to a flower lover. A beautiful camellia, with its blood-red, ball-shaped flowers, was already in bloom. Daffodils were rioting in the grassy bank that divides the garden from the path. Primroses were everywhere. But from a cook's point of view, the garden was a desert. It wasn't until the following year that I really got to grips with the challenge of making space to grow vegetables. But there was one thing I sorted out that very first weekend: the herb garden. I went straight to Groves garden center in Bridport and bought myself some growing herbs in pots: bay, rosemary, sage, thyme, marjoram, chives, basil, parsley, fennel, and mint. Four years later, all those original plants, except the fragile basil, are thriving. I use one or more of them almost every day. And I have added to them every year. I now also grow lovage, tarragon, lemon balm, lemon verbena, caraway, oregano, three more kinds of thyme, three of mint, plus bush basil, cilantro, and dill – the last three mainly in the polytunnel. That's twenty-four different edible plants – and most of them are crowded together in a space no bigger than a single bed.

I find herbs incredibly rewarding, and it's not just the cooking. To be in the garden and to be able to grab, on a whim, a few leaves to tear in the fingers, to release their distinctive, dependable scent, provides the gardener with regular tiny moments of quiet bliss. Bay is my very favorite smell of all. It's planned, not coincidental, that my bay tree at River Cottage is within touching distance of the porch. And touch it I do, especially in the winter when its leaves are at their most potent. A whoosh of bay up my nose every morning is as good as, well, a cup of coffee certainly.

Even when I lived full-time in London and the only outside space I had was two windowsills, I still managed to raise a quartet of essential herbs: rosemary, thyme, sage, and mint. I didn't have a bay tree, but on my walk back home from the tube station I used to pass one growing in a large tub outside an Italian restaurant and I'm afraid I used to plunder it regularly – I think perhaps that's where my addiction began.

In the kitchen, of course, herbs really go to work. It is often the heady aroma and just-released flavor of fresh herbs that transform a dish from the "interesting" category to the really sensational. For this reason, a good cook will always have a ready supply of herbs on hand.

buying herbs

Of course, herbs can be bought as well as grown. But while it is gratifying that supermarkets and even small grocery stores are now selling the better-known herbs fresh as well as dried, there are drawbacks to buying them in this way. First, cut herbs, especially those with delicate leaves such as chervil, cilantro, and tarragon, quickly lose condition. They will not last for more than a few days at best, and, even if they look all right, they will not have the same intensity of flavor as freshly picked herbs. Second, they tend to be packaged in quantities that are either too big or too small for the purposes you have in mind. If you require only a small sprig of thyme for a mushroom omelette, it seems extravagant to buy a hefty bunch, most of which will go to waste. If, on the other hand, you are making pesto, the amount of fresh basil that you need will cost you a small fortune at supermarket prices.

You can now buy herbs growing in pots in the supermarket. These may seem like the perfect solution, but they have their drawbacks. These pot herbs have been forced hard under glass; while basil and parsley grown like this can be fine, other herbs, like chervil, dill, and especially thyme, seem to have almost no flavor at all.

You will often get much better value buying big bunches of loose herbs from independent produce markets, farmers' markets, and Asian supermarkets. The life of bought cut herbs can be extended, though not for more than a few days, by putting the stems in a glass of water, or wrapping them loosely in a damp cloth and keeping them in the fridge.

By far the best option, however, is to grow herbs yourself. This is not merely a suggestion for those who already pride themselves on their green thumb. Anyone can grow herbs, as most of them are easy to look after and thrive in a temperate climate with minimal attention. And even if you don't have a garden, you can still grow herbs with ease in small pots or window boxes, inside or out. Used within minutes of being picked, the taste and aroma of the still-living leaves is beyond compare. The fact that they have been nurtured by your own loving hand gives an extra dimension of pleasure to your cooking.

growing herbs

Your herbs should be sited as close as possible to the kitchen; you have to be a very dedicated cook to put on your Wellington boots, put up your umbrella, and tramp to the other end of the garden for a sprig of mint.

Many herbs are natives of the Mediterranean, and, although most are frost-hardy, they need a sheltered situation and plenty of sun in order to thrive. Exceptions to this rule are golden marjoram, which needs a semi-shaded position to prevent the leaves from scorching, and chives, parsley, and mint, which will grow well in partial shade. For most other herbs, a south- or west-facing bed protected on the north or east side by a wall or hedge is ideal. At River Cottage, the herb garden is right beside the front door and goes around the corner of the house, so part of it is southwest facing and part of it northwest. The wooden panels of the porch provide some protection from easterly winds.

A very satisfying way to provide shelter for your herb patch if you don't have a handy wall or hedge is to get the hardier, bushier herbs to do the job for you. In a small area, a low hedge of rosemary, bay, or lavender will, once grown, provide enough shelter from cold winds. If your herb patch is badly windswept, you can use windbreak netting from the garden center until your bushy herbs can do the work for you.

Herbs do not need to be sited in a dedicated herb garden. In flower beds and the aptly named herbaceous borders, herb plants can be mixed in among the flowers and shrubs. The highly distinctive foliage of herbs such as lovage, rosemary, sage, and fennel offers dramatic shape and color to a border. And tough herbs like creeping thymes and marjoram can easily be grown in the cracks between paving stones on a terrace or path.

Besides sun and shelter, most herbs need well-drained soil. They are fairly easy to grow on sandy and limestone soils, but if your garden is on the dreaded clay, you may have to get busy digging plenty of grit and organic material, such as mushroom compost, into the herb bed before planting.

Most herbs can be bought as small plants to set out and grow in the garden, and some can be grown from seed. Garden centers and general nurseries have a selection of the more popular varieties, and others can be

obtained from herb specialists, sometimes by mail order. Once your plants are established, you can increase the supply of shrubby herbs such as rosemary and sage by taking cuttings in late summer. This is a somewhat miraculous and rather satisfying process. At its most simple, it means cutting a piece off your existing plant, sticking it in a pot, and watching it grow. For best results, choose a strong, slightly woody side stem that has fresh new growth at the top. Do not clip it off with hand pruners but break it, or cut halfway through it, then peel away a little strip from the parent plant. This slightly ragged little strip will throw roots faster and stronger than a clean horizontal cut. The cutting should then be placed in a small pot filled with moist potting compost, with the strip entirely buried beneath the surface and the compost covering the first 3/4 inch of the cutting. Keep cuttings under glass or indoors on a sunny windowsill, and make sure they are well watered until they are established.

As I mentioned above, you can buy small pots of growing herbs from some supermarkets. But, with the possible exception of basil, most of these are simply not suitable for planting out. Having been so mercilessly forced under glass, they tend to be lacking in resistance and sturdiness, and will almost certainly wither and die on you.

growing herbs in containers

You do not need a garden to grow herbs. Even a window ledge will provide space for a few 10-inch pots of herbs such as parsley, thyme, chives, and mint. And a small patio or balcony will be roomy enough for larger containers for growing more substantial plants such as rosemary, sage, lovage, and fennel. Clay pots look better than plastic ones but they dry out very quickly, so unless you are prepared to be vigilant and water every day in dry spells, put a plastic pot inside the clay one, or line it with polyethylene with a few drainage holes cut in the base. A general-purpose soil-based potting compost, organic if possible, will provide a suitable growing medium, and frequency of watering can be reduced by mixing water-retaining granules, sold in garden centers, with the compost. An occasional feed with liquid fertilizer will keep the plants growing well.

If you are growing herbs indoors, it helps to spray the plants with a fine mist of tepid water in hot weather, in addition to watering and feeding them.

In order to persuade the plants to produce plenty of fresh leaves for your cooking, it is important to prevent them from flowering by picking off any flower buds that appear. While a plant is young, it can be induced to branch and become bushy by pinching out the tips of the main shoots.

extending the season for your herbs

Perennial herbs like mint, chives, and fennel normally die down in winter and start to grow again in spring. However, they can be induced to continue growing through the winter months, and indeed to continue supplying you with leaves for the kitchen, by bringing them indoors or covering them with cloches in the garden. In early autumn, herbs growing in beds and borders can be dug up and planted into pots, while those already in pots are simply transferred from their outdoor positions to a greenhouse, conservatory, or a light but fairly cool room indoors, ideally near a window. The stems should be cut down to 2 to 4 inches in height to encourage new growth, and the plants kept watered and fed. Annual and biennial herbs (chervil, cilantro, dill, parsley) can be sown into pots toward the end of the summer and should be ready to use about three months later.

the most useful herbs

The herb gardener growing from seed can, like the vegetable gardener, get excellent results by following the care instructions on the packet of seeds. But not all garden shops and nurseries provide this information with pots of growing herbs. Here, then, is some basic advice about growing and using what I consider to be the most useful herbs:

BASIL *Ocimum basilicum* Basil is a half-hardy perennial but best treated as an annual in cold climates, since it is unlikely to survive frost. It is readily available as a growing pot herb and can also be grown from seed under glass, or on a sunny windowsill, or outside in a sunny, sheltered position when the danger of frost is past. Do not transplant outdoor sowings, but thin seedlings to 6 inches apart. Plants potted up carefully at the end of the summer can be kept and used through the winter, either in a heated greenhouse or on a sunny windowsill indoors

The best-flavored varieties are common basil and Italian basil, which has plumper, slightly curly leaves. Bush basil, which has very small leaves and is hardier and easier to grow, also has a good flavor. Alternative varieties tend to be less strongly flavored: purple basil and other variegated basils are pleasingly decorative but lack the punch of the best green basil. Dried basil provides a feeble shadow of the flavor of the fresh leaves.

From the cook's point of view, basil is the finest and most versatile of all herbs. When it is grown indoors, its sweet fragrance will fill your kitchen with the scent of summer. Its greatest friends are the Mediterranean vegetables – tomatoes, peppers, eggplant, and zucchini – but it also combines beautifully with fish: a simple olive oil and lemon juice dressing mixed with finely shredded basil leaves makes an excellent "drizzling sauce" for barbecued fish such as mackerel, red mullet, and bream.

Basil leaves are at their most fragrant when the plant is still young, between 6 and 10 inches high. Pick and tear the leaves as near to serving as possible before adding to a dish, to release their aroma at the last possible minute. This is especially important when using basil in hot dishes, as the flavor is quickly cooked out of the leaves.

BAY *Laurus nobilis* Bay is a slow-growing evergreen that can be grown outdoors in a sheltered position but is safest grown in a tub and brought inside in cold winter spells. It's a favorite for those with a penchant for topiary, and is traditionally clipped into cones or lollipop-shaped trees (clippings can be dried for use later). Bay can be grown from cuttings, or you can buy a small plant.

Producing, as they do, one of the most beautiful smells I know, it is no wonder that bay leaves, fresh or dried, are used in cooking all around the world to flavor stews, soups, stocks, and marinades, usually with red meat and game but also with fish. The flavor combines particularly well with oily fish such as mackerel and herring: fresh fillets rolled up with a bay leaf inside are fantastic broiled, grilled, or baked.

Dried bay leaves are almost as good as fresh, provided they are not kept too long.

CHIVES *Allium schoenoprasum* Chives make a good edging plant in the garden. They are readily available growing in pots, but they are also easy to grow from seed: sow in early spring – as early as Valentine's Day, if you like. Large clumps of chives can be increased by dividing them every few years and replanting bulblets in spring or autumn, in sun or light shade. The pretty purple pom-pom flowers are both decorative and edible, but nonflowering stems will have a better flavor than flowering ones. Lift the plants carefully, pot up, cut back, and bring indoors for winter use.

Chives have all the bite of their cousin, the onion, but none of the tears. They are most commonly used as a garnish, chopped and added freely to soups and sauces just before serving. A chive mayonnaise is perhaps the finest way to dress a potato salad, and excellent also with cold poached salmon. Snip into salads of summer leaves, or on a tomato salad as an alternative to basil.

CILANTRO *Coriandrum sativum* Cilantro has one of the most distinctive flavors of any herb. Its great and much-explored affinity with ingredients such as garlic, ginger, lemongrass, chiles, and coconut forms the backbone of much Eastern cooking, and it is also an essential flavor in any salsa (see page 104). It goes particularly well with fish and shellfish and also enlivens the taste of dull cultivated mushrooms and slightly sweet vegetables such as parsnips, carrots, pumpkins, and squashes. Its pronounced taste means that it is best used without other leafy herbs in cooking.

Cilantro is a hardy annual that can easily be grown from seed or bought in pots and transplanted. It will happily grow outside but thrives under glass.

DILL *Anethum graveolens* Its aniseed taste and frondy foliage indicate that dill is a close relative of fennel, but in fact the two flavors are quite distinct; try making gravlax (or gravmax – see page 328) with fennel instead of dill, as I once did, and you will see the difference. It works, sort of, but is nothing like as good.

Dill sold commercially, especially in supermarkets, is often feeble in flavor as a result of being forced under glass, so if you want a ready supply (you need lots of dill to make good gravlax) it's well worth growing your own. Seeds can be sown at intervals from spring onward, but pots of the growing herb can also be bought. In hot, dry weather it has a tendency to bolt if not well watered.

FENNEL *Foeniculum vulgare* The fresh, aniseed flavor of fennel makes it a natural companion to fish, and the plant is so easy to grow that every fish enthusiast should find a little space for it. In fact, the problem is likely to become containing it, as it is hugely vigorous: a small pot of fennel from the garden center can, if planted in a sunny spot in the spring, grow to a height of two yards or more in just a few months. The luxuriant, fleshy stalks can be cut back several times during the summer, and hung up to dry – they can then be thrown on a grill, where they will impart a dramatic flavor to fish (see the recipe for gray mullet on page 331). At River Cottage, several good sprigs of fennel also go in almost every foil parcel, court-bouillon, or stock where fish is involved.

Small clumps of cut-back fennel can be potted up and taken indoors for winter use. Its spectacular growth and distinctive frondy foliage make it a popular border plant. For wild fennel, see page 390.

LOVAGE *Levisticum officinale* Lovage is a smashing herb whose distinctive savory flavor – like celery with a light, curryish aftertaste – deserves wider recognition. It's almost impossible to buy as a cut herb, so you'll have to grow some: buy a young plant in a pot and transplant to a sunny or lightly shaded spot. Like fennel, it grows rapidly and tall – maybe two yards high in its second summer.

A few lovage leaves go a long way, as you will see if you make the Pea, Lettuce, and Lovage Soup on page 120. A small bundle of lovage does wonders for a chicken stock.

MARJORAM/OREGANO *Origanum* There are several varieties of marjoram, all native to the Mediterranean, one of the more pungent of which is commonly known as oregano. They are vigorous plants, which are easy to grow in a cold climate provided you can give them a sunny, fairly sheltered spot. They make excellent windowbox herbs. It is easier to buy a small marjoram plant in a pot than to grow it from seed.

Sweet marjoram is the most scented variety, but also the most delicate. It is best grown in a pot and moved indoors during the winter, where it will thrive on a sunny windowsill, continuing to give you a crop of leaves throughout the cold months.

In Italy, oregano is the herb used for flavoring pizzas but is also widely used in fish, meat, and vegetable dishes, often combined with thyme. The Greeks love oregano, and its addition, fresh, to the well-known salad of olives, feta, tomato, and cucumber, transforms it.

MINT *Mentha spp.* A hardy perennial, mint is difficult to grow from seed, so you will need to buy a small plant from a garden center. There are dozens of different kinds, some decorative, like the variegated green and white apple mint and the tiny-leafed, creeping Corsican mint. The ones most commonly grown for the kitchen are spearmint and apple mint. Both are excellent, and the rounded, hairy leaves of apple mint do indeed have a hint of the eponymous fruit. All will grow easily in light shade or full sun and are invasive plants: after a year or two, your problem is not likely to be how to grow mint but how to contain it. To restrain the running roots, plant in pots or in a bucket with the bottom removed, sunk into the soil. To increase the supply, just dig up one of the rooted offshoots from the parent plant and replant.

The unmistakable scent of mint is one of the great pleasures of an English summer and the perfect companion to spring lamb and young vegetables, in particular, peas, carrots, fava beans, and new potatoes. It is equally prized in the Mediterranean and makes a good alternative to basil, chopped on top of a simple tomato salad. It also goes beautifully, again instead of basil, with marinated grilled vegetables such as zucchini, eggplant, and peppers, or in a salad of cucumber dressed with yogurt

Mint's versatility extends to combinations with fruit, particularly grapefruit, pineapple, and melon, and, of course, in tall summer drinks. A cooling jug of Pimm's would be nothing without a few sprigs of mint. If you do use mint with fruit, combine it properly so the flavors of fruit and mint can marry. Try, for example, crushed strawberries with a few coarsely chopped mint leaves, a little superfine sugar, and maybe a dash of rum or kirsch. Serve chilled. The ubiquitous mint sprig atop an ice cream or sorbet, or on the side of a plate containing some other dessert to which the herb is irrelevant, is, by comparison, a pointless irritation.

Fresh mint tea is an invigorating delight; a couple of good sprigs with, say, a dozen leaves on each, makes a pot for two. Just pour over boiling water and leave for five to ten minutes.

PARSLEY *Petroselinum crispum* Parsley is one of the most commonly used herbs, probably because it is so friendly. Almost any savory dish, fish in particular, benefits from its mild, grassy taste, which also helps bring out the flavor of many other herbs – hence its use as a vital feature of a bouquet garni. There are curly-leaf and flat-leaf varieties. The latter, often known as continental or Italian parsley, usually has the best flavor.

A hardy biennial, parsley can be bought in pots from almost any garden center but is easy to grow from seed, too – just follow the instructions on the packet. Cut back in September and covered in cloches, it can be kept going through the winter. Or it can be potted up and brought indoors.

Parsley and garlic are one of the great culinary pairings: heated together with a little butter and wine, they will do wonders for virtually anything that has lived in the sea, and plenty of things that haven't, from frog's legs to chicken livers, spuds to snails. In Italy, a versatile mixture called *gremolata* is made by combining a tablespoon of finely chopped parsley with a teaspoon of finely grated lemon zest and half a clove of garlic, very finely chopped. This can either be sprinkled on food just before serving or stirred into a little olive oil and used as a dressing. It's excellent on broiled or grilled fish and de rigueur on osso buco.

For a recipe for Real Parsley Sauce, a great but much abused stalwart of English cooking, see page 119.

ROSEMARY *Rosmarinus officinalis* A beautiful evergreen shrub, hardy except in very cold winters, rosemary needs sunshine. Buy a small potted plant and transplant it. It flowers in early spring and off and on all summer, and is easily raised from cuttings (see page 64). Miss Jessopp's Upright is the best variety for hedging and grows over a yard high. There are white- and pink-flowered forms, and less hardy varieties such as Prostratus and Severn Sea. Rosemary can also be grown in pots, indoors and out. It will get too big for a window box after three or four years, so take cuttings for replacement plants every third year.

The marriage of rosemary and lamb is a blissful one with which most cooks are familiar, but there are many other uses for this pungent, twiggy herb, most of them pioneered by the Italians. They favor it with beef – inserting it with garlic into a filet for roasting in much the same way as we British do for a leg of lamb – and also with fish, especially red mullet, which is served with a rosemary and anchovy butter (simply cream 6 tablespoons soft butter with 8 mashed anchovy fillets and a tablespoon of finely chopped rosemary). Scallops can be threaded onto a twig of rosemary and barbecued or cooked on a grill pan. Whole new potatoes are delicious roasted in their skins in olive oil, with generous sprigs of rosemary thrown in for the last ten minutes of cooking time.

SAGE *Salvia officinalis* Sage is a hardy shrub that is best bought as a small plant. Besides having a distinctive flavor, sage is also a fantastic decorative plant, which forms a low cushion of evergreen leaves. Purple-leafed (Purpurascens) and variegated forms (Icterina and Tricolor) are among the prettiest, but they also have a full sage flavor for cooking with. Further, plants are easy to grow from cuttings, but can become straggly unless trimmed regularly. It's therefore best to replace plants every four or five years. Sage can be grown in pots indoors, but would much rather be outside in the summer.

Sage is the offal lover's best friend. Liver, sweetbreads, and brains are all transformed by the punchy, slightly camphoric flavour of sage leaves, a few of which should be finely chopped and mixed with the seasoned flour in which the offal is tossed before frying. A few more whole leaves can also be casually thrown into the frying pan for the last minute of cooking. They should accompany the offal onto the plate and definitely be eaten. If you are deep-frying anything in batter, a few sage leaves can be dipped and fried too, for a little *amuse-bouche*. Cook for just a few seconds until crisp. Sage also goes well with pork, veal, and poultry. When I have a "pig weekend" at River Cottage, I always make an herby sausage in which sage is the predominant flavor (see page 167).

THYME *Thymus vulgaris, T. serpyllum, T. praecox, T. x citriodorus* An evergreen, creeping plant with flowers varying in color from dark purple-red to pale pink and white, thyme produces shoots that make new roots as they travel along the ground. Start by buying one or two small plants and increase the ground cover by severing rooted shoots from the parent and replanting them. Some varieties have silver and gold variegated leaves.

A good edging and carpeting plant, as it tolerates being walked or sat on, thyme can also be grown in pots indoors. There are dozens of different varieties, many of which have very distinctive scents, but the best all-rounders for cooking are common thyme and lemon thyme.

With its powerful savory flavor and slight bitterness, thyme is an essential ingredient in a bouquet garni. But it also deserves an outing on its own occasionally. Unlike many herbs, its flavor infuses well during long, slow cooking, and a sprig of thyme is a worthwhile addition to many casseroles, in particular red meat and game, and for making most good stocks. A sprig in the cavity of a roasting game bird, or a whole fish such as red snapper, also pays dividends.

Thyme has an affinity with three other ingredients in particular: mushrooms, black olives, and artichokes. Mushrooms fried up with a little thyme can be eaten on toast, or with polenta and Parmesan cheese, or made into a fine omelette. I like to buy plain black kalamata olives and marinate them with olive oil and lemon thyme. Artichokes can be served hot with melted butter flavored with thyme and lemon juice.

garden fruit

If growing your own vegetables is satisfying, then growing your own fruit may feel positively decadent. And why not? It is no coincidence that fruit has come to be so loaded with sexual symbolism (Eve's apple, Tess of the d'Urbervilles' strawberry . . .). It is, after all, the product of the sexual congress of plants. Not only that, it seems it has actually evolved to provoke the sexual appetites of animals. Natural selection determines that it should be eaten, thereby ensuring the dispersal, and indeed composting, of the seeds it contains. And to this end fruits have adopted physical forms that unequivocally advertise their availability to the animal kingdom, particularly the higher mammals. So if the pinky yellow flush, gently contoured cleft, and soft downy skin of a ripe peach reminds you of a pert young bottom, and the inside of a cut fig of something even more intimate and arousing, it doesn't mean you should sign up for a course of Freudian analysis. It just means that fruits have learned the oldest marketing trick in the book: sex sells.

The taste experience offered by fruits merely compounds the visual provocation. They have in abundance that substance that sends the human taste buds into sensual overdrive: natural sugar. And as if that isn't enough, each fruit vies with the competition with its unique blend of seductive aromatics – what we call flavor. The result is that the experience of eating a fully ripe specimen of any given fruit is somehow complete, in a way that other foods do not achieve. There is nothing in so little need of further adornment or adulteration to pleasure the human palate than, say, a perfectly ripe pear, peach, or plum.

Underpinning their sensual benefits are indisputable physical ones. Fruits deliver one of the most useful and easily digestible forms of energy to the animals that eat them. Their carbohydrates are assimilated faster, and with less strain on the gut, than any other food.

No wonder, then, that the role of fruit in our own evolution is central. Our ancestors, the forest-dwelling primates, enjoyed a privileged symbiosis with the fruits of their habitat. Their intelligence and adaptability enabled them to feast on a wider range of fruits than any other species, and as they moved through the forest, dropping seeds in a tidy package of their own manure, they inadvertently assured the continued success of their favorite fruits in the forest habitat. When ape became human, the husbandry became conscious and calculated, as they quickly discovered that fruit could be cultivated. And when humans became civilized, it was not long before they were applying themselves scientifically not merely to the propagation of fruit in quantity but also, by means of hybridizing and grafting, to the improvement of their fruit's succulence, sweetness, and flavor. By the time the Romans were throwing fashionable orgies, cultivated fruit was the smartest thing on the menu: the fleshy products of plants' sexual activity were rated as among the highest oral pleasures.

In eighteenth-century Europe, another decadent society made the cultivation of fruit a symbol of wealth and status. Everybody grew vegetables. But the aristocracy proved its superiority and ingenuity by going to extraordinary lengths, and expense, to grow luscious fruits. In England, the climate is hardly suitable for growing peaches and grapes. But that was no obstacle. Wealthy landowners constructed glass hothouses with elaborate underground heating systems, fueled by charcoal or anthracite, for the cultivation of sweet and highly scented Muscat grapes. South-facing walls were built especially for the training of peach trees, and even had built-in furnaces, to warm the wall from the inside on the days when the sun didn't shine.

These days, such extravagant systems are largely redundant, as cheap air freight brings in exotic fruit from all over the world throughout the year. This is not something I'm inclined to moan about per se: I'm delighted to be able to buy mangoes, passion fruit, and papayas at the local grocery store – not to mention the oranges and bananas we have so long taken for granted. But the international market and huge global demand for fruit have taken their toll on quality and flavor. The goal of much hybridization now is long shelf life and regularity of shape and size. In the interests of the former, most fruits are harvested before they are ripe. And as if that weren't enough, scientists have begun to meddle with the basic genetic structure of fruits. In the good old days, they knew when to stop meddling: when something tasted right. Today, it seems, the supermarkets would pay scientists to cross a grapefruit with a spaniel puppy if they thought its furry ears and hangdog eyes would appeal to the housewife.

The problem with having strawberries in winter and mangoes in every corner shop is that it breeds complacency and ignorance on the part of the consumer: complacency – in that we think we can have whatever we want whenever we want; and ignorance – of the seasons of homegrown fruit, which, when grown to full ripeness outdoors in the summer, is quite unbeatable for taste. I'm not suggesting we all forgo bananas and pineapples from June to September. But the shopper who fails to notice the moment in the year when the infeasibly unblemished, hard, sour imported strawberries are briefly moved off the shelf in favor of properly ripened, fully fragrant local fruit is missing out on something very special: the real taste of a strawberry, for a start.

For those who wish to pursue a relationship with fruit that retains some of the sense of wonder and excitement that prevailed before the advent of the mass global market, an appreciation of seasonality is vital. And the best way to achieve that is to grow some fruit yourself. You don't have to build a fruit cage or learn how to train a dozen pear trees into an espalier. A single hanging basket of strawberries suspended from a sunny porch, or a dwarf cherry tree in the corner of a tiny town garden, will be enough to make a difference. You may harvest only a couple of dozen strawberries or a few bowls of cherries, but they will serve as a benchmark for quality and a symbol of seasonality that will make all the difference in the way you think about, shop for, and eat your fruit.

The garden at River Cottage is pretty tiny, and finding space to grow fruit in any quantity has been a problem. However, through stealth and determination I have managed to squeeze over a dozen fruit bushes into various awkward places. They all get a fair bit of sun, and this year I am anticipating, for the second season, reasonable pickings of strawberries, raspberries, red currants, white currants, black currants, gooseberries, and a lovely hybrid of these latter two called a worcesterberry. I've also planted two fruit trees – both greengages, which is my favorite of all the plums. The fruits I grow remain a tiny fraction of the fruits I consume. But the pleasure they give me is out of all proportion to the modest harvest I reap.

Before I share with you my limited but joyous experience of cultivating fruit (supplemented by a bit of wisdom gleaned from greater experts than I), I want to say a bit about the various ways you can buy fruit.

buying fruit

There is a fundamental difference between the mission to buy the best vegetables and the search for the most delicious fruit. Whereas most vegetables are at their best when the least time has elapsed since they were plucked from the ground, most fruits have a limited time span of perfection when the balance of sugars, water, and aroma-releasing enzymes makes them most pleasant to eat. This, of course, is what we call ripeness. And for the shopper, the search for truly ripe fruit can be immensely frustrating. The problem is that ripeness only briefly precedes the onset of decay, and therefore most properly ripe fruits are likely to be just a day or two away from deterioration. (A friend of mine swears that the window of opportunity for a real enthusiast to enjoy a pear at the height of aromatic succulence is to be measured in minutes rather than hours. I think that's a bit excessive – but only a bit.)

The supermarkets and grocery stores are reluctant to take delivery of properly ripe fruit, since within a few days they may have unsaleable mush and mold on their hands. The strategy of the trade for dealing with the ripeness "problem" is therefore to harvest, distribute, and sell almost all their fruit before it is ripe at all. This is good news and bad news. Some fruits actually ripen better off the parent plant than on. Tree-ripened bananas are mealy and starchy compared to those that have been picked green and left to ripen afterward. Avocados will not ripen at all until they have been picked – which is why the trade's method for "storing" avocados to spread the crop throughout the year is simply to leave them on the tree. And some varieties of pears are best picked green and left to ripen in warm air.

At the other end of the scale are fruits that will not ripen at all once picked. Melons, pineapples, and all citrus fruits fall into this category. Any attempt to sweeten them by leaving them on even the sunniest windowsill will be in vain. It therefore pays the shopper to know how to recognize when such fruits are ripe for eating. In the case of melons, smell and touch are the best indicators. The base of the fruit should give slightly to pressure from the thumb. And put the base, rather than the stalk end, to your nose: it should smell honeyed and temptingly aromatic. Another good sign is if there is no residual stalk attached to the melon: a clean break indicates the fruit was ripe for picking.

Pineapples offer a distinctly physical clue to ripeness: the size of the spiky plume of leaves on top of the fruit. Contrary to what you might expect, the smaller the plume, the riper the fruit. Unripe pineapples are also hard, with a greenish tinge, whereas a ripe fruit has softer, orange-brown skin. As ever, your nose is the final arbiter – it will smell fragrant and tempting.

As for citrus fruits, there is little the outward appearance of an orange, clementine, or grapefruit will tell you about its inner sweetness or juiciness. Any opportunity to taste before you buy is therefore to be welcomed. Some grocery stores, to their great credit, will allow this – with clementines and satsumas at least – especially if you are already in possession of a large basket of their fruit and vegetables that you are clearly planning to buy. But in any shop, there is nothing to prevent you from buying, tasting, then buying some more if you like what you taste. A pocket knife is a handy thing to have for cracking open your "sample" – and if you can suck on a wedge of orange in the doorway of your grocery store without feeling embarrassed, you may waste less money on substandard citrus fruit.

For the shopper, the most problematic fruits are those that fall between these two extremes – i.e., most of them. However, all fruits offer the shopper some clue as to their condition and readiness for eating. Here are a few brief notes on the ripeness/shopping issue for some more of the most popular fruits.

STRAWBERRIES The best strawberries you will taste are the ones you pick and eat straight from the plant on a warm day, when they are fully ripe and the flavor-giving molecules are still buzzing with the heat of the sun. This is why growing your own is such a joy – and the U-pick farm comes a very close second. After that, the best bet is to buy from local grocery stores, or even roadside stalls, which in peak season should be taking daily delivery of local, just-picked fruit. Fully ripe strawberries will last only about twenty-four hours before even the lightest of bruises take their toll and mold or decay set in. Eat them at once.

Most local strawberries picked for the supermarket are generally harvested a few days off full ripeness, and chilled immediately for transport. They will be a little more tart than fully ripe specimens but may be good nonetheless. Mold spreads fast in fruit piled up in a basket, so if you want to improve their flavor at home, spread them out on a tray and place them on a sunny windowsill – or outside on a really fine day. Direct sunlight will do more for them than a warm room, and even just a few hours of it can make a considerable difference.

Imported strawberries tend to be picked very hard and unripe for transport, and are then exposed to ethylene gas to color them up. This turns them red but does little for their flavor. Personally, I wait for the homegrown summer fruit to come on.

Strawberries do not recover well from freezing, so gluts from a hefty pick-your-own session are best made into purées, sorbets, or ice creams (see page 127) and then frozen. They do not keep their flavor in the freezer as well as other fruits, so should be consumed within three months at most.

RASPBERRIES Buying raspberries in small baskets in the shops is an expensive business, and the fruit is often disappointingly insipid. Again, the U-pick farm offers better value and better quality. July and early August are the high season, but some farms also grow excellent late-cropping varieties that are good in October. The sign of a ripe raspberry is that it comes easily away from the tough central core, leaving you with a clean fruit that is conveniently ready to eat. Very ripe raspberries of almost purple hue have more sugar and less acid. Tartness is a pleasing feature of the fruit, so taste as you pick, and favor fruit that has the balance about right.

Raspberries freeze well, either sieved and sweetened as a purée, in ices and sorbets (see page 130), or whole (see page 89).

Other BERRIES and CURRANTS Gooseberries, red currants, and black currants are among the easiest fruits to buy, as they keep better, even when ripe, than the more delicate soft fruits, and can be refrigerated without losing condition. However, they are all expensive to buy in any quantity, so once again the U-pick farm is a godsend for those who want to enjoy plenty of these fruits in peak season. They freeze well, either whole, or lightly cooked, sieved, and sweetened, then frozen as a purée, or best of all in many cases made into sorbets and ice creams (see page 130).

CHERRIES In England, the season for homegrown cherries is a short one: beginning in late June, it is often over by the end of July. The window of opportunity is extended by early imports from southern Europe and later ones from the U.S. and elsewhere. As ripe cherries tend to travel better than most soft fruits, these imports should not be ignored: the dark red cherries that start to arrive from Italy in early June can be particularly delicious. The best of the English cherries are the Merton Glory, which is pale yellow tinted with rose, and the Black Tartarian, which is very dark, sweet, and juicy. In the U.S., look for Bing, Black Gold, and Lapins Sweet.

There's not much you can do to sweeten an unripe cherry, once picked. Boxed cherries often come as a mix of ripe and less ripe fruit, so self-selection may allow you to favor the ripest fruit. In my opinion, no retailers of cherries should begrudge you the right to taste before you buy. I do this even in the supermarket, and I haven't been arrested yet.

PLUMS, DAMSONS, and GREENGAGES In England, these related fruits are one of the great pleasures of high summer. In mid-August, when the raspberries, strawberries, black currants, and gooseberries are over, the plums and gages start to come on. In their various different guises, they will last until October (some damsons can be very late). I love this seasonality, and although imported plums are available all year round, I much prefer to celebrate the British crop and forget about plums for the rest of the year. I try to buy as locally as possible and therefore much prefer local grocery stores and farm shops to the supermarket. Some U-pick farms extend their season to allow shoppers to pick their own early plums, where vast quantities can be had at knockdown prices. They also sometimes have more unusual varieties than the shops, which tend to stick to the ever-popular Victoria. Favorite dessert plums (i.e., sweet types that can be eaten without cooking) are Satsuma and Santa Rosa.

Gages – usually called greengages, though some are yellow when ripe and others have a pinky-purple flush – are a rounder form of plum. Most types are sweet and at their best eaten raw. A good, ripe greengage is one of the best of all homegrown English fruits, and the French imports aren't bad either.

Even the most sour plums become delicious when cooked gently with a little sugar. I love lightly stewed plums, sweet but still tart, chilled and served with crème fraîche.

APPLES Compared to all other fruits, most varieties of apples travel and store extremely well. In some cases, notably Fiesta, Jonagold, and Granny Smith, the flavor is actually improved by storage. This means the imported varieties are not to be ignored. But at the same time, homegrown apples, sought out seasonally and locally, deserve to be celebrated for their subtle, and sometimes not so subtle, variations in texture and flavor. Interest in traditional apple varieties is on the increase, and has been one of the causes championed with considerable success by the farmers' markets movement. Some of the supermarkets have earned themselves a rare plus point by getting in on the act, too. Safeway, in particular, always flags up such great British apples as the Russet, Worcester Pearmain, and Beauty of Bath as they arrive from September onward. I make a point of tasting any apple variety that I have never encountered before. At the Bridport farmers' market last autumn, I discovered for the first time the delights of the Lord Lambourne – a lovely crisp apple with a tart lemon tang and a hint of rosewater. In the U.S., look for Pink Lady and Jonathan.

People who really like apples tend to be quite fussy about the apples they like. Personally, I prefer a hard, crisp, sharp apple. Galas and Golden Delicious, sweet but bland, do nothing for me, whereas the first hard, sharp, homegrown Cox's Orange Pippins, with their unmistakable honeyed citrus flavor note, are unbeatable. The later Cox's are often too sweet and mealy, and the recent mass imports from New Zealand, which keep us in Cox's through our early summer months and have a yellow skin and suspiciously even tiger streaking of red, don't seem like real Cox's at all. Another favorite of mine is the early-cropping Discovery, often ready from mid-August, which stains a gorgeous rosy pink when bitten. Other good U.S. varieties include Gravensteins, Arkansas Black, and Braeburn.

The distinction between cookers and eaters can be a misleading one. From the cook's point of view, the more useful distinction is between apples that keep their shape when cooked and those that dissolve into a purée. In Britain, the best-known of the latter is the good old Bramley, still the best apple for making crumbles, pies, and delicious tart purées to serve with goose or pork. But if you want to make a classic French-style apple tart, with layers of thinly sliced apples overlapping in concentric circles, tart, early-season Cox's, Reinettes, or even Russets are the best bet. For a tarte Tatin, where whole halves of peeled apples need to keep their shape under assault from oozing hot caramel, Granny Smiths are just the thing.

Even the best storing apples, once exposed to warm air in the produce market or the house, will gradually begin to deteriorate. If the skin moves to form a wrinkle when pushed sideways with your thumb, it is starting to lose its crispness and, for me at least, is devoid of all interest. The pigs, however, love them.

Farmers' markets in the autumn are often a good place to discover interesting local varieties.

PEARS The best pears are those ripened off the tree. This should mean that the trade's policy of picking unripe fruit for transport fortuitously serves the consumer's best interests, but in fact a lot of pears are picked so green and hard that the journey to full ripeness is one they simply don't have the resources to complete.

It is impossible to be sure exactly what traumas of transport and storage a pear you encounter in the shops has been subjected to. But there are a few clues that can increase the chances of locating a good 'un and rejecting a bad 'un. Any sign of wrinkling around the stalk end while the bulb is still firm indicates a pear that will be mealy before it is ripe. A nearly ripe pear, on the other hand, will give a little around the stalk end when pressed with the fingertips, even when it is not wrinkled. A few days in a warm kitchen or, better still, on a sunny windowsill, should bring it to perfection.

The best-known varieties of pears in Britain are the elongated and slightly russeted Conference and the fatter, rounder Comice. In both cases, the skin changes from green to yellow as the fruit ripens, but the yellow of the ripe Comice is paler and brighter than that of the Conference. Williams (known in the U.S. as Bartlett) is another excellent dessert variety that has a reasonable distribution. British growers produce huge numbers of all these varieties, and the homegrown fruit, which stores well, is on the shelves from October to February. It is less likely to be prematurely picked than imported fruit, making the winter months the best for pear lovers.

There are dozens of other British pear varieties, some of tremendous character and flavour: Durondeau, Thompson's, Concorde, and Seckel, to name but four. It would be hugely gratifying and exciting to see the trade champion the best of these in our produce markets and supermarkets, as has happened to a limited extent with British apples in recent years. Sadly, there is precious little sign that such an initiative is imminent. For now, the best places to find unusual pear varieties are farmers' markets and farm shops near where they are grown.

APRICOTS In the U.K., the choice is not between different varieties of apricot but between whatever is available fresh and the dried product. Both kinds are imported – although a few enthusiasts grow apricots in this country, I have never found a commercial outlet for the homegrown product. As a fruit for eating raw, the fresh apricots we get here tend to be a big disappointment: insipid in taste and cotton-woolly in texture. Any exceptions seem to be a matter of good luck – being in the right shop at the right time. Fruits that have a warm, rosy-orange glow and are slightly soft to the touch are the best bet. You may still be disappointed, but the alternative – hard, yellowish fruits – is certainly good only for cooking.

Fresh apricots are well worth buying, though – they can be transformed by a simple procedure. Choose the nearest thing you can find to ripe fruit, cut them in half at right angles to the line between the stem end and the base of the fruit, and remove the pit. Arrange the apricot halves on a baking tray, cut side uppermost, and, with a teaspoon, tip a little heap of superfine sugar into the cavity of each. Then bake in a preheated 350°F oven for twenty minutes or so, until they are nicely tender and the juices are running. This is much more satisfactory than stewing apricots, as they retain their shape, at least partially. Prepared in this way, apricots are delicious eaten warm from the oven, or can be incorporated into many recipes – including the bread and butter pudding on page 132.

PEACHES and NECTARINES Finding a peach (or its smooth-skinned incarnation, the nectarine) that is perfectly ripe and ready to eat can be ridiculously hard in the U.K.. It's pretty tragic, as an indifferent peach is as uninspiring as a good one is delectable. Only an occasional encounter, as often as not on a foreign holiday, with a properly sun-ripened specimen, restores one's faith.

The problem is premature picking and a long stay in cold storage. Peaches can be ripened at home to an extent, especially if exposed to direct sunlight on a windowsill. But you can't expect miracles, and a rock-hard, sour-fleshed peach will never become good. An overlong stay in cold storage may also shut down the ripening process beyond the possibility of reactivation. Peaches and nectarines that have suffered this abuse may soften over time but will never sweeten, and their bland, mealy flesh is of even less interest than that of a tart, almost crunchy underripe peach, which can at least be made interesting by cooking (overlap thin slices of the peeled fruit in a layer in a heatproof dish, sprinkle with light brown sugar, and place under a broiler for three or four minutes until the sugar bubbles and the juices run; serve hot or chilled, with crème fraîche).

In my experience, the peaches from the Southern Hemisphere in the winter months and the earliest arrivals of the summer are the worst culprits. Peaches from Spain and Italy that start to arrive in England from August onward are a better bet. Choose plump ones that have a deep color with no yellow-green tinge. Squeezed gently with the fingertips, they should give a little beneath the skin. If you think you have found a properly ripe peach, buy it at once and eat it then and there. If your best expectations are confirmed, buy some more – as many, in fact, as you think you and your family can eat over the next couple of days.

labeling ripeness

British supermarkets (and some of their American counterparts) have recently introduced a policy of packaging some fruit – pears and peaches especially, but also mangoes and papayas – with the label "ripe and ready to eat," and charging a considerable premium for it. This little marketing ruse seems a bit nervy to me, since it's tantamount to a confession that most of their fruit is woefully unripe. And, in the same breath, they have the cheek to charge extra for delivering what you might reasonably have hoped they could offer you in the first place. What's more, some of the fruit packaged like this is still a day or two away from true ripeness – it has to be to allow for a three- or four-day shelf life. Still, the "ripe and ready to eat" fruit is usually the pick of the bunch, and should be good within a day or two of purchasing. For the undoubted pleasure of the perfect pear, or properly luscious peach, it may be worth shelling out the extra once in a while.

growing your own fruit

I hope the reasons I've given for growing your own fruit at the beginning of this chapter hardly need re-emphasizing. But for good measure, here's an extra one: it's really easy! Most fruits grow on hardy shrubs, bushes, and trees – plants that are essentially low maintenance. Choose a good site for them, plant them with a bit of love and care, and, apart from the odd drop of water in dry spells and perhaps an occasional feed, they will need serious attention only once a year, for pruning. Having said that, those who like to fiddle can find plenty of excuses to do so. Fruit trees and bushes can be trained and disciplined in all kinds of ways, some decorative, some aimed at increasing productivity and fruit size. But for lazy gardeners (like me), a laissez-faire attitude will still produce plenty of delicious fruits for you to revel in.

Beyond that, I have only one overriding caveat that should help you avoid any major disappointments. Many soft fruit and top fruit (i.e., fruit tree) species are susceptible to various diseases caused by viruses. At their worst, these can not merely decimate a harvest but kill off your entire rootstock. This sounds daunting, but the good news is that much work has been done over the years to breed plants that are reliable and disease resistant. It's well worth taking advantage of this, so when buying stock to start your fruit garden, it pays to visit a specialist fruit nursery or at least a large and well-stocked garden center, where well-informed staff can help you toward a sensible choice of virus-free stock. With this basic security in hand, your only major worry will be keeping the ever-hungry birds at bay. Suggestions about how best to do that appear below.

siting your fruit in the garden

It seems to me that one of the most charming features you can create in a garden is a good old-fashioned English fruit cage dedicated to growing soft fruits and berries. Draped with netting to keep out the birds, and planted up with a range of exciting fruits, a fruit cage is a little oasis of pleasure and fulfillment – or even the aforementioned decadence. Enter and you can run wild within its confines, feeding your senses with its tastes and smells.

You need a bit of space, of course. Five yards by five would be a minimum, and ten by ten would provide plenty of room for a bit of everything. Not that a fruit cage has to be square: a rectangle, triangle, circle, or even a trapezium may better suit your available space. Your planting plan needs a bit of thought. All your soft fruits will benefit from as much sunshine as possible, so to avoid the tall bushy plants shading the smaller ones, plant your rows in ascending order of height, from south to north. In practical terms, this means placing your strawberry beds at the south end, your gooseberries and currants in the middle, and your raspberry canes at the north end. Alternatively, if your fruit cage is fully south facing and gets the sun all day, simply create rows of fruits running from north to south and they will all get plenty of sun.

As for siting fruit trees, choose an open space away from the competing roots of other trees and shrubs. Pears and apples, damsons, sour cherry varieties, and cooking plums do not need full sun but will nevertheless benefit from all they get, producing bigger, sweeter fruit as a result. Sweet eating plums, gages, and cherries should be given as sunny a spot as possible. Peaches, apricots, and figs should really be trained against a south-facing wall: the heat reflected back from the wall will help to ripen these fruits, and in a cold climate they need all the help they can get. And finally, try to site your fruit within a reasonable walking distance of the house. You are sure to make better and more frequent use of it if it is a stroll away rather than a hike.

growing fruit in small spaces

Sadly, I have no room at River Cottage to build a fruit cage. I have therefore sneaked my fruit plants in and around the other fixed features of the garden. A row of gooseberry and currant bushes runs along the western edge of the long vegetable patch beside the house. My strawberries are layered in a south-facing "cascade" at the front of the steepest terrace. And I have raspberries and black currants growing rather clumsily together in a circular bed opposite the front door.

If, like me, you have a small but busy garden and want to find room for some fruit, you need to go on a little space hunt. Look for steep banks that can be terraced with bricks or railroad ties for the strawberry cascade. Perhaps you can use permanent fruit bushes to mark the ends or sides of vegetable rows that you plant with rotating crops. They can also be incorporated into herbaceous borders and flower beds. Even a small patch of lawn might benefit from the shade thrown by a fruit tree.

The town dweller need not miss out on the fruit harvest either. Almost all fruits can be grown successfully in tubs and pots. Indeed, gooseberries and currants will be exceedingly happy to be raised in this way, provided they are watered regularly and fed occasionally. Raspberry and tayberry canes can be grown in a large tub over a wigwam of poles, or trained against a fence or wall that faces any direction except north. Most strawberry varieties will thrive in a hanging basket; some strains, with fruit on long stems that tumble down from the plant, have been specially cultivated with this purpose in mind. There is also the strawberry pot – an ingeniously designed clay, metal, or plastic container that allows the plants to be staggered vertically and horizontally. These are now available in most good garden centers, and some such systems are modular, so you can make your pot as tall or as short as you like.

However tiny your patch, you needn't feel restricted to the soft fruits – dwarf apple, cherry, pear, or plum trees can be grown in a large pot on a patio or roof terrace. If space is really limited, they can also be fan-trained against a fence or wall.

All containers must have drainage holes to prevent waterlogging and consequent root rot in the all-too-inevitable wet spells. The inverse problem is that in hot weather even the largest containers dry out at an extraordinary rate. A partial solution is to mix in plenty of water-retaining granules (easy to find in any decent garden center) with the tree and shrub compost you put in the containers. But in long, dry spells even the most meticulously prepared containers will need a thorough soaking at least once every two days, if not daily. Container plants are the first casualty of the absentee gardener, and if you are away a lot and can't arrange a good-neighborly regular watering, then you may wish to consider an automated watering system controlled by a timer.

what to grow

Assuming you've cunningly located a number of fruit-planting opportunities in the garden, or alternatively invested in some suitable containers, what are you actually going to plant? This isn't such a tough one. As with vegetables, the golden rule is to grow what you most like to eat. If your space is seriously restricted, you might confine yourself to a single fruit that really excites you. On the other hand, the range of available soft fruits and fruit trees that thrive in cooler climates is nothing like as wide and bewildering as the vegetable options. And so if you are ready to devote a fair amount of space to your fruit growing, one might almost suggest, for the soft fruits at least, why not try a bit of everything?

Here are the principal options. I've listed them in order of personal preference – which seems a little harsh on the loganberries and tayberries. Actually, I like them both very much. I just don't happen to grow them at the moment. The varieties recommended for each fruit are reliable, disease resistant, and of excellent flavor.

RASPBERRIES If I grew only one fruit it would be the raspberry. Many people would put the strawberry above it, and as a child I probably would have myself. But to my palate, raspberries just seem to get better and better. I like acidity in my fruit, and the raspberry seems to me to offer the best possible sweet and sour tease, underpinned with a wonderful rosaceous aroma. As well as being delicious eaten straight from the bush, it also makes the best sorbet, the best ice cream, and the best jam. But my favorite way to eat raspberries is still warm from the garden, lightly squashed in a bowl with the back of a spoon, sprinkled with sugar, and dolloped with cold cream from the fridge.

Raspberries like the sun but will tolerate a little shade. They should be bought as growing plants from a nursery or garden center and planted in the autumn. Dry and twiggy, the plants look unpromising. But dug in with plenty of manure or compost, they will bullet skyward in the spring. Be ready for them. Bang in some light posts (about 2 inches square, 2 yards high) 2 or 3 yards apart along the row, and stretch thick gardening wire horizontally between them at heights of 20 inches, 1 yard, and 1 1/2 yards. Tie the new canes (as the stems are called) to the wires for support as they grow. The plants should be spread 20 inches apart and the rows a little over a yard apart so that you can walk comfortably between them.

That's the conventional technique – for producing long, straight rows of regimental raspberry canes. But raspberries are flexible climbers that can be trained in any number of ways to suit your space: tied up to bamboo poles arranged in a wigwam, for example, or grown up trellising like rambling roses.

However you choose to train your raspberries, any canes that have fruited should be cut down to the ground after harvesting. Those that have not can be left tied to the wires. Every spring the canes should be mulched generously with manure; this will both feed them and keep down the weeds.

Recommended varieties Amity, Latham, Meeker, and Autumn Bliss (an excellent late-fruiting variety).

GOOSEBERRIES The gooseberry doesn't have the best reputation of the soft fruits, perhaps because it doesn't lend itself to instant gratification in the same way that strawberries and raspberries do. Some varieties can be eaten straight from the bush when fully ripe. But in my view, gooseberries are at their best when picked hard and tart and cooked with plenty of sugar. Cooked, they are unbeatable, like rhubarb and apples, with a hint of strawberry. They are also wonderfully easy to grow and maintain, and after a couple of years a strong, healthy plant can produce a massive crop.

Buy young bushes in pots and plant them out, about 1 1/2 yards apart, in the autumn or early spring (March). Dig in plenty of manure when planting and mulch with manure again in the spring. In the winter, any gooseberry bushes over three years old should be pruned: remove one in three of the thickest, oldest stems by cutting cleanly at the base of the plant.

Recommended varieties Pixwell, Welcome, Downing, Oregon. A purple relation of the gooseberry, called the worcesterberry, is grown in exactly the same way, also crops heavily, and is extremely worthwhile. It has a flavor somewhere between the gooseberry and the black currant.

STRAWBERRIES They may be third on my list, but I still love strawberries with a passion. Young strawberry plants can be bought in pots and should be planted in early autumn or early spring. They won't crop well the first year, but should be highly productive for three or four years thereafter. They will then need to be replaced. In order to avoid having blank years, it pays to operate a "rotating rows" system, replacing a quarter of your crop every year.

It is essential to keep the weeds down around strawberries, and useful to keep the fruit from direct contact with the earth. The easiest way to achieve both these objectives is to keep the plants permanently mulched with black polyethylene. This can be laid, by pegging or weighting down with bricks, even before the plants are planted. They then go into the ground through X-shaped slits made in the polyethylene. Strawberries like a rich soil, so dig in plenty of manure or compost before the polyethylene goes down. This way of mulching makes watering a little troublesome: you need to direct your hose at the slits in the polyethylene right at the base of the plant.

The more traditional and esthetic technique, from which the strawberry gets its name, is to pack loose straw directly around the base of each plant as soon as they are in flower (early to mid-spring).

Early crops of strawberries can be grown very successfully in a polytunnel.

Recommended varieties Annapolis, Cabot, Cavendish, Chandler, Jewel, Surecrop.

BLACK CURRANTS My parents had half a dozen black currant bushes in their garden at one time. These bushes became so prolific that, even with the birds taking a healthy share, the glut was overwhelming. Black currant ice creams and sorbets took up over half the freezer, and we barely managed to eat it all up before next year's crop was upon us. Eventually, they pulled them out and gave the space back to the vegetable garden and a crop of late raspberries.

Despite this overexposure, I still like black currants, one of the strongest-flavored of all the soft fruits, and now have a couple of bushes at River Cottage. They are very easy to grow and should be cared for exactly as described for gooseberry bushes above.

Black currant leaves make a delicious, refreshing sorbet – follow the procedure for elderflower sorbet on page 391, infusing a handful of bruised leaves in place of the flowers.

Recommended varieties Ben Lomond, Ben Sarek.

RED and WHITE CURRANTS Usually less productive than either gooseberries or black currants, these bushes are nonetheless easy to grow and the fruit very worthwhile. Unlike the black currant, when fully ripened both are just about sweet enough to eat raw. A sorbet of either is a delight, and a trio of sorbets – red, white, and black currant – makes for intriguing flavor comparisons. Red currants combine well with raspberries, and a summer pudding made exclusively from those two fruits is rather special.

Red and white currants are grown much as for gooseberries and black currants, but as they are more delicate, slower-growing bushes they should be pruned more lightly. In winter, prune 3 to 4 inches off the tips of the main shoots. To encourage them to bush out and thereby increase the yield, cut off most of the side shoots from the main stems, leaving just one or two close to the base.

Recommended varieties Red: Rovada, Red Lake; White: Blanka.

RHUBARB Not really a fruit at all, but a herbaceous plant. Nevertheless, its stems, when cooked, have such a distinctly fruity taste (being very close to gooseberries in flavor) that it has come to be thought of almost exclusively as a dessert plant. Actually, a sieved compote of rhubarb, sweetened only slightly, makes an excellent sauce for oily fish such as herring and mackerel.

Rhubarb likes rich, well-drained soil and sun or partial shade. The more you compost it, the more productive it will be. A small plant planted on top of a whole heap of manure anytime between late autumn and early spring will be ready to harvest by early summer. Its huge leaves and pink red stems are very decorative and make a nice backdrop to more delicate flowers in a sunny border. You can increase your crop by dividing plants once a year and replanting.

To get longer, thinner stems that require less sweetening when cooked, you can blanch the rhubarb by excluding the light. Special blanching cloches (or, less glamorously, a trash can) are placed over the plant in early spring. Stems can be harvested four to six weeks later.

Recommended varieties Valentine, Hawke's Champagne, Victoria.

LOGANBERRIES A delicious fruit that is a hybrid of the raspberry and the blackberry. It is usually grown in the same way as raspberries, tied to wire or trellising. But being hardier, it can be left to go a bit wild, like a bramble, against a hedge, fence, or wall. An occasional, say, biweekly, shovelful of manure around the base of the main stem will keep it happy.

TAYBERRIES Another delicious variation of the bramble family, the tayberry plant can also be trained. But it has a stout woody stem and, left to its own devices, it will form an attractive bushy shrub that arches over as it becomes more substantial.

planting fruit bushes

The health and success of any of the fruit bushes above depends as much on careful initial planting as subsequent maintenance. In all cases, dig a hole at least twice as big in diameter as the pot from which you are transplanting. Work the soil nice and loose and mix it well with a generous shovelful of manure. Gently lower the plant's root ball into the center of the hole and bring in the loose soil from all sides, a little at a time, compacting a little but not too much (especially if it is clay). Try to make sure that the point at which the main stem leaves the soil is the same as it was in the pot. Water well after planting, and compact the soil a little more firmly the following day. Keep a circle of earth with a radius of 12 to 16 inches around the base of the plant weed-free and manure mulched, and your fruit bushes will thrive.

choosing fruit trees

Fruit trees are really no harder to grow than fruit bushes. They're just bigger. However, even size is ultimately at the dictate of the chooser. To choose the right tree, you need to understand a little about the way most fruit trees are cultivated these days. This is done by grafting fruit varietals onto various "rootstocks." The main rootstocks, which are different for apples, pears, and plums, are chosen because they are usually sturdier and more disease resistant than the natural rootstocks of the favored varietals – strange but true. You can see evidence of the process when you buy a young fruit tree: the graft union is identifiable by a noticeable kink in the stem, about 6 to 12 inches above the soil mark. The most important thing when planting a fruit tree is to keep the graft union scar well above the soil; otherwise, it may put out roots of its own and all the benefits of the rootstock will be lost.

In the trade, rootstock are known by numbers, not in themselves meaningful, so the more important terms to understand as a lay fruit-tree grower relate to the size of the mature tree they will grow into. Terms you will come across are *dwarfing, semi-dwarfing, vigorous,* and variations thereof. The M27 is not just a nightmarish bit of English highway but an "extremely dwarfing" rootstock used for growing small, bushy apple trees that will never grow higher than 2 yards – good for anyone who is scared of heights or incompetent with ladders. When it comes to the actual fruit, there are dozens, possibly hundreds, of different varieties that can be grown on this popular rootstock. The M25, by contrast, is classed as "very vigorous," suitable for planting in a dedicated orchard where you will, over the years, be happy to see your apple trees grow to 6 yards high or more.

As if the rootstock didn't make things complicated enough, there is also the vital but confusing issue of pollination. To produce good fruit, blossoms need pollinating, or fertilizing. Some fruits can do this themselves and are referred to as "self-fertile." Most require "partner trees" to pollinate them. Some may require at least two partner trees in order to fruit successfully. And just to add to the confusion, most trees require pollination by a fruit variety different from themselves. So, for example, the eating-apple varieties, such as Discovery, Fiesta, and James Grieve, need one of the other members of that group growing nearby to pollinate them. The British Bramley, by contrast, is classed as a triploid: it needs at least two of those eating varieties as neighbors for successful pollination. Another important rule is that trees chosen as pollinators must have "blossom overlap" with the ones they are supposed to be pollinating. There is a number system from one to five to help you with this: 1 is the earliest to blossom, 5 the latest. Compatible pollinators should be no more than one number apart: i.e., a 4 will do a 3 or a 5 but not a 1 or a 2.

I must say, it's a great relief to me that the greengage tree I have planted on the south-facing wall of the cottage is self-fertile. I'm not sure I could cope with the sex education.

There is, amazingly you might think, an upside to all this. Choose the right three apple trees, say, a Bramley, a Discovery, and a Sunset, and not only will they all pollinate each other but you'll have three different types of apples to enjoy – two eaters and a cooker.

All this means that choosing trees is often harder than actually growing them. With all these variations in play, it is a good idea to seek expert advice from a specialist fruit-tree nursery when buying your trees. If you are planning a wide variety of trees or a fully fledged orchard, such consultation would, I'd say, be bordering on the essential. The catalogs of all the best fruit-tree nurseries explain the pollination issue clearly and recommend appropriate sets of companion trees. It will pay you to ask them to send a catalog for a little leisurely study before your shopping trip. A good nursery should be only too happy to help you with your choices. Meanwhile, here are a few personal notes on the main fruit-tree crops, along with some varietal recommendations based on eating quality:

APPLES There are so many apple varieties available, some very local, that it's best to ask around and taste them in season before you buy your stock. If your neighbors have apple trees, ask them what variety they are, and find out if they are good pollinators for the type you have in mind. You may find the fertilization problem is solved before it has arisen. If you are more than 100 yards from such an obliging neighbor tree, you will need to either get two or more trees or buy what is called a "family" tree. This is a tree with two or more fruit varieties grafted onto a single rootstock – usually one cooker and one eater. The varieties will pollinate each other.

Discovery is an excellent, easy-to-grow apple that crops early and heavily and is delicious eaten straight from the tree. But it doesn't store at all, so fill your baskets while the going's good. For British lovers of tart, crisp apples, Lord Lambourne is tops. Beauty of Bath is another favorite, while here in Dorset everyone loves the Egremont Russet, and rightly so. Worcester Pearmain is highly productive and widely popular. The last two mentioned apples are also available in the U.S.

PEARS There's no doubt that really good pears are harder to grow in a colder climate than really good apples. This is basically because they need decent soil, shelter from the worst of the wind, and plenty of sunshine. If you can give them all that, there is no reason why you shouldn't succeed in growing fat, luscious fruit. But if you are deficient in any department, especially soil quality, you can expect smallish fruit that you may have trouble ripening. It's a good idea to dig in plenty of manure when you plant a pear tree. If you have very heavy clay soil, you can make partial amends by digging a simply enormous hole and filling it with good organic matter such as mushroom compost. Like apples, most pear trees need cross-pollination by compatible varieties.

Pears can be a good option for gardens with limited space, or a high-design concept, because they respond well to training. They can be fanned against walls and trained into long, flat espaliers, or even grown as "stepover" dwarf espaliers. For advice on such matters, you need to turn to a greater expert than me – such as one of the books listed under Gardening in the Bibliography on page 440.

Comice and Bartlett are rightly popular varieties, being reliable fruiters that are generally disease resistant. Other good U.S. choices are Anjou, Bosc, Seckel, and Foulle. There are dozens of other varieties, and if pears are your first choice of fruit tree, it is worth visiting a good fruit nursery and talking through your wants and needs with one of their experts.

CHERRIES Cherry trees thrive in most soils, but they do need sunshine, especially if they are going to produce sweet fruit that you can eat raw. You also need space for a cherry tree, as they cannot be grown on dwarf rootstock. They can, however, be trained by vigorous pruning. A fan-trained cherry tree on a south-facing wall should produce abundant sweet fruit. If you buy a tree that has been fan-trained from the beginning at the nursery, then maintaining it is easy: any branches growing flat, or nearly flat, against the wall can be kept and tied back. Anything pointing outward can be pruned.

The most beautiful British cherries are undoubtedly the translucent scarlet Morellos, but they are too sour to eat raw. They make superb jam and are very good for adding to game and pork dishes when tartness is required. In the U.S., Montmorency cherries, which are also sour, are the classic cherry for pies. Stateside, favorite sweet cherries are Bing, Rainier, and Royal Anne.

PLUMS, DAMSONS, and GAGES I think these are among the most rewarding fruits to grow, as they are so versatile. Many can be eaten straight from the tree, but they also lend themselves to puddings, in such irresistible forms as stewed plums with rice pudding, plum crumbles, Plum Bread and Butter Pudding (see page 132), and wonderful sorbets and ice creams.

Gages are a round variety of plum specially cultivated for eating raw. There are a number of varieties and not all of them are green, but pretty much all of them are delicious. Perhaps my favorite trees in the whole of the River Cottage garden are my two gages, one called Count Althann's Gage, which has lovely pinky-yellow fruit when ripe, the other Denniston's Superb, which is, as one might hope, superb. It is trained against the south-facing wall of the cottage next to the downstairs window. I can actually pluck myself a greengage from the comfort of my armchair.

There are over 300 varieties of plums and gages in the U.K., which is fairly mind-boggling. But if you only have room for one fruit tree in your garden, I would make it a plum. The following are some of the best varieties for U.S. gardens:

European plums grown in the United States include Pearl, known for its fine flavor; the late-season Salean, heavily grown in California; the hardy Mount Royal; and the sugar prune. The majority of plums grown successfully in the States are Japanese plums; they include Redheart, Santa Rosa (early season, partly self-fertile, and productive), Satsuma, Capelman, and Elephant Heart. Some of the U.S. plums are self-fertile, but others need to be planted near another variety of plum tree in order to produce fruit. Ask your nursery specialist for advice on which trees you need to plant.

PEACHES, NECTARINES, and APRICOTS Apricots are probably marginally easier to grow than peaches or nectarines, but all are difficult and require some special treatment – even to ripen just a few good pieces of fruit. Having said that, if you have good soil and a south-facing wall in a very sheltered spot, you may succeed as well as any. And if you fail, well, the blossoms of all three trees are very lovely.

The trees should be watered well in dry weather, and a good mulch around the base will help to conserve moisture in the roots. Watch out for signs of peach leaf curl (curling and rusty edges around the leaves), and treat with a copper fungicide as soon as diagnosed.

Peaches flower early (March or even February), and as there are likely to be few insects around you may have to pollinate them by hand. With self-fertile varieties, this can be done by dabbing the stamens of the flowers delicately with a small paintbrush, one after the other.

The following varieties are all self-fertile and all suitable for growing out of doors: apricot – Blenheim and Royal; nectarine – Sunglow and Redgold; peach – Redhaven and Bellaire.

QUINCE This lovely fruit deserves a mention, as it is easy to grow and has beautiful blossoms, as well as producing much underrated, and underused, fruit. In its raw state it is true that the quince is not promising – hard, gritty, and unpalatably sour. But cooked with sugar it is transformed, as its wonderful aromatic qualities are released. A little quince goes a long way: a single fruit, peeled, cored, and sliced, can be added to a pile of cooking apples, and its flavor will enhance the resulting pie, crumble, or compote. Always remove the seeds of a quince before cooking, as they can cause stomach upsets.

There are many varieties of quinces, but some are ornamental and have very small fruit that is not worthwhile. The best varieties for the kitchen are Maliformis, which produces round, apple-sized fruit, and Champion, with large, pear-shaped fruit. Both are partially self-fertile, but will crop better if allowed to self-pollinate.

Young quince trees need formative pruning for the first three or four years; each winter, cut back half the new season's growth. The best shape to aim for is an open center, so cut back any central, vertically pointing branches. Once the tree has a good framework, further pruning should not be necessary, except to cut out the dead wood.

freezing fruit

As with vegetables, the ready availability of the fresh product means that it is rarely necessary to buy frozen fruit. However, if you grow your own fruit, freezing any surplus is a useful home economy. And for U-pick enthusiasts, the trip is made all the more worthwhile if you pick for the freezer as well as for immediate consumption. Most fruits freeze well. Only a few, however, come close to retaining their structure. These are the single-berry fruits such as blueberries, bilberries, and gooseberries; the cluster berries such as blackberries, loganberries, and raspberries; and the currants, red, white, and black. If they are frozen carefully, they can, at a pinch, be thawed out and used as if fresh. Damage to the fruit can be minimized by selecting whole, unblemished berries and open-freezing them in a single layer spread on a large tray. As soon as they are frozen quite solid, and before they become encrusted with frozen condensed water, they should be carefully transferred to a polyethylene box with a lid. Spread them out in a single layer again for defrosting.

It is not worth the trouble of freezing large amounts of fruit in this way unless you really intend to use them in recipes that require the whole raw fruit. Instead, it is more economical of time and space to freeze fruit purées or, better still, homemade sorbets and ice creams. For real soft-fruit enthusiasts, an ice cream machine, far from being an extravagant luxury, may turn out to be a very economical item of kitchen hardware. For more on making sorbets and ice creams, see page 126.

Cooking apples, quinces, plums, greengages, and other fruits that are likely to end up being cooked anyway should be lightly stewed with a little sugar before freezing. You should err on the side of undercooking and undersweetening if you know the fruit is ultimately destined for pies, crumbles, and the like: it will undergo further cooking once thawed, and you can always add more sugar.

garden recipes

baby vegetables

When I pick the first harvest of baby peas and tiny beans, usually sometime in June, I like to serve them as a course on their own. If baby zucchini and small green onions or tiny, immature leeks are also available, it becomes something very special indeed.

You will need roughly equal quantities of the following, all picked immediately before cooking:
Small zucchini, cut into pea-size dice
Baby leeks or green onions, cut into ⅜-inch lengths
Young peas
Baby fava beans

PLUS
Olive oil
Sea salt

Gently sauté the zucchini and leeks or green onions in a little olive oil for a few minutes. The zucchini should still be al dente and the leeks/green onions just a little soft and sweet. At the same time, steam or blanch the peas and beans for just 2 minutes. Stir all the vegetables together and sprinkle with a little salt.

beet soup with feta

serves 4 to 6

This dish is about balancing the sweet, earthy taste of beets with the salty tang of crumbly feta cheese. The tomatoes add a little acidity and richness. In the winter, when tasty tomatoes are unavailable, you can substitute a couple of tablespoons of puréed, cooked apples. This is one of the posher dishes in the book and makes a very elegant dinner-party starter. It can be served chilled as well as hot; a sprinkling of grated raw beet makes a good garnish for the cold version.

3 to 4 medium (apple-sized) beets
(1 to 1¼ pounds total)
1 tablespoon olive or sunflower oil
1 onion, finely chopped
2 cups good strong stock
(beef is best, but chicken or vegetable will do)
½ recipe Roast Tomato Sauce (see page 102)
¾ cup (4 ounces) crumbled real (i.e., Greek, not Danish) feta cheese
Salt and freshly ground black pepper

Peel the beets and grate them coarsely, or chop them into small dice. Heat the oil in a large pan and sauté the onion in it for a few minutes, until soft. Add the beets and stock and bring to a boil. Season lightly with salt and pepper, then simmer gently for 7 to 10 minutes, until the beets are tender. Stir in the tomato sauce, transfer the soup to a blender, and process until completely smooth. Taste and adjust the seasoning if necessary.

Reheat the soup until thoroughly hot but not boiling. Divide between warmed bowls and sprinkle over the feta cheese, then serve with crusty bread.

purple sprouting broccoli with anchovy and chile dressing

serves 4

I serve this dish most often as a starter; the quantity below serves 4. The dish is a way of showing that purple sprouting broccoli, or even the humble curly kale, deserves an outing on its own, especially when homegrown. It's easily transformed into a more substantial supper dish by cutting the broccoli into smaller pieces and tossing them with hot buttered pasta – and, of course, the devilish dressing. The quantities for the dressing are deliberately excessive, designed to use up a whole can of anchovies. The leftover dressing keeps well in the fridge and can be used as a sort of gentleman's relish: serve as a quick-fix pasta sauce or try spreading it on toast, then topping with scrambled eggs.

1¼ pounds purple sprouting broccoli (or curly kale), ideally picked within hours of cooking
2 tablespoons butter – one for the broccoli, one for the dressing

FOR THE DRESSING
1 can anchovy fillets, drained
⅔ cup olive oil
2 garlic cloves, peeled
Leaves from a sprig of thyme
A few basil leaves
½ small red chile, or a pinch of red pepper flakes
1 teaspoon Dijon mustard
2 teaspoons red wine vinegar
A few twists of black pepper

Blend all the ingredients for the dressing in a blender until completely smooth. Alternatively, if you are using fresh chile, you can leave it out of the blender and chop it very finely by hand, then stir it into the dressing. This gives it a more substantial texture and nice flecks of red.

Steam the broccoli (or kale) for 3 to 4 minutes, so it still has a bit of crunch. Toss with a tablespoon of butter. Warm the sauce over a low heat, whisking in another tablespoon of butter as it heats up. This should help to emulsify it, but don't worry if it separates a bit; it'll still taste wonderful.

Arrange the broccoli on warmed plates and drizzle over a generous amount of the warmed dressing. Serve at once, with good hunks of soft brown bread to mop up the sauce.

variation broccoli with shrimp butter

We ate so much purple sprouting broccoli this spring that I tried this experiment as a change from the anchovy sauce. Take 4 tablespoons butter and melt in a small pan. Add 4 ounces bay shrimp (cocktail shrimp). Mash some of the shrimps to a paste with a fork or the back of a wooden spoon, leaving the rest whole. Add an extra tablespoon of butter, a good pinch of chile flakes, and a few drops of lemon juice. Heat through till the butter is completely melted, then serve, like the anchovy dressing, drizzled over lightly steamed broccoli.

In case you were wondering, it is this version of the dish that is illustrated opposite.

zucchini soufflé

serves 5 to 6

Soufflés are easier than people think. The difficulty lies not in getting them to rise but in getting the timing right, so they are still creamy, not cakey, in the middle. This is easier when you are making individual soufflés rather than a large one. Individual soufflé dishes (which are a little bit larger than ordinary ramekins) are perfect for this. If it suits you, the quantities below can also be used to make one large or two medium soufflés.

2 tablespoons olive oil
1 garlic clove, finely chopped
1 pound small zucchini, finely sliced
3 tablespoons butter, plus a little for greasing the soufflé dishes
¼ cup all-purpose flour
1¼ cups hot milk
Salt and freshly ground black pepper
3 egg yolks
½ cup shredded Cheddar or Gruyère cheese
4 egg whites

Heat the oil in a large saucepan, then add the garlic, zucchini, and a little salt. Cook the zucchini gently, on what I like to call a "slow sizzle," so that they soften without browning. Continue cooking, stirring frequently, until they are completely soft and almost all their water has evaporated (this may take 20 minutes or more). Then mash to a pulpy consistency (a coarse purée) with a wooden spoon or potato masher and set aside.

In a small pan, melt the butter and add the flour. Mix together, cook for 1 minute or so, then gradually stir in the hot milk to make a thick béchamel, stirring constantly to avoid lumps. Allow to bubble for 1 minute, then remove from the heat and season with salt and pepper.

Add the béchamel to the zucchini (or vice versa), along with the egg yolks, cheese, and a few twists of black pepper, and beat well to get a nice sticky mixture. Whisk the egg whites until stiff. Stir about a third of them into the zucchini mixture to loosen it, then carefully fold in the rest. Divide between 5 to 6 greased individual soufflé dishes or pile into 2 medium soufflé dishes or one large one (about 6 cups in capacity).

Bake in a preheated 375°F oven for 12 to 15 minutes for small soufflés, 20 to 25 minutes for medium soufflés, or up to 35 minutes for a large one – until well risen and golden brown but still slightly wobbly in the center. Serve straight from the oven, without delay.

four more ways to cook zucchini

The basic preparation of the zucchini for the soufflé opposite – stewed gently in olive oil until all the water has evaporated and they are soft, pulpy and wonderfully aromatic – is also an excellent way of preparing them to serve as a side vegetable. A little further embellishment makes for a number of interesting dishes:

zucchini bruschetta

Cook 2 pounds zucchini with 3 tablespoons of olive oil and 3 crushed cloves of garlic, as described for the soufflé opposite. Season with salt early in the cooking to help draw out their moisture. Stir whenever they begin to stick to the pan, and do not allow them to brown more than a shade. Keep cooking until they are concentrated and oily but not at all watery. They will partially break up, but don't mash them as much as for the soufflé. To make bruschetta, simply grill or toast thick slices of coarse country bread (Italians would use pugliese or ciabatta), rub one side with garlic, trickle with olive oil, and then pile a mound of the hot zucchini mixture on top. Grate over a little fresh Parmesan, if you like.

zucchini sauce for pasta

For 4 people, cook 2 pounds zucchini exactly as for the bruschetta, then stir in a couple of tablespoons of cream and at least 1/3 cup freshly grated Parmesan. Allow to bubble for just a minute so that the cream is incorporated and reduced a little. Meanwhile, cook your chosen pasta (spaghetti, penne, and tagliatelle are all good) in a large pan of boiling salted water until al dente. Drain the pasta, toss with the sauce, and serve. Bring some more Parmesan to the table. This is the dish shown on the next page.

deep-fried stuffed zucchini flowers

Cook the zucchini as described for the pasta sauce above (i.e., adding cream and Parmesan), then leave to cool. Check your zucchini flowers for insects (especially if any of your guests are vegetarian), then carefully scoop the cooked zucchini mixture inside them with a teaspoon. You should get 2 to 4 good teaspoons in each one, depending on the size of the zucchini flowers. Heat some oil for deep-frying until a small piece of bread thrown in takes about 1 minute to turn deep golden brown. Dip the stuffed flowers in batter (either your preferred recipe or the tempura batter described on page 340) and lower them carefully into the hot oil. Do not crowd the pan; cook 2 to 4 at a time, depending on their size and the size of the pan. Deep-fry for 1 to 2 minutes, until puffed up, crisp, and golden brown. Then drain on paper towels and serve sprinkled with sea salt. This, incidentally, is one of my all-time favorite vegetable dishes.

zucchini and milk soup

After cooking 2 pounds zucchini as for the bruschetta above, mash them with a potato masher to make a fairly smooth purée. Pour in up to 4 cups milk, stirring well, until the soup reaches the desired consistency (I like it fairly thick). Bring just to a boil, stir in 2 handfuls of freshly grated Parmesan, then season to taste with salt and pepper and serve at once, with a few torn basil leaves strewn over each bowl.

roast tomato sauce

This is really just a smooth purée of sieved roast tomatoes, but the flavor is so excellent, rich roasted, and garlicky that I often use it as a sauce. It's also an extremely useful way of dealing with a glut of tomatoes: make a large batch and freeze it. It then makes a versatile ingredient in all kinds of sauces and stews, or in soups such as Beet Soup with Feta (see page 92).

2 pounds ripe, full-flavored tomatoes, cut in half
2 to 3 garlic cloves, finely chopped
2 tablespoons olive oil
Salt and freshly ground black pepper

Arrange the tomato halves, tightly packed but not on top of each other, in an ovenproof dish. Mix the garlic with the olive oil and drizzle it evenly over the tomatoes. Season lightly with salt and pepper. Roast in a preheated 350°F oven for 35 to 45 minutes, until the tomatoes are soft, pulpy, and slightly charred. Rub through a sieve, discarding the skins and seeds.

Use as is, for an instant pasta sauce, or try one of the following variations.

variations cream of roast tomato soup
Put the sieved tomatoes in a blender with an equal quantity of good chicken or vegetable stock and 3 rice cakes or 3 tablespoons of cooked rice. Blend until smooth, then reheat, check the seasoning, and serve with a swirl of heavy cream or crème fraîche.

crostini Spread the sieved roast tomatoes on slices of stale bread drizzled with olive oil; top each one with a slice of fresh mozzarella and bake in a hot oven for 10 minutes, until the mozzarella melts.

rich tomato sauce with bacon

This is the sauce I make with canned tomatoes once my own tomato season is over (I prefer canned tomatoes to most out-of-season store-bought fresh varieties). I often have it with plain pasta, gnocchi, or polenta. The bacon/pancetta is optional, but I find that just a little bit of my homemade bacon (see page 154), which is very smoky and often on the salty side, gives it a huge flavor boost.

2 tablespoons olive oil
2 to 3 large garlic cloves, crushed
Two (14¼-ounce) cans of peeled plum tomatoes
2 ounces smoked bacon or pancetta, cut into small dice
2 tablespoons butter
Salt and freshly ground black pepper

Heat the olive oil in a large, heavy frying pan or shallow casserole and throw in the crushed garlic. Let it sizzle for a moment, but before it takes any color add both cans of tomatoes with all their juice. As the tomatoes come to a boil, break them up with a wooden spoon. Simmer the sauce hard, but not too hard, stirring regularly, until it becomes thick and pulpy (make sure it doesn't stick to the bottom of the pan).

Only when the sauce is finished should you adjust the seasoning with salt and black pepper, otherwise it will become overseasoned as it reduces.

If you want to add smoked bacon or pancetta, which will make the sauce rich and smoky, fry it in a separate pan with a little olive oil until nicely browned. Then throw it into the tomato sauce halfway through cooking. The addition of bacon will almost certainly mean no extra salt is needed.

Stir the butter into the sauce just before serving.

tomato, basil, and chile "sweet 'n' hot" dipping sauce

This recipe started out as a jelly, but it didn't set. As I'd made 30 jars of the stuff and was planning to sell it at the Bridport farmers' market, some hasty improvisation was called for. I added wine vinegar and chopped red chile and the result was an unexpected delight. This adapted version avoids the frustration of waiting for the jelly to fail to set, and gets you straight to the dipping sauce.

2 pounds tomatoes, quartered
2 pounds tart apples, peeled, cored, and sliced
A wineglass of water
Juice and finely grated zest of 1 orange
4 cups sugar
A large bunch of basil
⅔ cup good-quality white wine vinegar (it should be at least 5 percent acidity – check the label)
1 to 3 fresh red chiles (according to heat), very finely chopped

Put the tomatoes, apples, water, orange juice, and zest in a pan and cook over medium heat, stirring occasionally, until they are completely soft and pulpy. Rub the mixture through a fine nylon sieve – or, for a more translucent finish, let it drip through a jelly bag, if you have one. Return the liquid to a clean pan, add the sugar, and bring slowly to a boil, stirring to dissolve the sugar. Boil hard for 5 to 10 minutes, until thick and syrupy (on a sugar thermometer, the temperature should read 225°F). Take the pan off the heat and leave to cool.

Bruise the basil leaves by lightly twisting them and then tie them up in a square of cheesecloth. Push the bag into the hot syrup and leave to infuse as it cools. When the syrup is nearly cold, remove the bag and stir in the wine vinegar and some of the chopped chile. Leave for at least half an hour, then taste and add more chile if you think it needs it; the finished sauce should be hot, sweet, and sour, but still aromatic with tomato and basil.

Pour the sauce into small jars or bottles and seal with lids or corks. Like this, it will keep for several weeks in a fridge or cool pantry. If you want to keep it for longer, or sell it or give it as a gift, the sauce should be reboiled and poured into sterilized bottles or jars (see page 131).

fresh tomato salsa

This is somewhere between a salad and a sauce. It's good "cold on hot" – for example, served on plain, just-boiled pasta, with torn-up basil leaves and shaved Parmesan. It also makes a great accompaniment to plainly cooked (grilled or fried) fish such as mackerel, red snapper, and bass.

1 pound ripe, full-flavored tomatoes
2 tablespoons extra-virgin olive oil
1 medium shallot or small red onion, finely chopped
A squeeze of lemon juice or 1 teaspoon white wine vinegar
Salt and freshly ground black pepper

Put the tomatoes in a bowl, pour boiling water over them, and leave for 30 seconds, then drain. Peel them with a sharp knife and cut into quarters, then scoop out the seeds. You are left with skinless, seedless, delectably sweet tomato flesh. This can be finely chopped (for a salsa) or left in quarters (for a salady version). Either way, toss the tomatoes with the remaining ingredients and it is ready to serve.

variation bruschetta

Grill or toast slices of ciabatta or pugliese bread, rub with garlic, and drizzle with olive oil.

Mix the tomato salsa (chunky version) with a few chopped black olives and/or a couple of chopped anchovies and/or a few torn basil leaves. Pile onto the bread and serve as a starter, either on its own or with other antipasti.

fresh green tomato and cilantro salsa

This is a lovely zesty salsa, like a raw chutney, and is excellent with plain broiled fish or meat, or curries. To peel hard green tomatoes, don't try the boiling water technique described in the fresh tomato salsa above, but use a good potato peeler instead.

2 tablespoons olive oil
1 large onion, finely chopped
2 garlic cloves, very finely chopped
2 pounds green tomatoes, cored, peeled, and finely chopped
Juice of 1 lime
½ to 1 fresh red chile (depending on heat), deseeded and finely chopped
Leaves from a bunch of cilantro, coarsely chopped
Salt and freshly ground black pepper

Simply mix all the ingredients together in a large bowl. Leave for at least half an hour and then mix again. Taste and adjust the flavors according to whim (more chopped chile if you like it hot; more olive oil if you want it looser, etc.). This mixture will keep for a week in the fridge but doesn't freeze well.

tomato ketchup

This recipe is based on one from *The Big Red Book of Tomatoes* by Lindsey Bareham – a lovely book and a must for anyone with an excess of tomatoes. It was the central product at the launch of the River Cottage Glutton, my modest business enterprise at the local farmers' market. It is, quite simply, the best ketchup you'll ever taste. The vital thing is to keep cooking until it is thick and reduced – without burning. A large, heavy pan is essential. The spicing is a bit of a trade secret – all the spices I use are listed below, but I must confess that "1½ teaspoons" of each is a slight simplification; vary the amounts till you find your own "perfect" combination. Clue: mace is ace.

Use it as you would any commercial tomato ketchup – to accompany burgers, sausages, and plain grilled fish and chicken – but always with enormous self-satisfaction bordering on smugness.

6 pounds ripe tomatoes, coarsely chopped
4 onions, sliced
1 large red bell pepper, seeds and white membrane removed, chopped
½ cup brown sugar
¾ cup cider vinegar
¼ teaspoon dry mustard
A piece of cinnamon stick
1½ teaspoons whole allspice
1½ teaspoons whole cloves
1½ teaspoons ground mace
1½ teaspoons celery seeds
1½ teaspoons black peppercorns
1 bay leaf
1 garlic clove, peeled and bruised
Paprika to taste (optional)
Salt

Combine the tomatoes, onions, and red pepper in a large, heavy pan over medium heat and simmer, stirring occasionally, until very soft. Push through a coarse-meshed sieve and return to the pot with the sugar, vinegar, and mustard. Tie the cinnamon, allspice, cloves, mace, celery seeds, black peppercorns, bay leaf, and garlic in a square of cheesecloth and drop it into the stew. Bring the mixture to a boil, then reduce to a slow simmer. Cook, allowing it to bubble gently, stirring often and carefully, for 20 to 40 minutes. The time taken will depend on how juicy your tomatoes are, but in any case continue to cook until it is thick and pulpy. Taste a couple of times while it is cooking and remove the spice bag if the flavor becomes too strong.

Season to taste with salt and paprika, if using, then leave to cool. Pour the ketchup through a funnel into suitable bottles and seal. Stored in the fridge, this ketchup will keep for a month. If you follow the prescribed procedure for preserves (see the chutney recipe on page 117) and bottle it in sterilized jars while still warm, it should keep for a year.

ratatouille

serves 4 as a starter

Ratatouille can be delightful, but it can also be awful. Stewed in too much liquid, the different vegetables all start to taste the same instead of complementing each other. I have taken to cooking all the vegetables separately, then combining them at the end. There's only room for four pans on the average stovetop, so one of the usual five ratatouille vegetables has to go. I reckon that as long as you have the sweetness from the onions and tomatoes, you don't really need the peppers.

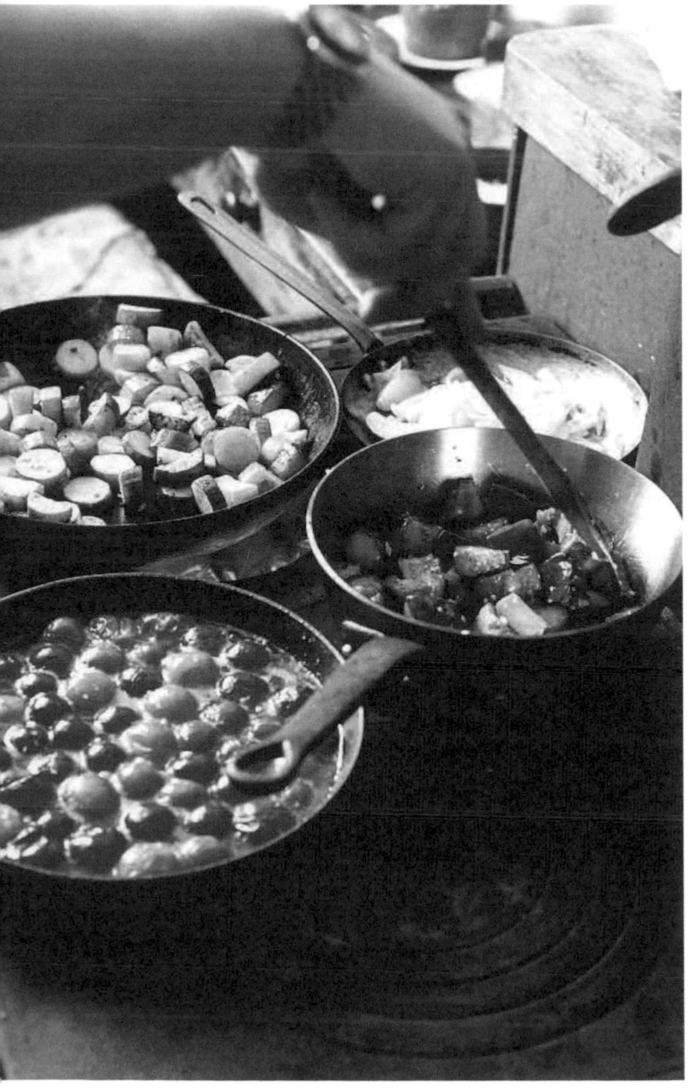

Olive oil
4 garlic cloves, finely chopped
About 8 ounces eggplant, cut into 1-inch cubes
About 8 ounces small zucchini, sliced ½-inch thick
About 8 ounces sweet cherry or Sungold tomatoes, left whole
About 8 ounces onions, in fairly thick slices
A few basil leaves, torn
Salt and freshly ground black pepper

Place 4 small pans over medium heat and cover the base of each with a little olive oil. Add a clove of chopped garlic to each pan, and one of the four vegetables. The eggplant takes a little longer than the others, so start that first if you like.

Cook the zucchini until tender, then turn up the heat a little to brown them lightly. The eggplant, when finished, should be completely soft and tender, almost creamy. The tomatoes should be wrinkled and sweet but still just about holding their shape. And the onions should be soft, sweet, and lightly caramelized. Season the vegetables toward the end of cooking and remove each pan from the heat when you are happy with it. When all the vegetables are ready, toss them gently together in a large pan and heat through for a few minutes, then add the torn basil leaves.

A ratatouille made this carefully deserves to be served as a course on its own. Bruschetta (slices of toasted bread rubbed with garlic and drizzled with olive oil) makes a good accompaniment.

radicchio and chile pasta sauce

serves 4

I learned to make this piquant and bitter pasta sauce many years ago at the River Café in London. It still gets a regular outing at home, as it is very quick and easy to prepare. Put your chosen pasta (try using penne, ridged pasta quills) on to boil just before you start to fry the pancetta, and by the time the sauce is finished the pasta will be ready. I prefer not to serve Parmesan cheese with this dish.

2 radicchio heads
About 3 ounces (2 thick slices) smoked pancetta or bacon
1 tablespoon olive oil
½ to 1 small fresh red chile (depending on strength), finely chopped
2 garlic cloves, finely chopped
½ wineglass of red wine
⅔ cup heavy cream
Salt and freshly ground black pepper

Wash and coarsely shred the radicchio, as you would a cabbage. Trim the rind off the pancetta and then cut the pancetta into thick matchsticks. Fry it in the oil in a large frying pan for a few minutes, until lightly browned, then throw in the chile and garlic. Cook for just 1 minute, then pile in the radicchio, stirring so that it cooks and wilts but does not burn. The pan will seem overloaded at first, but the radicchio quickly reduces in volume. Add the wine and let it bubble for a few minutes until it has almost disappeared, then pour in the cream and simmer to reduce a little further, until the sauce is thick and glossy. Season to taste with salt and pepper. Add the cooked, drained pasta (or add the sauce to the pasta dish, if your frying pan is too full), mix well, and heat through for 1 minute before serving.

celery root and chile gratin

serves 6

This dish seems to surprise and delight everyone who tastes it for the first time. I have taken to serving it as a course on its own, though it goes very nicely with lamb – either broiled chops or roast leg. Exactly the same procedure can be followed using sweet potatoes or a mixture of sweet potatoes and ordinary potatoes. There are several varieties of sweet potatoes available. The ones I like best are those with orange flesh.

2 pounds celery root
3 tablespoons olive oil
½ to 1 fresh red chile (depending on strength), finely chopped (or 1 teaspoon red pepper flakes – *not* powder)
3 garlic cloves, finely chopped
1 cup half-and-half
Salt and freshly ground black pepper

Peel the celery root and slice as thinly as possible – about the thickness of a dime is ideal; use the slicing blade of a food processor, if you like.

In a large mixing bowl, toss the slices with 2 tablespoons of the oil and all the other ingredients until the slices are evenly coated and the garlic and chile well distributed. Transfer to a lightly oiled gratin dish, spreading out the slices with your fingertips: you do not have to layer the gratin piece by piece, but try to ensure that the slices are mostly lying flat. Pour over any cream left in the bowl and trickle the remaining oil over the top. Bake in a preheated 375°F oven, for 40 to 50 minutes, until the celery root is completely tender and the top is browned and crisp. For extra crispness, you could finish it under the broiler for 1 to 2 minutes.

whole pumpkin baked with cream

serves 4 to 6

This is an incredibly simple and elegant dish, in which the finished "soup" is scooped out from the whole baked pumpkin – rich, filling, and satisfying, so ideal sustenance after some hard work in the garden on a cold autumn day. You can use as big a pumpkin as will fit in your oven, but be aware that if you use a real monster, judging the cooking time becomes hard and the risk of collapse increases greatly. You will use a huge amount of cream and cheese, too, so you need to have a lot of hungry people on hand. You can also make this recipe with small squash varieties, such as acorn or Sweet Mama, and serve one per person. A medium pumpkin serves 4 to 6, generously.

1 medium (1½- to 2-pound) pumpkin or several small squashes (1 per person)
Up to 1 pound Gruyère cheese, shredded (depending on the size of your pumpkin)
Up to 4 cups heavy cream (ditto)
Freshly grated nutmeg
Salt and freshly ground black pepper
1 tablespoon butter

Slice the top off the pumpkin or squashes three-quarters of the way up and retain; this is your lid. Scoop out all the seeds and surrounding fibers from the pumpkin. Place the scooped-out pumpkin on a baking sheet or in an ovenproof dish (which must have sides to catch any leaking cream – an accident that shouldn't, but can, happen).

Put enough shredded Gruyère into the empty cavity of the pumpkin to fill about a third of it, then pour in cream until the cavity is two-thirds full. Add a few gratings of nutmeg, a little salt, and plenty of black pepper. Throw in the butter and replace the lid, so the pumpkin is whole again.

Place in a fairly hot oven (375°F) and cook for 45 minutes to 1¼ hours, depending on the size of the pumpkin. Test for doneness by removing the lid and poking at the flesh from the inside. It should be nice and tender. At this point, the skin may be lightly burnt and the whole thing just beginning to sag a bit. Be wary: when the pumpkin is completely soft and cooked through, there is a real danger of collapse. The larger the pumpkin, the bigger the danger. Don't panic if it happens – it will look a bit deflated but will still taste delicious.

Serve small squashes individually in bowls, with spoons to scoop out the flesh. Serve the larger pumpkin by scooping plenty of flesh and the creamy, cheesy liquid (the Gruyère comes out in lovely long, messy strings) into warmed soup bowls. Either way, serve piping hot.

pumpkin risotto with crispy sage

serves 4 as a generous starter

Sage, which combines beautifully with the sweetness of pumpkin or squash, provides both a flavoring and a crispy edible garnish for this simple risotto. You can use various types of squash or pumpkin, but avoid the ones with stringy flesh. Butternut squash is particularly good.

2½ cups vegetable or chicken stock
1 small onion, chopped
2 tablespoons olive oil
A dozen sage leaves, chopped fairly finely
¾ cup arborio rice
8 ounces pumpkin or butternut squash (peeled weight), diced small
3 tablespoons butter
Salt and freshly ground black pepper

TO FINISH
2 tablespoons sunflower oil
12 to 16 sage leaves
A piece of fresh Parmesan or pecorino cheese

Heat the stock until almost boiling and then keep over very low heat. In a heavy saucepan, sauté the onion in the oil until soft but not browned. Add the chopped sage and cook for a couple of minutes. Add the rice and stir well for a few seconds to coat the grains with the oil, then pour in about a third of the stock and bring to a gentle simmer. Cook until almost all the stock has been absorbed, stirring regularly but not all the time. Add the pumpkin or squash and a little more stock and continue to simmer gently, stirring occasionally, until the stock has been absorbed. From then on, add more stock a little at a time until the pumpkin is soft and the rice nicely al dente. You may not need all the stock, but the texture of the risotto should be loose and creamy.

When it is almost ready, heat the sunflower oil in a small pan and quickly fry the sage leaves until crisp – this takes a matter of seconds.

Stir the butter into the risotto and season well with salt and pepper. Divide among 4 serving bowls and throw a few crispy sage leaves over each portion. Bring the cheese and a grater to the table for your guests to help themselves.

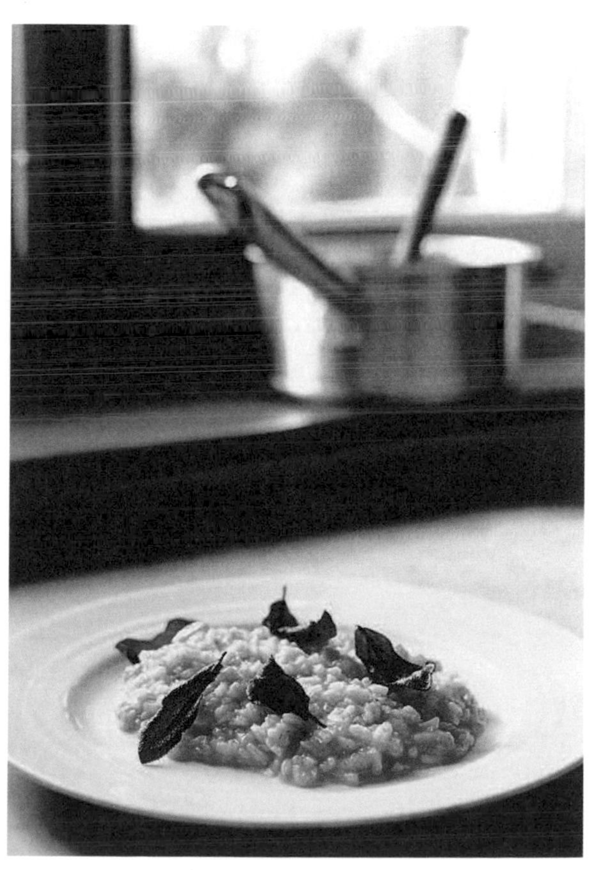

perfect mashed potatoes

serves 4

One of my favorite kitchen tools is an old Victorian potato ricer I picked up in Portobello Market. It's like a giant garlic crusher, from which your squeezed potatoes descend in little wiggly worms, guaranteed lump free. I use it several times a week, not just for making mash but also for squeezing the excess water out of lightly cooked spinach and even for extracting maximum juice from a fish stock. Potato ricers are still manufactured, and you will never regret buying one: avoid the cheap, tinny ones and pay a bit more for a large, robust stainless-steel model – it'll make you a lifetime's worth of perfect mashed potatoes.

The amount of butter and milk you use will determine the final texture of the potatoes. You can choose to have anything from a super-rich, almost pourable purée (serve sparingly with fried blood sausage for a fab starter) to a stiffer, more traditional mixture that you can pile high next to your sausages or on top of a shepherd's pie. The quantities below give you something between the two: appreciably rich and creamy but not absolutely sloppy.

2 pounds baking potatoes, peeled and chopped
½ cup whole milk
6 tablespoons butter
A pinch of freshly grated nutmeg (optional)
Salt and freshly ground black pepper

Add a level tablespoon of salt to a large pan of water (at least 8 cups) and bring to a boil. Peel the potatoes and cut into roughly equal pieces, no smaller than, say, a quarter of an apple. Pour cold water over them, stir briefly, then drain.

Add the potatoes to the pan of water when it is boiling or nearly boiling, bring back to a merry simmer, and cook until completely tender. Pour into a colander and leave for at least 3 minutes to "steam off" (this is important, as it will help to lower the final water content). Meanwhile, put the milk, butter, nutmeg, if you are using it, and some black pepper into the still-warm pan and put it over low heat to melt the butter. Keep hot, but not quite boiling, until the butter is completely melted. Pile the potatoes into a potato ricer and squeeze directly into the seasoned hot milk and butter mixture. Stir well with a wooden spoon to get a smooth, even texture, then taste for seasoning. Serve at once.

variations horseradish mash

This is particularly good with oxtails (see page 239). Add 2 tablespoons of freshly grated horseradish root to the hot milk and butter, then leave to infuse with a lid on for about half an hour. Do this in a separate pan just after the potatoes have started, and by the time they are cooked the horseradish flavor will be fully infused. Then proceed as above.

saffron and garlic mash I like serving this with simple fish dishes, such as plain broiled mackerel or red snapper, or whole bass, or sea trout baked in foil with wine, butter, and a few herbs.

As soon as you have put the potatoes on, crush 2 large or 4 small garlic cloves to a paste with a little coarse salt. Fry very gently in the butter for a few minutes (neither the garlic nor the butter should color at all), then pour in the milk and add a dozen strands of saffron. Heat until not quite boiling, then leave to infuse for 30 to 40 minutes. Finish as above.

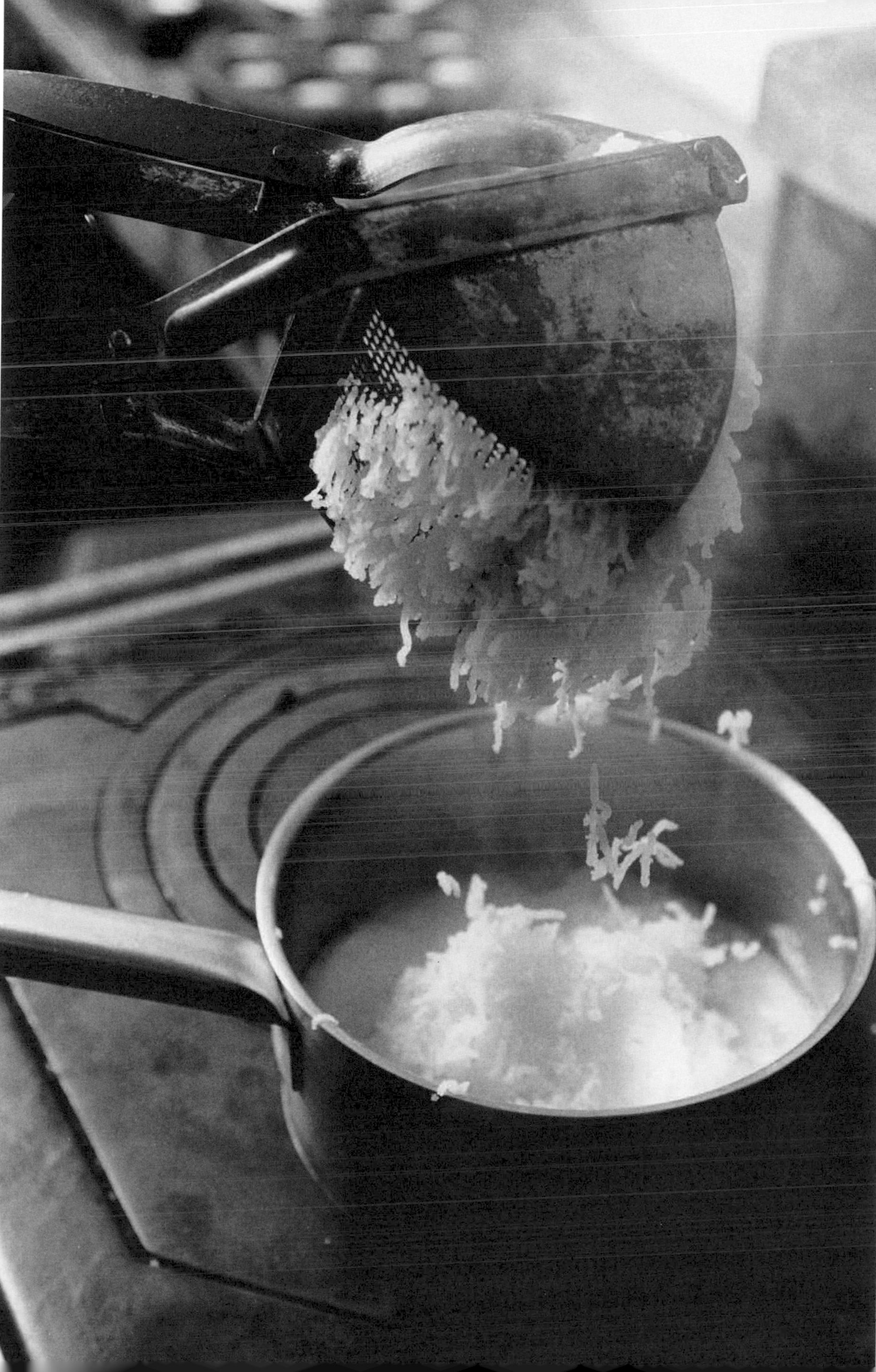

tortilla

serves 4

This recipe is a variation on the classic Spanish potato and onion omelette, making use of fresh spinach from the garden. It was designed partly as an "alcohol sponge" for a skittles evening with the Chideock Cider Circle, which makes one of the meanest brews in West Dorset. Judging by my hangover the next morning, it failed to perform this task with great efficiency!

2 tablespoons butter
1 tablespoon olive oil
2 large onions, finely sliced
1½ pounds boiling potatoes, peeled, parboiled, and cut into slices ⅜ inch thick
A handful of spinach (about 8 ounces), cooked, drained well, and coarsely chopped
10 freshly laid free-range eggs, lightly beaten
Salt and freshly ground black pepper

Heat the butter and oil in a large, heavy frying pan and cook the onions slowly until soft and translucent. Add the potato slices and fry gently for 2 minutes, then add the cooked spinach. Season the beaten eggs with salt and pepper and pour into the pan. Cook over low to medium heat for up to 10 minutes, until the bottom is nicely browned and the center has set; if the heat is too high, the bottom will burn before the middle is set. Now it is time to turn the tortilla over. This is done with a "double flip": place a plate (or the bottom of a tart pan) over the pan and flip it over once, so that the uncooked top of the tortilla is at the bottom. Take another plate and flip the tortilla again so the uncooked surface is on top again. Then place the frying pan back over the tortilla and flip one more time, so the uncooked bit is now in contact with the base of the pan.

Replace the pan over low heat and leave until the tortilla is cooked through. Serve hot, warm, or cold, cut into slices or cubes.

River Cottage chutney

makes six or seven 18-ounce jars

The summer's day you spend slaving away, peeling, chopping, and stirring, to make a mammoth batch of chutney is one you will be glad of for months to come. I have simply never tasted a commercial chutney that was anything like as good as those made by enthusiastic amateurs – i.e., you and me. A useful tip: chopping the fruit and vegetables by hand is laborious, but it does give you a much better texture in the end than using a food processor.

I have added an exotic note to this classic chutney recipe by using tomatillos, a zesty Mexican fruit/vegetable which, with its paper lantern covering, looks like a giant Chinese gooseberry. It has a taste somewhere between a tomato and a grapefruit. Tomatillos grow well in a sunny garden and are available in specialty foods stores and some supermarkets. But you could easily substitute green (unripe) tomatoes. The optional pepper flakes simply make for a hotter version.

As long as you get the basic ratio of fruit/vegetable bulk to sugar and vinegar right, chutney recipes are infinitely variable: pears, plums, pumpkins, peaches (anything beginning with "p," in fact) can all be used: personalizing a recipe is part of the satisfaction.

2 pounds overgrown zucchini, diced
2 pounds tomatillos or green tomatoes, peeled and diced
1 pound cooking apples, peeled, cored, and diced
1 pound onions, diced
1 pound golden raisins
1 pound light brown sugar
2½ cups white wine vinegar
2 teaspoons red pepper flakes (optional)
A pinch of salt

FOR THE SPICE BAG
1 ounce dried ginger pieces
12 cloves
2 teaspoons black peppercorns
1 teaspoon coriander seeds

Tie up all the ingredients for the spice bag in a piece of cheesecloth. Put it into a large, heavy saucepan with all the rest of the ingredients and bring slowly to a boil, stirring occasionally. Simmer gently for 2 to 3 hours, uncovered, stirring occasionally to ensure the chutney does not burn on the bottom of the pan. The chutney is ready when it is rich, thick, and reduced; if you draw a wooden spoon through it, the mixture should part to reveal the base of the pan.

Pot up the chutney while still warm (but not boiling hot) in sterilized jars (see page 131) with plastic-coated screw-top lids – which stop the vinegar from interacting with the metal. Leave to mature for at least 2 weeks – ideally 2 months – before using.

Using chutney This is a versatile, well-balanced chutney that you can serve with cheese, cold meats, pork pies, etc. But also remember what a useful ingredient chutney is, with its ready-mixed blend of sweet, sour, and spice. I frequently add it to curries and spicy soups and stews, such as the Tagine of Mutton and Apricots on page 251.

green herb sauce (salsa verde)

serves 4

This is one of the most useful and versatile sauces I know – it works for fish, meat, and poultry, hot and cold – and I'll probably include a version of it in every cookbook I ever write. Its three best companions are roast lamb, oily fish such as mackerel, tuna, salmon, or sea bass, and cold poached tongue with French lentils (add a little extra mustard for this last one).

Ingredients are variable, as are the quantities, but the basic idea is to make a mildly piquant sauce in which the explosive aromas of (ideally) just-picked herbs come shining through. Parsley is pretty much essential – indeed, you can make a good version using parsley alone. Add other herbs according to your own taste and what comes to hand: basil and tarragon are favorites of mine, but chives, marjoram, chervil, and oregano can all be used. I tend to avoid sage, cilantro, and rosemary, as they overpower the other ingredients. Here's a basic version as a guide:

1 small garlic clove
A small bunch of flat-leaf parsley, trimmed of coarse stalks
15 to 20 basil leaves
Leaves from 3 to 4 sprigs of tarragon
2 to 3 anchovy fillets
About 1 teaspoon capers
About 1 teaspoon mustard (Dijon or English)
A pinch of sugar
A few drops of lemon juice or vinegar
Freshly ground black pepper
1 to 2 tablespoons extra-virgin olive oil

Finely chop the garlic on a large chopping board. Then add the herbs, anchovies, and capers and chop all together until the ingredients are well mixed and fairly fine in texture. Transfer to a bowl and mix in a little mustard, sugar, lemon juice or vinegar, black pepper, and enough olive oil to give a glossy, spoonable consistency. As you add these last ingredients, taste and tweak the mixture till you get something you really like.

This sauce is best when made immediately before serving, but it will also keep for a few days, covered, in the fridge.

real parsley sauce

makes about 2½ cups

Good parsley sauce is hard to find but easy to make. The secret is to flavor the milk for the béchamel sauce with bay leaf and vegetables – in a perfect world, all béchamels would be made this way.

1 carrot
½ onion
1 celery stick
1 bay leaf
2 cups whole milk
3 tablespoons butter
⅓ cup all-purpose flour
A good bunch of parsley (about 3 cups leaves when stripped from the stalks), chopped
Salt and freshly ground black pepper

Shred the vegetables and place them in a saucepan with the bay leaf and milk. Bring to a boil, then take the pan off the heat and leave to infuse for about an hour. Strain out the vegetables and bay leaf.

Melt the butter in a separate pan and stir in the flour. Cook this roux gently for a couple of minutes, then whisk in the milk, a third at a time, to get a nice smooth sauce. Let it simmer very gently for 5 minutes. If it is too thick, thin it with a little more hot milk. Finish your sauce just before serving, by stirring in the chopped parsley and seasoning to taste with salt and pepper.

split pea and green peppercorn purée

serves 4

This is particularly recommended as an accompaniment to the Pigeon Pitas on page 417. The whole peppercorns make little punchy explosions in contrast to the smooth, slightly sweetish purée. The purée also goes very nicely with roast lamb.

1½ cups green or yellow split peas
1 onion, finely chopped
1 carrot, finely chopped
1 celery stalk, finely chopped
1 small leek, chopped
A sprig of thyme
1 bay leaf
3 tablespoons butter
A pinch of superfine sugar
Salt
1 tablespoon pickled green peppercorns (preserved in brine in a can or jar, not dried)

Soak the split peas overnight in plenty of cold water. Drain, rinse, and put into a saucepan with the vegetables, herbs, and enough water to cover. Bring to a boil, then reduce to a simmer and cook until tender. Drain off the water, discard the bay leaf and thyme, and put the peas and vegetables, with the butter, through a food mill, sieve, or food processor (although the latter makes a less interesting texture). Now, season to taste with the sugar and some salt, add the peppercorns, and mix well. Heat through before serving, thinning the purée with a little hot water if it is very thick.

pea, lettuce, and lovage soup

serves 4

Lovage is a much underrated herb that is easy to grow (see page 65) and gives a distinctive savory note with a hint of curry. It absolutely makes this soup, which is one of my all-time favorites. It can be served hot or chilled. I prefer the latter, especially on a warm summer's evening, when it makes the perfect starter for an al fresco dinner.

I tend to use the fatter, older peas from the garden for this soup, saving the tiny babies to eat whole. It's perfectly acceptable to use frozen peas instead.

1 onion, chopped
A little butter or olive oil
About 3 cups fresh or frozen peas
1 small romaine lettuce, or 2 Little Gems, shredded
About 2¾ cups good chicken or vegetable stock
5 to 6 lovage leaves, plus 4 sprigs to garnish
Salt and freshly ground black pepper

Sauté the onion in the butter or oil until soft, then add the peas and lettuce. Pour over the stock, bring to a boil, and simmer gently for 4 to 6 minutes, until the fattest of the peas are completely tender. Remove from the heat and add the lovage leaves, then blend the soup in a blender. I stop blending before it is completely smooth, as I like to see and feel some texture in the soup, but a completely smooth, velvety texture is also nice. If the soup is too thick, thin with a little extra stock or water. I like it quite thick, but again it's entirely a matter of personal taste.

To serve cold, chill in the fridge or, if you're in a hurry, transfer the soup to a cold bowl and place in a second, larger bowl half-filled with water and ice cubes. Stir until chilled, changing the water and adding more ice as necessary. To serve hot, reheat, stirring occasionally, but do not allow it to boil. In both cases, season to taste, then pour into individual bowls and garnish with a single lovage sprig.

strawberry sandwiches

makes 4 rounds

The idea of a strawberry sandwich may sound a bit odd, but I defy anyone who likes strawberries and sandwiches (that must be all of us, right?) not to be delighted by these. I like to think of them as a kind of summer dessert you can eat without a spoon. You don't have to add the pepper, but I think it makes them even more irresistible.

8 thin slices of good crusty white bread
Soft unsalted butter
2 cups ripe strawberries
A little superfine sugar
Freshly ground black pepper (optional)

Spread the bread sparingly with butter. Hull the strawberries and slice them fairly thickly. Arrange the strawberry slices on the bread, as close together as possible without overlapping. Sprinkle lightly with sugar and add a few twists of black pepper if you like. Place a round of buttered bread on top to complete the sandwich, then cut into halves or quarters. I prefer to leave the crusts on, but they become wonderfully dainty if you don't.

variation To make a summer teatime treat into an indulgent pudding, spread the bread thickly with clotted cream or crème fraiche (instead of thinly with butter) and be a bit more cavalier with the sugar.

cranachan trifle

serves 8

Cranachan, the Scottish answer to summer pudding, can be made with all kinds of soft fruit – either a single fruit or a mixture. Try strawberries, raspberries, blackberries, blueberries, or red currants. Wild strawberries are particularly delicious.

The Scots might not approve, but my version is an indulgent cross between a cranachan and a trifle. This also works well with a thick purée of stewed, sieved gooseberries instead of fresh soft fruits. If you prefer to keep it simple, however, omit the custard and just layer the fruit with the cream and the oatmeal mixture.

⅓ cup old-fashioned rolled oats, toasted in the oven until crisp
¼ cup mixed chopped nuts, toasted
1 ounce dark chocolate, grated
2 cups heavy cream
¼ cup Drambuie or whisky
A little sugar (optional)
1½ pounds soft fruit (see suggestions above)

FOR THE CUSTARD
1 vanilla bean
2 cups heavy cream
4 egg yolks
6 tablespoons superfine sugar

To make the custard, split the vanilla bean open lengthwise and put it in a pan with the cream. Bring almost to a boil, then remove from the heat and leave to infuse for a few minutes. Whisk the egg yolks and sugar together until thoroughly blended. Remove the vanilla bean, scraping the seeds back into the cream, then pour the cream over the eggs and sugar, whisking all the time. Return this mixture to the pan and stir constantly over low heat until it thickens enough to coat the back of the spoon. Strain through a sieve into a bowl and leave to cool, then chill in the fridge until nice and thick.

Mix together the oats, nuts, and chocolate. Whip the cream and stir in the alcohol, sweetening with a little sugar if you use whisky. Pick over and prepare the fruit (large strawberries, for instance, should be sliced), then divide half the fruit between 8 large wineglasses (or place in one large bowl).

Spoon some custard over the fruit and then sprinkle a layer of the oatmeal mixture over the custard. Add a layer of cream, then the remaining fruit. Finish off with cream and a final sprinkling of the oatmeal mixture on top. Do not wait long before serving or the oatmeal will lose its crispness.

floating islands with black currant sauce

serves 8 to 10

This is a simplified version of a French bourgeois classic: islands of fluffy poached meringue floating on a sea of cool custard, trickled with a nice sharp fruit purée. Black currant is my favorite fruit for the sauce, but raspberries, gooseberries, red currants, etc., will all do very nicely. The coffee in the meringue is optional, but it does help take the sickly edge off what is a very rich dish.

FOR THE CRÈME ANGLAISE (ENGLISH CUSTARD)
4 eggs
4 egg yolks
½ cup superfine sugar
2 cups heavy cream
2 cups whole milk
1 vanilla bean, split open lengthwise

FOR THE BLACK CURRANT SAUCE
2 pounds black currants
1 cup water
½ to 1 cup superfine sugar

FOR THE MERINGUE ISLANDS
4 egg whites
1 cup superfine sugar
1 tablespoon very strong black coffee (optional)

TO DECORATE (OPTIONAL)
Fresh fruit, such as raspberries and strawberries

To make the custard, beat the eggs and egg yolks together with the sugar until well mixed. Put the cream and milk in a heavy saucepan, add the vanilla bean, and scald (bring almost to a boil), then remove the bean and pour the cream and milk over the eggs, whisking all the time. Put this custard in a large, heavy pan over a low heat and stir gently until it starts to thicken enough to coat the back of the spoon. Remove from the heat,

stir for a further 1 to 2 minutes, strain through a fine sieve into a bowl, and let cool.

For the sauce, pick over the black currants, removing any twigs, leaves, or stalks, and wash thoroughly. Put them in a pan over low heat with the water and 1/2 cup of the sugar and cook, stirring occasionally, until they break up. Simmer gently for 5 minutes, then remove from the heat. Let cool a little and rub through a nylon sieve. Taste the resulting purée while it is still warm and stir in more sugar if you think it needs it (remember the custard is sweet, so the sauce should be quite tart). Let cool completely.

To make the meringue islands, whisk the egg whites until they form stiff peaks. Whisk in the sugar a third at a time, plus the coffee if using, and continue whisking until you have a thick, creamy meringue that will keep its shape when scooped. Using 2 tablespoons, form the meringue into quenelles (football shapes); this is done by scraping a little heap of the meringue from one spoon to the other – hard to describe but easy to do, with a little practice. Place the meringues 2 or 3 at a time in a wide pan of gently simmering water. Cover the pan and poach the meringues for about 2 minutes, until puffed up and lightly set. Remove from the pan with a slotted spoon.

While the meringues are poaching, have ready some individual serving plates or shallow bowls in which you have poured a pool of cold custard. Float a couple of meringues on each pool of custard and drizzle 2 or 3 tablespoons of the black currant sauce over the top. Decorate with extra fruit such as fresh raspberries or sliced strawberries, if you like.

cherry clafouti

serves 8

The simplest of dishes, a clafouti is really just a sweet batter pudding, fruit replacing the "toads" in the hole. The classic recipe, from the Limoges region of France, uses black cherries, but it works well with all kinds of fruit – try blueberries, apricots, or plums. The last two will need cutting in half and pitting, then placing cut side down in the dish; you can use the others whole like cherries.

A little butter for greasing
3 cups black or red cherries
⅓ cup superfine sugar
1 cup all-purpose flour
A pinch of salt
3 eggs, lightly beaten
1¼ cups milk
Confectioners' sugar for dusting

Lightly grease a 10-inch-diameter round ceramic or tin baking dish or a 10 by 8-inch rectangular one. Remove the stems from the cherries but do not pit them (you don't want the juices to run until the moment you bite into a cherry). Toss them with a third of the sugar and spread them out in a single layer in the dish.

Sift the flour and salt into a bowl and stir in the remaining sugar. Make a well in the middle and pour in the beaten eggs. Mix well, drawing in the flour from the sides, then beat in the milk, a little at a time, until you have a smooth batter (you can use a food processor to make the batter if you prefer). Pour the batter over the cherries and bake in a preheated 350°F oven for about 35 minutes, until lightly browned and puffed up like a Yorkshire pudding.

Clafouti is at its best eaten lukewarm, but not bad cold either. Dust with confectioners' sugar just before serving, and serve plain or with cream.

favorite fruit ices

One of the joys of a fruit garden – and one of the most effective solutions to a fruit glut – is making homemade sorbets and ice creams. They always have been (and, I suspect, always will be) one of my favorite things in the world. As a diehard enthusiast of the frozen dessert, I have made and eaten a lot of them over the years, and although these days I rarely measure ingredients precisely or follow written recipes, I have come to operate according to a set of reliable guidelines that serve me well. Here, then, are a few personal notes on the general business of making ice creams and ices:

- Ice cream machines are very useful indeed. Top-of-the-range ones can be expensive, but I wouldn't be without mine. If you like ice cream, they will enable you to make stuff that is better than *anything* you can buy in the shops. The hard work of making ice cream without a machine (taking it out of the freezer several times to whisk the partially frozen mixture by hand) is a pretty major disincentive.
- Fruit ice creams have a better flavor and texture if made with a custard or egg mousse base rather than just fruit purée mixed with heavy cream (Cheaty Peach Ice Cream, on page 130, is the exception that proves this rule). The mousse base, as described in Best-Ever Vanilla Ice Cream (opposite), is my preferred option.
- You need to bear in mind that flavors are muted at low temperatures. Mixes for sorbets and ice creams should, therefore, in their unfrozen state, taste a little *too* sweet, a little *too* sharp, and a little *too* fruity (if that's possible). By the same token, chocolate ice creams should be very chocolatey and coffee ones very coffeey. Once you have appreciated this principle, it becomes easy to improvise ice creams and sorbets with almost any flavor that comes to hand.
- Bear in mind that some fruits are much more strongly flavored than others. Black currants, for example, are extremely intense, and only a little black currant purée is needed to transform a mousse and cream mixture into strongly flavored ice cream. With strawberries, by contrast, much more purée will be needed.
- Avoid metal spoons, sieves, and bowls when using very acidic fruits such as raspberries and red currants. They can discolor the fruit and spoil the flavor.
- Fruits that are unpalatable raw, such as black currants, gooseberries, rhubarb, and sour plums, will need to be cooked before being made into ice cream. Cool and sieve the cooked fruit compote before adding it to the mousse base for ice cream or sweetening it for a sorbet.
- Confectioners' sugar is a very useful ingredient for instantly adjusting the sweetness of your mix. Lemon juice is equally handy for adjusting the acidity.
- If you don't have a machine, an easy way to make sorbets is to freeze your sweetened fruit pulp in a tray until solid, then scratch it up into frosty shards with a strong fork just before serving. This is what Italians call a granita. The texture is a little more crunchy than a sorbet, but still wonderful.

These guidelines should help the budding ice cream enthusiast to improvise all kinds of delights. Meanwhile, here are my top five tried-and-trusted frozen desserts, with accurate quantities for infallible reproduction.

best-ever vanilla ice cream

makes 1 quart

Made with the best eggs, the best cream, and a real vanilla bean, this should be one of the best vanilla ice creams you'll ever taste. I like it on its own, or with just a few fresh raspberries. Without the vanilla, this is the mousse base I use for most of my fruit ice creams.

2 cups heavy cream
1 vanilla bean, split lengthwise
½ cup superfine sugar
⅔ cup water
4 large egg yolks

Scald the cream (i.e., bring it almost to boiling, then remove from the heat) and add the vanilla bean. Leave to infuse until the cream is completely cool. Scrape out the tiny seeds from the bean and leave them in the cream.

Over low heat, dissolve the sugar in the water, then turn up the heat and boil rapidly to get a light syrup (it's ready when a little dropped onto a cold plate forms a thread when stretched between finger and thumb). Let the syrup cool for just a minute. Place the egg yolks in a bowl and begin whisking (ideally with an electric mixer), trickling in the hot syrup as you go. Continue whisking until the mixture is thick and mousselike, then whisk in the cream. Pour the mixture into an ice cream machine and churn until frozen.

strawberry gelato, Italian style

makes about 1 quart

Sweet, tart, and fruity, this is a real gelato, like the kind you get in the best Italian ice cream parlors.

About 2 pounds strawberries
6 tablespoons lemon juice (about 2 large lemons)
2 cups confectioners' sugar

Crush the strawberries and rub them through a nylon sieve to extract the seeds. Stir in the lemon juice, then whisk in the sugar. Pour into your ice cream machine and churn until frozen (or make granita style, as described on page 126). Strawberry ices tend to lose their flavor if stored for a long time in the freezer. This one is best eaten within a month of making – which, frankly, shouldn't be a struggle.

raspberry and red currant sorbet

makes about 1 quart

A fantastically tart and refreshing combination, which I like to serve alongside the Strawberry Gelato, Italian Style, on page 127. Moving from one to the other, then back again, trying to work out which of the two is more delicious, is my idea of sorbet heaven.

1 pound raspberries
1 pound red currants
2 cups confectioners' sugar

Crush the fruit and rub it through a nylon sieve to extract the seeds. Stir the sugar into the fruit purée. Pour it into your ice cream machine and churn until frozen (or make granita style, as described on page 126).

gooseberry and elderflower ice cream

makes about 1½ quarts

This is really a frozen version of the fool on page 427.

2 pounds gooseberries
4 to 5 elderflower heads
About 1 cup confectioners' sugar
1 recipe Best-Ever Vanilla Ice Cream mixture (see page 127), made without the vanilla bean (there is no need to scald the cream)

Gently stew the gooseberries and elderflower heads with a couple of tablespoons of water until soft and pulpy. Rub them through a nylon sieve to remove the elderflower bits and gooseberry skin and seeds. Stir the sugar into the resulting purée.

Stir the sweetened gooseberry purée into the ice cream mix until it is thoroughly blended. Check for sweetness, adding a little more sugar if it is very tart, then freeze in your ice cream machine. Serve with Scotch shortbread.

cheaty peach ice cream

makes about 1 quart

I use fresh seasonal fruit for all my ice creams – except this one, the easiest ice cream you'll ever make.

1 large can (about 26 ounces) of peaches in syrup
2 cups heavy cream

Empty the contents of the can into a blender and blend until smooth. Stir in the cream. Pour into your ice cream machine and churn until frozen. Yes, it's that easy.

raspberry jam

makes eight to ten 2-pint jars

I don't do a lot of jam making, as my excess fruit tends to go toward ice creams and sorbets. But I do have a terrible weakness for raspberry jam: a good one is as good as jam gets. The secret, I think, is to pick the raspberries on a hot, dry day, aiming for a good mixture of ripe and almost ripe fruit, then make the jam immediately. A light boiling produces a loose, almost pourable jam with a fresh, tangy flavor. I have to admit that this version was pretty much based on the instructions on the back of the jam sugar packet. But it took first prize at the Beaminster summer show, so I must have done something right.

1½ pounds (6 cups) raspberries

6 cups jam sugar (with added pectin), or 6 cups granulated sugar and 6 tablespoons fresh lemon juice

Pick over the raspberries carefully, discarding any leaves and stalks, along with any moldy or otherwise suspect fruit. Put half the fruit in a large bowl and coarsely crush the berries by hand, squeezing them with your fingers. Place them in a heavy stainless-steel or copper pan that is large enough not to be more than half full when all the ingredients are added. Add the remaining fruit, whole, and the sugar.

Stir over low heat for a few minutes to dissolve the sugar, then turn up the heat and bring to a boil. Boil hard for exactly 5 minutes. The jam can be taken off the heat and potted up at this point, and you will have a loose jam with an excellent, fresh flavor.

If you want a more traditional, jelled texture, boil the jam for 7 minutes in total, then test it for setting: using a teaspoon, let a few drops of jam fall onto a chilled plate. Let cool a moment, then push the jam sideways with your finger. It should crinkle slightly and, when taken between thumb and forefinger, it should be nicely tacky. As soon as it has reached this stage, remove the pan from the heat.

Pot up the jam in warm sterilized jars (see below) straight away.

Note To sterilize jam jars, just put them through a cycle of the dishwasher and leave them until dry. Alternatively, you can thoroughly wash them in hot soapy water, then put them in a very low oven for a couple of hours to dry.

plum bread and butter pudding

serves 6

I love bread and butter pudding and am always experimenting with variations on the theme. My experiments have convinced me that the addition of acidic fruit such as plums makes a far superior pudding to the traditional English version with raisins. This pudding works superbly well with any kind of plum, and also with peaches, nectarines, and apricots.

My bread and butter puddings tend to be fairly improvised affairs, and it's usually a question of scrabbling around for a dish that roughly fits the amount of stale bread I have lying around, then shoving in as much fruit as I can fit between the slices, pouring over the eggy custard, and banging it in the oven. It's nice to cook in this way – you can consider the quantities below a rough but reliable guideline until you feel confident doing it by eye. The one thing you can't stint on is the eggs and cream, or your pudding will be too dry. If in doubt, mix your custard first and pour it into your empty chosen dish: it should come at least halfway up the sides. If it doesn't, add an extra egg, another splash of milk and/or cream, a bit of sugar, and whisk it all up again.

6 to 8 large plums, halved and pitted
1 cup superfine sugar, plus extra for the plums
About ½ loaf of slightly stale white bread
2 tablespoons softened unsalted butter
1 vanilla bean
2 cups heavy cream
¾ cup whole milk
3 eggs
2 egg yolks

Lay the plum halves, cut side up, in an ovenproof dish and place 1/2 teaspoon superfine sugar in the center of each one. Bake in a preheated 400°F oven for 15 to 20 minutes, until they are tender and the juices have run. Remove from the oven and let cool.

Cut the crusts off the bread and cut it into slices that roughly correspond to the depth of the ovenproof dish you have chosen for the pudding: when laid in the dish at a slight angle from the vertical, the slices should come close to or level with the top. Spread the slices with the butter, then use any leftover butter to grease the dish.

Split the vanilla bean open lengthwise and place it in a pan with the cream and milk. Bring them almost to a boil, then remove from the heat and leave to infuse for a few minutes.

In a large bowl, whisk the eggs, egg yolks, and 1 cup of sugar together until they are thoroughly blended. Remove the vanilla bean from the hot cream mixture (you can rinse it, wrap it in plastic wrap, and use it again), then pour the cream over the eggs and sugar, whisking all the time, until you have a thin but smooth and well-blended custard. (If you're in a hurry or you just simply want to make your life easier, you can omit the vanilla bean and then you don't have to scald the cream and milk: simply whisk cold into the eggs and sugar.)

Arrange the buttered bread slices in your greased dish – if possible, at an angle somewhere between vertical and 45 degrees. Place the roasted plum halves between the bread slices, trying to distribute them fairly evenly throughout the pudding. Plug any glaring gaps by cutting leftover bread slices to fit; your dish should end up full but not overcrammed. Any syrupy juices from the dish in which the plums were baked can be poured over at this stage.

Strain the custard over the bread slowly and carefully, a little at a time, so it can seep and ooze between the cracks. If it looks like it may flood over the sides of the dish, wait a few minutes for it to soak into the bread before adding more. In any case, leave the pudding to infuse for at least half an hour before you put it in the oven. You don't have to use all the custard, but you should use enough to make sure that only 1/4 inch or so of unsoaked bread is at the top of the pudding.

Bake in a preheated 350°F oven for 30 to 40 minutes, until the top is golden brown and the custard is just set but still slightly wobbly in the center. This pudding is delicious hot, warm, or cold, and really needs no accompaniment.

variation For a super-indulgent winter version of this pudding, when fresh fruit is out of season, replace the plums with pitted prunes soaked overnight in brandy, Armagnac, or Calvados.

livestock

Given that I am always happy to nail my flag to the mast as an enthusiastic carnivore, what I have to say at the beginning of this section may seem a little illogical. I think we eat far too much meat in the U.K. There, I've said it.

It is too much in a number of different ways. Too much for our health, too much certainly for the welfare of our farmed animals, and far too much for the quality of the meat we eat to be consistently high. I say, eat less meat. And make sure that the meat you do eat is well cooked, well butchered, well slaughtered, and from animals that are well looked after, well fed, and, basically, well.

The problem started with the postwar boom in factory farming of livestock. The technology blossomed at the same time as the opening up of new communication channels. Through the use of intensive and aggressive marketing and dubious nutritional "education," government-backed agencies put out the message that every true Brit who wanted to stay happy and healthy should have a big slab of meat in the middle of his or her plate every mealtime. Soon, our butcher shops and supermarkets were filled to overflowing with cheap meat from animals who lived painful and stressful lives, fed on a diet scandalously inappropriate for their species – indeed, often it was their own species. Mad cow disease has demanded a radical rethink on that last policy, but the factory-farming system is alive and well and producing more meat than ever before.[2]

It is true that animal welfare in British farming is probably better than anywhere else in the world. But that doesn't mean we should feel happy to buy any old meat produced in Britain. Most of it is still produced by methods that would horrify consumers if they knew the truth. (The truth, incidentally, is graphically and compellingly spelled out in Audrey Eyton's book, *The Kind Food Guide*, now out of print, and, more recently, in Joanna Blythman's *The Food We Eat*.) What is a scandal and a disgrace, and a testament to gross government indifference to both the needs of British farmers and the wants of British consumers, is the way that meat is labeled in this country. It seems particularly ludicrous and insulting that our labels are allowed to tell us barefaced lies: that pork, for example, from pigs that have been reared abroad in conditions that would merit prosecution in this country, can, under a system condoned by our own Ministry of Agriculture, be labeled as British. No wonder the farmers are fuming. The situation in the U.S. is even more convoluted, insufficient, and frustrating.

What can we do about this? If we think that raising and killing animals for food is in itself morally wrong, then we can become vegetarians. If, on the other hand, we believe that breeding and raising animals that would otherwise not even come into existence, then slaughtering them just as they reach adulthood so that we can cook and eat them, is on balance an acceptable way to increase the pleasure of human lives, then we have another moral duty. That is, to be aware of just how fragile the claim to exercise this "right" really is. It stands and falls on our ability to respect the far less dubious rights of the animals themselves. I see no reason why animals' rights should be a complex moral issue. They are basic. Animals have, at the very least, the right to move, feed, and breed in a manner that more or less tallies with their natural instincts. Cows want to eat grass. Is it really asking too much that we should let them?

If, like me, you have been a somewhat troubled carnivore, the best possible way to reach an understanding of these issues, and perhaps find a little peace, is to raise some animals for meat yourself. It's worked for me at River Cottage. Since I took on first pigs, then sheep and cows, I am much clearer in my mind about where I stand on the meat issue. And the meat I have raised myself has been the meat I have most enjoyed eating and the meat that has least troubled my conscience.

In the pages that follow, I hope to persuade some of you that raising your own stock may not be so wildly impractical as perhaps you assume. In an ideal world, I think everyone who eats meat should care for, then kill and eat, an animal at least once in their lives, even if it is only a rabbit or a chicken. In the less ideal world we live in, most of us will continue to rely on the butcher and supermarket.[3] To you, I make an impassioned plea: try not to buy second-rate meat from badly treated animals. Learn a little (or even a lot) about the origins of the meat at the outlets where you shop regularly. If you are not happy, then go elsewhere. The chapters that follow include many suggestions to help you find meat that tastes better from animals that have led contented lives. Please use them. This meat will be more expensive, and perhaps you will be able to afford less of it. That may not be such a bad thing. And anyway, what's a clean conscience worth?

livestock | pigs and pork

Of all the culinary adventures I've had over the past few years, at River Cottage and elsewhere, one of the most satisfying – in the field, in the kitchen and, not least, at the table – is the rearing and processing of my own pigs. From the day of collecting a pair of wriggling, squealing piglets to the consumption of the last sliver of dry-cured ham from the same animals (anything up to two years later), I have found the entire process a complete joy. And gastronomically it's been a revelation.

Although, like most people, I have always had a weakness for bacon, I used to find "ordinary" (i.e., uncured) pork dull, flabby, and lifeless, the least interesting of all meats. That changed when I first came to River Cottage. A friend asked us over for Sunday lunch and served up a joint of roast pork with cracklings. As she carved, I could see it looked different from any pork I had ever seen before. A dark, close-grained meat, it was oozing with juice and had a thick layer of fat beneath the crackling. And it tasted quite divine: it was properly chewable without being tough and had a deep, porky flavor with just a hint of wildness about it. The cracklings were to die for. Our host explained that the meat had come from our local butcher in Beaminster, Frampton's, and that the butcher had told her it was from a rare breed called a Saddleback.

I later discovered that it had come from Peggy Darvill's rare-breed pig farm in Toller Whelme. And it was from Peggy, the following year, that I bought my first pair of pigs, two male Gloucester Old Spots, to rear at River Cottage. Pork is now my favorite meat. Indeed, these days, I find that pigs, pork, and charcuterie (the cured pork products that so magically extend both the shelf life and the culinary range of your pig carcass) seem to occupy a whole little culinary planet of their own. It's a beautiful place, and regular trips there, whether delivering a bucket of scraps to the pigs in their pen, or seeing their delight at being hosed down on a blistering hot day, or, to be brutally honest, tasting the first slice of blood sausage made on the very day of their slaughter, are among the most abiding pleasures of life at River Cottage.

The main aim of this chapter, then, is to try to share with you the passion and excitement that the very best pigs, and the very best pork, can inspire. To make a real success of them, you will need to master a number of important techniques, especially at the processing stage. They are not in the least difficult, but they should be strictly adhered to.

But before I go all-out to persuade you to take the porky plunge and buy your first pair of weaners, here are some thoughts about the pork you don't rear yourself.

buying pork

Central to my philosophy on meat is this basic principle: the quality of any meat relates directly to the lifestyle of the animal from which it comes. Sadly, no farm animal experiences such extremes of lifestyle as the poor pig. At its worst, husbandry of the pig is an abuse that is barely short of criminal; certainly, given the intelligence and sensitivity of the creature, it's morally abhorrent. Industrially farmed pigs are reared indoors on concrete, in their thousands, with no room to move and no opportunity to express any of their natural forms of behavior, such as rooting. They are fed a cocktail of chemicals and overprocessed high-protein feeds, the sole purpose of which is to ensure rapid growth and a minimal layer of fat. Their miserable lives may be short, but given the shoddy treatment that is meted out to them, you might say they are not short enough.

By contrast, pigs raised by real enthusiasts, who not only aim to produce pork of the highest quality but also take great pleasure in their animals, have a pretty good life. They live outdoors, with the option of shelter whenever they need it. They can root to their heart's content. They have a chance to express their social, gregarious nature in the uncrowded company of other pigs. And they have a natural, varied, additive-free diet. Their meat develops slowly, is surrounded by a natural layer of fat, and is made firm by a reasonable level of exercise. Consequently, it tastes quite delicious.

For the wised-up consumer in search of quality pork, the mission therefore is, in theory at least, relatively straightforward: just find the happy pig. A few years ago, this would have been like trying to find a broken nail in a heap of manure. But happily, thanks in large measure to the burgeoning organic movement and the dedication of rare-breed enthusiasts, it is starting to get a bit easier, in both the U.K. and the U.S.

Of course, between these two extremes there's plenty to choose from: pigs are farmed with varying degrees of intensity and conscientiousness. There are some very large outdoor pig farms rearing thousands of animals annually. These animals may not have the best, additive-free feeds and may have been fairly intensively farrowed from pretty miserable sows. But they have shelter, space, and real earth beneath their trotters, and that counts for a lot. In the search for happy pork, I would say that outdoor reared is a minimum requirement.

On the other hand, one should be able to do better than that. One of the most satisfactory ways to buy pork is to locate the nearest producer of seriously happy pigs and buy directly. This is increasingly possible, as small-scale producers, under pressure to compete with the industrial product, are looking for ways to sell directly to consumers without going through butchers or the trade. Some have their own farm stores, others sell by mail order or can deliver locally, and many take their pork to sell at farmers' markets. Buy in large quantities for the freezer, and you may find that prices are competitive with supermarkets and butcher shops. Anyway, the taste should allay any misgivings about paying a bit more.

Any pig farmer who is certified organic is likely to be producing excellent meat from happy animals (in the U.K. all the welfare requirements you could hope for follow directly from organic status).[4] But organic is not the be-all and end-all. There are many small farmers who have chosen not to jump through all the hoops that organic status requires, yet who are rearing free-range pork outdoors on a natural diet. Anyone raising rare breeds is pretty likely to be making a good job of it – they are probably genuine enthusiasts, and good welfare standards simply go with the territory. The most satisfying way to assess the means of production is to visit the farm yourself. If there's a chance of your becoming a regular customer, anyone selling directly should be more than happy to let you come to their farm and see how it's done. And anyone reluctant to show you around may be guilty of questionable husbandry. Openness is one of the strongest suits of those who practice good husbandry.

If you are having trouble tracking down a pig farmer, look online to find your nearest supplier of organic meat.

Those whose shopping activities must be confined to the main street and the supermarket needn't despair. Good butchers can find you good pork, even if they don't habitually stock it: ask if they can order organic or rare-breed pork for you. Even the supermarkets are at last joining in. Most of the big names now stock a range of organic meats. If organic is not available, look for other encouraging labels, such as *free range* or *outdoor reared*, but be aware that there are no legal definitions of these and welfare standards vary immensely. Terms like *farm fresh*, *traditional*, and *country* are meaningless marketing gibberish. Most supermarkets have their own schemes for premium pork and should be able to provide you with details of their welfare standards on request. In the States, naturally raised meats are becoming more and more available. Ask your butcher and look online for names like Niman Ranch, Winrose Farm, and Applecheek Farm.

Above all, wherever you shop, boycott the rubbish and champion those who really care about their pigs. We'll all benefit in the long run – and so will the pigs.

keeping pigs

The best way to ensure the pork you eat comes from contented, well-fed, properly cared-for stock is to buy and rear the pigs yourself. This is not such a wildly impractical option as most people might think, though equally, like all stock rearing, it's not to be undertaken "unadvisedly, lightly, or wantonly" (as the vicar might say).

Pigs are not willfully aggressive, but they are big, greedy, and not necessarily able to make a distinction between the carrot that is offered them and the hand that is holding it. They have powerful jaws, which can give a serious bite. There is no reason why small children cannot enjoy looking at and even touching your pigs, but they should be supervised at all times. Contented pigs are quiet, happy animals and shouldn't give you much trouble. Your neighbors may be more skeptical, but, provided they are forewarned, they may come to enjoy the presence of your pigs as much as you do. A little bit of noisy squealing at feeding time is the worst they will have to put up with.

The best way to get started in pigs is not to commit straight away to a breeding sow but to buy two or more "weaners" – piglets of seven to ten weeks old that have been weaned from their mothers and are ready to live independently. Buy them in spring and you can take them home, then fatten them up throughout the summer for slaughter as "baconers" in the autumn. A baconer is a pig of nine months or older and is usually at least 140 pounds carcass weight. "Porkers," by contrast, are killed at four to five months old and traditionally used entirely for fresh meat. Ironically, I have found the fresh meat from my baconers to be better than any commercially reared pork.

If you choose a pair of pigs (and as pigs are sociable, gregarious creatures you absolutely must have at least two) of a hardy breed, you will find them quite self-sufficient, and you won't have to worry about the finer points of farrowing (looking after a breeding sow and her piglets). Give the weaners the space they need, a proper shelter, clean fresh water every day, and the right diet, and there is every chance they will remain healthy and happy from the day they arrive to the day you take them to slaughter. If the pig bug bites, so to speak, and you have the confidence, time, and space, you can get yourself a breeding sow and take your porcine husbandry on to the next stage. But before you do that, get yourself a good pig manual (see the Bibliography on page 440) and talk at length to an experienced small-scale pig breeder about the art of successful farrowing.

choosing a breed

If you are planning to keep your pigs outdoors (which is the only way to do it that is of any interest to me), it makes sense to think in terms of a hardy breed that is well adapted to outdoor life. This includes just about all the old or "rare" breeds, such as the Gloucester Old Spot, the Saddleback, the Middle White, the Berkshire, the Tamworth, etc. These traditional breeds are very self-sufficient and far less susceptible to health problems than the modern commercial hybrids. Of course, unless you are interested in breeding and showing pedigree pigs, there is no reason why your chosen weaners should be purebred. The old breeds cross with each other extremely well. I started with a pair of purebred Gloucester Old Spots but since then have been experimenting with rare-breed crosses: Tamworth/Old Spot and Saddleback/Duroc. All have loved the outdoor life and, to date, touch wood, I have had no health problems with any of them. Ringing the changes with different breeds, and discerning the resulting differences in the taste and texture of their meat, is all part of the fun.

These kinds of pigs tend to be slower growing, and fatter at the finish, than commercial hybrids. But that shouldn't worry you in the least; they will taste outstanding, retain more moisture in the cooking, and your bacon especially will be all the better for the extra fat.

where to keep them

Because you will be providing them with other sources of feed than grazing, pigs do not need nearly as much space as sheep or cows. They do, however, need some room – enough to break into a trot every now and again – and ideally a little variety in their environment. For a pair of pigs, you should fence off an absolute minimum of 150 square yards. Light or free-draining soil is preferable to heavy clay. In wet weather, any pig run is sure to become a mud bath, but your pigs will be more comfortable if it dries out fairly quickly. The perfect pig run for the small farmer would be a little copse or patch of rough ground with a few trees in it – trees provide a bit of shade and something for the pigs to rub against (they love a good scratch). An orchard or the corner of an orchard would be heaven.

Not everyone has such a perfect porcine habitat at their disposal. On the other hand, with a bit of ingenuity, any patch of ground that is big enough can be made to work for you. A featureless patch of pasture can be made more pig-friendly by the addition of an old tree trunk to rub against and a large pile of brush wood to rest up in (pigs like to have alternatives to their regular shelter). An old dead tree dragged into their pen is better than no tree at all. An old tractor tire will provide amusement – but take it out again if they start eating it!

shelter

Pigs must have a secure shelter to sleep and rest in, but it doesn't have to be fancy. The specially made corrugated-iron pig arcs are not the prettiest of things, but they are economical and very practical options. The entrance of the arc should face away from the prevailing wind, and the inside should be well bedded down with fresh straw. More straw around and outside the entrance will help to keep the inside clean. Pigs like to keep their beds clean and tend to toss out any soiled straw. Give them fresh bedding every three to four weeks.

A traditional brick-built sty or a stable or another suitable outbuilding are other options for keeping pigs, but they are harder work to maintain, as they need weekly mucking out. They must also open out onto a decent outdoor run of soft, rootable ground (i.e., not concrete). A dedicated outbuilding of this kind, which should ideally have a supply of electricity, is essential for farrowing sows.

food

One of the great attractions of keeping pigs is that they will thrive on your kitchen and garden leftovers. They will eat just about anything you offer them, so the responsibility to make sure they do not consume anything inappropriate rests with you. The golden rule is NO MEAT OF ANY KIND.

Few households generate enough leftovers to keep two pigs properly fed, so your best option is to buy a supply of pelleted feed (pignuts), based on a good balance of cereal ingredients. Organic pignuts are available and highly recommended. A 12-pound bag of organic pignuts will last a pair of young weaners two to three weeks. Larger animals nearly ready for slaughter will get through that amount of feed in about half the time.

Pignuts can be used as a basic feed but replaced whenever you have a decent meal's worth of leftovers. We seem to average about one meal in four from household and garden scraps, and rather more than that in the summer when the vegetable garden is at its most productive. Pigs love greens, and ours tend to get all our bean and pea pods, over-the-top spinach, and any trimmings from kitchen vegetable preparation. They will even enjoy grass cuttings, but only a few handfuls: more will upset their stomachs. Stale or leftover bread, buns, biscuits, cereals, cooked rice, pasta, potatoes, and all starches go down well, as do dairy scraps such as cheese, milk, butter, etc. If you have neighbors who are prepared to contribute to your swill bin, so much the better. You can pay them back in bacon and chops at the end of the year. You will find it immensely satisfying to recycle and minimize waste in this way. The only loser is the compost heap – these days I struggle to maintain one, as practically all my vegetable waste goes to the chickens or pigs.

If you want to minimize the amount of bought-in feed you give to your pigs, you can set aside a patch for growing a dedicated fodder crop, such as wurzels, rutabagas, or the very fast-growing stubble turnips. Pigs love roots like these, and the green tops as well.

slaughter

Your first pair of pigs is likely to have given you so much pleasure that the prospect of taking them to slaughter will inevitably seem a little daunting. There is no doubt that people get attached to pigs. But there is one strategy for minimizing emotional trauma at "the end" that you can deploy throughout the time you spend looking after the pigs. It may sound a bit gruesome, but it works for me. Basically, it's to do with attitude and the way you think about your pigs. Put crudely: never stop thinking about your pigs as potential bacon. Even when you first bring them to their patch, have an eye on the future products you plan to get from them. Admire their growing hams, then go and research what kind of cure you might pickle them in. And as you watch them rooting for beech mast or tucking into a trough of windfall apples, think about what it will do for the flavor of their meat. As the time for slaughter draws near, size up the length of that side of bacon.

None of this means you need ever lose sight of your pigs' needs or that you cannot enjoy your contact with them or their behavioral antics. On the contrary, their happiness, and your ultimate plans for them, are inextricably linked: the happier your pigs, the better you can feel about taking them to slaughter, and the tastier the feast you have to look forward to.

That is said, of course, with the benefit of hindsight, and with three seasons of pig rearing under my belt. The first time is the hardest. My first pair of pigs were the first animals I ever took to slaughter, and the strange thing is I really didn't know how I was going to feel about it until I did it. As things turned out, and rather to my surprise, I didn't find it all that distressing. Efficiency is the order of the day, and that means help from at least one other person who really knows what they're doing. In my case, Peggy Darvill, who sold me the pigs in the first place, came over with her partner, Steve, to help me load them up. Incidentally, if you have only two pigs – or only two left – it is crucial welfare procedure to take them both to slaughter on the same day. It is even more unkind to leave a pig used to company on its own than to rear a lone pig in the first place.

My pigs had not been moved anywhere since the day they came to River Cottage seven months earlier. Now we had to get them out of their pen, across the bridge over the river, and into the back of the waiting trailer: all in all a potentially stressful procedure. The key, Steve explained, is to narrow their options for escape, keep them hungry, and lure them into the trailer with a bucket of feed. So we made a funnel-like path from the end of their pen to the bridge with old wooden boards and corrugated-iron sheets and lined the ground with straw all the way up the ramp and into the back of the trailer. I went ahead of them, rattling a bucket of feed (they hadn't been given their breakfast), while Peggy and Steve coaxed them gently from behind, ready to turn them if they tried to go back. It went like clockwork: they followed the bucket straight into the trailer, and hardly any pushing and shoving was required.

Steve and I took them to Snell's, a small local slaughterhouse outside Chard that gives an excellent and personal service. It's just a forty-minute drive from River Cottage. We unloaded them into the waiting pen, where they sniffed around inquisitively for a few minutes until the two slaughtermen came and walked them around the corner into the slaughter building. Almost as soon as they were out of sight I heard the clunk of the stunning tongs, and both pigs were gone without so much as a squeal.

I waited twenty minutes or so while they were "done." I didn't watch the process (although I could have if I'd wanted) but I did ask for an explanation of exactly what happens. I think everyone who takes an animal to slaughter should know this, so, for the record, here is the procedure: once stunned by an electric shock from the stunning tongs (after which they are unconscious), the pigs are hoisted up by their back legs to be carried down the "production line" on a moving chain. First of all, they have their throat cut and are bled out (the slaughterman will collect the blood for you on request). It is this process of bleeding that actually kills them. Next, they are dipped in near-boiling water for a matter of seconds to loosen the bristles, which are then removed by an automated "de-hairer" – this works by beating the body of the pig with rubber paddles. The belly of the carcass is then slit and the animal eviscerated. The liver, heart, and lights (lungs) are hung up for inspection, after which any edible innards requested by the client are removed and bagged up. Finally, the carcass is washed down inside and out with a powerful jet of warm water before being moved to the prechiller, and then the cold room, where it will hang until collected.

Throughout my first experience of taking home-reared animals to slaughter, I never really felt upset or guilty – just rather anxious that it should all go smoothly. That it did was a huge relief, and due in no small part to the calm efficiency of Steve, who was with me. I would certainly recommend any first-timer to go with someone who's been before and knows the ropes.

I went home that day with a bag of innards, a bucket of blood, and a clear conscience. Back at River Cottage, I made blood sausage and fried a slice of liver for my supper. The next time I saw my two pigs they were hanging in a butcher's cold room four days later. By that time I had really forgotten all about their charming personalities; they were nothing more nor less than the raw materials for a very exciting culinary challenge. I couldn't wait to get cracking. And, indeed, cracklings.

processing your pig

Careful planning of the processing of your pigs is essential: set aside at least a whole day, ideally two (a weekend is perfect), to be dedicated to the fast and efficient transformation of your carcasses. Remember that you are likely to be dealing with two carcasses, so the more you can process and preserve in the way of hams, bacon, salami, pâtés, brawn, confit, etc., the less valuable space you will take up in the freezer (you'll be needing that for the lamb and beef, which do not lend themselves so well to curing).

By all means, rope in friends and neighbors to help with your pigs – "pig weekends," as I call them, are great fun. A word of warning, though: as far as your chief helpers are concerned, try to invite people who will be genuinely interested, helpful, and, dare I say, competent. Three or four of you who know what you are doing will achieve far more than a dozen fair-weather helpers. The "only here for the beer" brigade can come at the end of the day, when the work's done and the real party starts. And they can bring the beer.

One thing you should not attempt to do yourself, or trust to a friend unless he or she is properly trained, is the basic butchering of the carcasses. The most important friend and ally a beginner can have is a good butcher. It is to him that the carcasses should go directly from the slaughterhouse. And to him that you must explain exactly how you want your animals cut up. This can all be a bit daunting the first time you do it, so the friendlier he is, the better! (I'm very lucky – they don't come any friendlier or more accommodating than my own local meat guru, freelance butcher Ray Smith.) You must give your butcher plenty of notice of the slaughter date of your pigs, as he will need to make time and space to deal with them. Ask him to quote for the job in advance.

timing and planning

If you have raised your pigs principally as "baconers" rather than "porkers" (which I would highly recommend), you can slaughter them any time between seven and ten months. So there is plenty of flexibility here: spring weaners can go for slaughter in autumn or early winter – late October/November is ideal.

To minimize the risk of contamination, it is very important that your raw pork remains as cold as possible throughout processing, so be ready to respond to the weather. The best possible conditions for working on your pigs are a cold, dry autumn day, but of course you can't always plan that. For the last two years, I have chosen a weekend in late October and been lucky both times. The joy of cold, dry weather is that it means you can work outdoors: I took my butcher's block and a trestle table outside, and we did almost all the work there. If you are going to work inside, a cool outbuilding may be preferable to a domestic kitchen. And if you have no choice but to work in the kitchen, two things are vital: clear the decks to make as much space as possible to work in, and turn off the heat and open the windows to keep the room cool and well ventilated. If that puts you and your helpers on the chilly side, then wrap up warm!

The best way to ensure the meat stays cold is simply to minimize the time it spends hanging around unrefrigerated. Of course, unless you are lucky enough to have a walk-in meat fridge at home, you will have to compromise a bit. There's no need to be obsessive about this temperature thing – just sensible. The best place for the meat to be is in the butcher's fridge, so let it stay there until you are ready to work on it (i.e., Saturday morning is a better time to collect it or have it delivered than Friday afternoon).

Here is a suggested timetable for a Slaughter Week, culminating in a Pig Weekend. Remember that you will need to book your animals in for slaughter several days in advance. If you want advice about choosing a local slaughterhouse (assuming you're lucky enough to have any choice at all), then talk to other local stock rearers or a butcher you know and trust.

Monday or Tuesday – slaughter

- Take pigs to slaughter, wait until they are done, and ask the slaughterer to save the liver, heart, lights, spleen, stomach, and blood (the kidneys will come back with the carcass). Take all these home with you.
- Make blood sausage the same day (see page 162).
- Refrigerate the remaining innards and ideally use within 72 hours – e.g., eat some liver fresh, then make pâté with the rest (see the recipe on page 228). Don't feel guilty if you end up giving some of the soft offals to the dog – he or she will love it. None of these soft offals freeze well raw – except as dog food – but the finished pâté will.

Wednesday or Thursday – butchery

- Have carcasses delivered to cold room of your chosen butcher (make sure he is expecting them). The butcher should have a written plan of how you want them done (see page 150). If at all possible, attend and assist at the butchering. You will learn a lot.

Friday (afternoon) – getting ready

- Make up the basic brine (see page 158) and cures for any special hams you are planning. Generally prepare your kit and the house. Make sure you have more than you think you need of the following: butcher's string, hooks, cheesecloth, large plastic containers or plastic bowls with lids, buckets (preferably with lids), sharp knives, sausage casings, and salt. You will also need at least one very large stockpot. Clean and check meat grinders and sausage-making tools.

- Make as much space in your fridge as you can and turn it on to maximum chill. Put tub(s) of finished brine in the coldest place you can find.

Saturday – order of play

- Put sausage casings to soak first thing in the morning.
- Prepare all work surfaces, knives, and containers by giving them a good scrub with standard cleaning products.
- Take delivery of butchered cuts and sort as follows:
- Any cuts destined for the freezer should go there as soon as they arrive.
- Put the relevant cuts for curing into the appropriate brine as cold as possible, as soon as possible.
- Put boned-out meat/ground meat for salami and sausages in the fridge until you are ready to use it.
- Anything destined to be cooked (the heads for headcheese, bellies for rillons, trotters and tails if you're not freezing them) is less urgent, but should be left in a cool place, or can go straight in the basic pickle brine if appropriate (see recipes), until needed.
- Bellies and hams for dry-curing have maximum priority: get to work on them as soon as possible. Box up the hams and bellies when done and get them out of the way.
- Get the headcheese ingredients on the stove, including tails and ears if you are using them (see page 230).
- Get to work on sausages and salamis: make up the basic mixes for each, and then return to the fridge all except the one you are using. (Sausage/salami making is quite tiring – you could save some batches for the following day.)
- If there is time, make Rillons (see page 232) and/or Chinese-Style Pig's Trotters (see page 229) for the freezer.
- Finish headcheese.
- Make/finish off dishes for supper: kidneys, crispy ears, blood sausage, first sausages, etc.
- Sometime before bed, make sure everything unfinished is as cold as possible. Ration fridge space. Check nothing is vulnerable to cats, dogs, foxes, etc.
- Eat, drink, and be merry. Take Alka-Seltzer before bed.

Sunday – finishing off

- Get up late and have a civilized breakfast of blood sausage.
- Finish off sausage/salami making. Make Rillons and Chinese-Style Pig's Trotters if you haven't already done so, plus a huge pot of stock with leftover pork bones (roasted first). This is not often encountered in recipes, but pork bones actually make an excellent, versatile stock that can be used wherever chicken stock is called for.
- Take sausages down from hanging and bag up in batches.
- Decide how much in the way of sausages, headcheese, Chinese trotters, stock, etc., you are likely to eat in the coming days, and freeze the rest.
- Relax. Have a drink. It's all over.
- Have another drink.

dealing with the carcass – a plan for your butcher

Sticking to some version of the above timetable will be easier if your pigs have been butchered exactly to your requirements. Bear in mind that pigs are always split down the middle. Two pigs will therefore give you four examples of each of the main cuts. That means plenty of opportunities for experimentation and variation with your various hams and bacon cuts.

It is technically possible to cure every part of a pig (even the trotters and tail are salted in some cultures), so that all of it ends up as bacon or ham of one kind or another, and the head as pickled headcheese. My own preference is to freeze a number of cuts to use later as "fresh" pork, dedicate certain others to making hams and bacon, and have plenty of ground meat for making salami and sausages. Before I explain how I use the various cuts, here is a diagram showing the basic way of dividing up a pig.

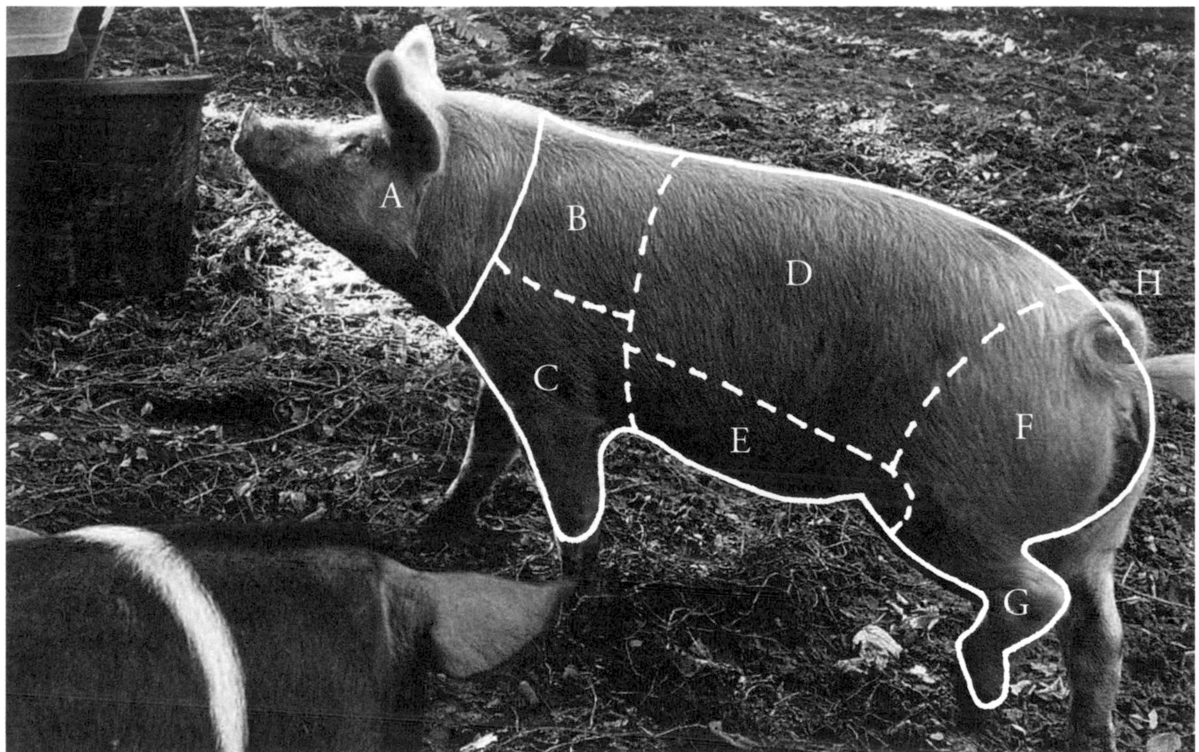

the cuts

Here's what I do with the various cuts from my two pigs:

Head (A) I have these split into quarters for making headcheese. This should be done with a saw, not a cleaver, to avoid splinters of bone ending up in your headcheese. You can either make a huge batch of headcheese using both heads and freeze some or put one of the heads in the freezer for making headcheese at a later date. (Ask the butcher to salvage the brains and put them in a bag – fry them in butter with a little sage and serve on toast.) If you want to try the recipe for Crispy Pig's Ears described on page 233 (and I dearly hope that you will), the ears should be cut away from the head at this stage, although they can be cooked in the same pot as the rest of the meat for the headcheese.

Boston butt (B) This piece, which contains the blade bone, is basically the shoulder. On a porker, this is often boned out and rolled up as a roasting joint. The same boneless joint can be cured as "collar bacon." I prefer to freeze two of my sparerib joints on the bone for roasting whole – it makes a fantastic large joint that would feed 15 easily – while the other two are boned out to provide the lean meat for salami.

Picnic shoulder (C) This is actually quite an impressive-sized piece on a large baconer. Cured on the bone, it makes what my friend Ray likes to call a "picnic ham." I make two of these, and the other two get boned out and go into the salami/sausage pile (leaner bits go in the salami pile, fattier bits for the sausages).

Loin (D) As you may guess from the diagram opposite, loins are very long on a mature baconer. Cured, they will give you what is called back bacon (the loin and belly are often cured together to give a whole "side" of bacon), but I prefer to divide the loin up for the freezer into a combination of roasting joints and chops. Loin chops, which have less bone in them, come from the hindquarter end. I get each loin divided into a long roasting joint, comprising the first half of the loin from the head end. Each of these can be easily subdivided into two smaller roasting joints if you like. The remainder of the loin I get cut into loin chops, although I sometimes leave two or three chops together as a mini roasting joint.

Belly (E) As you can see from the picture, the belly is about the same length as the loin, taken from the underside of the pig. You can cure all of it as bacon, but two pigs give you an awful lot of belly, so I like to divide each of the four bellies into two manageable pieces: the "thick end" is about the first third from the head end of the belly and makes my all-time favorite roasting joint; it can also be boned out and cut up for Rillons (see page 232). The "thin end," which comprises the remaining two-thirds of the belly, is my prime cut for bacon: I dry-cure all four of them and usually smoke three out of the four.

Hams (F) Just about any cut of pork can be cured, but, technically speaking, only the back leg is entitled to be called a ham. These are your pigs' greatest assets. If handled correctly they will provide four fine hams that will last you well into the year ahead. With my four legs, I usually make two dry-cured hams (one on the bone, one off) and two in some kind of "gourmet brine" (such as the Wiltshire cure – see page 159) for boiling and baking. In either case, I ask for them to be cut as "long" as possible, to maximize the amount of meat on each one. But unless you have an absolutely huge stockpot and a big enough burner to bring it to a boil, you might be better off with a shorter-cut ham for your brine cure; and the extra wedge that comes off makes an excellent small ham, often called a "corner ham," which only needs a few days in the brine. Any legs for the prosciutto-style dry cure need to be boned out, except for the knuckle, which is useful for hanging the ham – see page 155 for more details.

If you are not interested in dry-cure hams and want an easy life when it comes to carving your regular boiled/baked hams, the back legs can be boned out and cut into three more manageable pieces: the largest piece from the lower part of the leg is a traditional ham, and the remainder is subdivided into the slipper ham and the aforementioned corner ham.

Trotters (G) These will "come as they are," the ones from the front legs usually being cut longer than the ones from the back legs. However, eight of them gives you a chance to try all sorts of things. I usually freeze four and use the other four to make Chinese-Style Pig's Trotters (see page 229) over the Pig Weekend.

Tail (H) Don't forget to ask for this: it mustn't go to waste (see Variation, Crispy Pig's Ears, page 233).

The final pages of this chapter are devoted to the basic procedures for curing and preserving the various parts of your pig, to produce hams, bacon, salami, blood sausage, and various other "long-life" products that are generally covered by the useful French term *charcuterie*. For me, this is what keeping pigs is all about: simply butchering a pig and bunging it in the freezer would be of limited interest. But homemade bacon – now you're talking.

Of course, there is absolutely no reason why the pleasures of home-cured bacon and charcuterie should be restricted to those who are able to rear their own pigs. All the procedures that follow can be undertaken using the appropriate cuts of pork bought from the butcher. However, it is a good idea to order any pork for curing specially, and insist that it be as fresh as possible. If your butcher can lay his hands on meat from a larger animal (a baconer as opposed to a porker), then so much the better.

The best option, of course, is to buy directly from the producer. They can sell you a whole or half pig raised especially to your requirements, so you can even plan a fully fledged Pig Weekend with a bought-in pig.

By the way, there are a number of recipes using fresh pork among the recipes at the end of the livestock section. I have held over headcheese and rillons for this later section (though they would certainly be classed as charcuterie), as they are specific recipes rather than general procedures. As for the whole business of making fresh pork sausages, I will deal with it here for similar (i.e., opposite) reasons: it's the procedure, not the recipe, that matters.

dry-cured bacon

Just about any part of the pig can be made into bacon, but the bit that gets my juices flowing is the belly. Four "thin ends" (see page 151) from my two pigs produce very manageable pieces – easy to cure, easy to smoke, and easy to cut – and give me enough bacon to last a good few months.

Although flavorings such as brown sugar and pepper can be added to the cure, I don't usually bother if I'm going to smoke the bellies (which these days I almost always do), as the oaky smoke flavor overrides the subtleties of the cure. Saltpeter (sodium nitrate) is hard to get hold of now, but as its main purpose is to preserve the color of the meat it can be omitted.

Pork bellies (thin ends)
Salt

OPTIONAL
Saltpeter (available from some chemists)
Brown sugar
Black pepper

It's hard to give exact quantities for your dry-cure mix, but for 4 thin ends, 2 pounds fine salt mixed with a teaspoon of saltpeter will get you started. Add 1/2 cup brown sugar and a tablespoon of cracked black pepper if you like. You may need to make up a little more cure mix after the first few days.

The process couldn't be more simple. Place one belly at a time on a clean work surface and, with clean hands, just grab a handful of the dry-cure mix and start rubbing it with your fingers into all the surfaces of the meat. When it is thoroughly salted all over, place in a clean wooden or plastic box, move on to the next belly, and follow the same procedure.

The finished bellies can be stacked on top of each other and left, covered, in a cool place safe from flies. Keep the leftover cure mix. After twenty-four hours, you will notice that the meat has leached salty liquid into the bottom of the container. Remove the bellies, pour off this liquid, and rub the bellies with handfuls of fresh cure mix. Restack the bellies, preferably moving the two from the bottom onto the top.

Repeat the process daily. Your bacon will be ready after just five days, though if you cure it for longer (up to two weeks) it will keep longer.

Smoking This will not only add a superb flavor to your bacon but will also improve its keeping quality. Bellies salted as above for just five days should be rinsed and hung to dry for one to three days before smoking. Then hang them high in a chimney above an open fire or place them in your smoker; twenty-four hours of near-continuous cold smoking will do the trick. Or, if the smoking is intermittent (i.e., you are lighting the fire for a few hours each day), you can leave it for up to a week. For more details about smoking techniques, see page 273.

Storing and using bacon Unsmoked bellies cured in this way should be rinsed of excess salt, patted dry, wrapped in clean cheesecloth, and left to hang in a cool place, such as a cool, well-ventilated cellar or outbuilding. Cut pieces off the belly as you need them, then rewrap and rehang. Alternatively, wrap the belly in cotton, cheesecloth, or waxed paper and store in the fridge. Bellies cured for more than ten days can keep for months in this way, but will tend to be unpalatably salty. Pieces cut from them can be soaked in fresh water for a few hours to counteract this. My preference is for a lighter (five-day) cure, and any bellies that I am not likely to use within a couple of weeks go in the freezer.

I have kept smoked bellies in the fridge for up to two months, cutting bits off when I needed them. A little mold began to appear after a while, but I scraped that off and my bacon was none the worse.

Cooking with home-cured bacon The finished bacon is in the style of Italian pancetta: quite salty with a very concentrated flavor and particularly fine when smoked. I find a little goes a long way, and although I use my bacon all the time, I rarely cut whole slices off my belly for frying in traditional breakfast fashion. Rather, I find myself throwing it, usually cut into small chunks, into all kinds of other dishes, such as soups, stews, and sauces. A classic quiche made with home-cured smoked bacon is a revelation, and the Rich Tomato Sauce with Bacon on page 102 is a regular favorite. The Tartiflette (see page 225) is another winner, where the quality of the bacon makes all the difference. All recipes calling for bacon or pancetta in this book will be extra tasty and extra satisfying if you use your home-cured belly.

air-dried ham, prosciutto style

Air-dried hams rely simply on salt and air to produce their finished texture and taste. The basic procedure is a two-stage affair: curing, then drying. For the cure, the whole leg is completely packed in salt and pressed under a substantial weight to accelerate the moisture loss and salt penetration. This pressing also contributes to the dense texture of the ham. Once cured, the ham is hung to dry and mature in a cool, airy place for several months.

Air-dried hams are eaten "raw," and at their best must rank as one of the greatest delicacies you can make with a pig. In Italy, every region has its special air-dried ham, of which Parma ham is the most famous. The Alpine hams of Haute-Savoie and the serrano hams of Spain can also be delectably distinctive, demonstrating that the taste and texture of an air-dried ham varies according to the diet and variety of the pig and the length and conditions of the curing and hanging.

In making your own dry-cured ham, it is best not to think in terms of imitating European regional classics but rather enjoying whatever turns out to be distinctive about your own idiosyncratic version. As long as you don't salt it too much or cut it too early, it is very likely to be delicious.

The secret of success is to be well organized: read the instructions below carefully before you even take your pigs to slaughter. Get your ham-making kit together well in advance, and talk to your butcher about your needs. Work out where you are going to store your ham while it cures and where you are going to hang it. Attend to the details and you have every chance of first-time success. Once in a while, and sometimes for no good reason one can think of, a hanging ham will go rotten on you. It's heartbreaking when it does, but all you can do is get back in the saddle and try again.

The kit For each ham you will need: a wooden wine case or similar-shaped box (plastic will do, but don't use a metal one) with a few small holes in the base for drainage; a 20- to 30-pound weight; a wooden or plastic board; and plenty of cheesecloth. Unless you have managed to get your leg carefully tunnel-boned (see below), you will also need butcher's string, a darning needle, and a sharp skewer.

1 leg of pork
About 6 pounds fine table salt (not sea salt)
1 tablespoon black peppercorns, cracked
1 tablespoon coriander seeds, cracked
White wine vinegar

Preparing the meat Ask your butcher to cut legs for dry-curing as "long" as possible, to maximize the size of the ham. Italian-style prosciutto is boned out, so that it can be sliced very finely with an automatic circular meat slicer. You can make air-dried ham on the bone (see page 157), but for the beginner a boned-out ham has less risk of going bad, as you can rub plenty of salt into the cavity to help cure it from the inside as well as the outside.

There are two ways to bone out a ham for dry-curing. The simplest is to slit through the skin and meat on the "short" side of the leg (i.e., the side where most of the meat is exposed by cutting from the main carcass) right along the length of the bone. Use the point of a very sharp knife to nick the meat away from the bone until you can lift the whole thing out. It takes patience and practice, but is something an amateur can make a reasonably tidy job of. Once you have removed the bone, take a handful of salt and rub it well into the cut surface of the meat from which the bone was taken. After salting the inside of the leg, you will need to stitch it up again. This is done by bringing back together the edges of the cut you made to access the bone, to re-form the shape of the ham, and stitching it with good butcher's string. First, use a sharp skewer to make the holes for stitching, and then run the string through the holes with the darning needle. You need a good tight blanket stitch.

You can avoid the stitching process by asking your butcher to "tunnel-bone" the leg for you. This is a highly skilled technique that not all of today's butchers are up to, but it does create a natural cavity to rub the salt into without the need for stitching.

Packing the meat in salt Whether tunnel-boned or stitched, and in either case salted on the inside, your leg should now be weighed: make a note of the weight. Pour salt in a layer about ¾ inch thick over the base of the wine case. Sprinkle the cracked peppercorns and coriander seeds over the salt and place the leg in the box with the lean, meaty side down and wide skin side facing up. Pour the rest of the salt in an even layer over the leg until every bit of it is covered by at least ¾ inch of salt.

Cover with a piece of wood or plastic that just fits inside the wine box and covers as much as possible of the leg. Place a large weight (a stone or a concrete block will do) weighing 1½ to 2 times the weight of the leg on top of the board. Leave the box in a cool, dry pantry or cellar and check regularly to ensure that no mice or rats have been burrowing into the salt to get at your ham! The weight of the ham will determine how long it should be salted: it should be left for no fewer than three days per 2 pounds and no more than four (the latter is "safer," but your ham may turn out a little on the salty side).

Hanging the ham When you have left the ham for the allotted time, remove it from the box and wash thoroughly with fresh cold water to remove excess salt. Rub the whole joint with white wine vinegar and wrap completely in a double layer of cheesecloth, tied tightly with butcher's string. Hang in a cool, well-ventilated place for four to six months to "wind-dry." Ventilation is essential, and the more "wind," the faster and better the cure. A drafty barn or garage would be a suitable location; I hang mine in the porch at River Cottage. Or, like my friend Victor, you could construct a rainproof frame for your hams and hang them in a tree. Surround the frame with chicken wire to make it bird- and squirrel-proof, but not windproof.

A squeeze with the fingertips will tell you when your ham is ready: it should be very firm but not quite rock hard – still giving just a little.

Unwrapping and serving Taking down your ham after many months is a moment of high excitement. Don't be alarmed to find, on unwrapping it, that it is covered in mold. This doesn't mean it has gone rotten, and the mold is easily scrubbed off with a nailbrush dipped in vinegar. If it is rotten you will know: it will smell bad and be black in parts.

Slice the ham as finely as you can (you'll see why a circular meat slicer is such a godsend). Pour yourself a glass of fine wine and sample away. It's possible you will find hams cured in this way a little on the salty side. Having something sweet on hand to balance this often enhances the pleasure. Fresh melon or figs are the classic accompaniments to Parma ham, but cherry tomatoes, as sweet as possible, are also excellent. Or try dried figs, gently poached with a few pickling spices, as described in the recipe on page 226.

Air-dried ham on the bone The Spanish prefer their serrano ham on the bone, and like to cut shards and slivers off it with a very sharp knife. I like this version very much, but it is slightly higher risk: bacteria and bugs seem to find a "way in" more easily.

To minimize this risk, it is a good idea to inject brine into the meat at several points. Use a syringe and inject about 1/4 cup brine (see page 158) in five or six places down the length of the leg as close as possible to the bone. Then pack the meat in salt and weight it, exactly as above. Give it just three days per 2 pounds, then prepare for hanging as above. I like to leave this ham as long as possible – at least eight months.

Molasses cure My friend Victor likes to give the on-the-bone version a "molasses bath" for two weeks after salting and before drying. Raw molasses is thinned with an equal quantity of warm water and left to cool completely. The ham is immersed in this solution for two weeks, then scrubbed and prepared for drying as above. The molasses bath must stay as cool as possible (ideally below 41°F), which makes this a suitable cure for a ham slaughtered in November and salted until December. During warm spells, frozen gel packs (the kind you put in cooler bags), can be dropped in the bath to keep the temperature down.

hams for boiling and baking

As well as the dry cure, you will want to have in your repertoire the technique for the more traditional British ham for boiling and baking. At the most basic level, you can make unsmoked "green" bacon (or pickled pork, as it used to be called) simply by placing your chosen cut of pork in a plain salt and water brine. This basic brine is also useful for brief pickling (not more than twelve hours) of heads, ears, tails, and trotters before more elaborate dishes, such as headcheese, are prepared from them.

FOR THE BASIC BRINE
4 pounds coarse salt
1½ ounces saltpeter (optional)
1½ gallons water

Bring all the above to a boil, stirring to dissolve the salt, then boil hard for ten minutes, skimming off any froth. Let cool and then transfer to a container made of glass, earthenware, stoneware, or plastic but *definitely not* metal. (If you want to buy a cheap brine tub, a large (5-gallon) plastic box with a lid will do for smaller cuts of meat and has the advantage that it will fit in a large fridge.)

Before you add your meat to the brine, both should be thoroughly chilled, ideally to 37 to 39°F, at which temperature they should remain throughout the cure. If you don't have a fridge big enough to contain your brine tub, you can bring the temperature down by adding those frozen gel packs from the freezer. Keep the brine tub in a cool cellar or larder and change the gel packs for newly frozen ones morning and evening, and you should be able to keep the temperature right down.

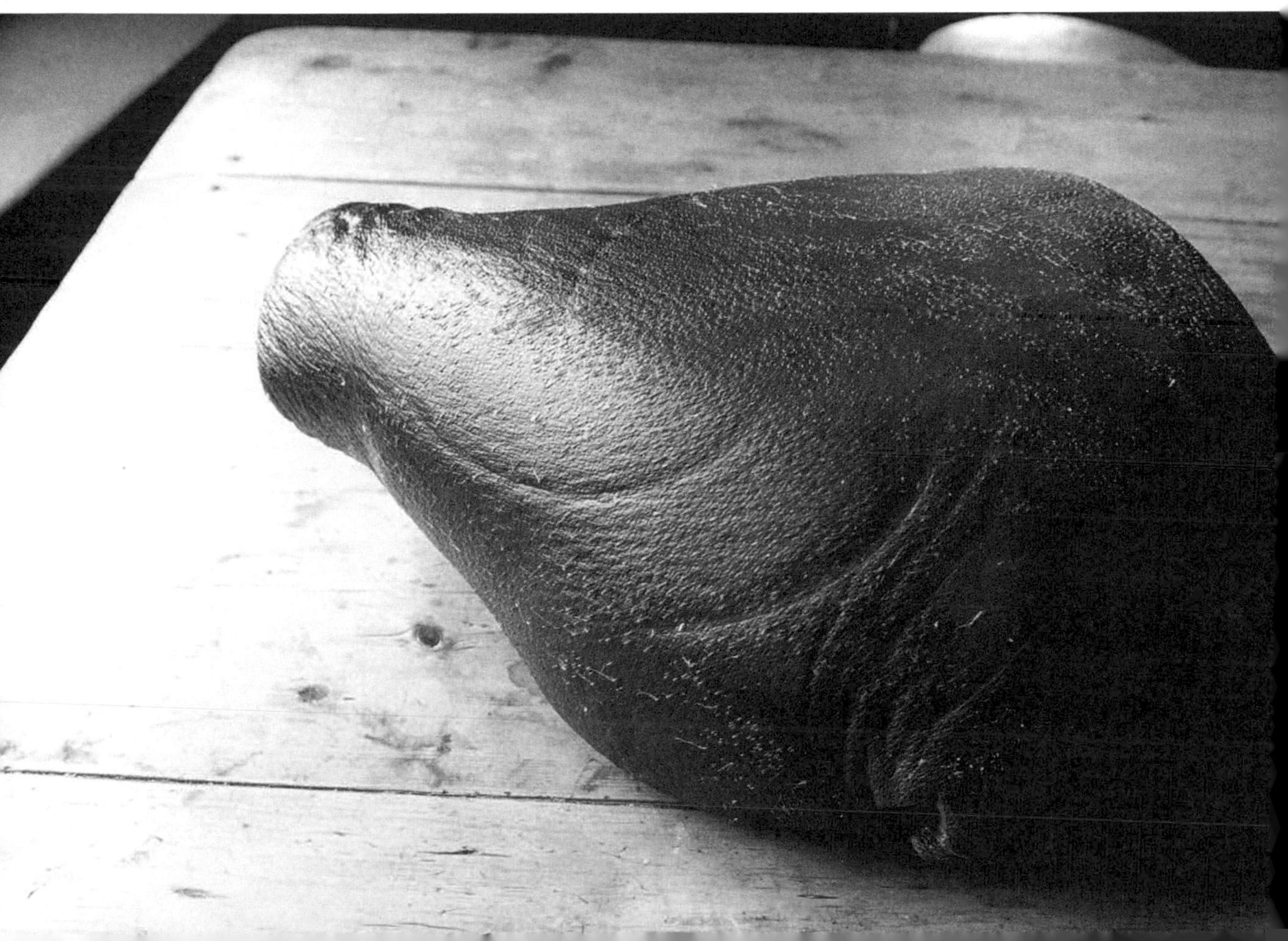

Your chosen cuts (the flank, belly, or collar makes good green bacon) must then be completely immersed in the brine, for which a heavy wooden or plastic board or some other nonmetallic weight may prove useful. To cure a piece of belly, or any piece of pork under 4 pounds, twenty-four hours is sufficient. Add twelve hours per each 2 pounds thereafter.

The pickled pieces of green bacon should then be removed from the brine and squeezed as dry as possible in a cotton cloth. Hang them in a cool, well-ventilated place for up to twenty-four hours to dry further. They can then be stored in the fridge for up to two weeks.

Bellies cured in the above fashion make good green bacon and can also be cut into chunks and added to stews and casseroles of beef, poultry, and game, where they will help to lubricate these sometimes dry meats. Larger, "squarer" pieces such as collars and corner hams can be boiled whole with stock vegetables and eaten hot or cold. Try cooking yellow split peas in the stock from boiling the bacon until they dissolve into a thick purée. Serve with the hot meat for an authentic pease pudding with bacon.

flavored cures

For centuries all around England, strong flavorings such as spices, cider, beer, hops, and sugar have been added to the basic salt and water brine to produce highly distinctive regional cures. When whole back legs are immersed in these cures, then hung to mature or sometimes smoked, some of Britain's most famous regional hams are produced: the Suffolk and the Wiltshire, for example. Here are the recipes for these two: the Wiltshire cure is my favorite, as it achieves an exquisite bittersweet flavor from the presence of molasses and beer in the brine.

You don't have to use a whole leg (which may weigh over 20 pounds), and an important consideration is whether you have a stockpot big enough to accommodate such a huge piece of meat or, indeed, an oven big enough to bake it in. I have finally invested in both, and as you can see from the photograph opposite, the resulting baked, glazed hams can be rather spectacular.

The Wiltshire cure The quantities below for the brine for the Wiltshire cure are for a small boned-out leg or half a large leg. For a large leg of pork from a mature baconer, on the bone, you may need to double the amount.

1 whole or half leg of fresh pork, on or off the bone
1 recipe basic brine (see opposite)

BRINE FOR THE WILTSHIRE CURE
3 pounds salt
1½ ounces saltpeter (optional)
3 quarts beer
2 pounds black treacle or molasses
20 to 30 juniper berries
2 tablespoons black peppercorns, crushed

Ideally, your piece of pork should spend a couple of hours in the basic brine before being transferred to the Wiltshire cure.

Boil all the ingredients for the Wiltshire cure together in a large pan and then let it cool. Transfer to a nonmetallic brine tub and chill to 37 to 39°F. Place your piece of pork, also chilled, in the tub and submerge completely, using a nonmetallic weight. Leave the pork in the brine for three days (minimum) or four days (maximum) for every 2 pounds. The maximum time is for a ham you intend to keep for a long while; the minimum will suffice if you plan to cook and eat it soon after it is finished.

After its allotted time, remove the ham from the cure, wipe dry with a cotton cloth, put it in a cheesecloth bag, string bag, or old cotton pillowcase, and hang it to dry in a cool, well-ventilated place for twenty-four hours. Then hang it high above a hardwood fire or place it in your smoker and either smoke it continuously for twenty-four hours or intermittently (six to twelve hours a day) for about five to seven days. Ideally, the air temperature where the ham is smoking should not exceed 105°F (81°F is "perfect," but a little variation will not hurt). For more details about smoking techniques, see page 273.

In late autumn and winter, a finished smoked ham (with a maximum cure time) can hang in a well-ventilated outbuilding for up to four months or in refrigerated cold storage (at 37 to 39°F) for six months at any time of year. In warmer weather, hams are at risk from flies and other bugs; best get them cooked before too long. A ham that has been cured for the minimum time should be kept in the fridge and cooked within two weeks of smoking.

The Suffolk cure The procedure is the same as above, using the following ingredients for the brine:

8 cups beer
8 cups malt vinegar
3 pounds salt
2 tablespoons peppercorns
2 tablespoons cloves
2 tablespoons saltpeter (optional)
2 pounds brown sugar

salami

My experiments with salami and chorizo have been, though I say so myself, an unqualified success. I attribute this in large measure to the advice of my friend Victor Borg, who insists that the golden rule for all cured sausages is simple: they must contain exactly 2 percent salt, by weight. As long as you get this bit right, you can experiment with all sorts of flavorings and additions. You therefore need an accurate set of scales when making salami.

Unlike sausage meat, the meat for salami should be as lean as possible. Mine is usually taken from the shoulders and front legs of the animal (i.e., Boston butt and the picnic shoulder – see the diagram on page 150) and trimmed of excess fat. Fat is then added to the mix in the form of finely diced back fat: the thick, gristle-free fat from just under the skin of the pig. It doesn't have to come from the back, but it must be from this firm, evenly textured subcutaneous layer (i.e., not flare fat, or leaf fat, from inside the carcass, or rendered fat or lard).

The recipe below is for the simplest possible salami. The only flavorings are a little garlic and some red wine. This is the basic mixture to which all extra flavorings are added – see Variations opposite for some suggestions. The hardest thing of all will probably be finding the ox-runners. These extra-large natural casings, made from salted cow's intestines, are the perfect size and strength for making small salami, which end up 1¼ to 1½ inches in diameter when ready to eat. For a larger salami, you could also use "beef middles" (taken from farther down the intestines), which gives a diameter of about 3 inches. I stick to the smaller ones, as they mature quicker, and if ones goes bad I have lost less. Both these types of casings are much harder to come by than ordinary sausage casings. Luckily, they are available by mail order. Even packed in salt, they do not keep forever. It is normal for them to smell a bit tripey, but if they absolutely honk of ammonia they will wreck the taste of your salami and you must throw them away. Any casings left over from a salami-making session can be frozen and used next time.

At a pinch, you can make salami using the larger-size sausage casings (hog casings), but they will be very thin by the time they have dried and will not keep as well.

For large quantities of salami, a sausage-making machine, either with a crank handle or a modern electric one, is invaluable. But if you're making just a few, you can use a plastic funnel to fill your casings.

Acidophilus is a natural enzyme that helps the skin of the salami to develop the correct (nonthreatening) mold. It is available as a powder in pharmacies and natural foods stores (if you can only get tablets, they can be ground up in a mortar). It's not essential, and an alternative way to encourage the mold is to hang your salami with mature specimens that already have a bloom of mold on a natural casing.

Make up your batch of salami mix in multiples of the following quantities:

12 ounces lean pork, coarsely ground
3 ounces back fat, cut into small pea-sized pieces
1 teaspoon fine cooking salt
6 tablespoons red wine
½ garlic clove, crushed to a paste
(1 clove for every 2 pounds of mix)
½ teaspoon acidophilus

YOU WILL ALSO NEED
Small sausage casings
Butcher's string

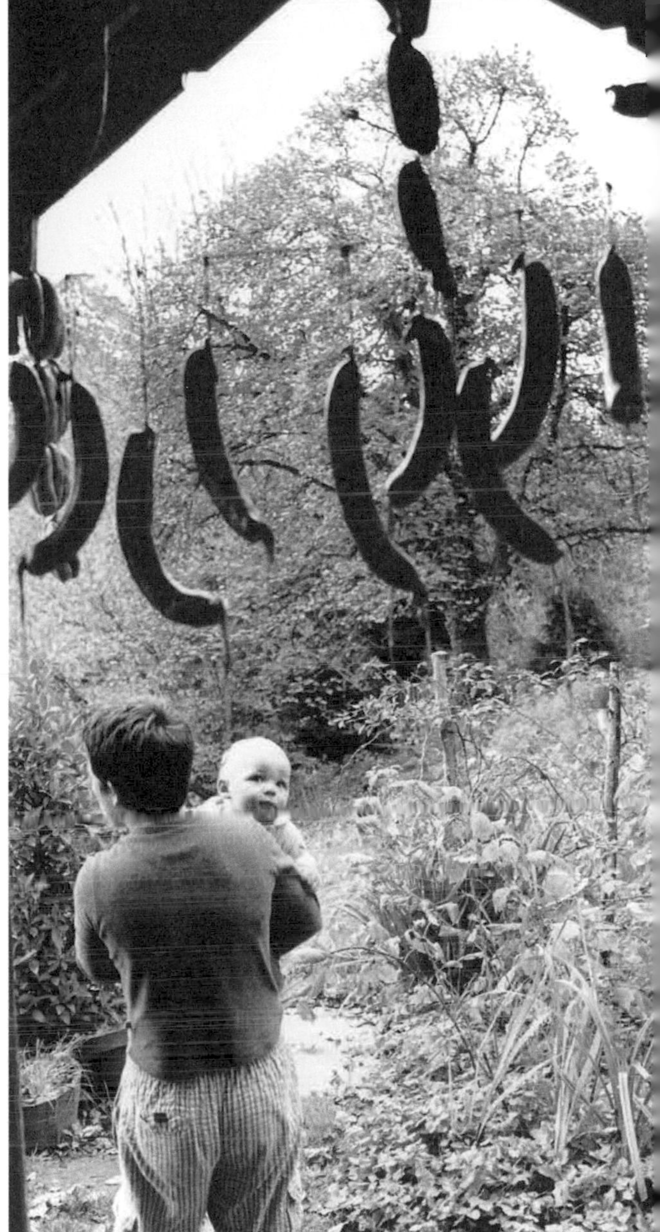

Before you get to work on your salami mix, put the casings in a large bowl of fresh water to soak. Slosh them about to rinse off the salt, then run the tap through the inside of them to flush them clean. When they are slippery, flexible, and thoroughly rinsed of salt, they are ready to use.

Variations You can add all kinds of things to the basic mix above, such as hazelnuts or pistachios, herbs and spices. Personally, the only embellishments I like are a sprinkling of cracked black peppercorns (about one teaspoon per 2 pounds) or the same quantity of dried fennel seeds.

Filling the casings Mix all the ingredients together thoroughly – with your bare (but clean) hands, if you like – so that the salt and fat are well distributed throughout the mix. Load up your sausage-making machine with the mix, slide a length of casing onto the nozzle, and tie the end of the casing into a knot, as you would tie a balloon. Then tie a short length of butcher's string in an ordinary granny knot inside the knot in the casing. Stuff the casing with the mix until you have a filled length of 16 to 20 inches. Then cut this length off, leaving enough unfilled runner at the end to tie another knot.

Hold the filled casing up with the knotted end at the bottom and squeeze the mixture down the casing gently, so it is nice and tight. Then tie another knot in the top of the casing and another length of string inside that knot. The compacted sausage, tied securely at both ends, will now be about 12 to 16 inches long, although you can make shorter ones if you like. It's useful to have two people on the job for an efficient production line: one to do the filling and cutting off of lengths, the other to do the knots and hang up the filled casings.

Maturing salami The salami should be hung individually by the string loops in a cool, well-ventilated place where the temperature is not likely to rise above 53°F. Make sure they are not touching a wall, or each other. Over the coming weeks, a number of molds, ranging in color from gray-green to white and even orange, may form on the casings. None of these should worry you.

The salami may take anything from four to ten weeks to mature, depending on the conditions and, indeed, on how you like them. They can be tried as soon as they are fairly firm to the touch and dry looking, but they will continue to dry out and harden until they are practically rock hard. I like them "medium hard." When they reach the stage you like, the process of further hardening can be slowed down by rubbing off the mold with a screwed-up piece of paper towel, then rolling the salami in dry wood ash. Then wrap loosely in paper and store in a cool pantry or the fridge. Eat within a month of this process.

I cut my salami into slices 1⁄16 to 1⁄8 inch thick with a sharp knife, and I peel off the ring of casing from each salami before I eat them, although it is perfectly safe to eat.

Chorizo This spicy, Spanish-style sausage is flavored with paprika, and the very best version with smoked paprika (pimentón), which gives it a quite wonderful taste. You should be able to find this magical substance – which makes it taste as if the whole sausage has been smoked – from good Spanish-run delis.

The mix for chorizo doesn't have to be quite as lean, and I usually add about 1 pound regular sausage meat to 2 pounds of the salami mix. It is important to keep the salt level at 2 percent, so add an extra 2 teaspoons salt for your 1 pound sausage meat.

To this 3 pounds of mix, add a generous tablespoon of paprika (smoked, if you can get it), two to three more garlic cloves, crushed to a paste, and a generous teaspoon of fennel seeds. Fill up the casings and hang as for salami.

Chorizo can be eaten raw when fully matured, like salami, but it is also delicious sliced and fried after hanging for just a week. See especially the recipe for Clams with Pork Tenderloin and Chorizo on page 341.

boudin noir and other blood sausage

Making your own blood sausage is not for the faint-hearted. You may be dealing with the blood of your own pigs, ideally on the very day of their slaughter, while it is still warm. For me, however, getting straight down to business and making blood sausage is the best therapy for the inevitable stresses of slaughter day. It is also the best possible affirmation of your intention to make good use of every last bit of your pig – everything but the oink, as the old butchers like to say.

Making blood sausage can be messy, but it is not too difficult. Perhaps the most important thing is to keep your pan of water on the gentlest of simmers when poaching the sausages – anything too vigorous and they are liable to burst, filling your pan with a mass of black gunge and froth. The first time I made blood sausage, and before I had gleaned this vital tip from Jane Grigson's *Charcuterie* book, I lost about one in three, which I found very distressing. If you want to avoid such anxieties, check the "oven method" at the end of this recipe.

Note If you don't keep your own pigs but want to make some blood sausage, your butcher may be able to get some fresh blood for you, as he is likely to be taking regular deliveries from a slaughterhouse.

Classic boudin noir There are many variations on the blood sausage theme. The French version, *boudin noir*, has so many regional variations that it would take an entire book to list them all. The recipe below is based on a classic French boudin, which is richer and more delicate than a British blood sausage, called black pudding here. My favorite variations, including good, oatmealy British breakfast black pudding, appear at the end.

8 cups fresh pig's blood
A bundle of small natural casings, though large sausage-size (hog casings) will do at a pinch
3 tablespoons salt
1 teaspoon brown sugar
1 teaspoon freshly ground black pepper
½ teaspoon ground mace
1 tablespoon rum or brandy
½ cup milk
1½ cups fine fresh bread crumbs
2 pounds pork fat (ideally fatback, or the fat end of a cured belly, or pancetta, with most of the lean meat trimmed out)
2 pounds onions, finely chopped
2 cups heavy cream

EQUIPMENT
A plastic funnel with a ¾-inch nozzle
A deep-frying basket or steamer basket
A sharp needle or pin

Preparing the blood and intestines If you are collecting the blood from a slaughterhouse, it will need to be stirred while still warm to remove the "strings" – natural clots that form as it cools. Some small slaughterhouses may do this for you, but if you have to stir it yourself, do it before you leave the slaughterhouse – a clean wooden stick or the handle of a long wooden spoon is all you need. Keep stirring, lifting up, and discarding the strings as they attach themselves to the stick. Don't worry about any small clots that fail to attach; they can be sieved out when you get home.

Destringed blood can be kept in the fridge for up to forty-eight hours; or it can be frozen, then defrosted gently in a large bowl over a pan of barely simmering water. This will allow you to make your blood sausage as part of your Pig Weekend (the help may be appreciated), and you will also be able to use the fat from your own carcass. Having said that, I still prefer to use fresh blood on slaughter day – these days I always have spare fat in the freezer from a previous pig.

Soak the casings in cold water for an hour, then rinse them thoroughly. Put one end over the cold tap and flush out with plenty of water to remove all the salt. Cut into suitable lengths (about 16 inches suits me, giving a boudin of about 10 to 12 inches when knotted at both ends). Knot one end of each length and leave in a pile in a bowl of cold water.

Making the mixture Sieve the blood into a large clean bowl or bucket and stir in the salt, sugar, spices, and alcohol. Warm the milk slightly, take off the heat, then add the bread crumbs and let soak.

Finely dice the fat, and put about a quarter of it to sauté in a large, heavy stockpot that is big enough to contain all the ingredients. When the fat has run a little, add the onions and sauté very gently until soft but not colored at all. Add the rest of the fat and sauté until the pieces are slightly translucent and more fat has run. Stir in the milk-soaked bread crumbs and the cream, then slowly pour in the seasoned blood, still stirring all the time, until it is thoroughly incorporated. The mixture will still be quite liquid.

Filling the casings Take a length of casing and pull the unknotted open end over the opening of the nozzle. Hold the casing in place with one hand and ladle the mixture into the funnel with the other. Have something handy to unclog the nozzle (I use a chopstick), as it may occasionally get blocked with pieces of fat. Fill over a clean bowl to catch any overflow and the occasional, inevitable dropped boudin. Don't overfill, and leave a good 2 to 3 inches at the top to tie a second knot in the casing. Tie the knot and place the boudin gently on a large plate. Stir the mixture well before each filling to make sure the fat pieces are well distributed. Keep filling and tying off your boudins until all the mixture, including the overspill, is used up.

Cooking the boudins Bring a large pan two-thirds full of unsalted water to a boil, then turn the heat down until the water has settled to the gentlest of simmers. Place two or three boudins in your deep-frying basket or steamer basket and lower gently into the water. Wait patiently for them to return to a simmer; then after about five minutes of very gentle simmering, lift the basket to the top of the water and prick each boudin two or three times with a needle or pin. If a brown liquid comes out, they are cooked. If the liquid is still pink, put them back in the pan for a few more minutes. If at any point during the cooking a boudin floats to the top, prick it with the needle. This should prevent it from bursting. When the boudins are done, remove from the pan and lower into a bowl of cold water. Leave for just a minute, then lay them on a cotton cloth to cool.

How many boudins you cook at a time is a matter of confidence and experience. You can speed up the operation by using two pans, or a large fish kettle, and poaching six, eight, or more at a time. You can dispense with the deep-frying basket and simply use a slotted spoon to remove them as they are ready. But, please, go gently at first, or you may lose a lot of boudins through bursting. And believe me, a burst boudin breaks your heart, it really does.

Cooked boudins, once cool, should be wrapped in plastic wrap (or better still, vacuum packed) and stored in the fridge. In a properly cold fridge (39°F or less) they will last for a fortnight – or a month if vac-packed. (For the amateur *charcutier*, a vac-packing kit is very handy.) Unfortunately, boudins do not freeze well.

Serving The best homemade boudins (such as the ones above) are delicious cold, just sliced and served with a glass of wine. But to make a meal out of them (or an excellent starter), they should be thickly sliced and gently fried for a minute or two on each side, then served on a warm plate with very buttery mashed potatoes and/or slices of apple (Granny Smith's are best) that have been lightly fried in butter.

Small boudins (4 to 16 inches) are labor-intensive to make but nice to have, as they can be cooked and served whole, one per person: fry gently in a little pork fat or butter, turning frequently, for about fifteen minutes.

Normandy boudin Follow the recipe above, replacing the rum/brandy with Calvados and adding 1 pound firm dessert apples such as Granny Smith or Cox's, peeled and finely diced, then sautéed gently for a few minutes in a little butter. Stir into the mix just before filling up the casings. Fill and finish as above.

Spinach boudin This recipe from Poitou makes for a "healthy" boudin (relatively speaking) because of the much-reduced fat content – it is nonetheless delicious. Follow the recipe above, omitting the diced pork fat (use a little pork fat or butter to sauté the onions) and reducing the weight of onions to a scant 8 ounces. Make a batch of creamed spinach with 2 pounds spinach leaves, thoroughly washed, lightly cooked, squeezed as dry as possible, then finely chopped and stirred into 2 cups light béchamel sauce. Stir this creamed spinach into the sautéed onions, then stir in the soaked bread crumbs, cream, and seasoned blood. Add a little grated nutmeg to the mixture before filling and finishing as above.

Spanish morcilla I think this is my favorite of all blood sausages. Replace the milk-soaked bread with 1¾ cups cooked long-grain rice. Add one teaspoon of mixed spice and one tablespoon of paprika to the spice mix for the blood. Replace the rum/brandy with a wineglass of sweet sherry. Soak 2¾ cups seedless raisins in boiling water for one hour, then drain and add to the mix just before filling the casings.

This mixture needs to be particularly well stirred up before each boudin is filled, so the rice and raisins don't all sink to the bottom. The filled boudins should be gently rolled back and forth with the palm of your hand before poaching: again, this helps to achieve an even distribution of rice and raisins.

This is the best blood sausage for eating cold but is also delicious sliced and fried.

British breakfast black pudding A stodgier sausage, because of the addition of cereals, but still the best for a breakfast fry-up. Omit the bread crumbs and milk from the basic recipe. Soak 5½ cups rolled oats overnight the day before you make your black pudding. Boil the same quantity of pearl barley until tender (about thirty to forty minutes) and drain. Stir the oatmeal into the sautéed onions and fat and cook for a few minutes before adding the cream. Season the blood with extra black pepper and a teaspoon each of ground coriander and cayenne pepper. Stir in the seasoned blood, then the pearl barley. Fill and finish as above.

This version works well as an oven-baked blood cake (see page 166), but if you go for this option, you should stir the finished mixture gently over low heat until it starts to thicken, like custard, before pouring it into your pans or molds. This will prevent all the oatmeal and pearl barley from sinking to the bottom, and the fat floating to the top.

Oven-cooking method If you can't find a supply of natural casings, or simply want to save time and avoid the possible trauma of bursting boudins, any of the above recipes can be baked as "blood cakes." Simply pour the mixture into greased loaf tins or long terrine dishes and cover loosely with buttered foil. Place in a pan of hot water and cook in a fairly moderate oven (350°F) for forty-five minutes to an hour, until set firm. Slice and eat straight from the oven, or let cool and then fry slices to order.

various fresh pork sausages

Making fresh sausages (as opposed to salami) is one of the central activities of a River Cottage Pig Weekend, and one of the most sociable, as everybody gets to have a go. Everybody loves a sausage, and the opportunity to customize your own is usually seized with zeal, even by those who are normally inclined to shun the pleasures of the kitchen. The results offer instant gratification, as sample batches of the various seasoning combinations are fried up and their various merits hotly debated.

To make my sausages, I use the same old-fashioned crank-handle machine that I use to make salami, but with a smaller nozzle attachment. Less-cumbersome modern alternatives are available from good kitchen stores, including electric-powered machines that will also grind your pork for you.

I don't usually bother with small sausages, so I choose the larger size of natural sausage casings, called "hog casings," which make good old butcher's bangers (as opposed to the extra-large casings, which I use for salami). These casings come packed in salt and need to be soaked, rinsed, and flushed through with fresh water before use.

Sausage meat Before you can make any sausages, you have to make sausage meat. If you are using home-reared pork and you have employed a butcher to sort out the carcass for you, you may want him to make up your sausage meat as well: his big industrial grinders will make light work of it. You will need to specify which parts of the pig you want your sausage meat made from. My preference is for a fifty-fifty combination of belly and leaner meat, usually taken from the boned-out Boston butt. Any trimmings arising from the general cutting up of the beast can also be added.

Another important decision is how finely you want your meat ground. Most modern butchers' sausage meat is ground on the finest setting. I find the resulting sausages too fine and pâté-like in consistency, so I prefer the next setting up. This gives a more old-fashioned "butcher's banger" consistency.

Of course, you don't have to keep your own pigs to make your own sausages. But if you want really good homemade sausages, it won't be enough just to buy the standard ready-made sausage meat. Choose fresh, quality belly and lean Boston butt and either grind it yourself or ask your butcher to do it according to your requirements.

You can make good sausages from 100 percent ground pork, plus your chosen seasonings, but there is no shame in adding a little cereal to the mix. This tradition is not merely a matter of bulking out the mixture with a cheap additive. A little "rusk," as it is called, improves the texture, as it helps to retain a little more fat in the sausage. I like to add about 5 percent by weight – so 2 ounces per 2 pounds of sausage meat. You can use various cereal-based products for rusk, including rice flour, fine oatmeal, or fine white bread crumbs. I actually use a multigrain organic baby cereal, with excellent results.

When planning a sausage-making session, bear in mind that 2 pounds of sausage meat will give you about fifteen to twenty large sausages, depending on their length and how tightly you stuff them.

Seasonings There are unlimited ways to season your sausages, and inventing new and original spice and/or herb combinations is all part of the fun. The best way to try out new ideas is to take a small amount of sausage meat, add your experimental seasonings, and mix well. Then fry up a bit of the mixture in a little patty and taste the result. When you get something you like, make up a big quantity and do another taste test and a final seasoning adjustment before you commit to the casings.

One thing that all your sausages will need is salt. About 1 to 2 teaspoons per 2 pounds of meat is a good rough guide, but you can make any final adjustments after your taste test.

Here are three of my favorite combinations. In each case, the quantities are enough for 2 pounds of sausage meat.

Hugh's herb sausage Sage dominates this mixture, to produce a sausage that is my favorite for bangers and mash. Finely chop all the herbs together, then mix thoroughly into the sausage meat with the pepper and salt.

About 20 sage leaves
About 20 chives
Leaves from 5 sprigs of thyme
A small bunch of marjoram
1 teaspoon freshly ground black pepper
Salt

Spiced apple sausage Mix all the ingredients together with your sausage meat.

1 small Golden Delicious or Granny Smith apple, peeled, cored, and finely diced
2 tablespoons Calvados
2 teaspoons mixed spices (ground cinnamon, nutmeg, and allspice)
1 teaspoon finely grated lemon zest
2 teaspoons brown sugar
1 teaspoon freshly ground black pepper
Salt

Ivan's white pepper sausage My friend Ivan insisted on making a sausage with no other seasoning than 2 teaspoons of ground white pepper, plus salt. It was outstanding.

Making the sausages For a beginner, the only real difficulty in making sausages is getting to grips with the sausage-making machine and avoiding too many air pockets. This is largely a matter of trial and error. Electric sausage-making machines will come with their own set of instructions. A crank-handled machine like mine can be a bit temperamental, and it is sometimes easier to have two people operating it – one turning the handle, the other controlling the casing as it fills.

The basic idea is to fill a long length of casing – as long as you like, really – then twist it into individual sausages of your chosen length. It is important not to overfill the sausages, or they will burst when you twist them. There are various clever twisting techniques devised by butchers over the years, where the sausages are twisted together to make long strings of twos and threes. These techniques are impossible to describe in words!

If wrapped or boxed immediately after being made, sausages will leach a considerable amount of liquid. To avoid this, the finished sausages should be hung in a cool place for a few hours or overnight. They can then be wrapped in waxed paper or plastic wrap, or placed in plastic containers, and stored in a refrigerator. Freshly made sausages kept in the fridge should be used within five days. If you want to keep them longer, either vacuum pack them (see page 105) or bag them up in freezer bags, in small batches. Defrost completely at room temperature before cooking.

Cooking sausages There is more to cooking sausages than you might think. They can be broiled, fried, grilled, or cooked in the oven, but in all cases the most common mistake is to cook them at too high a temperature for too short a time. Personally, I prefer to fry them, unpricked, at a gentle sizzle, turning every couple of minutes, for at least twenty minutes or even half an hour. By this time they should be darkly browned (but not blackened) and cooked right through, but still very juicy

Alternatively, place them in a roasting pan and bake in a preheated 350°F oven for thirty-five to forty-five minutes, turning and basting them with their own fat two or three times during cooking.

It is on the grill that sausages receive the worst abuse – everyone has experienced the piece of sausage-shaped charcoal that, astonishingly, turns out to be still raw in the middle. Grilled sausages can be delicious, but you must find an area with a low fire where they can cook more slowly, so that after ten to fifteen minutes they are nicely cooked through, a little blackened maybe, but not absolutely nuked. Practically, the solution is to wait until you've done your steaks, lamb chops, and burgers (where black on the outside and pink in the middle is the way to go), and then put the sausages – and indeed the chicken drumsticks – on when the grill has some residual heat but is basically on the wane.

livestock | cows and beef

The cow is, of course, the ultimate dual-purpose animal for the small farmer, since it is able to provide both meat and milk – the latter being the starting point for all kinds of delectable products, including two things that most of us eat almost every day: butter and cheese.

Having said that, I have to come clean about my very limited experience of the dairy side of cattle. Marge, the River Cottage house cow, arrived here in the spring of 1999 with her two-month-old calf, for whom she was producing a plentiful supply of milk – enough, I had hoped, for me to tax the odd couple of quarts for personal consumption. This was not necessarily an unrealistic aim. There is a small-farming tradition of sharing a house cow's milk with her unweaned calf, especially in the spring when the lush grass can help her produce enough milk to cope with this extra demand. But to be carried out successfully, this strategy requires a degree of organization on the part of the farmer, and no little cooperation on the part of cow and calf. The routine (which needs to be daily, and regular as clockwork, if cow and calf are to tolerate it) is to walk them into your shelter at night, into separate compartments where they are close enough for the calf to derive comfort from its mother's presence but far enough apart so that it cannot suckle. The following morning, the farmer milks the cow's bulging udder, leaving enough for a modest breakfast for her calf. Cow and calf then run together all day, when the calf will be able to get all the milk it needs, and they are separated again in the evening.

Surprise, surprise, I wasn't quite able to get to grips with this routine. My milking sessions with Marge were confined to surreptitious raids in the field at random times of day. Once in a while, I could get her settled enough on a trough of rolled barley to extract a pint or two, while her calf stood by glaring at me resentfully. And pretty soon I gave up even on this. These days, I buy locally produced organic milk from the village shop in Beaminster. My consolation is that Marge's calf, who eventually had the full benefit of an untaxed milk supply, is starting to look like a superb bit of beef.

The lesson I learned is that the dairy side of farming, be it with cows, goats, or even milk sheep, is perhaps the most demanding of time and energy, and the one that requires the greatest commitment. If you want to take a short break once in a while, or go on holiday, you may be able ask a neighbor to feed the pigs and water the garden, but I fear they will be loath to take on your milking responsibilities.

If I were to pretend that I had anything to teach you about dairy farming, beyond that simple caveat, I would be guilty of gross hypocrisy. (And my friend and neighbor, Frank, who experiences the trials and tribulations of modern commercial dairy farming on a daily basis, would be sorely peeved, and who could blame him?) So for those who wish to pursue, with more tenacity and success than I have been able to, the dairy side of farming, I would highly recommend John Seymour's seminal work, *The Complete Book of Self-Sufficiency*. It is clear that

the dairy cow is Seymour's personal favorite on the farm (as the pig is mine), and his pages on it are both thorough and truly inspirational.

The side of cattle that now interests me most at River Cottage is small-scale beef production. And by small-scale, I mean tiny: the raising and slaughter of a single beef steer per year. I can't pretend to be any great expert on that either, but the joy of it is that you don't really need to be. If your interest in beef production is not commercial or competitive, you can have a very relaxing time of it. For two-thirds of the year, your cattle will take care of their own dietary needs, while a little bit of good pasture management may provide you with enough hay to take care of the remaining third. And when the time comes to slaughter, there is no reason why your steer should not provide you with beef as good as any you have ever tasted.

But before I say anymore on the agreeable subject of home-reared beef, here are some thoughts on the not-always-so-agreeable commercially available product.

buying beef

Like all meat, the quality of beef varies hugely. But the British have always been enthusiastic beef-eaters, so the demand for good beef has always been high here. And the consumer has tended to be more knowledgeable about beef than other meats. The result is that there has always been a fair amount of good-quality beef around. On the other hand, most beef remains a by-product of the dairy industry. This is because dairy cattle, which in the U.K. are mostly high-yielding Friesians, need to produce a calf every year if they are going to go on producing milk. Potentially, only half of these calves will be milk-producing females, and only half (if that) of the female calves will be required as replacements for the dairy herd. This means that at least three out of every four calves born to dairy cattle are immediately excluded from the dairy loop. The options are simple: either sell them shortly after birth or try to find a market for their meat. But since they are from dairy cattle, they are never going to produce great beef. The farmer's incentive is therefore to get as much weight on them as quickly as possible and get shut of them. This means feeding them cheaply and rearing them intensively, often indoors without much room to move.[5] And that makes for miserable cattle, and lousy beef. The search for ever-cheaper feeds and ever-more-intensive rearing systems has not only led to a decline in the quality of much beef, it has also led to the most disastrous event in the history of Western food production: the outbreak of mad cow disease – a direct result of giving super-cheap, high-protein feeds made from recycled cow parts back to their own kind.

But the good beef/bad beef routine isn't quite so black and white. Not all beef from beef cattle is good, and not all beef from dairy cattle is bad. For a start, mindful of the commercial limitations of pure dairy beef, most dairy farmers these days use beef-breed bulls, such as Aberdeen Angus and Hereford, for the essential annual impregnation of their dairy cows. These then produce cross-bred calves which, given the right conditions, can turn into a pretty decent bit of beef. Indeed, for the small farmer who wants to fatten up a calf for slaughter, buying a dairy-beef cross calf is a good economic and gastronomic option – more of that below.

At the same time, on the pure beef side, breeding alone does not ensure quality. Thus, as well as good-quality dairy beef, there is also very poor-quality beef-herd beef. Such is the premium attached to the name of the Aberdeen Angus that farmers who can produce a lot of it, at low cost, can make fantastic profits. Intensively farmed Angus is therefore in plentiful supply. Some of this is taken all the way from the south of England to Scotland for a brief stay before slaughter, simply so that it can come back with the proud label "Scotch Aberdeen Angus." Once, this was a meaningful guarantee of quality. It is no longer set in stone.

The biggest problem of all for the consumer is not that the beef market is a mixture of good, bad, and indifferent meat – that's sadly inevitable – but that current retailing practice and labeling laws make it extremely hard to identify the good stuff. The good news is that, since the mad cow disease crisis, it has been a legal requirement to label all beef from cattle reared in this country as British beef.[6] As the best British beef is still the best beef in the world, this is at least a useful start. I buy only British beef. Apart from that, you are pretty much at the mercy of your butcher – or local supermarket. A good butcher should know exactly where his beef comes from and how long it has been hung. If he can answer your questions about his beef in a convincing and friendly manner, then it is certainly worth giving it a whirl. If he can name his producers and if he knows a bit about how their steers are fed and finished, then he clearly cares about his beef as much as you do. You could be in for a treat.

One policy that I have noticed in a couple of top butcher shops here in the West Country, which I heartily applaud, is a weekly bulletin board giving salient details of the animal(s) from which the current stock of beef has come – for example, "grass-fed, barley-finished Devon Rubys from Babwell Farm, Somerset, slaughtered at 22 to 24 months and hung for 3 weeks." This is exactly the kind of information we consumers would like to know.

At the supermarket, there is no such personal contact to reassure you. There is, however, a confusing array of labels.[7] Very few of these are independently monitored. Usually, it is fairly easy to pick out the premium branded beef – it will be sporting a fancy label saying "traditionally reared" or some such, and will be about 20 percent more expensive. In fairness, some of these labels do offer beef that has been reared with better husbandry, and indeed prepared with more skillful butchery, than the lowest-common-denominator products surrounding it. But the rule with all such labels is, assume the worst. In other words, unless it makes specific and palpable claims about the welfare and diet of the animals, assume it is as bad as anyone else's beef.

If you are concerned about the welfare of the cattle from which your beef has come (and you should be), the one reliably meaningful label at the current time is the organic, or "naturally raised," one.[8] Most of the larger chains of the leading supermarkets now stock organic beef, and most good butchers can find it for you if you ask.

Welfare is one thing, taste is another. I know from personal experience that the eating quality of organic beef is very variable. At its best it is unbeatable, but at its worst it is no better than average. In Britain, the Soil Association gives awards for meat every year, and the winners are producing some of the finest meat you will find in this country.

Another good way to make contact with good beef producers is at any farmers' market. They may be organic, or they may not, but as they personally produce the meat they are selling, they should be able to tell you all about it. Once you have made friends with a producer of good beef, you can cultivate your relationship to get the very best from them, ordering in advance, specifying what cuts you would like, and even exactly how long you would like them hung.

Whoever you buy from, it will always pay you to know what good beef looks like in the raw state. The supermarkets, and even some butchers, would have us believe that good beef is pink, bloody, and "fresh" looking. In fact, excessive moisture is a sign of poor-quality, under-matured beef. The best beef should be neither too dark, nor too pale (though certainly darker than is commonly seen in our supermarkets). And it should be shiny rather than wet. Generally speaking, it should be firm and elastic. Very well-matured beef for fast cooking, such as tenderloin, sirloin, and rib roast, may be darker, and the prod of a finger should leave an indentation that doesn't spring back. Even the leanest cuts should show "marbling" – a distribution through the flesh of small threads of fat.

When it comes to presenting beef to the customer, the small independent producers who sell top-quality meat directly, either through farmers' markets or by mail order, have a tendency to one unfortunate habit. For ease of transport and handling, they usually vacuum-pack their meat. In the case of beef, this is particularly sad. Vaccuum-packed beef sweats a lot, leaching blood, which can soak back into the fat and meat, spoiling its texture and flavor. If you can persuade your favorite beef supplier not to vac-pack your order, so much the better. If you can't, then at least remove the meat from the pack as soon as possible, and let it breathe uncovered in the fridge.

veal

There is much anxiety and outrage about the way that dairy calves have been (and in some countries still are) raised for veal – and rightly so. But veal is not per se a morally suspect product, any more than lamb or pork is (most pigs are slaughtered at a similar age to veal calves). And, of course, veal can be delicious. Tracking down veal from animals that have lived well and free is, however, a challenge. Organic certification provides the answer. Organic veal is from calves who have run free in the field and grazed and suckled until slaughter. Animals that have lived this sort of life produce what is often referred to as "pink veal."[9]

home-rearing beef

Cattle is the generic term for all cows, whether beef or dairy, but individual animals go by various names according to their age, sex, and purpose. To avoid confusion, it's worth explaining these terms at the outset:

Cow An adult female, for producing milk and calves
Bull An adult male, usually a stud animal
Bullock A young bull
Steer A castrated male
Heifer A young female; technically, a cow that has not yet had a calf, though she may be referred to as a "calved heifer" until she has had her second calf

Unlike lambs and piglets, beef calves are usually expensive. The best way to acquire one is therefore through possession of a fertile cow who, provided she is introduced at the appropriate time to a bull with a fully leaded pencil, will provide you with one free of charge. I say that through slightly clenched teeth, because despite the best efforts of both Knotting Regulus the First (a pure-bred Dexter bull), and the local artificial inseminator, Margo, the River Cottage cow, has this year failed to produce a calf. And so it is not without a sense of irony that I offer the following tips on how to acquire a fertile cow that will deliver you a fine calf every spring.

choosing a cow

An ideal way to start out with cattle is to buy a cow and calf. Buy in spring or early summer, when the calf is still just a couple of months old and not yet weaned, and you have the option of taking milk from the cow as well (see page 171 for how this can be achieved or, in my case, not achieved). The calf should itself be proof of the cow's fertility. In terms of assessing her general health, look for a richly colored, shiny coat, a bright eye, and a placid, easygoing temperament. You should certainly inspect her udder, feeling both the bag and the teats very carefully. If there are any hard lumps there, she has probably had mastitis, and may get it again. This means she will have trouble feeding her calf, and any milk you get will be useless. She is best avoided.

In Britain, any cow, steer, or calf you buy must have an ear tag and documentation showing she is TT (tuberculosis tested) and brucellosis free. You will also have to register your "herd" with the Department for Environment, Food, and Rural Affairs (DEFRA) and follow their veterinary requirements.[10] And you will have to present documentation at slaughter. In the U.S., regulations vary from state to state, and there is currently no national I.D. system.

You need to make friends with your resident house cow, whether or not you are going to milk her. She should be happy to let you touch her, scratch her muzzle, even put your arms around her neck. If she is already trained to be led by a halter, so much the better. You can tell the age of a cow by the number of, and wear on, her teeth. But that's a matter for experts. The bottom line is, if you are buying your first cow, take someone with you who knows what to look for. It is a fact of rural life that good-natured, healthy, fertile cows with a few good years left in them are hard to buy – not least because their owners will be understandably reluctant to part with them. If a farmer with a herd of cows is ready to sell you one, you can be sure he or she will want to sell you the worst in the herd. There are one or two exceptions to this rule. Farmers who are selling up an entire herd will be selling the good as well as the bad. And some farmers will deliberately raise good heifers and then get them in calf with a view to selling them on with their calf, at a small profit, to the likes of you. There is no reason why these girls should not be excellent cows, but the slight drawback is she is likely to be sold with her first-ever calf, which means that she and you will both be beginners. You will have to work hard at your bond with the cow, perhaps halter-training her yourself. The upside is that, if all goes well and the two of you become firm friends, she has over a decade of loyal service in her and perhaps as many as a dozen calves to give you.

what breed?

There are a number of breeds to choose from, and the most common distinctions drawn between them are whether they are native British or American or Continental breeds, and whether they are beef, dairy, or dual purpose. Native British and American breeds are the obvious choice for the cold-climate farmer because they are hardier than Continentals. They do not have to be housed over the winter (though they do need an accessible shelter in their pasture), and they do not need as much extra processed feed (called "concentrate") as a Continental breed will during these cold months. As for the beef/dairy/dual-purpose issue, that depends whether milking is part of your plan. Here are some of your options:

Dexter Marge is a Dexter, a hardy, native, miniature, dual-purpose cow now officially designated as a rare breed. I can't say I've sampled a great deal of her milk, for reasons discussed earlier, but the beef from a distant relative of hers (my first steer was a pure-bred Dexter) was quite superb. The small carcass size makes for easier butchery and storage. I highly recommend Dexters, with the mild caveat that they can be willful and occasionally uncooperative. If I get another Dexter, I will choose one without horns.

Jersey The obvious choice if you are after milk. The yield is not as high as a Friesian, but the milk is superb and the temperament of Jerseys is second to none. Good animals to bond with. Because of the very yellow color of the fat, Jersey beef has no commercial viability, but in fact it is very good eating.

Red Poll A good old-fashioned dual-purpose cow – a useful trade-off between good milk and good beef.

American Milking Devon First cousin to the Ruby Red Devon, this dual-purpose breed produces both abundant milk and well-marbled meat.

Holstein The most popular dairy cow in the U.S., this black and white spotted cow is a classic milk producer.

Angus The legendary beef animal. Hardy and happy on more marginal or hill grazing. The bulls are good for crossing with dairy animals for beef.

Hereford The other classic beef breed. Bulls have an unusually good temperament and are therefore a favorite for crossing with dairy cows for a good beef cross.

breeding

Your aim should be to get your cow to produce one calf every year. Commercial beef farmers aim for a mixture of autumn and spring calves, which gives them a range of animals to take to slaughter at staggered intervals throughout the year. For small farmers, spring is the simplest option, as the calf should have an easier time of it, adapting instantly to outdoor life. And mum will have plenty of good grass to make milk.

The gestation period for a cow is nine months, so for a March calf a June insemination is ideal. The tradition is to give a cow six weeks after calving before "serving" her again – i.e., putting her in with a bull. She will be "bulling" (in heat) every twenty-one days, so should get pregnant within three months of her last calf and hit roughly the same date the following year.

You need to be able to recognize the signs of bulling. You can then get your cow to a bull, or a bull to your cow, as soon as they start. Or, better still, plan ahead. Make a note of the date she starts bulling, and bring in the bull a day or two before she is due to start again. There are a number of clear-cut signs that a cow is bulling: she may be mounted by other cattle, including her own calf; she may do a bit of mounting herself; she bellows more frequently, in a somewhat wistful manner; she lifts her tail a lot; at the peak of her bulling (which lasts about eighteen hours) she may show a trail of clear mucus coming from her vagina. This is known as the "bulling string."

The alternative to running her with a bull is to bring in the AI – artificial insemination – man. The downside is that your cow will miss out on the romance. But from the farmer's point of view, it has to be said that AI is a pretty attractive option. You don't have to arrange transport for either your cow or the bull. You don't have to run the gauntlet of an angry bull in your pasture. You can choose from a whole range of pedigree bull sperm. And, my experience with Marge notwithstanding, the success rate is extremely high (usually over 90 percent).

Whichever route you choose, you will need to make a decision about what breed of bull is going to father your next calf. You may wish to keep the breed pure – in which case the AI man should have the right sperm in the bank if you can't find the right bull nearby. Or you can simply choose a good beef bull, such as a Hereford or Angus, both of whose calves have a reputation for easy calving, even for dairy cows. There is no reason why you can't ring the changes from year to year and see how the beef turns out each time.

Most cows who are bulling should be happy to be served by any bull – or any AI man, come to that – and should get pregnant without any trouble. But there is a piece of cattle-breeding wisdom that says it is easier to get a lean cow pregnant than a fat one. When the vet broke the bad news to me about Marge – that she wasn't pregnant after all – he raised this as a possible cause of the problem. Small farmers' cattle can be somewhat pampered. We tend to err on the side of overfeeding during the winter months, so the extra benefit of the spring grass can put them a little on the fat side. This doesn't mean you should starve your cow to ensure a pregnancy – absolutely not – but if, like Marge, she fails to produce a calf one year, you can either trade her in for a younger model or, like me, take the soft-hearted approach and see her carefully through the winter without overdoing it, hoping for better luck the following year

calving

Cows don't generally need any help at all with calving, which in springtime they will do quite happily outdoors. The chances are you will walk out one morning and find the new arrival contentedly suckling, while getting a firm licking from its mother. Very occasionally, a cow may get into problems delivering her calf. If this happens, call the vet at once. If you see hind feet and a tail coming out first, you are looking at a breech delivery. An experienced stockperson will know how to deal with this – usually by tying a rope around the back legs of the calf and pulling hard. But ideally, you should not attempt this without the help of someone who has done it before. Calves in breech can drown if not quickly dealt with, so if you have no choice but to tackle the situation unassisted, the key thing is to pull down (i.e., toward the ground) as well as out. And you will have to pull hard.

A more likely problem, but still a rare one, is that a calf may have difficulty finding its mother's milk and getting started. If it hasn't started to suckle within an hour of being born, you should intervene. Help the calf to stand up and direct its muzzle to the teat. If the cow keeps wandering off, tie her up. You really want to make this work, as a calf who does not get the first colostrum (extra-rich milk full of essential organisms and antibodies) is very vulnerable to falling ill. A calf should have three quarts of colostrum in its first six hours.

If beef is your only concern, once your calf is up and feeding well, you can forget about it for a while. It's in safe hands. But if you want to get its mother back on the full-time milk rotation, you will have to intervene. You need to separate calf and mother, and ideally put them out of earshot of each other. You can only do this when the calf has had its fill of colostrum, plus a good dose of mother's milk – this means at least three days after birth. But unless you have more than one cow, and more than one calf, so that you can make two separate little herds, one for milk and one for beef, then it is not fair to mother or calf to do this.

ooo56

A single cow and calf unit should stay together, and if you want to milk the cow, you will have to do it by the temporary separation system described at the beginning of this chapter. I hope you have more success than I did!

If you don't want your calf to have horns (and horns can be dangerous – to you, to your family, and to livestock) he or she will have to be de-budded. Get a vet to show you how to do this the first time, and you should be able to manage it yourself the next. You can avoid the horn problem by choosing a hornless ("polled") breed of cow. You will also have to put a hornless bull on her, or you run a fifty-fifty risk of a horned calf.

Male calves can be castrated at the same time. The testicles of a young calf are small, but delicious enough not to waste. I fry them up in butter with a bit of sage and have them on toast.

In Britain, all calves must be registered with the BCMS (British Cattle Movement Service) and ear-tagged within twenty-eight days of birth. Farmers are sent a passport and have to keep hold of it in order to move, show, or take their cattle to slaughter. There is no similar program in the U.S. at this time.

maintaining your herd

The size of your herd depends on how many animals you want to slaughter each year. In my case, it's just the one. This means that at any given time I have either two or three animals on the pasture, depending on whether the newer calf has been born or the older one has gone to slaughter.

The only problem is in year one. If, like me, you start with a cow and her young calf, you will not realistically be wanting to slaughter the calf until the summer or autumn of its second year at the earliest. My solution was to buy a yearling steer (also a Dexter) at the same time as my cow and calf, for slaughter at the end of just one summer. This dealt with my year-one needs very nicely. Marge's first calf will be ready for slaughter this autumn, and had she calved this spring I would also have a steer or heifer for slaughter next year. As it is, she has let me down, so I have bought another beef animal at auction for slaughter next year.

Once it's up and running, and provided your cow delivers, this is a very neat and economical system for the small farmer. It means that from spring until late summer you will have three animals feeding on your lush pasture (a cow, a beef animal, and a young calf), but when the beef animal has gone for slaughter you just have two to see through the winter. She calves again in the spring and the cycle goes around again.

Summer feeding is easy: provided you can offer them some good grazing, your cattle should look after themselves from March until October or even November in a mild year. The general stocking rate for summer grazing is one cow per acre (half an acre for a calf). So as long as they have this much or more, they will be fine. Unless you are trying to maintain your cow for milking (in which case there is a prescribed formula of feeding for hay, silage, and/or concentrates to maintain the milk yield), the winter months are not much harder. The grass is growing much more slowly, but your cattle will continue to graze. A bale of hay every couple of days will keep a cow and calf happy. A couple of kilos of rolled oats, and the same of wurzels or stubble turnips, would make a nice weekly treat. If the weather gets very cold, increase the frequency of the treats.

Ideally, your calf should be fully weaned before the winter feeding starts. This is achieved by separating cow and calf for at least three or four weeks until the mother has dried up. Then they can be put back together again. If you don't wean your calf it will go on suckling through the winter and will end up muscling in on mother's milk even after the next calf has been born.

In Britain, post–mad cow disease legislation means that all beef cattle must now be slaughtered before thirty months of age. If you operate a two-calf rotation as I do, you will be slaughtering at around eighteen to twenty months – in the autumn of the calf's second year. The legislation does allow room for a three-calf rotation, which lets you take your calf to its full adult weight before slaughtering it in the summer of its third year, just before its thirty months are up. At the time they go to slaughter, they will have two calves following behind, one aged about sixteen to eighteen months, the other about four to six. The same standards do not apply to U.S.-grown beef.

finishing beef

Most serious beef farmers aiming for the top end of the market will have a formula of extra feed, usually some cocktail of molassed sugar beet, rolled oats, and barley, which they will feed to their stock for six to eight weeks before slaughter. This is designed to increase the weight of the animals and the fat content of the beef to make it more attractive at market, and is particularly important when finishing beef in the winter months. There is no harm in dabbling with finishing formulas of this kind, and if you do want to slaughter in winter it will certainly improve the quality of the beef. But for the timetable outlined above, where your beef animal is taken to slaughter at the end of a summer on lush grass, it isn't really essential.

slaughter

Taking a single beef animal to slaughter is not the easiest of things. If it has never been separated from its mother, it is hardly going to want to leave. For this reason, a weaned animal can be taken away more easily than an unweaned one. And an animal that is used to, and accepting of, human contact will be much easier to load up than one that has been running wild. So it is a good idea for the farmer to bond with a beef calf as well as a breeding cow. I know this from experience. I have made the mistake of having minimal contact with Marge's calf, and when the vet comes to give him his TB jab he can hardly get near him. It takes three of us to walk him into the shed and close the gate on him so the job can be done. I am not looking forward to slaughter day one bit. Now I am working on my beef steer by bringing him into the shed for a little extra feed every couple of days. But had I done this early on, or even halter-trained him as a calf, he would be a lot easier to manage.

When you do take a beef animal to slaughter, make sure you have the manpower to load up the trailer with a minimum of fuss. If you can shut up the animal in your shed or shelter, alone, for a few nights before slaughter, it should be more passive or accepting. Make sure it has water and a little feed.

Small slaughterhouses, especially those with organic accreditation, tend to offer the small farmer a far more friendly and personal service.[11] Book your animal in for slaughter at a specified time and try not to be too early or too late. Wait to see it into the slaughter room, and wait while it is done, so you can take away the various offals. Sadly, the only part of the head you are now allowed to keep is the tongue. This you should definitely take, along with the liver, kidneys, heart, lungs, and tripe. This latter should be rinsed for you, but it will need a further clean and scrub when you get home. Beef blood can be used to make blood sausage (see page 162), so take a bucket for that too if you want to make some.

For more details on going to slaughter, see Pigs and Pork, page 144.

dealing with the carcass

The carcass of a beef cow is big, and dealing with it is correspondingly a big job. You need help, and the best help you can have is from a qualified butcher. So if you can strike a deal, book the friendliest butcher you know for half a day, watch him and work with him, follow his lead, and try to learn as much as you can.

But even before butchering, there is a problem to be solved. You want your beef to be as delicious as possible. This means that, ideally, you want it hung for at least three weeks – four or five if you are very confident of its quality. The problem is, where is that going to happen? Not at your place, unless you have invested in a meat fridge where a whole carcass can hang undisturbed at 36 to 39°F. This is a further favor you will have to ask of your butcher friend. But space is often at a premium in a busy butcher's meat store, and you may have to reach a compromise. The bits that you really want to hang well are the steaks you are going to fry and the joints you are going to roast. In other words, the rump, the sirloin, and the ribs. These cuts all happen to link up on the carcass (see diagram below) and it is possible to butcher it so that you have two large sides of beef comprising all these prime cuts. If these parts of the carcass can be set aside for longer hanging, then the rest can be divvied up for salting, grinding, or freezing without too great a loss to your gastronomic plans. Incidentally, hanging means hanging – you cannot hope to mature a piece of beef simply by letting it sit in a fridge.

One way or another, your beef carcass must be rationalized and brought to heel. This is a good time to think about outstanding debts and favors owed: beef may be a welcome form of payment. Inevitably, you are going to freeze a lot of it. Do the hard work of dividing it into manageable pieces before it goes in the freezer. An entire hindquarter of fresh beef may look daunting, but an entire hindquarter of frozen beef is downright impossible. Remember that the freezer is not the only option. The brine tub can pickle a lot of beef and save you a lot of freezer space. See page 241 for the wisdom on corned beef. A lot of the carcass will only really be good for stewing and grinding: albeit excellent stews and top-quality ground beef. Time spent getting meat off the bone now, trimming it and bagging it up for stew, or grinding it and bagging it up for burgers and bolognese will be space saved now and time saved later. The bones can be cleaved into manageable sizes, roasted, and used to make the finest beef stock you have ever had – strain it and reduce it, then bag it up and freeze it.

There is no getting away from the fact that you will have to become a bit of a butcher and master the basic anatomy of the beast, as well as know which cuts are suitable for what kind of cooking. Here are some pointers.

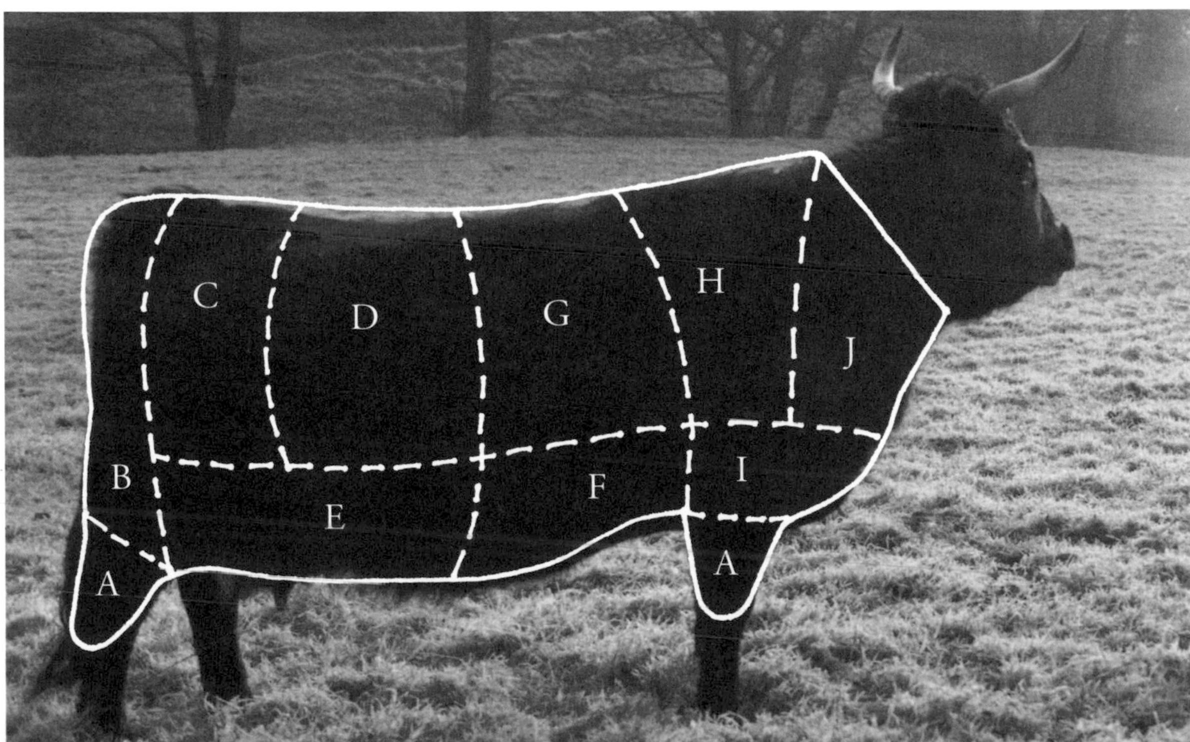

Tail In theory the most gristly, bony, sinewy, unpromising part of the animal; in practice, once transformed by slow cooking and a few well-chosen flavorings (see page 239), one of the most sublime.

Hind shank and shin (A) A cut from the top of the back leg, the *hind shank* is tough but lean, and can yield plenty of meat for long, slow cooking. I prefer to cook it in the piece and on the bone, with vegetables, as a kind of pot-au-feu, or to bone it out and salt it (see page 241). Trimmed and cut up, the meat can be used, along with shin, for well-flavored stews. It's good for making your own ground meat, too. The shank is also known as the *hock* or, in Scotland, the *hough*.

The *shin*, or top of the foreleg of an animal, is a bargain cut that is quite delicious if cooked very slowly in a flavorsome liquor. On the bone, it can be braised with wine and vegetables; off the bone it makes excellent stew. In younger animals, cross-sections of the shin, sawn through the bone about ¾ inch thick, can be prepared Italian style, as osso buco: cooked very slowly with wine, herbs, and tomatoes until the meat is completely tender. The little morsel of marrow in the bone is a particular delicacy.

Round (lower B) The heel of round or *round tip* is the cut immediately above the leg, which yields a greater amount of similarly tough meat. Still good value for slow-cooked daubes and pot-au-feu. Boned, it makes a great piece for corned beef and stews.

Top round (middle B) The long inner muscle of the cow's massive thigh. It is a little more tender than bottom round. In the best quality of animal, and where the meat has been well hung and properly aged, roasting is rewarding and the meat can be served just pink. It should not be roasted fast, however, like a filet or sirloin, but slowly, with a little stock or water in the pan. Braising, on a bed of vegetables moistened with stock, is also appropriate. (Roasted or braised, a good piece is excellent served cold – ideally left uncut until completely cool.) Eye of round is a classic cut for French daubes, particularly if kept whole or in large pieces.

Bottom round (upper B) A classic cut from the back of the thigh, comprising a pair of overlapping muscles, whose wide-grained texture is a testament to the hard work they do in propelling its owner from one place to another; it is tough. In the butcher's shop, it is often sold as a cheap roasting joint. Such a treatment is, in my view, a complete waste of time. It may seem extravagant to use bottom round for stews, but if it's your animal, you can do what you like with it. I use it for stews and also for marinating in powerful spices (for example, as for Rabbit Satay on page 412) before stir-frying. It ends up a little bit chewy but wonderfully tasty. Coarsely ground bottom round makes excellent burgers, which can be served as pink as you like.

Rump roast and rump steak (top B) Considerably cheaper than filet, rump roast and steak (which are not to be confused with top round) are also tastier and chewier, though if they are not properly matured they can be less than tasty and far too chewy. Rump meat is suitable for frying, grilling, and barbecuing, in thickish slices. When you are really sure of the quality and maturity of a piece of rump, then a large piece of the "eye" – a muscle that can be separated from the rest of the rump – makes a fabulous roast, which can be cooked fast and served rare. The meat from the lower muscle of the rump is rather tougher. It should be separated from the piece from which you cut your rump steak and used as bottom round. Good, well-hung rump steak makes the best steak tartare (see page 237).

Full loin (C, D) The full loin is a large piece taken from the lower middle of an animal's back, which includes the much-prized *filet*. The full loin is typically divided into the *sirloin* (C) and *short loin* (D), subprimal cuts that share two main muscles: the top sirloin/top loin, a long muscle along the top of an animal's back, and the *tenderloin*, or *filet*, which lies right below it. The sirloin also contains part of the same muscle found in the adjoining round.

Sirloin (C) The sirloin portion of the loin muscle, known as *bottom sirloin*, yields the *sirloin tip*, or *tri-tip*. Bone-in sirloin provides excellent *sirloin steak*.

Short Loin (D) This subprimal cut contains many of the choicest cuts: *filet/tenderloin*, *T-bone*, and *New York/Delmonico*. A *T-bone*, or *porterhouse*, steak is a cross section of the unfileted sirloin. On one side of the T-bone is a piece of filet, on the other the meat, which, when taken off the bone, is the entrecote or "sirloin steak" of common butchers shop parlance (aka *New York steak* and *strip steak*, among others).

When the entrecote side of the sirloin is removed from the bone, trimmed of all gristle and excess (but, please, not all) fat, and neatly parceled up, it is a fine joint for roasting. This is the eye of the sirloin, what the French call *contre-filet* (because it is on the opposite side of the bone from the filet). A little cheaper and a little tastier than the filet, it is almost as tender, and should be roasted fast and served pink.

A great cut of beef for roasting on the bone is a large cross section of sirloin, i.e., potential T-bone steaks as yet uncut, with the filet on one side and the contre-filet on the other. The joy of this cut is that it retains and absorbs flavor from the bone, and you can offer your guests a choice of incredibly tender filet and especially tasty contre-filet.

Filet (inside D) In a 600- to 700-pound beef carcass, there is a scant 4 to 5 pounds of filet, which is the least exercised muscle of a castrated young bull – no wonder it is so expensive. In fact, one of the reasons beef bullocks are castrated is that, as you might imagine, it makes them less inclined to mate, or even to practice mating, and so prevents a rigorous form of exercise that would strengthen (and toughen) a great number of muscles, the filet in particular. Filet is therefore supremely tender, especially from a well-hung carcass, and consequently much prized by chefs. But it has less flavor than other cuts – and an overcooked filet has practically no taste at all. Frying, grilling, and quick roasting (of a whole or large piece) are all appropriate cooking methods. I would never freeze a filet, but like to roast it whole in a very hot oven and serve it very bloody and rare – almost fridge cold in the middle.

Flank (E) This is the chunk immediately below the sirloin, before the ribs begin – in other words, the belly. It is boneless, cheap, very fatty, but quite delicious if cooked very slowly in casseroles or a pot-au-feu. It makes a fatty but extremely tasty cut of corned beef.

Plate (F) This is a similar cut to the hindquarter flank, with the principal difference being that the plate has ribs in it. Some may see this as an inconvenience, but flavorwise it is definitely a plus. *Short ribs* are fine in a pot-au-feu, and can also be salted. I have my own rather greedy way of doing them: tenderized by long, slow cooking, they are then crisped up briefly in a hot oven and served rather like spareribs, sometimes with Horseradish Mash (see page 114).

Ribs (G) The bovine equivalent of a rack of lamb is *roast rib of beef*, or *standing rib roast*. There is plenty of lean meat in the eye of these "chops," and a single rib "cutlet" makes a good two-person portion. A three- or four-rib piece from a well-hung, quality animal makes, to my mind, the ultimate roasting joint. It has the fat to keep it lubricated, the bone to keep in moisture and flavor, and, in a slow-grown, grass-fed animal, excellent marbling in the eye of the meat. Boned, the roast is called a rolled *rib roast* or *rib-eye roast*. The trimmed filet, or eye, of the rib gives a cut that is particularly popular in America – the *rib-eye steak*.

Chuck (H) This is the meat taken from around the blade bone in the animal's shoulder. In the butchers shop it is sold, usually ready-cut, for stews and casseroles. Larger pieces of chuck steak (often sold as braising steak) are good for daubes and stews. Or it can be ground and used for bolognese.

Brisket (I) A cut from farther up the ribcage, brisket is marginally leaner than flank, but still pretty fatty. It is the ultimate cut for corned beef, and this is what I do with it every time.

Stew meat/ground meat (J) What's left of the carcass meat – mainly from around the neck and shoulder – is what would find its way into a butcher's tray labeled "stewing steak." But since I have already set aside some excellent cuts from my carcass for long, slow cooking, I am more than happy that the rest should go for grinding. I find that commercial ground meat is usually too finely ground – the juices run out when it is cooked and it becomes insipid. I get my own grind done on a coarser setting, which gives more body and texture to the bolognese, lasagne, chili, and other slow-cooked dishes I make from it.

Tongue (not visible) Sadly, the only part of the head one is now allowed to take from the slaughterhouse. So take it you must. It can be salted and boiled (exactly as the Corned Beef on page 241), or try the recipe on page 239.

livestock | sheep and lambs

Some people may find it hard to get excited about sheep – compared to, say, pigs or cattle – and if you see no charm at all in the animals you should not get involved with them. But my experience with sheep at River Cottage has convinced me that they are in no way short on character. They can be cheeky, affectionate, and playful, and ready to form a lasting bond with their owner. And the small farmer, whose flock may be measured in single figures, has the advantage of being able to get to know the quirks and character of each individual – the greedy one, the friendly one, the shy one, the leader. Sheep can be good with young children, and are usually safe with them – not that you should leave them together unsupervised. But if they have been used to close human contact since birth, they will not merely tolerate but actually enjoy a pat, a scratch, and a hug.

The River Cottage flock has been the source of considerable pleasure for me and my family. And the way they gently crowd and jostle me every time I walk into the field still brings a smile to my face.

But there are other reasons, besides their underappreciated affability, to consider keeping sheep. They are extremely efficient grazers, and if you have even a small paddock or field, a few sheep will take care of it very nicely. On a slightly bigger scale, their grazing efficiency can be very complementary to cattle. They graze much closer than cows, and tidy up pasture that would otherwise be left very patchy by cattle. Most breeds of sheep are hardy and can overwinter out of doors without any trouble at all. Given enough grazing, they will not even need any extra winter fodder. In this sense, they are relatively low maintenance, though of course they do need to be sheared, and may also require a little more routine veterinary attention than other stock.

Of course, there is one overarching reason for rearing a few sheep: good lamb and mutton are quite delicious, and the stuff you raise yourself is sure to be the best you've ever tasted.

If the practicalities of home-rearing sheep are not compatible with your lifestyle, the good news is that, for once, we can say that the commercially reared product is usually of reasonable quality and often excellent – provided you exercise a little rigor in your shopping.[12]

buying lamb and mutton

Thanks to the sheep's ability to thrive on fairly marginal land, British sheep have not, generally speaking, been subjected to the horrors of intensive farming – growth promoters, hormones, unnatural feeds – that have so threatened the quality of our beef and pork. But different breeds of stock, and the variable quality of the land on which they graze, mean there are still vast differences in flavor and texture from one piece of lamb to the next – and who would have it any other way? Life would be exceptionally dull if a Scottish sheep that had grazed among the heather tasted exactly the same as a West Country animal that had spent its days on the chalky soils of the Dorset Downs.

Although the quality of British lamb at its best is something to be proud of, it would be misleading to imply that a second-rate British product does not exist. It does, and I have tasted it – bland meat with gristly spots that is too tough when served pink, and rather dry and tasteless when overdone to compensate. Such meat is the product of farms where sheep are not a priority but a seasonal stopgap, usually an adjunct to intensive arable farming. Lambs are reared on impoverished arable land, and fed up on cheap feeds or arable by-products.

Spotting poor-quality lamb at the butcher's is not always easy. Enquiring about its origins is a start, though there is no guarantee that the response will be either honest or significant. But butchers who have proved their worth in other areas are unlikely to fail you when it comes to providing a good piece of lamb, while country butchers whose beef and pork are not especially outstanding may nevertheless have access to better-quality local lamb. When buying spring lamb, look for light pink meat with a general plumpness in any leg or shoulder and a generous amount of creamy-white fat. The butchers and supermarkets may have you believe that lean lamb is what you want but, believe me, the fattier animals are the tastier ones.

Certified organic lamb is from animals that have been raised exclusively on organic feed – mainly organic pasture – and it is often excellent. But in terms of quality, the distinction from other lamb is not as obvious. Much of the best lamb is grazed on land that is effectively organic, even if it is not certified – for example, the Welsh and Scottish hills and moors. From the gastronomic point of view, the best nonorganic lamb may be as interesting as the organic product. On the other hand, the usual assurances over welfare – particularly the way sheep are transported and slaughtered – are always a compelling reason for choosing organic.

The other great variable with lamb is, of course, age.[13] Young spring lambs will be tender, sweet, and require little hanging to develop the meat. From midsummer onward, lambs will not only be larger and have a more developed flavor, they will be inclined to toughness. There is nothing wrong with this meat – indeed, personally I prefer it – but older lambs need to be hung properly to develop tenderness and flavor; often they are not. Blood spots and wet-looking meat are signs of underhanging. If your butcher is friendly, it is worth specifying that you like your lamb well hung – a couple of weeks is not excessive for a summer lamb.

In fact, a whole leg of lamb is one of the few take-home cuts of meat that it may be practical to mature further at home, though you must have the necessary cool space to do this properly. A leg of lamb should be hung, preferably covered in cheesecloth or a clean cotton cloth, from a butcher's hook, hip down, knuckle up, in a well-aired place where the temperature is reliably less than 46°F. In the summer months, only a very cool cellar is likely to fulfill these requirements, though in autumn and winter a cold stone outbuilding should just about fit the bill. Butchers hang meat in carefully regulated walk-in fridges where the temperature is never more than 39°F (or at least they should). Since the temperature at home is likely to be much less reliable, it would be unwise to hang a leg of lamb for more than a week.

My real bugbear with commercial lamb is that there is almost no market for what I would consider the finest "lamb" of all – mutton.[14] The problem is that lambs are never a great money maker, as farmers want to cash in as quickly as possible. The result is that few animals go beyond their sixth month, and most are killed at around their fourth. The exceptions to this rule are the lambs of the wilder, late-lambing hill sheep. These are often born too late to finish in their first year. Overwintered on roots and other fodder crops, they are fattened on early spring grass and often slaughtered at around a year old. I would consider such animals far better eating than most young spring suck-lambs. The irony is that most butchers would rather pass them off as "spring lamb," because that's what the consumer traditionally demands.

It's a pity, because without doubt the best sheep meat I have ever eaten has come from animals over a year old. It is a mistake to think of mutton as coming from some worn-out old ewe that is no longer productive or an exhausted ram that is being retired. Mutton "wethers" (castrated male sheep) are usually slaughtered (by those in the know) in their second or third year after fattening on spring and summer grass, when they will be physically mature but still young animals in the prime of life. Their meat is quite superb, and far from requiring marinating or slow cooking, it can be roasted and served pink, like the best cuts of prime beef. But it does need to be properly hung – ideally, like the best beef, for at least three weeks.

All this is too much to deal with for most butchers, and certainly the supermarkets. But with a bit of detective work, top-quality mutton of this kind can be found. As ever, the answer lies in direct contact with producers who are butchering and retailing their own meat. You may find them at farmers' markets or through the Internet. Some, but not all, of them will be organic. Some of them may require you to take possession of half an animal. But they will portion it up for you, ready for the freezer, and probably deliver it, too. These are the people to talk to about mutton, and when you mention the "m" word, the chances are you will get an appreciative, knowing response. It's probably what they prefer to eat themselves.

The word about mutton is starting to get around. Smart chefs are putting it on their menus. Smart butchers are beginning to market it as something rather special. The winning "lamb" entry in this year's organic meat awards, organized by the Soil Association, was a leg from an animal three years old! It was roasted fast in a hot oven and served nice and pink, and it well deserved its gong.

Mutton will catch on, which will be a treat for all of us. But the biggest treat of all will always be the mutton you rear yourself.

starting a flock

To the uneducated eye, a sheep is a sheep. But as with pigs and cattle, there are actually dozens of different breeds, usually regional in their origins, and each suited to different kinds of pasture (though most are pretty adaptable). Physically, they can be very different from each other. In fact, it is often the discovery of a particularly distinctive breed, which is deemed to have more "character" than most, that charms the first-timer into giving sheep-keeping a whirl.

Hobby-farming sheep on a small scale is already a surprisingly popular enterprise – as you will quickly discover if you take yourself into the fold. The result is that in any given part of the country you are never far away from knowledgeable and, for the most part, friendly people ready to offer you help and advice. The best possible start you can have in sheep-keeping is to make firm friends with such a figure, and adopt them as your mentor. You then have someone you can turn to when you have questions and, most importantly, when you have problems. If they keep the same kind of sheep as you, so much the better, and if they sell you your stock in the first place, then better still – they have a vested interest in helping you get off to a good start.

It is worth taking a bit of time to choose a breed of sheep that you like, that will meet your needs, and that is suitable for the land you can offer them. But before you start talking to sheep people, and possibly acquiring their stock, you will need to know the very basic sheep vocabulary. Here is a brief glossary:

Ewe A mature female, usually a stock breeder
Ram A mature, physically intact male, usually a stock breeder
Lamb Any young sheep, especially those destined for early slaughter

Wether, or mutton wether A castrated young adult male being reared for meat
Chilver A young ewe that has not yet had a lamb
Hogget A yearling sheep of either sex (also "ewe hog" and "ram hog")

The most sensible way to start a small flock is to buy some ewes that have lambed before and will lamb for several years to come. The reasons for this are fairly obvious: if you are a beginner it is better to buy ewes that are not also beginners; on the other hand, you don't want animals whose lamb-producing days are all but over.

The best times of year to buy – not least because this is when others are inclined to sell – are, as with most stock, spring and autumn. In spring, you should buy ewes that have newborn lambs, whereas in autumn you should buy ones that are already carrying next year's lambs. It is hard to be absolutely sure of the latter, but any healthy ewe that has been running with the ram ought to be pregnant – and with a bit of luck she should have the raddle mark (see page 194) to prove she has been "tupped" (the shepherd's term for *mated*). Less scrupulous vendors have been known to rub a raddle mark on barren sheep – so beware!

As with most stock, the aging of sheep is done by looking at their teeth. A lamb will have eight immature teeth on the bottom jaw, which are used to cut grass by closing them against the "pad" (palate) of the toothless upper jaw. The middle two teeth are the first to grow, and at one year old these should be noticeably longer than the surrounding teeth. At two years, four teeth will be prominent, at three years six, and at four years she will have a full mouth of eight fully grown teeth. After five or six years, the teeth will be showing a considerable amount of wear and some may be missing altogether. Once their teeth are gone, sheep will not feed well and quickly lose condition – most are therefore sent for slaughter in their sixth or seventh year.

Good sheep are rarely given away, and you should therefore have no compunction about looking them in the mouth before parting with money for them. As well as aging them by the teeth, check that the teeth are nice and straight and come up level with the front of the pad. Teeth that stick out (overshot jaw) or do not reach the front of the pad (undershot jaw) will not last as well, and neither will their owner.

So, the best ewe to buy is one that is two or three years old and has already had one or two lambs. You should get two, three, or even four more lambing years from her. An older ewe whose teeth are in good shape may also be worth a look, but if she has already lambed three times you should be ready to haggle a bit.

Check the udder too. Hard lumps of tissue indicate that she has had mastitis, which means that one or both of her teats might have trouble delivering milk to her lambs. Of course, if you are buying in spring she should have her lamb(s) with her, and you should be able to see that they are suckling well.

How many ewes you buy depends on the amount of pasture you can offer them and how many animals you wish to kill each year. On summer grass, stocking rates are about five sheep per acre, but if you wish to overwinter your sheep without too much extra feeding you should think in terms of about half that. If you wish to kill two or three animals a year for your own use, and are not particularly concerned about selling any meat, then four ewes is probably a good number to start with. They should give you three to six lambs in the spring, and you can keep one or two ewe-lambs as replacement stock. Or you can start by buying two or three ewes and two or three chilvers from the same flock. The chilvers (who may be the daughters of the ewes) will lamb in your second spring of sheep-keeping, by which time you will not be such a beginner and they will have seen from the senior ewes how it is done. A larger flock will allow you to keep on top of a larger amount of grazing, but will require more concerted management. You will need to sell your excess lambs or use them for barter.

what breed?

With over fifty different breeds registered in the U.K., it's almost impossible to answer this question. There is nothing wrong with allowing personal prejudice to be your guide, and buying sheep that you simply like the look of – provided they are suitable for the land you can offer them. Don't put soft sheep (i.e., down and short wool breeds) on very tough hill country – they won't be able to hack it and will quickly lose condition. The reverse, on the other hand – mountain and hill breeds on lush lowland pastures – is not necessarily a problem, although they may run to fat and therefore not breed as well as you had hoped. They may also be more averse to handling and less respectful of fencing than soft southerners!

If you are not attracted by the physical characteristics of any particular breed, but simply want some good, healthy sheep that will be largely trouble-free and provide you with strong lambs, then one of the commercial breeds of ewe will suit you very well. These are hybrids, usually known as half-breds or mules. The most popular are those known as North of England mules. Scottish and Welsh half-breds are particularly popular in their respective countries. Mules and half-breds don't breed true, so they are always crossed with purebred rams – the most popular being the black-faced Suffolk or the white-faced Texel.

If you do go for something a little more fancy, there is still much to be said for starting with a breed that is, if not common, at least locally popular. You will then be able to tap into a good support network of fellow enthusiasts. My own choice at River Cottage has been the Dorset Down. I love them to look at, I love them to manage, and I love them to eat. And I have been positively spoiled with support and encouragement from local enthusiasts. Best of all, borrowing a ram is never a problem . . .

tupping

Ewes cannot lamb on their own. They need servicing – tupping – from a reliable ram. If your breeding ewes number in double figures, you may want to keep a resident ram. When buying a ram you can age him in the same way as a ewe. You should also check his testicles with your hand. There should be two of them.

But good rams are expensive, and if you have only half a dozen sheep, then buying and maintaining a ram will put the economics of your little flock out of kilter. What you need is a helpful sheep-keeping neighbor who is prepared to lend you a ram for long enough to be sure that all your ewes have been tupped – though this can be a problem if you have chosen some exotic rare breed of sheep and want to keep the bloodline pure. How far will you have to go to borrow a ram? There is another problem. Those who own rams keep them primarily for the benefit of their own ewes. They won't want to lend them out until they are confident that all their own ewes have been covered. This may not be until sometime in November, which means that your lambs may not be born until April (gestation time is a few days short of five months). That is not necessarily a problem. But if anyone else has gotten ahead of you in the queue, then you may be pushing your lambing period impractically late. Book early to avoid disappointment. And if you can get the ram in by Bonfire Night, or November 5 (traditionally for lambs on April Fool's Day), then so much the better. Those managing commercial flocks like early lambs (often from late February), so they may be a good bet for a timely loan of a ram. Incidentally, the going rate around our way for the loan of a ram is a bottle of good Scotch if you pick it up yourself, two if it's delivered.

It is traditional to ensure the fertility of your ewes by "flushing" the flock before putting in the ram. This means putting them on your poorest pasture for three or four weeks, then putting them on very good pasture, and introducing the ram a few days later. This technique works by appealing to the ewes' sense of maternal opportunism: a lush period after a lean period says to them "Get pregnant quick, while the going's good." It is also believed to increase the chances of twin lambs.

Unless you happen to have two or more suitably sized paddocks, the easiest way for small farmers to flush is by strip-feeding (see Organic Pasture Management on page 196 for more on this), using an electric fence to concentrate the ewes on a small patch of pasture while giving a neighboring patch a chance to grow. You can artfully boost the "good" pasture by feeding them a little extra hay, sheep nuts, or rolled barley. Whether you flush or not, the bottom line is that fat sheep are less likely to conceive, so make sure they are not too pampered in the month running up to tupping.

Those used to loaning rams will normally be happy to deliver him wearing a "raddle" – a harness that holds a large piece of colored crayon across his chest. This leaves a clear mark on the backside of any ewe that he has tupped. When they've all been done you can send him home again, although sometimes not all ewes will have got pregnant from one tupping. Ideally, you should leave him in for another three weeks (the ewes come into season every sixteen days) to pick up any ewes who failed to conceive the first time around. A ram will not tup a ewe who is not in season (i.e., those already pregnant), so by changing the color of the crayon you can see who gets done the second time around and mark them down as late lambers.

Commercial breeders use a veterinary technique called "sponging" to bring on estrus in ewes. This can be useful to concentrate lambing times, but it is probably not worth worrying about for the small-scale sheep-keeper. Not quite knowing is all part of the fun.

lambing

Having said that, you must be ever vigilant come lambing time. All lambs are precious – they are what your sheep-keeping is all about – and in a small flock they are doubly so. When lambing time is a week or two away, start inspecting your ewes twice daily. Watch, and occasionally feel, their udder. It will, quite suddenly sometimes, inflate with milk. In this state, a ewe is probably only days – a week at most – away from lambing. If the weather is very cold, bring your ewes into their shelter, laid with fresh clean straw, at night. The shelter should also be prepared as a lambing area, with hurdles ready to make small compartments, one for each ewe and her lamb(s).

But until they lamb, let your ewes out again for all but the chilliest, wettest days, so they can graze and move around. Leave the gate to the shelter open, so that they can go in there to lamb should they choose. Once lambing starts, you should be looking out for your ewes every few hours. The first sign that lambing is actually under way is usually a colored bag of opaque fluid hanging down from the back end of the ewe. The lamb will not be far behind.

Most ewes can manage quite well on their own, but occasionally they will need help. Normal delivery is front feet first, then nose. If you see front feet poking out, or front feet and a head, but nothing further happens within, say, half an hour, you should pull the lamb out. This may be easier in a confined space, and ideally you should walk the ewe into a pen or your prepared lambing area, then help her to lie down. But if she is already lying down in some corner of the field, don't try to move her. The feet of a lamb are very slippery, and a soft cord can be tied around them to help your grip (old neckties seem to be a favorite tool for this job). Ideally, time your pulling to the ewe's pushing – pull down, toward the ewe's back feet, as well as out – and never pull up or you may damage the lamb.

As the lamb's body emerges, support it with your free hand. When it is half out, a gentle twist as you ease the lamb downward may help to relieve the pressure and free the back end of the lamb. As soon as the lamb is out, check that it is breathing. If necessary, wipe away any mucus from the nose and mouth. Then gently poke a piece of hay or straw into the nostril to encourage the lamb to sniff or sneeze, which should help to trigger normal breathing. If there is still no sign of life, hold the lamb up by the back legs and gently massage its throat with finger and thumb, then try the nose tickle again. As soon as you are confident that all is well, present the lamb to its mother and back off. She should lick it for a while, and pretty soon it will stand up and find her teats. If this hasn't happened within an hour of its birth, some gentle coaxing may be required. Place the ewe's teat inside the lamb's mouth. If it doesn't start to suck, trying milking a little milk onto your fingertips and getting the lamb to suck your fingers. A lamb should respond quickly to the taste of milk and soon get the hang of suckling.

If things are still not working, the problem may be with the ewe – check by gentle squeezing that the milk is flowing. Once the lamb is sorted and settled, keep an eye on the mother to see if there is another to follow.

The above procedure is for assisting a ewe with a normally presented lamb. Unfortunately, there are also a number of abnormal presentations. There is the breech birth, where the lamb comes out tail end first. There are lambs presented with their heads thrown back. And things can get especially complicated where twins and triplets are concerned. There are procedures for the correction and delivery of all malpresented lambs, and they involve putting your hand inside the vagina of the ewe and back into the womb, where the position of the lamb can be corrected. Such maneuvers are best not practiced by the novice without the attendance of a vet or experienced stockperson (i.e., your local sheep-keeping mentor, as suggested above). Such a figure should be alerted some days before you are due to start lambing, and called immediately if you suspect a ewe is having difficulty delivering.

Sooner or later, you will have to learn to deal with such problems yourself. With that in mind, there are two excellent ways to gain valuable lambing experience before your flock is due to lamb. One is to book yourself on a registered lambing course, which you can do through your local agricultural college. The other is to assist a local sheep farmer or small farmer who is lambing before you. I would urge you to do either or both of these things. When it comes to lambing, there is no substitute for hands-on experience.

Once you have delivered healthy lambs to healthy ewes, you can stop worrying for a while. Your ewes will thrive on the spring grass and their lambs on mother's milk. If the weather is very cold or wet, keep mother and lamb in their shelter for a few days until the lambs look strong. Keep mum well fed with hay and/or a little concentrate, and give her fresh water twice a day. Remember, what she really wants to do is get out there on that spring grass, so as soon as the weather improves let her out with her lamb. You can always bring them in again at night.

Two or three days after lambing, your ram lambs should be castrated. Tails on all lambs can be docked, if you like – it will definitely help prevent fly strike (see page 198). For both castration and docking, the rubber band method is the best – and the most humane. Kits can be bought from an agricultural supply store, but get the vet, or your sheep mentor, to show you how to do it the first time.

Lambing can be tense, and it is certainly tiring. Occasionally, it can be heartbreaking. But when it's finally over, and your flock, perhaps now doubled in number, is out on the spring grass, the satisfaction is immeasurable. It's what being a small farmer is all about.

bottle-rearing orphan lambs

It is extremely rare to lose a ewe who has successfully lambed. "Orphan" lambs are usually the weakest of three triplets, who are losing the battle to share two teats. Very occasionally, a twin or even a singleton may be rejected by the ewe, or simply fail to find the teat. Such lambs can be hand-reared by bottle, using a formula powder bought specially for the purpose. Goat's milk can also be used, but they do not do well on cow's milk.

Lambs reared in this way will grow up thinking they are humans – affectionate creatures who like physical contact and may therefore be emotionally difficult to take to slaughter. Female orphans can, however, go on to be good breeding ewes. Because they are expensive and time-consuming to feed, and usually lag behind the rest of the flock in terms of weight gain, orphans can often be bought very cheaply from commercial sheep farms. They can be a good way for the smallholder to build up a flock, or, if your own lambing has not gone well, to fatten up a couple of lambs to plug the meat gap.

shearing

I have one simple piece of advice on shearing – get somebody else to do it. The pros make it look easy, but personally I make it look very difficult indeed. Of course, in the long term, it would be an excellent idea for any sheep-keeper to know how to shear his or her sheep. If you wish to learn, find someone who can do it well and who also has the patience to teach you – this probably excludes most professional shearers.

Shearing should be done in the spring and not later than early May if you wish to avoid the dreaded fly strike (see page 198). At this time, professional shearers – either locals or (often in Britain) Antipodean itinerants – can be hired and will usually charge by the sheep. Small farmers are not usually their top priority, and you may have to pay a little extra to get a small flock done. For this reason, it may be a good idea to make friends with your shearer – flagrant offers of cold beer usually help.

organic pasture management

Whether you are grazing sheep, cows, or a combination of both, it is the quality of your pasture that ensures the good health, and ultimately the good meat, of your stock. Simply having these animals on the land is itself your basic management strategy. But in terms of the way you allow your animals access to grazing during the year, you have a number of options.

If you want to maximize your stocking density over the period of lush summer grass growth (at two or three times the standard annual stocking rate of about one cow and five sheep per acre), that's fine. But come late autumn and winter, when the growth slows down, you will have to feed your animals with extra hay, roots, or cereal. This can, of course, be bought. However, if you want your pasture and stock to be self-supporting, there is another way: understock your acreage during the summer months and set aside the extra land for growing the winter feed. The easiest crop, of course, is hay: you do nothing except cut the grass. But you can also set aside a strip of land to grow stubble turnips or other fodder beets for your animals.

It is impossible to give a set formula for such pasture juggling, but it is something you will get a feel for over time. At the outset, the best policy is to err on the side of understocking, and making more hay than you think you need for winter.

Unless your land is divided tidily into small fields, the easiest way to move your stock from one patch to another, and indeed to set aside a patch for hay, is by the use of a battery-powered electric fence. These are

easily set up and dismantled, and both sheep and cattle learn to respect them pretty fast. At River Cottage, my one long field, of a little over five acres, is divided into notional thirds. During the winter, the stock has the run of the entire field. When the spring grass gets going, they will be confined first to one third, then to another, then to another. From, say, mid-April, one of the thirds is set aside for a June hay harvest. The other two thirds are then alternated. A few weeks after the hay crop, when the grass starts to return, the hay patch comes back into play as grazing. This system, which basically treats your pasture as a staggered crop of grass, is known as "strip-grazing," and there are many variations on the theme. The basic idea is simple: every bit of land gets an occasional break, for a few weeks at least, to allow some growth to come back.

All pasture that is constantly or regularly grazed will start to lose condition, as the underlying soil loses nutrients to the demands of the grass. The quick-fix solution to this problem is artificial fertilizers – chemical nitrates that are spread on the pasture annually – and many farmers have a rather gung-ho attitude on their use. You can often spot a field that has been blitzed with nitrates: the grass is suspiciously even in length and almost artificially dark green in color. Clover leaves among the grass are unnaturally large. Pasture treated in this way becomes more and more dependent on its annual nitrate fix. Eventually, even heavy doses will not do the job, and the land has to be ploughed up and reseeded.

There is a gentler, nonchemical, organic alternative to pasture management, which has to be preferable for the small farmer. It involves maximizing the pasture's natural ability to self-sustain. The use of clover, a vitally important leguminous plant that actually fixes the natural nitrates in the soil, is part of it. Feeding a small amount of clover seed to your stock is a cunning way to increase the clover presence in your pasture. The seed comes out intact in the dung, which not only gives it the moisture to germinate and the nutrients to thrive but also acts as a mulch to suppress the growth of the grass beneath. Annual harrowing, with a large, spiky chain dragged behind a tractor, will help tear out tired grass and make way for new growth, as well as distributing your animals' nutrient-rich dung more evenly through the field. Occasionally, a larger dose of purchased manure will be necessary to give an extra boost to soil nutrition. To find out more about organic pasture management in the U.S., contact the National Sustainable Agriculture Information Service (*www.attra.ncat.org*).

maintaining health

Sheep are susceptible to a number of health problems. For trouble-free sheep-keeping, regular inspections and routine preventative treatments are essential. Here are the most common problems and the best ways to deal with them:

Feet Sheep's feet can suffer various problems, especially on damp lowland pastures (hill sheep are not so bad). They need to be trimmed regularly – say, three or four times a year – and this is a job you should learn to master; again, get your sheep mentor or the vet to show you how. As well as trimming, regular footbaths should help eliminate the risk of foot infections. You can buy portable footbaths and use hurdles to contain your sheep long enough for them to stand in them properly – a few minutes is prescribed for most treatments, and simply running them through it is not enough.

Even with these preventative measures, you may still find a sheep limping from time to time. The cause is likely to be some form of foot rot, a general term for bacterial infections in the feet, or "scald," a specific foot injury caused by long grass chafing between the claws. Both problems can be treated with antibiotic spray. Nevertheless, call the vet to examine your first lame sheep and talk you through the diagnosis and treatment. Thereafter, you may be able to deal with the problem yourself.

Worms Sheep can be infected by various parasitic worms, especially on land that does not get a decent break (ideally, a continuous six months every two years or so) from being sheep-grazed. The simplest solution is regular preventative worming. Ewes should be wormed roughly three times a year, including six weeks before lambing, then again two or three weeks after, and again in midsummer. Lambs should not be wormed until they are at least eight weeks old, thereafter with the rest of the flock.

Fly strike This is a very nasty infestation of maggots from eggs laid by greenbottle flies, which usually affects the dirty rear end of a sheep around and under the docked tail (undocked tails are even more at risk). Dipping used to be the preventative treatment for this and various other ailments, but it is a lot of trouble and not very practical for the small-scale sheep-keeper. (Organic sheep-keepers regard dipping as an unnecessarily high dose of rather dangerous chemicals.) For undipped sheep, timely shearing, before the weather gets too hot, is very important. A preventative spray can be administered at the same time, which generally lasts a couple of months. The warm summer months are the riskiest time, so inspect your sheep regularly then. If caught early, fly strike can be effectively dealt with by a spray treatment. But if left unchecked, it will kill a sheep in the most horrible way imaginable.

There are a number of other problems you may encounter, including pneumonia and something called "twin lamb disease," which sometimes strikes ewes expecting multiple lambs in the month before lambing. I shan't go into detail over these, but it is useful to be aware of the general symptoms of an unwell sheep: standing apart from the rest of the flock (though this is normal during lambing); intermittent head shaking or twitching (not just occasionally but repeatedly); coughing or wheezy breathing. These are all signs that an animal is not well, and the vet should be called at once.

The best preventative is general vigilance. Spend time with your sheep, daily if possible, even if only for a few minutes. Sheep are easily trained to come to a bucket of feed, when most can be scratched and petted a little. Sheep that enjoy or at least tolerate being handled are easier to inspect, easier to treat when they are ill, and ultimately easier, physically if not emotionally, to take to slaughter.

slaughter

You can kill a lamb or mutton wether at any time, but personally I favor late spring and late autumn. In the autumn I will kill either a mutton wether of around eighteen to twenty months or a large lamb of six to eight months, and in spring a wether of just over a year (once it's had a couple of months of good grass). In either case, I like to hang the carcass for at least a fortnight, ideally three to four weeks for the older animals. This usually means calling in a favor from a friendly butcher so I can keep the animal hanging in his cold storage. I've pushed this one a bit far over the last couple of years, and am beginning to think it's about time I got my own cold storage! A tall fridge of the kind that doesn't have a freezer at the top, with the shelves removed, might be just about big enough to hang a lamb carcass in.

There is no reason not to kill sheep in the winter months. They may be slightly out of condition, depending on your winter feed policy, but they will still be good eating. If you are singling out an animal for winter killing and you really want it fat, you can lure it into the shed for a daily treat of extra hay or oats for three or four weeks prior to slaughter. The advantage of winter killing is that you may be able to hang the animal yourself, if you have a reliably cool outbuilding to do the job in. (In the U.K., you could even kill the animal yourself, and spare it the stress of the slaughterhouse, but you will need to know how to skin it, and you will not legally be able to sell, or even barter with, any of the meat.)

If you go to the slaughterhouse (see Pigs and Pork, page 144, for more details of this), wait while your animal is done, then take home the soft offals and the tongue, plus the blood if you want to make blood sausage (see page 162). Fresh lamb's liver is delicious, as are the heart and kidneys – try the recipe for Lamb's Kidneys with Chile and Lentils on page 248. The lungs (lights) can be used for making haggis.

It is much easier to butcher a lamb than a pig or a cow, and it is well worth getting a butcher to show you how it's done so you can do it yourself next time. Even on a summer's day, if you take delivery of an animal straight from cold storage you should be able to get it done in a cool outbuilding, or even a large domestic kitchen, before the meat gets dangerously warm. But you do need proper equipment: a butcher's block, a meat hacksaw, and very sharp knives. A sheep's carcass is easily divided, either into two symmetrical halves (sides), or, as displayed on pages 204–205, across the body into legs, saddle, and shoulders. I prefer the latter approach, as it can be done on a (large, sturdy) table without hanging up the carcass. But however you make the first cuts, the resulting pieces are fairly easily subdivided, to give you the cuts favored by the butcher (and his customers). I divide my mutton into the traditional lamb cuts and treat them in much the same way.

UHY

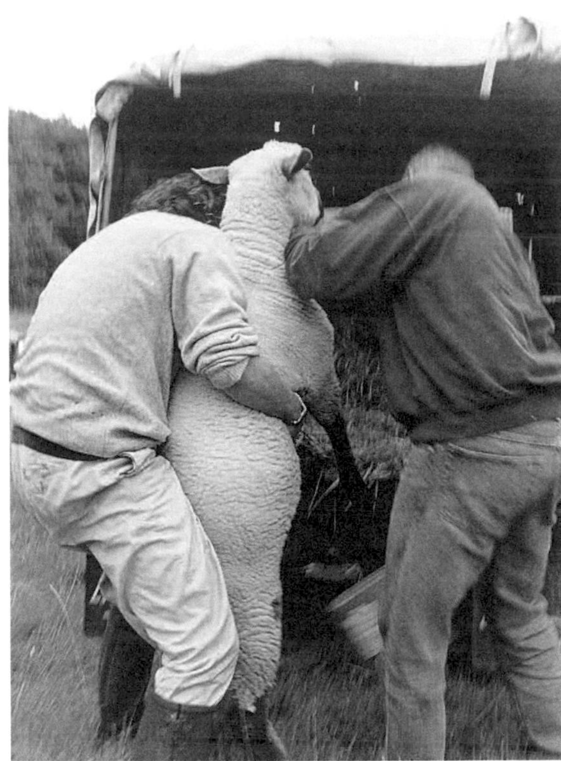

the cuts

Leg (A) Everyone knows what a leg of lamb looks like and everyone knows, more or less, how to cook it. There is no doubt that a good leg of lamb makes a fabulous roast (and a good leg of mutton an even better one). But an overcooked roast, dry and gray, is a terrible disappointment. I do not insist that those who like their lamb well done are gastronomic philistines, but I do think that they would enjoy it all the more if it were succulent and tender to boot. Roast your leg fast and hot, and it will never take more than an hour and a half. Even if the very center of it is a tiny bit pink, there will still be plenty of well-done meat all around it, and it will be moist. Alternatively, try the recipe for Leg of Mutton or Lamb Baked in Hay (see page 245), which remains fabulously moist even if you cook it for half an hour longer than I suggest.

The sirloin end of the leg is the equivalent of the rump of beef, and in the butcher's shop is most often encountered in the form of lean and generous *sirloin chops*, which are slightly more expensive than loin chops or neck cutlets. In fact, the *sirloin* can also yield a fantastic small roasting joint, especially from an older animal, which can be cooked either on or off the bone. Or it can be left on the leg for a giant roasting joint.

Shank (B) The shank can be left on the leg, but it is a tough and sinewy piece of meat that is transformed by slow cooking on the bone. I usually remove and freeze the shanks of my sheep along with the shins (see below), and when I kill the next one I have eight pieces altogether – perfect for long, slow cooking with wine and stock vegetables. You end up with a muttony equivalent of an oxtail stew, meltingly tender meat falling off the bone and into a rich, winey gravy.

Loin (C) A loin is the ovine equivalent of the sirloin of beef: it is where *loin chops* are taken from, but it is also, in its entirety, a prime roasting cut. Two loins still joined together, one from each side of the animal, is called a saddle. It makes a spectacular roasting joint, especially from a good mutton wether – see the photograph on pages 206–207. With more lean meat than a single leg or shoulder, a whole roast saddle of a good-sized mutton wether should serve up to ten people. Roast a saddle loosely covered in well-buttered foil in a preheated 375°F oven for 1 to 1¼ hours. Then remove the foil, turn the oven down to 350°F and cook for a further twenty to thirty minutes. Baste the joint regularly during this last half-hour, if possible with a cup of good strong stock made from lamb bones and trimmings. The shorter cooking times are for smaller lamb saddles and/or pinker meat.

Rib (D) The best end of the neck is the part that is most remote from the head. A versatile cut, it is trimmed and subdivided in various ways. It can be cut into tidy little *rib chops*, which, when trimmed of excess fat and the chine bone to which they were attached, are known as *cutlets*. When the little nugget of meat from a single cutlet is removed and further trimmed, you have a *noisette*. If all eight cutlets on a best-end joint remain attached, you have a joint called *rack of lamb*.

As with the saddle, two racks of lamb, one from either side of a carcass, can be left joined together and deftly cut by the butcher to form a circle, then trimmed so you have that great party piece known as a *crown roast*. Those miniature paper chef's hats to go on the end of each chop are a traditional decoration – but, I'd like to think, an optional one!

Breast (E) An underused and underrated cut, the breast (which includes part of the belly) is not ideally suited to the Jack Sprats of this world, being undeniably fatty. But rolled up around a dry stuffing (say, of bread crumbs, garlic, and herbs) to absorb the fat, it makes an economical roast, with lots of tasty crispy bits on the outside and succulent, naturally basted meat on the inside. A more time-consuming, but ultimately very rewarding, treatment is the French method known as Sainte-Ménéhould: the breast is simmered very gently for a couple of hours with stock vegetables, then the ribs are pulled out and the meat is pressed under a weight and left until cold. It is then cut into fingers, which are tossed in melted butter, coated in bread crumbs, and crisped up in a very hot oven. Delicious served with Salsa Verde (see page 118).

Shoulder (F) Wrongly thought of as the poor man's leg, the shoulder offers plenty of tender meat, albeit in a form that is not as easy to carve. One way around this is to bone and roll it to make a *shoulder roast* – it roasts particularly well in this shape, as some of the plentiful fat on the shoulder is rolled into the inside of the joint and bastes it from within. My favorite way of doing it is as weeping lamb (see page 250).

Neck (G) As the neck continues toward the head, the meat becomes tougher and a little more sparse, but no less tasty. Fileted neck makes great stewing meat, but I think it is even better if cooked on the bone. Lancashire hotpot is perhaps the most celebrated use of neck and is properly made with cross sections of ¾ inch thick, with the bone still in. Cooked long and slow enough (for about two hours at 300°F), the bone will be tender enough for those so inclined to chew it up with everything else. My personal favorite treatment for this underrated bit of the animal is Ivan's Neck of Lamb with Lemon and Thyme (see page 244).

Fore shank (H) The top part of a sheep's foreleg, which you will encounter on a roast shoulder as the thin, tapering bit that becomes very crisp, is barely recognized as a cut in its own right. But saw it off, bag it up, and freeze it along with the shank, then use in the same way – see shank, opposite.

Note If you have a big oven, the whole front end of a lamb (i.e., cuts D, F, and G) can be left whole as a wonderful and generous roasting joint, with crispy bits, lean bits, and fatty bits to satisfy every large family's tastes. It is, however, the devil to carve.

Ground lamb If you want to save freezer space, and have ready supplies of delicious lamb mince on hand for moussakas, shepherd's pies, and the like, middle neck, scrag end, and the leaner parts of the belly can all be ground and bagged up for the freezer.

livestock | poultry

If you want to make a modest start in the business of keeping livestock, chickens are an obvious option. You may never graduate to ducks, geese, or turkeys, let alone sheep, pigs, or cattle, but once you have started to keep a few chickens – once you have seen the color of home-laid yolks, and tasted the best-ever breakfast egg – you may find it very hard to give them up. And if you explore the further possibility of raising chickens for the table, you will find it equally hard to roast a bird that has not run free, fed on corn, and generally had the kind of life a chicken was born to have.

You don't need much space to keep chickens. I know several townies who do it, including a bachelor friend of mine who has only two (keeping a single chicken is not kind). They only have about three yards of his tiny garden to run in, but they are a cosseted pair who seem to enjoy life, and between them they give him a breakfast egg every single day of the year. And he gets enough two-egg days to keep him in scrambled eggs whenever he has company – as he often seems to on a Saturday morning. Whether or not the promise of fresh-laid eggs for breakfast is a factor in this, I couldn't say.

It may seem a cop-out, but my chapter on poultry will not be giving instructions for keeping ducks, geese, or even turkeys. I'm afraid I have no experience of any of these things, as yet. And although I'm guilty of pretending to be much more of an expert than I really am in a number of places in this book (no, I won't confess where, but you can probably guess), I feel I have to draw the line somewhere. As it happens, I'm thinking of getting some ducks next spring to raise for the table. To be honest, I don't fancy geese much, as they make such a racket. I love to cook and eat them, though, and I usually buy mine direct from local producers. They take orders for Christmas weeks, or even months, in advance, so book early to avoid disappointment.

buying eggs

If you don't and can't keep chickens, you may still wish to eat eggs that have been laid by contented hens leading a natural, stress-free life. Unfortunately, these are not as easy to find as one would hope. One thing is sure: any eggs that do not say "free range" on the box, or otherwise describe in detail the method of production, have been laid by chickens who lead a very miserable life indeed. They are fed on rubbish, too – usually fish meal, which sometimes imparts a distinctly fishy taste to the eggs. But even if it doesn't, that's hardly the point. The only way you could justify buying such eggs is if you either thought that chickens were incapable of feeling stress and pain or you simply didn't care – which would make you either an idiot or a heartless soul. It amazes me that the battery chicken means of egg production is still legal. But I'm afraid it is us, the consumers, who are allowing it to thrive. The good news is that the battery system is scheduled to be phased out completely by 2012 in E.U. countries. And good riddance.

The bad news is that the words "free range" don't offer much guarantee of a happy life for the layers either. E.U. regulations set standards that are pitifully low.[15] They impose no limit on the number of birds that can be kept in a "free-range" chicken house, and that number is sometimes in excess of 5,000. Technically, the birds may have access to some scrawny patch of ground outside, but often they live their short, stressful lives in complete ignorance of this. "Free-range" layers can also legally be subjected to long periods under artificial light to increase their productivity; they can be routinely debeaked (beaks are clipped to prevent stressed and frightened birds damaging other stressed and frightened birds); they may be fed as inappropriately as any battery hen; and their feed will often include a yellow dye to give the yolks that "free-range" look.

Of course, not all free-range producers are so cynical. But it's hard to tell from a box of "free-range" eggs just how free the chickens have ranged. So where does that leave the consumer? Scratching around for other clues, I guess. Some of the supermarkets have independently come up with labels that offer some reassurance on issues of both welfare and feed. I have seen labels touting the merits of "four-grain" eggs and "barn-laid" or "perchery" eggs, which typically mention some of the good points of the hens' lifestyle, such as that they are free to "perch and scratch" or "dust bathe." It all sounds very reassuring, but the labels tend to keep quiet about such factors as stocking density and mortality rates.

As mentioned in the Pigs and Pork chapter, in Britain there is also the RSPCA's label, Freedom Food, which has been adopted by a number of supermarkets.[16] It certainly adds a feel-good factor to the packs on which the symbol is flashed. But the scheme has been widely criticized for not going far enough: eggs can sport the symbol even though they have been laid by chickens that have never seen natural light. Debeaking is also allowed.

As ever, the most meaningful labels you can turn to are those that award eggs organic certification. The welfare requirements required by organic bodies such as the British Soil Association far outstrip those of any other label.[17] They insist, among other things, on sensible rates of stocking, fully organic cereal-based feeds, and no debeaking. An honorable mention must also go to Martin Pitt, who supplies free-range eggs to a number of independent retailers nationwide. His eggs are not organic, but the chickens are naturally fed and are free-range in the genuine sense of the phrase. He sports an admirably honest label that actually shows a picture of his own hens enjoying a stroll outdoors.

Labels aside, there are still many country households keeping a few happy hens in the yard or garden, fed naturally on grain and vegetable scraps from the kitchen, who produce a few more eggs than they need. If you can't quite bring yourself to join this happy throng and get your own hens, you may nevertheless find some egg-producing neighbors who will give you first crack at their surplus.

buying chickens

When it comes to buying a chicken for the table, the statutory labeling is marginally more helpful than it is with eggs. Once again, it would be a mistake to interpret the term "free range" as implying a bird that has led a happy or natural life. But in Britain it is subdivided into more rigorous legal categories: "traditional free range" and "free range, total freedom." Only the latter offers the kind of assurance that really means free range to me – that the chickens have complete and unrestricted outdoor access all the time. On the other hand, no guarantees are given about feed – and even if such a chicken is sold as "corn fed," one should assume that the routine use of antibiotics and other drugs is standard.

Again, the organic alternative offers the best possible assurances about the lifestyle and diet of the bird you are going to eat, and in most cases you will definitely taste the difference.[18] Farmers' markets are a good source of organic chickens, as well as birds that may not be organic but are nevertheless genuinely free range. The people selling them are the people who reared them, so they should be able to answer all your questions about how it was done.

As for the many millions of broiler chickens that cannot even muster enough welfare points to call themselves free range, I'm afraid you would be right to assume the very worst.[19] They are so abused that a high proportion of them don't even make it to the supermarket. I know from my own investigations that many of the biggest broiler producers allow for a routine premature mortality rate of a staggering 20 to 30 percent. These immature chickens, which often die, lemminglike, in massive suicidal "smothers," are shipped out for pet food, fertilizer, or maggot farming (yes, maggot farming). Those responsible for these atrocities might be less adept at bringing smiles to the faces of boy scouts if the boy scouts knew what had happened to the chickens they're eating. Not so bootiful.

keeping chickens

If you're going to take the plunge and get yourself some chickens, the first thing to decide is where you are going to keep them. The more space you can devote to them, the happier they will be. Personally, I like to see my chickens break into a trot every now and then, so I would never give them a run less than five yards long, even if it was only a couple of yards wide.

Obviously, edges and corners of your garden will be easiest to fence off and are likely to be your best options. But you need to be aware that chickens not only eat grass, they also scratch and peck the ground. Even a small number of birds will reduce a small patch of grass to bare earth in a month or two. This is not necessarily a problem, provided you keep your chickens supplied with scraps of green vegetables as a substitute for the fresh grass they would otherwise eat. But eventually the same patch of bare earth may start to harbor parasites and disease. A chicken run that is scratched to bare earth should be relieved, and reseeded, annually.

Better still, you can avoid the bare-earth syndrome with a simple two-patch rotation: divide your allotted grass down the middle with a low fence and move the hens from one side to the other every two or three weeks. If you can organize your fencing so that the henhouse straddles both strips, so much the better. Alternatively, if you are keeping a small number of hens, the traditional portable ark may be a neat solution. This is a small, pitch-roofed henhouse with a wired-over run attached. Stout handles at either end mean that two people can easily move the structure from one patch of ground to the next. This is a simple way to give chickens constant fresh grass even within a very limited piece of ground. Of course, it places a strict limit on the extent to which the birds can roam, but the regular fresh grass will go a long way toward compensating for that, and provided you keep the numbers well within the figure recommended for the ark, you will have happy, healthy hens.

Chickens don't have to be kept on grass, although it is what they like best. If you are going to put them on hard ground, such as concrete or paving, you should lay down a generously thick layer of wood or bark chips, or straw. This can be changed every few months and incorporated into your composting system (see page 42). And again, fresh greens should be part of your feed program, to compensate for the lack of grass.

Chicken wire, as the name suggests, is the preferred form of fencing, although a fence that will keep chickens in is a very different matter from a fence that will keep foxes, and other predators, out. To be completely predator-proof, you would need fencing so high, dug in so deep, made of wire so strong, that you would inevitably be installing an expensive, time-consuming eyesore. Best to concentrate on making your henhouse predator-proof. If you are vigilant about shutting up your hens at night and do not let them out too early in the morning, then foxes should not give you too much trouble. Further suggestions for deterring predators, including the ladder system, appear below.

If you have the space, you may not wish to confine your chickens at all. Provided they know their henhouse is home, and will come to it at night, they can run free during the day. Such farmyard birds are the happiest of all hens – they can go where they please. But be aware that one of the places they most like to go is a well-ordered flower garden or vegetable patch – and they will find plenty to eat in either. Even if you don't want to fence your chickens in, there are sure to be areas you will want to fence them out of.

housing

Simplicity is the order of the day, and anyone half-competent with a hammer and nails should be able to knock up a small henhouse for up to half a dozen birds. Any weatherproof, windproof structure with space to perch and to nest will keep your chickens happy. A wooden box about a yard square, with a slightly sloping roof, is about as basic as it gets. It should be deep enough to run perches at least 8 inches above the floor, with a decent bit of headroom for a tall chicken on the highest perch. Shallow nesting compartments can run along one end of the box, although these are often arranged as a bolt-on affair at the back of the henhouse. This has a twofold advantage. It makes them attractively dark and snug for the chickens on the inside (they like a bit of privacy). And it makes for easy egg-collecting access, via a simple hinged flap, for the people on the outside. Both nesting boxes and the floor of the henhouse should be lined generously with straw or wood shavings.

The henhouse should be raised a couple of bricks above the ground, to protect the wooden floor from damp and frost and to discourage rats, who otherwise greatly favor such opportunities to make a new home.

Ready-made henhouses of all shapes and sizes can be bought at agricultural suppliers and large garden centers, but shop around, as they can be pricey.

the ladder system

The idea of the ladder system (which I found out about from a photograph sent to me by someone who had seen it used in France) is to give unconfined chickens a degree of independence and safety from predators, without the need to round them up and shut them in on a nightly basis. And they can also come out when they choose in the mornings. In theory, this allows your chickens to be completely free range, running in a field alongside your other livestock. I will explain my cautious use of the phrase "in theory" in a moment.

The basic system becomes instantly comprehensible from the picture opposite. The henhouse is raised on an old telegraph pole or similarly stout support to a height of about two yards. Access to the henhouse is via a ladder, made by knocking simple steps into a long, stout pole. The design of the ladder is deliberately crude and rickety: a chicken will be able to use it but a fox or badger (the two most common chicken killers) will not. The nesting box, and therefore the eggs, are accessed by means of a conventional, person-supporting, ladder, which is laid on the ground when not in use.

Chickens do not automatically grasp the ladder system. They have to be trained. The way to do this is to shut them in the henhouse every night to begin with. Open the door in the morning, and they will soon learn that the only way down to the ground is by means of an awkward shuffle down the ladder, or a kamikaze leap from the top step. Over time they will come to prefer the shuffle. Teaching the upward climb requires a little more patience. Food, as ever, is the best incentive to learn. If the only grain available is placed on a temporary platform nailed to one of the lower steps, they will soon learn how to climb a step or two to get to it. Once they have mastered this trick, raise the feed platform a couple more steps. Eventually, usually within a week, they will be happy to make the climb all the way to the top – and happy to go into the high-rise henhouse to lay.

Note that the ladder system works best when it is the only housing system on offer. No matter how adept your chickens become at climbing the ladder, once you offer them any low-rise alternative they may soon come to prefer it, and you will be back to nightly shut-ins.

In terms of security from predators, I am convinced the system is effective – at least against badgers and foxes, during the hours of darkness. Of course, some foxes are cheeky enough to take a chicken in daylight hours, and unconfined birds are at the greatest risk. But in such cases, you are likely to lose solitary birds. The idea of the ladder system is to avoid the wholesale slaughter that almost always happens when a fox gets into a conventional chicken run. I am not so sure that my high-rise henhouse is mink-proof. I haven't suffered a mink attack since I did the conversion, but I have a hunch they could climb my ladder if they wanted to.

In terms of the ideal of running the chickens among all the other livestock, the practice isn't quite as satisfactory as the aforementioned theory! The problem is the uncontainable desire of sheep and cows to rub themselves against anything that promises to scratch their itches. As far as they are concerned, the henhouse ladder might have been designed for no other purpose. Such a deliberately delicate structure lasts about four rubs from a cow or five minutes of determined work by a sheep before it comes crashing to the ground. There is a solution, but it is an ugly one: a ring of electric fencing, under which the chickens can happily run, and through which even the itchiest cows and sheep are reluctant to venture.

the human hair deterrent

We may be straying into old wives' territory here, but the theory at least makes sense. Foxes and other predators are smart enough to realize that people are their biggest enemy. Consequently, they tend to avoid them. Our scent is a dead giveaway. We are an odorous species at the best of times, and our hair is a particularly rich source of the oils and secretions that give us our scent. So, balls of human hair, stuffed into stockings and tied onto the fence of your chicken run, should keep the bad guys away.

choosing chickens

When choosing your chickens, before you can answer the vital questions of how many and what breed, there are a number of other things to think about:

How many eggs do I want? The best layers, which are specially bred hybrids, really will lay an egg almost every day. It is worth thinking about how many eggs you use every week (are you a keen maker of cakes and custards, or just a "scrambled eggs for Sunday supper" kind of person?). Fresh eggs from happy hens are lovely things to give away, or even barter with, so it's fine to produce a few more than you need. But don't go mad. Get as many chickens as you think you need for a generous personal supply of eggs, plus one more for luck.

Do I want to eat my chickens? If the answer is no, my question is "Why not?" Okay, not everyone wants to wring a chicken's neck and put it in the pot, and a lot of people do keep chickens only for their eggs. But almost everyone likes eating chicken, and once you have your own hens you are only a few steps away from the tastiest roast chicken you'll ever have. If I'm convincing you here, then at least one of the hens you buy should be a "dual-purpose" bird – a bulky breed that puts on a bit of meat and is therefore suitable for eating. It will, of course, lay eggs as well – that's how your roasters get started.

The main reason for not raising at least a few birds for the pot is if you think your circumstances do not realistically allow you to keep a rooster. For example, if you're a light sleeper who doesn't like to wake up early in the morning. Or if you have neighbors like that.

Do I want a rooster? If the answer to the above question is yes, then so is the answer to this one. Contrary to the beliefs of most ignorant townies – no offense, I used to be one of them – you don't need a rooster for your chickens to lay eggs. Not even to get started. Hens will start laying spontaneously as soon as they are sexually mature (about four months).

A rooster is recommended not just for providing fertile eggs but for keeping the hens in good order. Hens will fight, especially if space is restricted or if newcomers join the flock. Roosters will tend to keep the peace.

If, on balance, you would rather not have a rooster, but you would like to get some eggs fertilized, either for replacement egg-laying stock or for table birds, you can sometimes borrow a rooster short-term, as you would a ram or a bull. In Britain, contact your local branch of the Poultry Club. In the U.S., contact a national or local poultry organization (*www.poultryhelp.com*), or simply ask around among local fellow poultry-keepers. If you want a rooster of a specific breed, most traditional breeds have their own enthusiasts' association and should be happy to help. A good rooster will cover all your hens within a day or two, and their eggs will be fertile for up to a week after his visit. If you can leave him in for two or three weeks, so much the better.

Do I want bantams? The bantam is a miniature chicken that comes in many different breeds, often following the same breed patterns as ordinary chickens. They lay smaller eggs and are slightly wilder and more independent by nature – happily roosting in trees or on the beams of outbuildings. These charming creatures particularly suit those who wish to let their poultry run free. (If you keep only bantams, and can offer them some suitable outbuilding to perch and lay in, then you don't need a henhouse at all.) Another reason they are popular is that they make excellent broody surrogates, sitting better and tighter on the eggs and earlier in the year than most chicken varieties. Some breeds of bantams, such as the Light Sussex, make good eating, but they will always be on the small side.

These are some of the considerations. Here are some of the breeds that can help you meet your needs.

good layers

Isa Brown Also known simply as a "brown hen," this is the hybrid that has been bred to produce brown eggs in battery cage systems. Given a proper home, it will be a happy, healthy hen, and a fantastic layer. Some barely miss a day all year, though like any hen most will tend to slow down in the winter (officially, they average 200 to 250 eggs per year). They are very light-bodied birds and therefore poor eating.

Welsomer Best known for the beauty of its egg, which is the darkest brown of any hen, and often very large. They are charming, hardy birds that lay well through the summer, less well in winter. They average about 100 eggs per year. Pure-bred Welsomers are light birds, but if crossed with a meaty rooster, such as a Light Sussex or Indian Game, they will eat well.

dual purpose

Cuckoo Maran A large, hardy bird that matures slowly but is ultimately excellent eating. Reasonable layer (average 100 eggs per year).

Light Sussex A much-favored dual-purpose bird, hardy and strong. Good layer (average 100 to 150 eggs per year).

Dorking One of the oldest breeds around, possibly introduced by the Romans; tough, adaptable, and excellent eating. Poor layer (40 to 50 eggs per year).

Wyandott A charming white powder puff of a bird, with a good weighty carcass under the fluffy feathers. Poor layer (40 to 50 eggs per year).

Dumpy A favorite Scottish breed, hardy and tolerant. Good eating. Poor layer (40 to 50 eggs per year).

Rhode Island Red The bird from which the brown-egg-laying hybrids originate. A good layer (100-plus eggs per year) and a reasonable eater.

especially for eating

Ross Cobb The Cobb (often known as a Ross Cobb, as the frozen food company of that name did much to develop the breed) has been bred to put on weight at an astonishing rate. Most of the factory-farmed broilers are variations on the Cobb theme. Intensively farmed, with the "benefit" of drugs, hormones, and dubious feeds, they can be table-ready within twelve weeks of hatching. They also have a tendency to "go off their legs": putting on so much breast weight without being able to develop their leg musculature effectively cripples them, and they cannot even walk. But restored to a more natural environment, Cobbs do well and make good eaters. Crossing Cobb hens with roosters of a hardier dual-purpose breed, such as the Light Sussex or Maran, makes for a slower-growing, more balanced eating bird.

Indian Game A "fancy" breed related to the fighting cock, the Indian Game is a big, powerful bird. The purebred bird is indeed slightly gamy, and tougher than a normal eating chicken, but those who like the idea of a real farmyard bird to roast will love it. Indian Games cross well with other, softer eating hens, such as the Wyandott and Ross Cobb. The Indian Game cock was the chosen "stud" in my attempt to breed fine table birds. After a couple of dud roosters, I finally got hold of a "perfomer" that crossed with my own mixed flock of dual-purpose birds. All the resulting birds were good eating. The Wyandott cross was the best, closely followed by the Dorking. I was recently informed that I should have done this the other way around, using Indian Game hens to cross with roosters of other dual-purpose breeds.

hatching eggs under the hen

If you want to hatch some eggs, either to replace your egg-laying stock or to raise some birds for the table (or to do a bit of both), and you have a rooster, the simplest thing is to let nature take its course – almost. Sometime during the spring and summer, one or more of your hens is sure to go broody. This is easy to spot, as she will sit tight on one of the nesting boxes and move only with great reluctance. If you try to lift her, she will give a rather irritable broody "cluck." And you may get a peck or two.

She is ready to hatch some eggs, and if you want her to do so, it is best to transfer her to a broody coop – a private little nesting box with its own wire-enclosed run, like a miniature version of the ark described on page 211. In here, she will not be disturbed while she looks after her eggs.

Put ten to twelve fertile eggs under her (if you have a rooster, and he has been seen to be doing his job, you can assume that almost all your eggs will be fertile). They need not be freshly laid. But if you are storing eggs with a view to incubating them, or waiting for a hen to go broody, they should be stored on their side and turned 180 degrees every day. Fertile eggs may remain viable, but dormant, for weeks – but it is best to use eggs that have been laid within the last ten days for incubating. Once they go under the broody hen (or in the incubator – see below) they start to develop, so that eggs laid a week or more apart should still hatch out at the same time. Of course, the eggs you place under the broody hen need not necessarily be her own but those you would most like to hatch – i.e., your prime eating crosses, if you have gone in for a bit of that. Bantams, especially the Silky, are widely thought to make the best broodies and mothers, and many poultry enthusiasts keep a few just to do this job.

She should now sit tight until her eggs are hatched. She must have fresh water and some grain in her run, and once a day you should shoo her off the eggs to make sure she has a drink, a nibble, and ideally a crap (most broodies are very clean, and rarely get their eggs messy). Make sure she is back on the eggs within half an hour (physically put her back on if you have to).

In order not to waste time trying to hatch infertile or "addled" (dead) eggs, after eight or nine days of incubation they can be "candled" to check the developing embryo. In a dark place, or at least shaded from direct sunlight, hold each egg up to a bright light from a torch or candle. If the egg is fertile, you should see a distinct webbing of veins inside the shell. If not, it is a dud and can be discarded. Note, however, that some dark brown eggs are difficult to see through. If in doubt, leave the eggs under. If in the end they don't hatch, you can simply throw them away.

In twenty-one days the eggs will hatch. The chicks will have the safe run of the coop, and their mother will keep them warm when they need it. They should be fed on commercial chick crumbs or a little whole-wheat flour mixed with warm milk. After a few days, and provided the weather is good, you can let mother and chicks out to run with the rest of the flock. She will show the chicks how to feed. But they should all go back into the broody coop at night, for the first month at least. Thereafter, they can take their chances with the rest of the flock. If you are rearing large numbers of birds you will, of course, have to expand your accommodation.

hatching by incubator

If you wish to control the timing of your hatch and you prefer to avoid the uncertainty of waiting for your hens to go broody, you can turn to the artificial alternative – an electrically heated incubator. These come in various shapes and sizes, and each will have its own set of instructions. Even the smallest ones will usually hatch about twenty eggs. Incubators can often be borrowed, or bought second-hand, so ask around and check the local papers if you want to pick one up cheaply. They are all different, so be sure to ask the previous owner exactly how it works.

A broody hen will turn her eggs from time to time, which is essential if the embryo is to develop properly. With artificially incubated eggs, you will have to perform this important task yourself (although some incubators have an egg-turning or tilt mechanism on a timer that does it for you).

If all goes well, and your machine is a good one, the eggs should start to hatch after twenty-one days. You must resist any temptation to "help along" the chicks as they struggle to chip away at their shell. Nor should you take off the lid to try to watch all the action. A constant temperature and humidity are very important, and any interference may result in lost chicks. Okay, you're allowed the occasional peek, but don't overdo it.

Hatched chicks should be left in the incubator until they are completely dry and fluffy – several hours minimum. They should then be transferred to a suitable first home: a stout cardboard box lined with several layers of newspaper is ideal. They don't need to eat for twenty-four hours but should have fresh water from the start. From day two they should be kept well supplied with chick crumblers. The warm temperature they are used to must be maintained for several weeks after hatching, until the chicks are "feathered up" (i.e., have real feathers instead of fluff), and the best way to do this is with the use of a heat lamp. They need to be weaned off the heat lamp gradually: start raising the lamp (i.e., lowering the temperature) after two weeks and after about four weeks switch off the lamp by day. By about six weeks they should be "off heat" – ready to face the real world. This is just a rough guide. The chicks will tell you if they need more or less heat – panting and lying with their wings stretched out if they are too hot, huddling together and shivering if they are too cold.

Once you've weaned your chicks off the lamp, transfer them to a covered run outside (near the other chickens if you like) for the day. But put them back in their box and bring them inside at night. After a couple of weeks of this routine, they should be strong and independent enough to fend for themselves and take their chances with the rest of the flock.

feeding your chickens

The healthiest diet for all chickens, both layers and eaters, is a simple mixture of grain, grass, and occasional fresh greens – particularly when the grass runs short (i.e., in a confined space or in winter). Trimmings and outer leaves from kale, cabbage, lettuces, spinach, bean stalks or pods, or any other greens that have gone over the top, plus any scraps and peelings from the kitchen, will all be avidly devoured. The birds whose eggs have the most beautiful yellow-orange yolks are the ones who get plenty of grass or greens.

For their main feed, the best mixture is a combination of flaked corn and whole-wheat grains. Grain for birds running free does not need to be measured. It can be constantly available and they will not overeat. Self-feeding hoppers are therefore very useful. (Unfortunately, jackdaws and other birds can also become quite adept at self-feeding, in which case the air gun may come in handy – see page 362.) They will also enjoy any leftover bread mixed with leftover milk, plus pasta scraps and any other cereal-based leftovers.

One thing all chickens need is calcium, to help make their eggs. Free-running chickens with a varied diet and plenty of greens should get all the calcium and minerals they need, but just to be sure you can place a little ground oyster shell in a tray in their run. They will take it as they need it. Grit is also required for proper functioning of the gizzard. This is likely to be present in sufficient quantities in most soils, but poultry grit can be bought and added if in doubt.

Chickens fed in this way will stay healthy and lay well. However, if you want to maximize egg productivity, you can buy some layers' pellets to include in their diet. It certainly helps them to get kick-started with their laying in the spring. I would use only organic pellets, as other kinds have unnecessary chemical additives. Some are intended to be a complete food, but I would always mix them fifty-fifty with a pure-grain feed, as I feel that's what chickens should be eating.

If you are raising some birds for the table, there's no need to force the pace at which they're feeding and growing. Indeed, it's precisely because you're not forcing the pace that they're going to be so tasty. But you can, if you like, give them a little bit of special treatment. If you wish to, separate your eaters from your layers. Take all the roosters and any hens that you don't want as replacement layers. Fix them up a run on fresh grass, and they will do really well. Give them a grain-based diet of wheat and corn, ideally organic, supplemented with any vegetable trimmings from the garden and kitchen. A high-corn diet will fatten them more quickly and give them that characteristic yellow fat. Spoil them mildly but not wildly.

chicken health

Unlike intensively reared chickens, who have a different disease for every day of the week, naturally reared birds have few health problems, especially if their patch is kept fresh by one of the rotation systems described above. To avoid a build-up of parasites, their accommodation must also be kept clean. The floor of the henhouse should be lined with straw or wood shavings, which will make it much easier to clean. Scrape out the henhouse every two to four weeks, depending on the number of birds using it, and spread fresh straw or shavings. The old stuff makes fantastic fertilizer. Sling it straight on the compost heap.

killing a chicken

People like to say that certain breeds will be ready to kill after a certain number of weeks, usually fourteen, sixteen, or eighteen. It's all relative. A chicken is not ready to kill for the table until you think it is. Pick it up, feel its weight, and feel its breast. If it feels tempting, then you should kill it if you want to. You may not be able to resist at ten weeks, when it is still only a poussin. Or you may want to wait until it is super-heavyweight at thirty weeks. Any older than this and most chickens would be in the "old-boiler" rather than "good-roaster" category.

When you decide to kill a chicken, catch it as quickly and efficiently as you can – a long-handled fisherman's landing net can be invaluable for this – and take it out of the vicinity of its fellows immediately. Then wring its neck. For a right-hander, this is most easily done by holding the bird's feet in your left hand so it hangs head down, breast toward you, back away. Grab the head with your right hand, so the neck is between your two middle fingers and the head is in the palm of your hand. Pull the head down while rotating your wrist upward, so the neck is stretched tight and the head pulled back. You should hear a crunch as the neck vertebrae break. As you can probably guess, there's a knack to this. Always err on the side of firmness, to get the job done. It's not the end of the world if its head comes off (although in a sense I suppose it is).

Ideally, a chicken should be bled: as soon as you've killed it, slit its neck vertically, i.e., from above the crop (the pouch where it stores undigested food) to the base of the beak. Let it hang above a bucket for half an hour, then pluck it (as for pigeon, see page 373) while it is still warm – the feathers come out easily this way.

drawing

The neck, head, and feet of a chicken are usually removed before sale, but when you kill your own bird you don't have to do this. In many parts of France, they are roasted along with the rest of the bird: the head is tucked under the wing, and the feet are singed on a gas flame to burn off the tough scales, then popped into the cavity of the bird with the claws. They are taken out for the last twenty minutes or so to get nice and crisp. Done like this, head and feet are among the most fought-over bits of the roast.

If you don't want to try this, you should at least keep the head, neck, and feet, along with the giblets, for making stock.

The giblets are removed by drawing (i.e., gutting) the bird: make a small incision between the vent and the tail (just below the parson's nose), then cut carefully around the rectum to detach it from the rest of the body. With a bit of practice, you can do this in such a way that when you lift it out, most of the guts will come away with it, followed by the gizzard, heart, liver, and lungs. But initially you may have to delve in for a bit of a scrape. Once you've gotten everything out, give the inside of the bird a good wipe.

Identify the heart and liver and put these on one side: fried or grilled, they are delicious plucker's perks. Identify the gizzard – a large, gristly muscle below the crop – rinse it thoroughly, and put it with the neck and bits for stock. The rest of the guts should be thrown away. Then turn your attention to the neck end of the bird, and carefully scrape out the crop.

Once prepared in this way, a chicken can be cooked immediately, but it may be a little on the tough side. It will be improved if hung by the feet in a cool place for at least twenty-four hours – and not more than four days.

Then consult the recipes starting on page 252.

livestock recipes

roast belly of pork

serves about 10

This is one of my favorite pork dishes, and one of the simplest. The leftovers, served cold with a little homemade mayonnaise, are arguably even more delicious.

The thick end of the belly (last 6 ribs)
Fresh thyme leaves
Salt

Score the skin of the belly, in slashes about ⅜ inch apart, with a sharp knife (a box cutter is surprisingly handy) and rub vigorously with salt and thyme leaves, getting them right into the cracks.

Roast in the oven at 425°F for the first 30 minutes, then turn the temperature down to 350°F and cook for a further 45 minutes, until the juices run clear when the meat is pierced with a skewer and the crackling has crackled to an irresistible golden brown.

Remove the crackling before carving, then cut the joint into thick slices. Serve each person one or two slices of meat with a good piece of crackling. I like to serve this roast with mashed potatoes (see page 114) and some simple, lightly steamed greens such as savoy cabbage, spinach, or curly kale.

tartiflette

serves 4

This is my adaptation of a classic dish from the Haute-Savoie. It's a great stand-by when there's nothing much left in the fridge but you can somehow rustle up a bit of bacon, an onion or two, a couple of spuds, and some cheese. Traditionally, it should be made with Tomme de Savoie, a sweet, nutty cheese that melts beautifully into a stringy goo. Gruyère, Emmental, or Beaufort would be an excellent substitute, but even a Cheddar or Edam would do.

A little oil for frying
About 8 ounces good bacon or pancetta, coarsely diced
2 onions, sliced
1 pound parboiled or leftover potatoes, sliced
⅔ cup heavy cream
About 8 ounces good, meltable cheese (see above), sliced

Heat the oil in a large frying pan and cook the bacon in it until slightly crisp. Add the sliced onions and cook gently until soft and sweet. Add the potatoes and cook for a few minutes longer, until the potatoes are lightly browned and the onions slightly caramelized. Transfer to an ovenproof dish. Pour over the cream and lay the slices of cheese on top. Bake in a hot oven until the cream is bubbling and the cheese melted. Serve at once, with good red wine and crusty bread. (That's not a serving suggestion, that's compulsory.)

glazed baked ham with spiced figs and parsley sauce

There are few more spectacular things to put on a table than a whole ham on the bone glazed with an almost black crust of sugar and mustard. It deserves very special accompaniments: sweet, spicy poached figs cut the saltiness of the ham (prunes or pineapple are traditional alternatives), and a real parsley sauce, creamy and soothing, mollifies the whole combination into the ultimate comfort food.

9- to 18-pound ham, Wiltshire or Suffolk cure, ideally on the bone (see pages 159–160)
A few stock vegetables, e.g., onion, carrot, and celery
10 black peppercorns
3 to 4 bay leaves
5 to 6 sprigs of thyme
A small bunch of parsley stalks
Real Parsley Sauce (see page 119)

FOR THE SPICED FIGS
1 pound dried figs
½ cup light brown sugar
6 cardamom pods
1 teaspoon coriander seeds
1 teaspoon mustard seeds
1 small dried chile

FOR THE GLAZE
1 tablespoon English mustard
1 cup brown sugar
½ cup rum or whisky
15 to 20 cloves

Put the ham in a large bucket of cold water to soak 24 to 48 hours before cooking (depending on the size of the ham and the length of the original cure – i.e., saltiness). Change the water every 12 hours.

Rinse the soaked ham and place it in a large stockpot. Cover with fresh cold water and add the stock vegetables and peppercorns, plus the herbs, tied in a bouquet. Bring the water to a boil, then reduce the heat, cover partially with the lid, and simmer very gently for 4 to 5 hours. If after an hour of simmering the water tastes unpalatably salty, discard it and replace with fresh boiling water – this will help to reduce the saltiness of the finished ham.

While the ham is simmering away, separate the dried figs if they are stuck together in a block and rinse in cold water to remove any rice flour. Put them in a heatproof bowl and pour over just enough boiling water to cover them. Cover the bowl with a plate and leave for 3 to 4 hours.

Remove the ham from the pot and allow it to cool slightly. Meanwhile, place the mustard and sugar for the glaze in a small mixing bowl and add just enough of the rum or whisky to mix it to a thick, sludgy paste. Carefully cut away the skin of the ham, leaving a smooth, even layer of fat over the meat. Place the ham in a large roasting pan, then score the fat layer with the point of a sharp knife in a coarse diamond pattern, but not so deeply as to go right through the fat to the meat. Slosh the remaining alcohol over the fat and then spread the glaze mixture all over it in an even layer. Stud the fat with cloves at regularly spaced intervals. Roast the ham in an oven preheated to 350°F for 1 to 1½ hours, until the glaze is a dark, golden-brown, bubbling crust.

Meanwhile, strain the water in which the figs have been soaking into a clean saucepan and add the sugar and spices. Stir over low heat to dissolve the sugar, then bring to a merry simmer and cook until reduced to a light syrup. Add the figs and poach gently in the syrup until completely tender. Remove the chile – the other spices can be left in. If the syrup gets too thick, add a little warm water.

Carve the ham while piping hot from the oven and serve on hot plates with 2 or 3 figs, a spoonful of their syrup on the meat, and a generous pool of parsley sauce on the side. There won't be much room on the plate for it, but since this meal should be a feast in the best sense, have also on the table a large dish of creamy mashed potatoes (see page 114), some lightly steamed cabbage tossed in butter and sprinkled with a few caraway seeds, some plain boiled carrots, still a bit crunchy, lightly buttered and tossed with a few mustard seeds and just a pinch of brown sugar, and some good English mustard.

Ray's liver pâté

This simple recipe was given to me by Ray Smith, who butchers my pigs for me. A whole pig's liver can weigh up to 4 pounds, but doesn't freeze well, so unless you have a huge appetite for fresh liver it's good to have a recipe that offers a variation on the theme and extends its life by a week or two. A whole calf's liver will present you with a similar problem and also makes an excellent pâté. Pig's liver is so cheap that it's well worth buying just to make this dish, but it must be *really* fresh.

This quantity makes 2 pâtés of just under 2 pounds each. I usually eat one fresh and freeze the other.

2 pounds very fresh pig's or calf's liver
1 pound pork belly
1 onion
3 to 4 garlic cloves, crushed
1½ cups fresh bread crumbs
2 tablespoons chopped fresh sage
A wineglass of port or brandy
A good pinch of nutmeg
Salt and freshly ground black pepper
8 to 10 slices of bacon to line the dishes, "stretched" with the back of a knife (optional)

Peel any membrane from the liver and trim out any tough ventricles. Put the pork belly, onion, and liver through a grinder on the coarse plate, or process together in a food processor – but not too finely, as you want your pâté to have some texture. Transfer to a bowl, add all the other ingredients, and mix well.

Line two 4-cup ovenproof dishes or terrine dishes with the bacon (or simply grease them with a bit of butter or lard). Divide the mixture between them and cover with greased foil. Place the dishes in a hot-water bath and cook in the center of a moderate oven (350°F) for about 1½ hours. The pâté is cooked when it comes away from the side of the dish and is firm to the touch.

Allow to cool in the dish, then refrigerate and turn out when thoroughly chilled. The pâté is best if kept for a day or two before serving.

Chinese-style pig's trotters

serves about 10

I picked up this recipe from the delightful Rose Billaud, with whom I cooked on *TV Dinners.* Not everyone likes pig's trotters, or thinks they like them. This is the perfect dish to make enthusiastic converts of skeptics. For those who enjoy Chinese sweet-and-sour flavors and the sticky-fingered pleasures of gnawing meat off the bone, this recipe is an absolute delight.

Make sure that you remove all the hairs from the trotters – shave them with a razor if necessary.

4 pig's trotters
2 tablespoons sunflower oil
1 pound shoulder or spareribs of pork, cut into large cubes, skin still on
1-inch piece of fresh ginger, crushed
4 large garlic cloves, crushed
Salt
6 tablespoons dark soy sauce
3 tablespoons light soy sauce
¼ cup packed light brown sugar
¼ cup malt vinegar or white wine vinegar

Using a meat cleaver, split each pig's trotter into 4 or 6 pieces (i.e., once down the middle, then once or twice across). Your butcher could do this for you.

Heat the oil in a large, heavy pan, add the pig's trotters and pork shoulder or spareribs, and fry until browned. Add the ginger, garlic, and a little salt and continue to fry to release the aromatic flavors. Add the soy sauces, sugar, and vinegar and just enough water to cover. Bring to a gentle simmer, cover with a lid, and let cook until the trotters are tender (2 to 2½ hours). Check occasionally to make sure the liquid is not too low.

When the trotters are cooked, remove all the meat (i.e., trotters and shoulder or spareribs) from the pan with a slotted spoon and put in a bowl on one side. Continue to simmer the cooking liquid gently until it has reduced to a rich, syrupy texture. Return the meat to the pan and heat through in the sauce.

The trotters can be served immediately, though the flavor will continue to improve if they are left overnight in the refrigerator. They can then be eaten cold, in the jelly in which they have set, or reheated.

Serve with plain boiled rice and simple stir-fried vegetables (such as crunchy green beans with carrots and green onions), or as a course in any Chinese-style banquet. Eating with the fingers has to be allowed, as does spitting out any knuckly pieces of bone from the trotters!

headcheese

serves about 10

This classic dish uses all the meat from the head of the pig, including the tongue, cheeks, and ears (unless you want to keep these for Crispy Pig's Ears, see page 233). The natural gelatin in the bone of the head should be enough to set the headcheese in its own jelly, but an extra pig's trotter will make sure.

I usually have the brains removed from the head before making headcheese and fry them up with a bit of sage as chef's perks, but they can be included in the headcheese if you like.

1 pig's head, quartered (brined for up to 24 hours if you like – see pages 158–159)
1 or 2 pig's trotters
2 onions, peeled and quartered
A large bundle of fresh herbs – parsley, bay leaves, thyme, marjoram
A cheesecloth bag of spices (1 to 2 teaspoons each of cloves, coriander, and mixed peppercorns)
A handful of chopped parsley
Juice of ½ lemon
Salt and freshly ground black pepper

Place the quartered head, trotters, onions, bundle of herbs, and bag of spices in a large stockpot. Cover with water and bring slowly to a gentle simmer. For the first half hour of cooking, skim off any bubbly scum that rises to the surface. Cook, uncovered, at a very gentle simmer for about 4 hours altogether, until all the meat is completely tender and coming away from the bones. Top up the pan occasionally as the water level drops (remove the ears after about 2½ hours if you want to use them for Crispy Pig's Ears).

When cooked, lift out the meat and let cool enough to handle. Pick all the meat (plus the brains, if you haven't already removed them), skin, and fat off the head bones; it should fall off quite easily. Remove any bristly hairs with tweezers. Carefully remove the tongue in one piece, peel off the skin, and set aside. Coarsely chop all the bits of meat, including the fat and skin, and toss them together with the chopped parsley and the lemon juice. (Everything except the bone and bristles can go into a headcheese, but if you want to make it less fatty, just discard some of the really fatty pieces at this stage.) Season to taste with a little salt and pepper.

Place a layer of this seasoned mixture in a terrine dish at least 8 cups in capacity, or in 2 or 3 smaller ones. Place the boiled tongue on top and then finish off with the remaining meat mixture.

Remove the herbs, onions, and spices from the cooking liquid and strain it if cloudy. Boil until reduced by about two-thirds and then spoon about 6 tablespoons of this gelatin-rich liquid over the terrine to help it set as it cools. Put a plate or board on top, weight it down, and put in the refrigerator to set.

Serve cold in slices, with pickles and gherkins. Or make a delicious *salade de tête* in the style of the best French charcuteries: cut the headcheese into 1-inch dice and toss with cold cooked green lentils, chopped parsley, and a mustardy vinaigrette.

rillons

Rillons are the big brother of rillettes, being whole rather than shredded. Another way of describing them would be confit of pork belly. Like duck or goose legs in the classic confit, large cubes of pork belly are cooked slowly in seasoned fat (in this case, largely their own) and, once cooled, can be stored for months beneath a layer of this fat. Personally, I've never been able to store them for more than a couple of weeks without eating them all. Luckily, the leftover lard, highly seasoned by the cooking process, is great for roast potatoes.

The quantities in this recipe are deliberately approximate. It is the process and principles that are important. The garlic is optional, because I once left it out by mistake and rather liked the result: the thyme and bay and the natural porky flavor shone through.

2 to 4 pounds pork belly (ideally from the thick end, the ribs removed)
A generous spoonful of lard
Some sprigs of thyme
2 to 3 garlic cloves, whole but lightly crushed (optional)
A large glass of red wine
A small glass of water
Sea salt and black pepper

Cut the belly into large cubes, about 2 inches, leaving the skin on. Heat the lard in a large pan and throw in the meat. Brown fast and hard, turning occasionally, then transfer to a large ovenproof dish in which, ideally, the pieces should fit fairly snugly without being piled on top of each other. Use 2 smaller dishes if you're doing a really big batch. Throw in all the other ingredients, including a generous sprinkling of salt and plenty of black pepper, and place the dish in a hot oven (400°F). Check on them every 8 to 10 minutes, turning the pieces when you do so. After about 30 minutes, the fat rendered from them should be at least halfway up the pieces, which will be getting very nicely browned. Turn the oven down to 325°F and cook the rillons for at least another hour, turning them once or twice during that time. You can't really overcook rillons (although you can burn them to a crisp if you forget to turn the oven down), but they are basically done when the skin is tender enough to chew without *too* much effort!

You can eat rillons hot, but they are at their best cold, from the fridge in fact. Cut each rillon into 3 or 4 slices and sprinkle with a few extra flakes of salt. Eat just as they are, with a glass of rosé or a kir.

Rillons can be stored for months, like confit of duck or goose, if completely covered in their own fat and kept in sealed jars in a cool place. Alternatively, if you think you're going to use them up within a couple of weeks, keep them in a sealed plastic box in the fridge. Leave any fat that clings to them, as it will help to keep them moist. If you don't like eating cold fat, just wipe it off before you slice them.

The fat strained off from the rillons will set to form a highly flavored lard (because of the garlic and herbs). If you're not using this to store the rillons, keep it in a sealed tub in the fridge and use it for roast potatoes, fried bread, etc.

crispy pig's ears with Hugh's tartar sauce

The slightly gristly texture of a pig's ear may present a problem for the squeamish, but the mustard and crumb treatment turns it into a real delicacy. My own cheaty recipe for tartar sauce finishes it off nicely. Serves about 10 as a snack or canapé, 4 to 5 as a starter.

2 pig's ears, simmered gently with the head (see Headcheese, page 230), then removed from the liquid and cooled, with any hairs removed
2 to 3 tablespoons English mustard
Fresh bread crumbs for coating
3 tablespoons butter, melted

FOR HUGH'S TARTAR SAUCE
2 generous tablespoons mayonnaise (ideally homemade)
1 to 2 hard-boiled eggs, finely chopped
1 tablespoon coarsely chopped parsley
2 to 3 gherkins, finely chopped
2 teaspoons capers, finely chopped
1 teaspoon English mustard

For the tartar sauce, combine all the ingredients thoroughly in a small bowl.

Slice the pig's ears lengthwise into finger-sized pieces. With a knife or pastry brush, give them a light coating of mustard, then roll them in bread crumbs and brush or drizzle with the melted butter. Place on a baking sheet and bake in an oven preheated to 425°F for 30 to 40 minutes, until crisp and golden. Serve immediately, with the tartar sauce.

variation This is a classic from the Parisian brasserie, La Coupole, which also serves the tail in the same way. Take a whole cold cooked ear (or tail), as above, but forgo the mustard and bread crumb treatment and simply cook it on a hot griddle, turning once or twice, until it is blistered and blackened. Serve whole, with the tartar sauce. One ear serves one as a main course. See the picture on the next page. You'll either fancy it, or you won't.

steak tartare

A really good steak tartare is one of the treats I look forward to when I first get to grips with a very well-hung side of my own home-reared beef. It can be made from rump, sirloin, or tenderloin – though personally I don't really think the latter has enough flavor for it. Steak tartare is like a Bloody Mary – no two aficionados can agree on how it should be made. I therefore prefer not to premix a steak tartare but to present all the traditional flavorings on the table for everyone to fix their own. Tartare virgins can be shown the way by more experienced diners.

Rump or sirloin steak, about 5 ounces per person
1 egg yolk per person
Some shallots, finely chopped
Some salted capers (preferable to vinegar-pickled, but these will do), rinsed and coarsely chopped
Some gherkins, finely chopped
Flat-leaf parsley, finely chopped
Dijon mustard
Worcestershire sauce
Tabasco sauce
Salt and freshly ground black pepper

Trim the meat of all fat and sinew, then process or grind it finely. The best way to do this is to scrape the meat with the blade of a large, sharp knife. It's a labor of love, but it does remove any sinews. Shape the meat into patties, one per person. Make a dip in each patty and tip the egg yolk into it. Place all the other ingredients in individual bowls and take them to the table. Encourage everyone to mix their own.

Steak tartare is traditionally served with either Melba toast or *pommes frites* (French fries).

cold roast beef with fresh horseradish sauce

serves 8 to 10

Beef cooked in this way ends up nice and pink in the middle, perfect for serving cold. Horseradish is easy to grow in the garden, but can also be found growing wild on roadsides and in empty lots (see page 390). A sauce made with fresh horseradish is a revelation – better than anything you can buy in a jar.

Olive oil
1 large piece (about 6 pounds) aged sirloin
Salt and freshly ground black pepper

FOR THE HORSERADISH SAUCE
A piece of fresh horseradish root, weighing about 6 ounces
1 cup crème fraîche
2 tablespoons strong English mustard
2 teaspoons white wine vinegar

Massage a little olive oil into the beef, then sprinkle with salt and pepper. Heat a little more olive oil in a large frying pan, place the joint in the pan, and fry, turning occasionally, until it is well browned all over. Transfer to a roasting dish and place in a hot oven (425°F) for 20 minutes. Turn the oven down to 375°F and cook for a further 11 minutes per pound.

Remove from the oven, cover with foil, and let cool at room temperature. Keep in a cool place until it is time for your picnic (or in the fridge, wrapped in waxed paper, not foil or plastic wrap, if you're keeping it for more than 24 hours).

For the horseradish sauce, wash and peel the horseradish root and grate it finely. Mix together the crème fraîche, mustard, and vinegar, then stir in grated horseradish to taste; you might not need it all, depending on how fiery you like your sauce. Season with salt and pepper.

Carve the beef into thin slices and serve with the horseradish sauce, some buttered brown bread, and various salads.

tail and tongue of beef with rich red wine sauce

serves 4 to 6

When I killed my first beef steer, a little Dexter, the tail wasn't really big enough to make a decent dish on its own, so I added the tongue to the pot and otherwise proceeded as if I was making a classic oxtail stew (a favorite of mine). The result was a revelation, the distinctly different textures of the meats combining beautifully. If you're a die-hard oxtail fan but not so keen on tongue, you could substitute a second oxtail for it. On the other hand, this might be the dish that converts you to the joys of tongue.

1 oxtail, cut into 1-inch lengths
1 whole fresh (not pickled) ox tongue
1 marrow bone (optional, but it beefs up the stock)
2 large carrots, coarsely chopped
1 onion, coarsely chopped
2 celery stalks, coarsely chopped
1 small turnip, coarsely chopped
Thinly pared zest of ½ orange
A bouquet of fresh herbs (bay, thyme, parsley stalks)
½ bottle of good red wine
Salt and freshly ground black pepper

The oxtail and tongue will both benefit from a couple of hours in the plain brine described on page 158, though you can omit this step if you are short of time. Then rinse well, and scrub the oxtail pieces under cold running water. Place them in a large casserole with the tongue, marrow bone if using, vegetables, orange zest, and herbs. Add enough cold water to cover everything completely and bring slowly to a simmer, skimming off any brown scum as it rises to the surface. Cover the casserole and simmer very gently (or put it in a slow oven, 300°F, if you like) for at least 3 hours, until the oxtail meat is tender and coming away from the bone and the tongue can be easily pierced with a skewer.

Remove the tongue and pieces of oxtail from the pot with a slotted spoon. Remove and discard the bone and the vegetables and strain the stock through cheesecloth or a clean cotton cloth into a clean pan. Add the wine and boil fiercely over high heat to reduce. Just how much you want to reduce the sauce is a matter of personal taste. I like it fairly intense and rich, but I stop short of those very sticky reductions that seem to be de rigueur in expensive restaurants. When you have reached the level of reduction you require, season to taste (do not do so earlier; if you judge the saltiness to be right before you reduce it, it will be far too salty afterward). Add a few more drops of wine if liked, to refresh the flavor.

While the sauce is reducing, remove the oxtail meat from the bones, peel the coarse skin from the tongue, and cut the tongue meat into 1-inch pieces. Return the tongue and oxtail pieces to the sauce and heat through thoroughly in the sauce, stirring occasionally and allowing it to bubble for just a couple of minutes.

Serve with Perfect Mash or Horseradish Mash (see page 114) and steamed seasonal greens such as spring greens, savoy cabbage, or kale.

tripe with chickpeas and chorizo

serves 4

The first time I took a beef steer to slaughter I forgot to ask for the tripe. I was kicking myself for weeks. This year I took the tripe home and rinsed it in the stream before giving it a thorough scrubbing under cold water. Home-prepared tripe like this is very tripey indeed. The recipe below can equally easily be made with blanched ox tripe from the butcher's or even the supermarket.

I discovered this dish in a restaurant in Buenos Aires and improvised it when I got home. The spiciness of the chorizo means that the distinctive flavor of the tripe is not *too* prominent. But it's still a dish for, shall we say, enthusiasts.

1½ pounds blanched beef tripe
2 tablespoons olive oil
2 garlic cloves, finely chopped
Two 14½-ounce cans of tomatoes
8 ounces Spanish chorizo, cut into slices ¼ inch thick
1 small onion, thinly sliced
1 large carrot, cut into thick matchsticks
⅔ cup white wine
1⅓ cups beef or chicken stock
2 teaspoons tomato paste
1 cup cooked chickpeas
A good pinch of cayenne pepper
Salt and freshly ground black pepper

Wash the tripe thoroughly and cut it into slices ¾ inch thick. Heat all but ½ tablespoon of the oil in a pan and add the garlic. Just before the garlic turns golden, add the tomatoes, then turn up the heat and cook until most of the liquid has evaporated and the tomatoes are reduced to a thick, pulpy sauce. Stir the tomatoes frequently while they are cooking to break them up and prevent the sauce from sticking to the bottom of the pan. When you think you cannot reduce them any further without risk of burning, remove from the heat and set aside.

Heat the remaining oil in a separate pan and fry the chorizo gently until it is lightly browned and some of the fat has been released. Add the onion and carrot and cook for a few minutes until the onion has softened a little.

Add the wine, stock, and tomato paste, bring to a boil, and allow to bubble vigorously until the liquid is reduced by a third. Then add the tripe, cooked chickpeas, cayenne, and tomato sauce, mixing them all together well. Turn down the heat and simmer gently for 25 minutes, uncovered, until the tripe is tender. Season with a little black pepper, and salt if necessary.

Serve in warmed soup bowls so that everyone gets plenty of sauce.

corned beef

Conventional wisdom has it that the best cuts for corned beef are bottom round and brisket, the former being much superior. I've experimented with various cuts, including the flank steak and even a large chunk of foreshank. They all work well, but in my book the fattiest, cheapest cuts, such as brisket, give the most open-grained texture in the end, which is what I like. The tongue, when salted, has a taste and texture all its own – perhaps better even than the muscle meat cuts. It can be served hot or cold with the sauce accompaniments recommended below. The coarse skin of the tongue should be peeled and discarded before the meat is sliced.

FOR THE BRINE

5 quarts water
2 cups light brown sugar
4 cups coarse sea salt
1 teaspoon black peppercorns
1 teaspoon juniper berries
5 cloves
2 bay leaves
A sprig of thyme
A bunch of parsley sprigs
¾ cup saltpeter (optional)

A 4- to 6-pound piece of beef (brisket, bottom round, flank steak, foreshank, or a whole tongue)
1 bouquet garni: 1 bay leaf, 3 or 4 parsley sprigs, 3 or 4 thyme sprigs, tied in a square of cheesecloth
1 carrot, chopped
1 onion, chopped
1 celery stalk, chopped
1 leek (white part only), chopped and rinsed
1 head garlic, cut in half across the middle

Put all the ingredients for the brine in a large saucepan and stir well over low heat until the sugar and salt have dissolved. Bring to a boil, allow to bubble for 1 to 2 minutes, then remove from the heat and let cool completely. Cover your piece of beef completely with the cold brine, weighting the meat down if necessary. Leave the meat in the brine for 5 to 10 days in a reliably cool place (joints of less than 6 pounds should not be left for more than a week or they will become too pickled).

Before cooking, removed the beef from the brine and soak it in fresh cold water for 24 hours, changing the water at least once. Then put it in a pan with the bouquet garni, vegetables, and garlic, cover with fresh water, and poach very gently on top of the stove – or in a low oven (300°F) if you prefer. A 6-pound piece of beef will take 2½ to 3 hours.

Serve the salted beef carved into fairly thick slices, with French lentils, Horseradish Mash (see page 114), and good English mustard. It is also excellent cold. Let it cool in the liquid, then take it out and store it in the fridge, wrapped in waxed paper. Serve with River Cottage Chutney (see page 117). Leftover corned beef makes great hash – see page 242.

corned beef hash

serves 4

This is a lovely, comforting supper dish to make with corned beef leftovers. It also works well with the meat from a leftover beef stew or pot-au-feu. For a real treat, serve with a fried egg on top and a pile of wilted spinach on the side.

About 2½ cups corned beef trimmings (or leftover stewed beef)
Beef drippings or canola oil for frying
1 large or 2 medium onions, sliced
About 1 pound potatoes, cooked and coarsely chopped
Salt and freshly ground black pepper

Chop the meat into fairly fine shreds. Heat the fat in a large, heavy frying pan and gently fry the onions in it until lightly browned. Throw in the meat and potatoes and continue to fry, turning or tossing occasionally, until everything becomes a bit browned and crispy (when it looks right, it'll taste right). Season with pepper (and salt if necessary, depending on the saltiness of your beef).

liver and bacon

This is a classic. You could use very fresh lamb's or calf's liver. Most beef liver, as sold by most butchers shops, is too coarse to serve in this way. But fresh liver from a fairly young beef steer of good quality (such as you might raise yourself) will be perfect. The liver in the picture opposite came from my first Dexter steer and was cooked on the day of slaughter. It was outstanding.

FOR EACH PERSON YOU WILL NEED
1 onion, sliced
Canola oil for frying
Bacon, 2 slices
A generous slice of liver, about ½ inch thick

PLUS
Perfect Mashed Potatoes (see page 114)
Dijon or English mustard, to serve

Cook the onion gently in a little oil until it is translucent and tender, then turn up the heat a little so that it browns slightly – be careful that you don't burn it.

At the same time, start frying your bacon in a separate pan. When it is done how you like it, transfer it from the pan to a warmed plate in the oven. Fry the liver in the bacon fat for 3 to 4 minutes (or more if you don't like it pink), turning once.

Serve the liver on the warmed plate with a spoonful of fried onions, the bacon, a good dollop of mashed potatoes, and some mustard.

Ivan's neck of lamb with lemon and thyme

serves 5 to 6

This recipe comes from a Russian friend of mine, Ivan Samarine. Its origins, he tells me, are Greek. One of the joys of eating it is mopping up the juices with bread. The combination of lamb fat, olive oil, and lemon juice, infused with thyme, is quite delicious.

Neck is the cheapest cut to use: the bones and fat all add to the flavor, and the meat will emerge quite tender at the end of cooking. Ask the butcher to cut the neck into slices 1 inch thick. Any really fatty bits can be trimmed away, but a certain amount of fat is crucial to the success of the dish.

¼ cup olive oil
2 pounds neck of lamb, on the bone, or chops from the neck, or a mixture of the two
Juice of 1½ lemons
7 to 8 sprigs of thyme
A wineglass of water or lamb stock
Salt and freshly ground black pepper

Heat the oil in a heavy saucepan or sauté pan. Add the lamb and allow it to sizzle and spit for a few minutes, turning until it is lightly browned all over. Add the lemon juice, thyme, water or stock, and some salt and pepper to the pan, then turn down the heat, bringing the mixture to a gentle simmer. Let simmer, with the lid on, for 45 to 50 minutes, until the meat is tender.

Serve with plenty of good white bread and perhaps a simple tomato salad.

leg of mutton or lamb baked in hay

Hay was originally used in cooking as an insulator. In grand Victorian kitchens, roasts were taken from the oven and packed in boxes lined with hay, to keep them hot when transported to shooting lunches and elaborate picnics. It was noted that the hay imparted a distinctive and delightful flavor – worth exploring for its own sake. Mutton or lamb baked in hay like this is not just tasty but unusually moist and tender.

A few handfuls of hay
½ cup (1 stick) soft butter
Leaves from several good sprigs each of rosemary, marjoram, and thyme, chopped
2 garlic cloves, crushed
Salt and freshly ground black pepper
1 leg of mutton or good-sized leg of lamb

Preheat the oven to 425°F. Choose a deep roasting pan, preferably with a lid (if you don't have one with a lid, you can use foil). Line it generously with loose hay, about 2 to 2½ inches deep.

Put the soft butter in a bowl, add the chopped herbs, garlic, plenty of black pepper, and a little salt and mix well. Smear in a thick and even layer all over the mutton or lamb. Place the meat on its nest of hay and then cover with the rest of the hay. Cover with the lid, or a double layer of foil wrapped well around the edge of the pan. Make sure there are no loose bits of hay poking out (they may catch fire).

Bake in the center of the oven for 2 to 2½ hours, depending on the size of the leg. Remove from the oven and let rest for at least 20 minutes. Then take off the lid, scrape away the blackened hay, and carve as usual.

Any juices from the pan can be poured off, skimmed of excess fat, and used for making gravy, although I tend to forgo the gravy, preferring to serve this dish with boiled flageolet beans heated through in the juices and fat from the meat.

lamb's kidneys with chile and lentils

serves 4

This recipe produces quite a fiery dish. If you prefer a milder piquancy, substitute 2 teaspoons of Dijon mustard for the chile. The whole dish is done quickly, over high heat, and should be ready in just a few minutes if the kidneys are not to be overdone. Always cook it at the last moment.

1 pound fresh lamb's kidneys
2 tablespoons olive oil
2 garlic cloves, finely chopped
1 to 2 small fresh red chiles, finely chopped
A wineglass of red wine
⅔ cup heavy cream
Salt and freshly ground black pepper
5 ounces French lentils, cooked until slightly al dente, then drained
1 tablespoon finely chopped parsley

Rinse the kidneys in cold water, then pat them dry and cut in half. Trim away any membrane from the outside and any gristly core from the center.

Heat the oil in a large, heavy frying pan over high heat. Throw in the garlic and, a few seconds later, the kidneys. Sauté for barely a minute, tossing them in the pan until they are nicely browned. Add the chile and pour in the wine – it should bubble vigorously and quickly reduce to about half its volume. Add the cream, a good pinch of salt, and a few twists of pepper, and boil to reduce still further. When the sauce is glossy and nicely coating the kidneys (not much more than 6 to 7 minutes after the kidneys first went in), add the lentils, mix well, and heat through for just 1 minute. Serve at once, sprinkled with the parsley. Plain steamed rice and a salad of watercress dressed only with olive oil and a squeeze of lemon make good accompaniments.

weeping leg of lamb or mutton with root vegetables

serves 6 to 10

In this dish, which I have adapted from a recipe of Sheila Kidd's at the Ark restaurant in Norfolk, a pan of root vegetables is enriched and flavored by the fat and juices dripping from the lamb, which roasts immediately above it. The result is that your vegetables end up almost like a gratin, infused with the flavor of meat. Delicious. Serves 6 to 10, depending on the size of the lamb joint.

1 well-hung whole leg (or shoulder) of autumn lamb or mutton
3 garlic cloves, cut into thin slivers, plus some chopped garlic for the vegetables if you wish
A few sprigs each of thyme and rosemary
2 tablespoons olive oil
Salt and freshly ground black pepper
2 onions
About 2 pounds potatoes
About 1 pound large carrots
About 1 pound parsnips
About 1 pound leeks
1 cup lamb stock or water

With a sharp, thin-bladed knife, make a dozen or more incisions about 1 inch deep through the skin and into the meat of the lamb joint and insert a sliver of garlic and a little piece of thyme and rosemary into each one. Massage the olive oil all over the lamb. Put in a roasting pan and season with salt and pepper. Place in a preheated 425°F oven.

Meanwhile, slice the onions. Cut the potatoes into fairly thick (1/4-inch) slices and the carrots, parsnips, and leeks into 3/4-inch chunks. Mix them all together in a bowl and season with salt, pepper, and a bit more garlic, if you like. Gently heat up the stock or water.

When the lamb has been roasting for about 30 minutes, remove from the oven and lift it out of the pan. Pour off some/most of the fat that has run off so far; the amount you discard depends on the overall fattiness of the joint – my lambs are very fat, so I pour off quite a lot at this stage, knowing that there's plenty more to come. Don't throw away the juices, though. Add all the vegetables to the pan and toss them in the remaining fatty juices. Pour over the stock or water. Put the leg of lamb in a large roasting rack that will fit in the pan above the vegetables, or place it directly on an oven shelf above the pan so that it "weeps" onto them. Roast at a slightly reduced temperature (375°F) for about an hour more, or 1 1/2 hours if it is a very large leg. Turn the vegetables in the pan occasionally and add a little more water or stock if they are very dry.

Remove the lamb from the oven and let rest for 10 to 20 minutes before carving. Meanwhile, turn up the oven (or turn on the broiler) and give the vegetables a quick sizzle to crisp them up before serving. I find that with an overall cooking time of just under 2 hours, a large leg of mutton is still just pink in the middle, which is how I like it. You may have to reduce the cooking time for smaller legs.

variation Sheila's original version of this dish uses only potatoes, onions, and mushrooms for the vegetable gratin. I like my version because I'm lazy, and it means I don't have to cook any extra veggies!

tagine of mutton and apricots

serves 6

This is a North African–style dish of the kind that would be cooked long and slowly in a tagine in the embers of a fire. By all means, use a tagine if you have one. My large stainless-steel stockpot seems to deliver the goods. Half a leg of mutton serves 6, but you could use the whole leg to make a mammoth stew that will feed over a dozen – just double up the quantities below.

If you don't have the bone from the meat to make stock and you don't have any lamb stock at hand, you can, at a pinch, use a chicken stock cube and water.

½ leg of mutton or roughly 2 pounds stewing lamb
A few stock vegetables (carrots, onion, celery), coarsely chopped
1 bay leaf
¾ cup organic unsulphured dried apricots
2 tablespoons olive or sunflower oil
3 garlic cloves, crushed
2 large onions, sliced
3 large carrots, cut into ¾-inch chunks
2 cinnamon sticks
2 teaspoons ground cumin
1 tablespoon coriander seeds, lightly crushed
6 cardamom pods, lightly crushed
A few small pieces of dried ginger (or 1 teaspoon ground ginger)
A pinch of ground mace
A glass of white wine
⅓ cup good fruit chutney
Salt and freshly ground black pepper

If you are using half a leg of mutton, bone it out, leaving the very tough meat at the end of the knuckle on the bone. As the meat is to be cut into pieces, no great subtlety is required in taking it off the bone – just try to keep the pieces as large as possible to begin with. Trim any major fat and gristle off the meat and cut it into large – about 2-inch – pieces. Roast the bone and the knuckle in a preheated 400°F oven for 10 minutes, then put it in a pan with the stock vegetables, bay leaf, and water to cover and bring to a boil. Simmer very gently for 1½ to 2 hours, then strain the stock through a fine sieve.

Rinse the apricots well in cold water, then place in a bowl. Pour over enough boiling water from the kettle to barely cover them and let them soak for at least an hour.

Heat half the oil in a large frying pan over medium heat. Add the garlic, onions, and carrots and cook for a few minutes until softened. Add all the spices and fry for a few more minutes. Transfer to your tagine or stockpot. Turn up the heat under the (now empty) frying pan and add the rest of the oil. Brown the meat quickly in it, in small batches, and add to the vegetables. Pour the wine into the pan and bring to a boil, stirring to deglaze, then add it to the meat, together with the water from the soaked apricots, the chutney, and enough stock just (and only just) to cover the meat. Bring to a boil, then lower the heat immediately to a very slow simmer. Add some salt and pepper and simmer, uncovered, for 1½ hours (or cook in a 325°F oven with a lid on, if you prefer). Add the apricots and cook for a further half an hour. By this time the meat should be extremely tender. Taste a bit – if in doubt, cook for a little longer.

Serve with steamed rice, into which you have stirred a teaspoon of whole cumin or caraway seeds.

roast chicken with honey and couscous

serves 4 to 5

I don't normally like stuffing a chicken, as it lengthens the cooking time and the breast meat is often dry by the time the stuffing is cooked. In this case, perhaps because the couscous goes in hot and itself carries plenty of moisture, that never seems to happen. With its subtle spicing and honeyed juices, this is a dish that seems to charm everyone who tries it.

It should ideally be cooked in a clay pot or tagine, but any casserole in which a whole chicken will fit snugly can be used.

¼ cup raisins
½ cup couscous
⅞ cup boiling water
1 onion, finely chopped
3 tablespoons butter
2 tablespoons sliced almonds
2 generous teaspoons runny honey
1 teaspoon ground cinnamon
The liver of the chicken, chopped (optional)
Salt and freshly ground black pepper
1 large free-range roasting chicken, about 5 pounds
A little olive oil (optional)

Mix the raisins with the couscous in a heatproof bowl and pour over the boiling water. Cover the bowl with a plate and let the couscous swell for 5 to 10 minutes. Meanwhile, cook the onion in half the butter until soft but barely colored. Add to the couscous. Return the empty onion pan to the heat and lightly toast the almonds in it until golden. Add them to the couscous, too, then stir in the honey, cinnamon, and the chicken liver, if you have it. Season with salt and pepper and mix well.

Stuff the chicken with the couscous, but don't fill it too full. You may not get all the couscous in, but save any remaining to serve with the bird. Place the chicken in a presoaked clay pot, a tagine, or casserole (if the latter, then add a glass of water to help keep it moist during cooking). Spread the remaining butter over the breast of the bird and season with a little more salt and pepper. Cover and place in a preheated 350°F oven (unless your clay pot requires starting in a cold oven, in which case follow instructions). Cook for 70 to 80 minutes, until the chicken is tender and the juices run clear when the thigh is pierced close to the bone with a sharp knife. A clay-pot-cooked chicken is lovely and moist, but the skin will not crisp up. So if you like a crisp skin (who doesn't?), brush it with olive oil, sprinkle with salt, and place under the broiler for 5 to 10 minutes.

Carve the bird and spoon the stuffing from the cavity and the juices from the bottom of the chicken pot or casserole. No accompaniment is really necessary, but you might like to serve a lightly dressed green salad, such as watercress, or some plain steamed green beans with or after the chicken.

pot-roast chicken and vegetables

serves 4 to 5

This is my favorite one-pot dish and can be adapted for both young roasting birds and old stewing chickens – the difference being in the length and temperature of cooking. When I want to feed a lot of people with minimum effort, I sometimes cook 2 whole chickens by this method – I have an enamel dish with a lid in which 2 birds fit rather snugly. After 10 minutes' preparation and 1½ hours' cooking, to be able to put dinner for 10 on the table – meat, vegetables, and gravy all from the same pot – causes me a measure of satisfaction bordering on smugness.

The vegetables can (and should) be varied according to the seasons. Celery, fennel, parsnips, squashes, kohlrabi, etc., can all come and go.

1 chicken, weighing 4 to 6 pounds
2 onions
3 large carrots
3 leeks
3 potatoes
2 bay leaves
2 to 3 sprigs of thyme
1 tablespoon soft butter
A glass of white wine
A glass of water
2 teaspoons salt
Freshly ground black pepper

Place the chicken in a large casserole, a clay pot, or a deep roasting pan with a lid. Slice the onions and cut all the other vegetables into chunks. Arrange the vegetables and herbs around the bird. Rub the butter over the breast of the bird and pour over the wine and water, then season well with the salt and some pepper. Place the lid on the dish and put it in a preheated 375°F oven. Remove the lid after about 50 minutes and give the vegetables a good stir. Baste the chicken with the fat on top of the juices in the dish. Leave the lid off and return to the oven for 25 to 35 minutes, until the breast is nicely browned and the juices run clear when the thigh is pierced with a skewer.

To serve, transfer the chicken to a large warmed plate and carve it up fairly chunkily. Spoon vegetables from the roasting pot and plenty of buttery juices onto each plate beside the meat.

Note If using a stewing chicken, turn the oven down to 300°F after the first half an hour, then cook for 1½ to 2 hours without removing the lid. Turn the bird over on its back halfway through cooking and give the vegetables a good stir at the same time.

variation I once cooked a whole chicken like this for just two of us and, knowing that there would be far more of everything than we could manage, I spooned some of the vegetables and juices into the blender along with a couple of fistfuls of sorrel leaves from the garden. I whizzed it all up and the result was a particularly fine, creamy sorrel soup, which I served as a starter. This was such a success that I have done it many times since, varying the extra ingredient for the soup: nettles, fresh peas and lovage, and watercress have all worked very nicely.

Ukrainian chicken borscht

serves 10 to 12 as a main course

A huge cauldron of this lovely peasant dish was originally prepared on the first River Cottage television series by a team of Eastern European cooks to feed an army of raspberry pickers (of whom I was one). Using 6 chickens, it served over 30 people, but I have scaled the recipe down to a more modest 2 to 3 chickens for 10 to 12. This is a good dish for using up stewing chickens (retired layers) or roosters that won't perform, and I have also made it very successfully with rabbit and with frozen pheasants that needed using up – although it's no insult to a nice fresh roasting chicken.

3 ounces pork or goose fat (preferably) or 6 tablespoons canola oil
2 to 3 chickens, depending on size (or 4 pheasants), cut into serving pieces
A piece of bacon or salt pork, weighing about 1 pound, cut into ¾-inch cubes (optional)
2 large onions, sliced
4 garlic cloves, coarsely chopped
1 whole tube of concentrated tomato paste
1 green cabbage, cored and shredded
2 pounds potatoes, cut into cubes
5 carrots, peeled and shredded
5 beets, peeled and shredded
1 level tablespoon paprika
Salt and freshly ground black pepper
2 cups sour cream, to serve

Heat the fat or oil in a large, heavy frying pan and brown the chicken pieces in batches. Transfer the chicken to a large stockpot, along with the bacon or salt pork if you are using it. Turn the heat down under the frying pan and, using the same fat, cook the onions and garlic until they are soft. Add them to the stockpot.

Mix the tomato paste with a little water and pour it over the meat and onions. Add all the other ingredients, including at least 2 teaspoons each of salt and pepper. Pour in enough cold water just to cover the meat and vegetables. Bring to a boil, turn down the heat, and simmer very gently for at least 2 hours, stirring occasionally, until the meat is completely tender (you can reduce the cooking time by 30 to 40 minutes if using fresh roasting chickens). Taste and adjust the seasoning.

Serve in deep bowls with plenty of the soupy liquid, a big dollop of sour cream, and hunks of crusty bread.

top three leftover-chicken recipes

I believe that the best-quality fresh chicken deserves to be cooked whole and simply – see pages 252 and 253 for roast chicken variations. Once you have found your favorite way of roasting a bird, recipes for leftover chicken may ultimately prove more useful than treatments for the whole bird. We often roast a chicken at home for just the two of us, knowing that during the following days we'll be feasting on leftovers and making use of a first-rate stock. Here are three of my favorite ways of using up chicken:

cold chicken with potatoes and anchovies

Cold chicken is always tasty, but sometimes dry. This delicious and well-lubricated dish can be thrown together in a matter of minutes.

Leftover cooked chicken
½ to 1 small can of anchovies, drained
½ garlic clove, crushed
1 tablespoon olive oil
Lemon juice
A few green onions, or 1 small red onion
Boiling potatoes
Chopped parsley

Cut up the cold chicken, but not too small. Coarsely chop 1/2 to 1 can of anchovies, depending on the amount of chicken you have. Mix the anchovies with the garlic, olive oil, and a squeeze of lemon juice. Toss this mixture with the chicken and onions and let macerate while you boil some potatoes until tender. Slice them when still warm and toss immediately with the chicken mixture and some chopped parsley.

chicken with bacon, peas, and cream (a sauce for pasta)

serves 2 to 3

For me this is Sunday or Monday supper in front of the telly. Better hope something good's on.

2 to 3 thick slices of bacon or pancetta, cut into small dice
Olive oil
1 onion, chopped
1 garlic clove, chopped
About 1 cup fresh or frozen peas
Leftover cooked chicken, chopped fairly small
A few tablespoons of heavy cream
Salt and freshly ground black pepper
Freshly grated Parmesan cheese, to serve

In a heavy frying pan, fry the bacon or pancetta in a little olive oil until just crisp. Turn the heat down, add the onion and garlic, and cook until soft but not colored. Add the peas and a splash of water and allow to bubble for a couple of minutes. When the pan is almost dry again, add the chicken and heat through. Pour in the cream and season well with salt and pepper.

Let it bubble until the cream has reduced a little and the sauce has thickened. Serve tossed with your chosen pasta, with plenty of freshly grated Parmesan on the table.

croquetas de gallina (Elena's chicken croquettes)

makes about 20

This is a Mallorcan dish, and something of a labor of love for mere leftovers. However, the satisfying crunch of the crisp coating, followed by the creamy, almost bland, chicken middle, makes this irresistible comfort food that is worth all the trouble. It's well worth mastering the basic technique for this dish, as there are lots of delicious variations (see below).

1⅔ cups whole milk
3 tablespoons butter
¼ cup all-purpose flour
1 small onion, finely chopped
1 small garlic clove, crushed
A little olive oil
2 cups chopped or ground leftover cooked chicken meat
2 teaspoons chopped parsley
2 teaspoons chopped chives
A pinch of nutmeg
Salt and freshly ground black pepper
1 egg, beaten
1¼ cups fresh bread crumbs
Sunflower, peanut, or olive oil for frying

Heat the milk in one small pan and melt the butter in another. Add the flour to the butter and stir to make a roux, then cook gently for a couple of minutes. Add the milk, hot but not boiling, a little at a time to the roux, stirring vigorously to get a thick, smooth béchamel sauce. Allow to bubble gently for a couple of minutes, stirring all the time.

In a separate pan, cook the onion and garlic in a little olive oil until soft, then add the chicken and stir for a few minutes. Add this mixture to the béchamel and let cool. Add the herbs, nutmeg, and some seasoning and mix together well with a wooden spoon. Transfer the mixture to the fridge for an hour or two until completely cold and set firm.

Take spoonfuls of the cold mixture and roll them into balls with floured hands. Dip into the beaten egg, then roll in the bread crumbs until thoroughly coated. Deep-fry in hot oil for 4 to 5 minutes, until nicely browned and crisp, or panfry in about 3/8 inch oil, turning occasionally.

Serve the croquettes either on their own or with a simple tomato sauce (e.g., either of those on page 102).

variations curried croquetas

Cook the finely chopped onion until soft and then add curry spices and cook for a few minutes longer. Add to the béchamel with the chicken, as above, omitting the herbs and nutmeg.

fish croquetas Leftover fish or fresh fish trimmings of almost any kind (as long as they are bone-free) can be substituted for the chicken. Crabmeat and chopped shrimp are particularly delicious. Omit the nutmeg and herbs and use a pinch each of ground coriander and red pepper flakes instead.

NN 92

fish

Although several valleys and ridges away from any possibility of a sea view, River Cottage is only about five miles, as the gull flies, from the sea. This sometimes seems odd to me, as when I am puttering in the garden I tend to feel that I am entrenched deep in an inland rural arcadia so all-consuming that there is barely time, or mental space, to make room for the idea of a spectacular, lime-cliffed coastline, dropping vertiginously to the gently contoured shingle beaches below – not to mention a vast expanse of sea beyond. So when, on some sunny summer evening, the pigs are fed and the day's work is done, and the thought of a trip down to the coast strikes like a bolt from the green, it's hard to believe it's really an option – but it is!

On the drive from River Cottage to the coast, the shoreline gets closer, but the landscape doesn't dish out much in the way of clues. The rolling hills and gullies and the lush, loamy verges continue until I'm almost there. Winding my way through the pretty village of Eype, on the way to my favorite beach, only the quaint house names – Sea Glimpse, or Shingle Tops – hint at what is imminent. Then comes the unmistakable taste of salt air. And as I sometimes forget around which bend it is that the sea can first be seen, I tend to brace myself. The final revelation still comes like a wave of light and noise that tingles the hair roots, just as it did when I arrived here as a child on holiday – after a drive of some four hours, not fifteen minutes.

I like it like that. And though I would prefer to spend a lot more time on the coast and on the sea, it still seems an unfeasible treat that it is there at all. When I do make it to the shore, I can revel in the rhythm of the waves sipping at the shingle, then lift my eyes to the horizon and marvel at the sheer size and power of the water. It keeps me transfixed for, oh, minutes. And then I start to think about supper. . . .

But seriously, I still find it incredible, and inspiring, that from such a vast expanse of sameness – water, water, water, with a large dose of added salt – comes such an astonishing variety of edible creatures, including most of my favorite foods. I'd probably shoot the messenger that came to tell me I had to choose, once and for all, between fish and meat. But having done so, I'd definitely go for fish – provided, of course, that crustacea, bivalves, mollusks, and cephalopods were all included in the deal.

Now that I have a small boat for potting and fishing, I try to make more time to get out to sea. Returning home with a few mackerel, a spider crab, or even a couple of cuttlefish to combine in the kitchen with some fresh vegetables from the garden is the best possible way to forge a link between land and sea. And returning home empty-handed, as I not infrequently do, is not so bad either. At the very least, I bring back a raging hunger. And there's always the ham hanging in the porch, or the bag of mutton chops in the freezer (the messenger hasn't come yet). The fish supper can wait until another day and will be all the more cherished when it comes.

I always feel immensely sorry for anyone who claims that they don't like fish. But I'm suspicious, too. Their blanket condemnation of the entire marine larder stems from what exactly? A bad childhood experience in the school canteen? A ropey piece of cod in a pasty "parsley sauce" served up by an overbearing aunt whose kitchen exploits were always a source of anxiety? The fatal assertion that the fish on the plate must be finished because it is good for you? I was exposed to all of the above. But somehow I got through it. Bird's Eye's finest fish fingers, with a good splosh of ketchup on the side, certainly helped. My mother's wonderful kedgerees and fish pies, much-loved Saturday-night specials, helped to wean me gently off the orange–bread crumb school of fish cookery. And a dish of crisply fried tiny red mullet, known locally as *barbounia*, ordered for me at a beachside taverna on our first foreign holiday, to Greece, was a turning point. Our Greek friend, Spiros, dared me to munch up the salty, crispy heads I'd left on my plate. I did, and I loved them. It was explained to me then that freshness is everything. And as, on the same holiday, I went on to catch a small garfish from the beach, which Spiros himself cooked for me within hours, tossed in flour and fried in olive oil, I became hooked: on catching fish, on eating them, and, best of all, on cooking my own catch.

I don't know if I can come up with a prescription for those who remain doubtful of the potential pleasures of fish at their table. If their negative piscine experiences have been outright Freudian in intensity, there may be no hope. But I would like to think that for every horror story concerning stale haddock, dodgy mussels, or insipid trout fed on rubbish in some slimy pond, there is an antidote tale of fishy joy: of a boy's first self-caught mackerel, grilled over a fire on the beach; of prawns caught in rock pools, boiled in sea water and eaten with brown bread and butter; of opalescent strips of squid spiked with garlic and chile, slapped on a grill under a blistering summer sun. . . . Does that sound tempting? I hope so.

fish | sea fish

Despite my sincere eulogy to the romance and satisfaction of cooking self-caught fish, I still buy a lot more fish than I catch. If I didn't, I simply wouldn't get to eat fish that often. But for me, the pleasure of fish shopping is not so far removed from the pleasure of trying to catch fish. In both cases, I rarely have any idea what I'm going to end up with. But when I take my wallet instead of my rod, the likelihood of returning home with something for supper is increased dramatically.

I am very spoiled, in that even my fish shopping trips take me right to the sea's edge. I buy most of my fish in the harbor at West Bay – and almost always directly off the boats belonging to the fishermen who work there. Jack Woolmington is my most regular supplier. But since the harbor at West Bay is tidal, and Jack throws his bottom nets at varying distances away from the shore, I never know what time he's going to get back into port. If I'm well organized (or, more likely, if my wife Marie reminds me), I ring him up the night before for an ETA. Even then, the estimate is necessarily a rough one. The time I consequently spend loitering around the harbor is somehow rather special: scuffing my heels against the moorings; looking covetously at the nets and pots piled up on the harbor wall; watching the gulls watching the tourists licking their ice creams and eating their chips. And finally, watching Jack's boat transform from a dot in the distance to the tackle-laden hefty tub that comes chugging through the harbor entrance. I love it.

Jack's main cash catch is Dover sole and skate, but we only rarely treat ourselves to such extravagances. My passion is his by-catch: a few plaice, the occasional flounder, and some amazing brill. He also catches crabs, both brown and spider, in his nets. A large spider crab feeds two of us very nicely, and only costs a couple of quid. Once in a while I buy an enormous cod, like the one shown opposite. I have a ritual for using these. I cut off the head generously, leaving a fair amount of meat on the shoulders, and then take off the fillets for salting and sometimes smoking. I usually simmer the head with a few stock vegetables and herbs – see the picture on page 267. The meat from the head makes a simple supper, served warm with a drizzled dressing of olive oil, lemon juice, and a few chopped herbs (and sometimes a bashed-up anchovy or two). We usually eat it with a mound of buttery mashed potatoes, or plain boiled new potatoes when they're ready in the garden, and the resulting stock goes for next day's soups or risottos, or straight into the freezer. Recently, I tried another tack: roasting the head – first studded with slivers of garlic and sprigs of thyme, then brushed with olive oil, then sprinkled generously with flaky sea salt – in a hot oven for about half an hour. It was a spectacular success, feeding four of us with meat to spare for my son Oscar's lunch the next day. I can't wait to do it again.

With a few grumpy exceptions, I have found that most fishermen are delighted to sell their fish direct from the boat to harbor-hangers like me. The middlemen who trade their fish for them tend to drive a hard bargain, so fishermen can improve their profit margins considerably by selling direct, and still offer the likes of us a very generous discount on retail prices. If you live near a fishing port, I would urge you to take advantage.

fishmongers

Having this ready supply of just-caught fish is a great privilege. As my dad likes to say, "If it were any fresher, it would be insolent." But I still buy fish at the fishmonger's and even occasionally in the supermarket. A good fishmonger offers a very different experience from Jack and his boat, but it can be thrilling nonetheless. Buying fish in the city a long way from the gulls and the salt air, I am still, in a sense, going fishing. The hunt is on – but rarely for something prescribed in advance by a shopping list for a particular recipe. I am looking for nothing less than the freshest fish in the shop. One hopes to be spoiled for choice, and in a really good establishment one is. It's a pleasure to do business with someone who knows and cares about their fish. If you are lucky enough to have such a character in business near you, then get to know them, honor them with your regular business, ask them anything you want to know about the fish they sell: where and how it was caught and even, when you feel confident, how long it has been on ice. If something disappoints you, let them know – gently. Find out what's due in when – and be there to pick it up when it is really fresh. And if you want something special – a large sea trout, a wild salmon, or a line-caught sea bass of a certain size – order it in advance. Make it your aim to become their most treasured customer, and savor the special treatment you receive. You will have earned it.

supermarkets

If, despite your best efforts, you find that your local fishmonger simply doesn't deliver on quality, you may even be better off in the supermarket. Buying good fish in the supermarket is less of a thrill and more of a skill, but it can be done. Many of the larger superstores now have their own fish counters. Most of these are no better and no worse than an indifferent fishmonger's – a lot of the fish they sell has been previously frozen (they are obliged to label this, but the labels tend to be a little on the small side). Like any fishmonger's, at any given time, they will have some good fish. The problem is that you will probably not be allowed – and certainly not encouraged – to prod and poke until you find it.

But be aware of one thing a supermarket offers you that the fishmonger doesn't: a "use-by," or "best before" date. You won't find this with the fish on the ice. But there is often a refrigerated case for packaged fresh fish. The best of this is the stuff presented in plastic-wrapped polystyrene trays, ready cleaned and perhaps filleted. Contrary to what you might assume, experience has taught me that these are sometimes the freshest fish to be found in the whole supermarket. And the use-by date is a pretty reliable guide to freshness. The reason is that the whole business of packaging fresh fish really puts the supermarket on its mettle. In order to give their packaged fish a four-day shelf life, which is what they favor, they simply have to be dealing with really fresh fish to start with, otherwise the health inspectors would be down on them fast and hard. Chilling procedures have to be scrupulous, and distribution speedy and efficient. If you, the shopper, can lay your hands on a pack of fresh fish that has arrived in the refrigerated case within the last twenty-four hours, there is a very real chance that it will be good and fresh – in better shape, more than likely, than much of what is sold, fishmonger style, at the fish counter.

With this in mind, my policy is to work backward from the date on the pack: I would never hand over money for fish on the same day as the use-by date, and would be reluctant to do so the day before. A two-day leeway is

probably worth thinking about, a three-day margin a very good bet, and four days the best you are likely to find. In fairness to supermarkets, I should say that when I have found packaged fish well within the use-by date I have often been impressed by its condition. I have bought sushi-worthy mackerel fillets in this way, lovely fresh herrings, excellent cod steaks, and fine tiger prawns. Consequently, I now tend to favor the fresh fish in the refrigerated case to fish at the fish counter.

However, do be aware of another form of supermarket packaging, where the fish is not as fresh as it might appear. "Modified-atmosphere" packaging is used to prolong the shelf life of a number of "fresh" foods – especially fish and meat. You can spot the packs by the way the transparent top is sealed onto the tray below (which is also usually stamped-out transparent plastic). It has to be peeled off from a little flap in the corner. These packs contain a special mix of harmless gases that impair the ability of bacteria to do nasty things to the fish inside. As far as I'm concerned, the jury is still out on whether this is good, bad, or irrelevant, but it does call into question the real meaning of the word "fresh." What is particularly irritating is that it is happening without us even being told.

There is one further supermarket tip, which I would hesitate to cast in stone but which may prove useful. The old tradition of eating fish on a Friday has a residual but dependable following in the U.K. Most supermarkets will expect to sell significantly more fish on a Friday than on any other weekday. They will also expect to sell a fair bit on a Saturday, simply because it is such a busy shopping day. Most supermarkets therefore take their largest delivery on a Friday morning – probably of enough fish to last for Saturday as well. Buy your fish on a Friday, and the chances are you will have a wider choice of fresher fish.

clues to freshness

Wherever you buy your fish, if you want value and quality you must become a confident judge of freshness. Handling a fish will quickly tell you whether it is in good condition, and a good fishmonger should not begrudge you the right to have a little prod. Look for a bright, clear eye, as opposed to a sunken, cloudy one. Look behind the gill covers at the gills; in most species these should be pink, wet, and possibly (in a very fresh fish) bloody. As the fish loses condition the gills become dull, gray-brown, and gummed up with slimy mucus. Sniff behind the gills, too. Any whiff of tainted fishiness and you should look for another specimen.

Press your finger gently but firmly into the thickest part of the fish. It should be firm and resistant to pressure, and not leave a soggy indentation. This is a particularly good test for flat fish: plaice can look quite decent even when they are rather past it; soles and dabs, on the other hand, often appear drab and unhappy even when they are still quite fresh. Incidentally, freshness, as in "how long dead," is not the only issue. Badly treated fish will rapidly lose condition, whereas a well-packed, carefully transported, firm-fleshed white fish, such as turbot or even cod, will still be worthwhile after four or five days. The press test is a good indication of pot-worthiness, not just age.

A dry skin is no indication that a fish is past its prime, just as "the wet look" does not guarantee freshness. Fishmongers are adept at cosmeticizing their counters with a regular splash of water; this is why it is important to examine the fish closely. Once you have inspected a good few fish, including some that are less than fresh, you will soon become proficient at discarding doubtful specimens and returning home with a catch to be proud of.

catching fish

Fish can, of course, be had for free. But as a means of providing fish for the table, I cannot possibly recommend sea angling to anyone who isn't genuinely excited at the idea of standing on a beach in a howling gale, watching seaweed accumulate on a fine nylon thread that stretches from the end of an overpriced carbon stick to a lump of lead beneath the waves, and finally to an unfortunate marine worm impaled on a bent piece of wire. That I happen to love doing precisely that is something I've never been able to explain convincingly to someone else who doesn't. Fishermen never seem to make converts of their nonfishing friends, though if they're very lucky they may make friends with other fishermen.

Even anglers who eat what they catch know better than to look too closely at the economics of their hobby. For if one fishing friend should ever be fool enough to say to another that he reckons he has caught and eaten enough fish to offset the costs of equipping himself for his hobby, he will be drummed out of the fraternity as too big a liar even for the very generous allowances of mendacity customarily afforded by his peers.

Even more efficient methods of catching fish that are open to the amateur, such as laying long lines or putting out nets, will still not appeal to anyone who basically lacks the fishing instinct, or gene, or whatever it is we are blessed and cursed with. I therefore have no intention of launching into a lengthy section on fishing techniques that would no doubt bore the nonenthusiast into a stupor, while simultaneously infuriating fellow fishermen into paroxysms of "I wouldn't do it like that myself."

I do, however, reserve some harsh words for those fishermen who take not a jot of interest in the culinary possibilities of their catch. Especially those fools who kill and then discard their catch – and then have the nerve to buy fish and chips on the way home. The waste is criminal. If you're "one of them," and you've somehow mistakenly picked up a copy of this book, perhaps because your enthusiasm for fishing goes beyond the sea and

you saw the word *river* in the title, then may I politely refer you to the All-Purpose Fish Batter on page 345. It's as good as anything you'll find in a fish and chips shop. If you like the results, you may wish to experiment further with the recipes at the end of this section. I may not be able to bring nonanglers into the fold, but I'd be thrilled to think I might lure a few reluctant fish cooks into the kitchen to make something more out of their catch.

preserving fish

Whether the fish you buy is mainly bought or caught, there are excellent reasons, both economic and gastronomic, to learn a little about methods of preserving it. This basically means salting, smoking, and pickling. These techniques offer more than just an opportunity to extend the shelf life of fish acquired in any quantity. They create sensations of texture and flavor that will hugely expand the repertoire of the enthusiastic fish eater. Personally, I prefer salt cod to fresh. Smoking eels turns them from a fish of borderline gastronomic interest into a really worthwhile delicacy. And for even fair-weather holiday anglers, who find themselves with more mackerel than they know what to do with, the recipe for dill-cured mackerel (or Gravmax, as I like to call it – see page 328) means they can take their catch home with them without filling up the freezer with bags of fish that won't get used or inflicting a surfeit of fish on the cat.

salting

As well as being the most straightforward means of preserving fish, salting is also the usual preliminary treatment for all kinds of fish prior to smoking or pickling. But the best fish for straight salting, in which no other flavorings are to be used, are undoubtedly the cod and its round-bodied relatives, the haddock, ling, and pollack. They all have large sides of white flesh that are easy to fillet and rapidly give up their moisture to salt. Oily fish such as mackerel and herring can be simply salted, but to my mind are much more interesting if taken on to the next stage and smoked, or pickled and cured with some highly aromatic flavorings.

Here is my procedure for salting white fish:

Choose only very fresh fish; buy large fillets, or preferably a whole large fish and fillet it yourself. The flesh of big fish has bigger flakes, which makes for a better texture when salted.

In a large, shallow dish or tray, in which your fillets will fit without overlapping the ends or sides (they can, of course, be cut to fit), sprinkle a thin, even layer of rock salt or coarse sea salt (the cheaper the better – you will need about 8 ounces of salt for every 2 pounds of fish). Lay the fillets skin-down on the salt, touching but not overlapping. Cover generously with more salt – a thicker layer this time, say, about 2 inches. Place in a cool pantry or cellar, or in the fridge. After twenty-four hours, the salt will have dissolved in the water drawn from the fish, to form a brine. The salt cod can now be used, and in this form will keep for up to a week. If you want to keep it longer, top it up with half as much salt again and make sure that the brine completely covers the fish. Cod thus preserved can be kept for over a month. If you want to keep it even longer, then the fillets should be hung to dry in a cool, well-ventilated place. Once completely dry and hard, and if stored in a dry place, salt cod can be kept indefinitely – literally for years.

Using salt cod "Wet" salt cod (i.e., preserved in a brine according to the first two methods described above) should be soaked in cold water for twenty-four hours before use, and the water changed at least three times. Dry salt cod will take about forty-eight hours and several more changes of water. Always taste salt cod raw before you use it, and if it is unpalatably salty, soak it for a little longer.

Prime fillets of wet salt cod can be soaked, marinated, and eaten raw (see Provençal Marinated Salt Cod on page 333). Dry salt cod really should be cooked.

Short salting This is a little trick I use to improve the texture of cod, pollack, and ling, which can all be a little on the mushy, or bland, side. Proceed exactly as above, but rinse off the salt with fresh cold water after only one to two hours (depending on the thickness of the fillet). The texture of fish treated in this way is subtly tightened, since much of the moisture will have been drawn out by the salt. The flavor is pleasantly salty, but the freshness still shines through. For battering and deep-frying, I even prefer cod prepared in this way to unadulterated fresh cod.

smoking

There is something incredibly palate-tickling and addictive about smoked food of any kind, but smoked fish is the best of all. Home smoking therefore has to be one of the most satisfying and exciting projects for any fish enthusiast, which is why I'm about to devote a number of pages to it. The crudest way to smoke food is simply to hang it above, or slightly to the side of, an ordinary log fire. One shouldn't ignore the possibilities of such a basic technique: it served many cultures all over the world for centuries, and in some places still does. But if you want to achieve consistent results and avoid the risk of occasionally ruining a piece of fish or meat, it will pay you to understand a little more about the principles of smoking and construct a system that allows you to generate plenty of good smoke while retaining some control over the only other vital factor: temperature.

I have adapted the fireplace and chimney at River Cottage as the most basic kind of smoker, and, while sadly it is not quite big enough for smoking a whole leg of ham, it serves me extremely well for sausages, smaller cuts of meat, and, above all, fish. The fireplace is pretty tiny, which is useful as it makes it easier to regulate the heat. The fish or meat is hung directly about two and a half yards above the fire, by means of a hatch I have knocked into the chimney flue on the outside of the house. I have to climb up a ladder to put the fish in and take it out, but it's all part of the fun, and I haven't fallen off yet.

building smokers

If you don't have a suitable fireplace, home smokers can be adapted from all kinds of junk, such as old oil drums, metal trash cans, tall filing cabinets, and even, I have heard, old fridges – although I have never quite understood that one, as every fridge I have ever had has been lined with plastic. I guess you have to strip that out!

However you set about building a smoker, there is one important principle to understand. There are essentially two ways to smoke: hot and cold. Hot smoking is effectively a way of cooking food: the temperature of the chamber is usually approaching or above 225°F, and any fish fillets or whole small fish will be cooked through in about half an hour to an hour. The presence of smoke in the chamber is simply a flavoring. The advantage, of course, is that any food cooked in this way is ready for immediate eating – and it should still taste deliciously smoky. The disadvantage of hot-smoked fish is that it retains a fair amount of moisture, and is therefore not really preserved in any significant way by the process. Vacuum packed and refrigerated, it should keep for a week or two, but it is not suitable for long-term storage – unless frozen. The kind of patented box smokers you can find in fishing and camping shops are only suitable for hot smoking. They are nevertheless very handy for traveling anglers, campers, and beach barbecues – hot-smoked mackerel or trout, fresh from the sea or river, is hard to beat.

Cold smoking is a more subtle procedure that requires a bit more attention to detail. It's worth it, though, as it gives you such great delicacies as the finest smoked salmon, herring, eels, cod, and haddock. The texture of cold-smoked fish is distinctly different from hot-smoked. Try cold-smoking mackerel, and you will see what I mean: it produces a very different animal from the ubiquitous hot-smoked version and, in my view, an even better one. Long, slow cold smoking is also the route to the finest smoked hams and bacon (see pages 155 and 159–160 for more on that). The aim of cold smoking is to produce a chamber of smoke at a temperature of about 77° to 86°F. Dedicated enthusiasts of the art of cold smoking often fit temperature gauges to their smokers. I judge the temperature of my chimney by placing my hand in it where the fish are going to be hanging. It should feel pleasantly warm but not hot – the temperature of an overheated room. Another good indicator is that if the steel bars that I have fitted to hang my fish on are too hot to touch, then the air in the chimney is too hot for cold smoking. It's time for a fiddle with the fire.

For a chimney smoker, adjusting the temperature for cold smoking is a matter of experience and a readiness to improvise. I used to simply make a fire, wait until it had burned down to hot coals, and then smother it with damp oak sawdust. This basically worked, but had a tendency to flare up if I was not vigilant, and ready to throw on more damp sawdust or spray it with water. I have now made a shelf about 1 foot above the fire onto which I can slide a stainless-steel plate. Over a small charcoal or kindling wood fire, this "baffle-plate," as it's known technically, quickly reaches a temperature where any damp sawdust placed on it will smoulder nicely. It also has the effect of reflecting heat back into the fire, keeping the chimney above at a lower temperature. The whole system is now more stable.

Most home-built cold-smoking systems use a similar baffle-plate technique to achieve a stable temperature and a long, slow smoulder of the smoking material. Heat sources can vary from a wood or charcoal fire to a portable gas ring or even an electric element. An ingeniously simple, homemade cold-smoking system I have seen uses two metal trash cans and a small portable grill. The top trash can is smaller than the bottom one, which has a number of small holes drilled in the center of its base. The smaller trash can has the bottom completely knocked out of it (i.e., it's basically a cylinder, with a lid). The barbecue (which is less than 18 inches high) goes on the ground and is lighted as if for cooking. When the coals are nicely hot, an old roasting pan scattered with damp sawdust is placed on top of the grill. As soon as the sawdust starts to smoulder, the larger trash can goes on top, upside down. The smaller one, which has a couple of metal rods bolted across the top as hanging bars, goes on top – the right way up, and with the lid on. Smoke generated in the bottom can travels up through the holes into the top can, where the fish is hanging from the bars. A few adjustable ventilation holes in the top (i.e., bottom) of the bottom can and the lid of the top can help to adjust the draw of the smoke and the heat of the fire. Very simple, but it works.

Having made the important distinction between hot and cold smoking, it's only fair to add that I actually do a lot of "rough smoking" – hanging fish above an untampered-with fire on which I am simply burning logs. It's the old-fashioned way, and a much more hit-and-miss affair, since the temperature will vary as the fire is stoked, burns down, and is stoked again. But, generally speaking, the temperature in the chimney seems to be around 104° to 140°F – neither one thing nor the other, you would have thought. However, for mackerel, eels, and white fish such as cod and pollack, it seems to work very well. I give them three to six hours, and just make sure they come out before they are too frazzled. My point is that smoking is by its nature an inexact craft, not a science, and therefore ripe for experimentation. A fish is "properly" smoked if you like its finished taste and texture. If it is not smoky enough, smoke it some more. If it's too firm or raw, whack up the heat a bit. And if it's burned to a frazzle, better luck next time.

If building a smoker seems too much trouble, and you don't have a chimney that lends itself to the job, then commercially produced hot and cold smokers are available.

choosing wood for smoking

Apart from temperature and length of smoking time, the other way to influence the results of your smoking is to vary the type of wood you use to produce the smoke. Almost all hardwoods are suitable for smoking. Soft woods, on the other hand, especially pine and fir, tend to produce a smoke that is not only unpleasantly acrid in taste but may also be carcinogenic. Stick to hardwoods. Of these, oak has long been the favorite in Britain, and certainly has a distinctive and unmistakable flavor. But beech is also good, as are most fruitwoods, especially apple and cherry. Some woods are especially aromatic, and if combined with other woods, even in small quantities, they will add their inimitable savor. Notable among such scented woods are bay, juniper, and hickory – the latter is especially popular in America. You can also smoke very successfully over a peat fire.

The exact form in which your wood is burned depends on what kind of smoking you are doing. For hot smoking and rough smoking (as described above) over an open fire, large logs, or kindling, can be used as they come, but smaller wood chips or sawdust thrown on in addition will help increase the quantity of smoke, and therefore boost the final flavor of your fish. But for more closely controlled cold smoking, fine wood shavings or sawdust are easier to work with. And if using the baffle-plate system described above, they are pretty much essential, as larger pieces will not smoulder without direct contact with flames. Hardwood sawdust mixes designed especially for smoking can be bought, but they are expensive, especially if you do a lot of smoking. Timber yards and joiners may let you pick up a few bags of sawdust from their floor for nothing – but be sure you know what kind of wood you are getting. (Once you have used it a few times, you should be able to recognize oak sawdust by the smell.)

the smoker in use

Maintaining your home smoker while it smokes is largely a matter of trial and error, until you get the hang of the quirks of your own particular model. The objective, however, is straightforward: to generate a steady supply of smoke at a reasonably constant temperature. In the case of cold smoking, this is never likely to be much less than five or six hours (for mackerel, eels, and herring or salmon) and may be as much as a week (for a 20-pound ham on the bone). Damp sawdust burns slower, smokier, and at a lower temperature than dry sawdust, so always dampen your sawdust to maximize your "smoulder time."

Sometimes climatic conditions or too-damp sawdust can result in problems getting your sawdust going. In such circumstances, an excellent trick to kick-start your smoker is to heat some sawdust in a heavy frying pan on the stovetop until it starts to smoulder really well, then dash outside to the smoker and tip the smouldering stuff on top of the damp stuff. Once the sawdust is on the go, you should keep the fire under it low and the air fairly restricted: too much oxygen or too much heat and the sawdust will dry out, flare up, and be gone in a matter of minutes. If it's going too fast, add more damp sawdust and stir the pile a little. If the chamber is too hot, sprinkle a little water on the fire. For both these jobs, one of those gardening spray cans filled with water is a handy thing to have around a smoker.

Even the best-designed home smokers rarely burn for more than about three hours without needing topping up with sawdust or adjusting in some way, so you will have to check it fairly regularly. On the other hand, the supply of smoke doesn't have to be constant. If you need to go out (or go to sleep!) while the smoker is on the go, don't worry about it. Just let it fizzle out, then relight it when you come back. Beware, though, in the summer months: an extinguished smoker left outside and unattended for more than a few hours with food inside it may be found by flies, who will do their worst.

preparing fish for smoking

Fish can be smoked whole or in fillets, as you prefer. Generally speaking, any whole fish for smoking, such as mackerel, herring, and small trout, should be gutted first. The exception to this is bloaters – herrings smoked whole with their guts still in, for a wonderful gamy flavour. Herrings for bloaters must be really fresh.

Whatever the size or cut of your fish, one essential ingredient must be added before it is smoked: salt. Salt and smoke are a magic combination – the flavor of smoke without salt, on the other hand, I find not merely uninteresting but unpleasant. All fish for smoking must therefore be salted, however briefly. This can be done in a brine, the quantities for which are 2/3 cup salt for every quart of water. Boil the two together for a few minutes and then let cool completely before adding the fish. Half an hour in the brine will be enough for whole fish or fillets of anything up to about 1 pound. Thereafter, give them an extra half an hour per 2 pounds.

Personally, I prefer to dry-salt my fish, exactly as described in Short Salting on page 273. The timings are roughly as for the brine method. Then rinse the salt off thoroughly and pat the fish dry with a clean cotton cloth. Whether you use dry salt or a brine to prepare your fish for smoking, don't make it too salty: it will be even saltier when it comes out of the smoker. I always taste the raw fish before smoking, and if I've accidentally overdone it I soak some of the salt out in fresh water for a couple of hours, then dry it and taste again.

There are a few idiosyncrasies in preparing different fish for smoking, and some regional variations, so here are a few simple notes on the fish I smoke most often, in vague order of delectability, with a few suggestions for how to eat them thrown in:

EELS For me, eels are the apogee of the smoking experience. Mine are alive when I get them – either from the River Brit in the garden or from other local waters. I kill them with a blow to the head and then gut them but leave the skin on. Then I throw them straight into a bucket and shake several handfuls of coarse salt on them. They are "self-brining," in the sense that although they are technically dead, their nervous system tends to react to the salt, and they can writhe and wriggle for anything up to a couple of hours. When they've finally stopped wriggling, I wash off the slimy salt and dry them carefully with a cotton cloth. Then I tie them up singly by the head and cold-smoke them – head up, tail down – for five to seven hours, or longer with real monsters (anything above 3 pounds). Cold smoking is the best way to get a fine smoky flavor into your eels, but the texture of cold-smoked eels is not very palatable, being somewhat chewy. For this reason, they are traditionally finished with a half-hour blast of hot smoking, achieved by removing the baffle-plate of the smoker and stoking up the fire. If you are not confident of regulating the heat in your smoker in this way, then you can simply place the cold-smoked eels on a tray in a medium-hot oven (350°F) for ten to fifteen minutes.

The skin becomes very hard and leathery as the eels smoke, but smoking preserves much of the fish's natural oiliness. Once the finished eels are cold, the skin can usually be peeled off and discarded quite easily. A blade run close to the backbone should then remove the soft, smoky flesh in neat fillets. I like to eat smoked eel cold with horseradish sauce (see page 238), brown bread and butter, and a salad of plain crisp lettuce, such as romaine.

If the flesh of your smoked fillets turns out still a little on the firm side, then simply fry them very gently in butter for a few minutes. They will soon become meltingly soft and yielding.

MACKEREL My biggest regular catches are of mackerel, and although I more often make Gravad Max (see page 328), I also smoke a fair few. I don't usually fillet them, but do cut their heads off and gut them. I salt them for about thirty or forty minutes, then tie them up in pairs by the tail and rough-smoke them for a few hours. I usually stoke up the fire at the end, as for eels, to finish cooking them through. Then I either eat them straight away, with hot buttered toast, or let them cool and store them in the fridge for later. They are delicious cold, with lemon and black pepper, and also make a fine pâté: simply separate the flesh from all bones and skin and mash it with a little lemon juice, olive oil, and a pinch of cayenne pepper. Add crème fraîche for a looser consistency and a great sandwich filling.

HERRINGS I don't catch many herrings, and when I buy them it tends to be for pickling or eating fresh. However, I have smoked a few, and once made a pair of kippers I was very proud of. The secret seems to me to be keeping them on the bone. This is why kippers are split rather than filleted. To split a herring, open the cavity with a blade to remove the guts, then extend the opening to the tail and head. Place the herring on a board, open belly spread apart and facing down, and flatten it out by pressing with the base of your palm. Dry-salt it for at least an hour, then rinse and dry it. Hang by the tail, and smoke it as cold as possible for as long as possible – ideally about twelve hours. I like kippers poached in milk, then served with melted butter.

COD FAMILY The fish I smoke most often are cod, whiting, and pollack, in that order (which happens also to be descending order of eating quality). I would smoke haddock, but there's not much caught on this coast. Nevertheless, it is haddock I use as a model for the smaller fish (anything under about 1$^1/_4$ pounds). In Scotland, small haddock are made into delightful creatures called Arbroath smokies, and my imitation River Cottage smokies are made with similar-sized fish of the available species. The procedure is to remove the heads and guts of the fish but otherwise leave them whole. They are brined or salted for about an hour, then tied by the tail in pairs and hung to cold-smoke for five to seven hours. They are finished, like eels, with a blast of hot smoke to cook them through (which again can be done in the oven if you like). After they have been poached in milk for just five minutes, the skin can easily be removed, and the succulent meat picked from the bones. It's excellent as is, but particularly fine stirred into scrambled eggs and served on toast, or mixed with a cheesy béchamel and made into a smokie and cheese soufflé.

Fillets from large cod and pollack are excellent smoked in the more conventional manner: leave the skin on, salt or brine for about an hour, then tie tightly (using the skin to get a good hold) at the thinner (tail) end of the fillet. Cold-smoke for five to seven hours, then let cool, and use like smoked haddock, for kedgerees, etc. Or rough-smoke over an oak log fire for a shorter time, but make sure it doesn't get too cooked.

COD ROE When Jack brings in large, late-winter cod laden with heavy roe, my smoker – and I – get one of the big treats of the year: homemade smoked cod roe. Try to get the roe unbroken in its sac. It should be salted or brined for ten minutes per quarter pound. Then wrap carefully in cheesecloth, tie up, and cold-smoke for five to seven hours. Eat cold in very thin slices, with a squeeze of lime and a shot of iced vodka or aquavit to wash it down. Or make into homemade taramasalata (see page 332) – the best you'll ever eat.

TROUT and SALMON I caught but a solitary salmon this year, and what I did with it is described on page 321. Next time I catch one, I have pledged to smoke it. I plan to split it carefully and brine it for an hour per 2 pounds. I will then cold-smoke the two sides, tail end up, for ten to fifteen hours, tasting little morsels from the fat end until I think it is just right. I will slice it myself and serve it to my family and friends in the time-honored fashion, with lemon, black pepper, brown bread, and butter. Then I may very well die and go to heaven.

I had a trial run last year with a 6-pound rainbow trout, which came out very fine. I didn't die, though.

pickling

Salting is the simplest form of pickling, but in this context I mean to refer to pickling processes where other substances are added, both for their preserving properties and their flavors. Vinegar is the principal practical additive, though. Any number of exotic flavorings may also be used.

What follows is a simple procedure for pickling fillets of either herring or mackerel, using one of my favorite spices, juniper berries, as the main flavoring. I've adapted it from Rick Stein's great book, *English Seafood Cookery*, but I've been doing it for so long that I sometimes forget that. Cheers, Rick! You will need:

3 to 4 herrings or small mackerel, filleted
A quantity of brine (see page 158)
¾ cup white wine
¾ cup white wine vinegar
10 juniper berries, whole but lightly crushed
1 teaspoon coriander seeds
2 bay leaves
¼ cup light brown sugar
½ onion, sliced

Place the fish fillets in the brine and leave for half an hour. Place all the remaining ingredients in a pan and bring to a boil. Simmer for just a couple of minutes, then let cool completely.

Remove the fillets from the brine, then cut each one diagonally into three or four slices and transfer to a bowl or plastic container. Cover the fish completely with the cold pickle, put a plate over the bowl (or a lid on the container), and transfer to the fridge. Let pickle for at least twenty-four hours, but ideally eat within three days. To serve the fish, drain it from the pickle, then make a sauce by mixing a little of the pickle with some crème fraîche or sour cream and a dab of mustard. Finely slice an onion (ideally red), then scatter the slices over the fish and generously spoon over the sauce. For a more substantial offering, serve with a salad of waxy new potatoes.

freezing

I never freeze white fish, such as cod or haddock, unless it has first been salted and/or smoked. The problem is the water content, which makes large crystals that break up the texture of the flesh. On thawing, it is pretty much ruined for anything except fish cakes. Salting and smoking take the liquid out, and fish cured in this way suffer much less when thawed. Oily fish like mackerel and herrings freeze a little better when fresh, but tend to be readily available anyway, so why bother? I do freeze mackerel when I have a lot, but they tend to get used for bait rather than cooking. So any fish that goes in my freezer for subsequent human consumption tends to have been smoked, pickled, or cured in some way first.

top five underrated fish

It is not my plan to go into detailed discussion of the culinary merits of the myriad fish species you may encounter – there's just too much to say. Instead, I'm going to give you a highly personal "top five" sea fish, those that offer the best value for the money and don't always get the recognition they deserve.

MACKEREL Easy to catch, cheap, and plentiful, mackerel is still one of the most delicious, and underrated, of any sea fish. It has a remarkable affinity with bay leaves; one should be on every dish, pan, or griddle on which a mackerel is baked, fried, or grilled. And no fish is better on an outdoor grill or beach fire than a just-caught mackerel.

BLACK BREAM At least the equal of, if not superior to, the more frequently lauded and highly priced bass, bream can often be had cheaply, especially in the summer months, in British south-coast fish shops near to the ports where they are landed. The flesh is beautifully textured and slightly oily – somewhere between a mullet and a mackerel. A fish of 12 to 14 ounces is a perfect one-person frying-pan fish: throw salt on it and fry in olive oil to crisp up the skin. Add a few sprigs of thyme for a special flavor. Black bream is now being farmed in the Mediterranean, and although the farmed ones are nothing like as good as wild, they are a lot better than farmed salmon.

GRAY MULLET (WHITE AND STRIPED IN U.S.) A great, and usually inexpensive, fish. Smaller ones are perfect for the grill (see page 331), but bigger fish are also ideal for baking and braising: trying cutting a good-sized (2- to 3-pound) gray mullet into four or five pieces and stewing gently in olive oil with onions, tomatoes, garlic, fennel, and olives for about forty minutes.

GURNARD Gurnard was once dismissed as good for nothing but bait. Now British fishmongers and chefs are starting to realize (as the French and Spanish have for years) that this bizarre-looking fish, with its massive triangular head and tapering tail, carries excellent flesh. I like a whole gurnard baked in foil with a knob of butter, a splash of wine, salt, pepper, a bay leaf, and a few sprigs of fennel. I predict a rise in popularity, so get them while they're still cheap. The U.S. version is called a sea robin.

SPRATS If you happen to be walking on one of Dorset's beautiful beaches at the moment when a shoal of sprats, harried by dive-bombing seagulls, start to throw themselves onto the beach, then sprats will no doubt enter your top five too. This has happened to me in September for the last two years, and the resulting free meals have been among the most exciting fish feasts I have had. In the U.S., sardines take their place.

NEW AQUARIUS

shellfish

My first trip to Dorset was as a five-year-old boy on holiday. We stayed at a farm in the Char Valley, which turns out to be just a few miles from River Cottage, and I fell in love with three things: Topsy, the donkey; Caroline, the landlady's granddaughter, and the rock pools at the western end of Seatown Beach. One of these, known locally as the Fairy Ring Pool, seemed to me like a vast lake – uncrossable, it was so huge. I would paddle in it with my shrimping net for as long as the tide would allow, and in the course of a session compile a menagerie of rock-pool exotica in my plastic bucket: shrimp, crabs, blennies, periwinkles, limpets. When it was time to leave the beach I would, on parental insistence and with some reluctance, release my captives back into the sea. And the next day I'd come back and start all over again.

On the last day of that holiday, my father joined me in the rock pool, armed with an altogether more businesslike net, and urged me to focus my attention on a single quarry: shrimp. We caught hundreds of them and, after a meticulous size-grading by my father, took the best and fattest of them back to the farmhouse for tea. The smaller ones went back into the pool alive. "We'll get them next year," said my dad, giving me much to look forward to.

I remember watching the shrimp turn pink within seconds of hitting the boiling water. It was macabre, but thrilling. I had no qualms about tucking into these creatures, which, only the day before, I had wanted to keep as pets. And I thought they were delicious.

That was the first free meal I gleaned from a beach, and I've been at it ever since. Thirty years later, I still go back to the Fairy Ring Pool. I fish for shrimp the lazy way: dropping a baited trap into a deep part of the pool and returning to collect it after the next tide. And I might stop off to pick up some periwinkles. They're particularly fat and juicy at Seatown, and there are billions of them.

These days I also go farther afield for my shellfish. I have a small fishing boat in West Bay Harbor, which means I can put out pots to catch crabs, lobsters, and even cuttlefish, and pull on my wet suit to dive for scallops. Pulling and throwing the pots is usually combined with an hour or two's fishing for mackerel or trolling for bass. I've never had a lobster and a bass on the same day, but I live in hope.

buying shellfish

As with fish, if I didn't supplement my own modest catches of shellfish with those brought in by the professionals, I wouldn't eat as much shellfish as I'd like. So I buy quite a lot, and, as with other fish, I prefer to buy directly from the boats: it's fresher (usually alive, in fact) and cheaper. Lobsters and scallops in particular are now fiendishly expensive. If you can intercept them before the retailer has a chance to add his markup, you will save a considerable amount of money. This is, of course, difficult for anyone who is not within striking distance of a port where shellfish are regularly landed, but there is another tactic for those who are prepared to do a little detective work. Good restaurants take frequent deliveries of fresh fish and shellfish, and will of course be paying wholesale prices for them. If you are a regular of some nearby establishment, you might discreetly inquire where they get their fish. Perhaps the wholesalers might be able to include you in their rounds. Or perhaps the chef in the restaurant might be prepared, once in a while, to add something for you onto his or her order. If you manage to work out such an arrangement, make sure you don't abuse it. Be loyal and regular in your orders, and try not to mess around with piffling quantities that mean it is barely worthwhile for these busy professionals to help you out.

If you are purchasing shellfish at the fishmonger's or the supermarket, buy it alive if you possibly can. And if you want something special, such as a lobster or a few dozen oysters, order it in advance to make sure it is as fresh as possible (if it turns out not to be, you are certainly under no obligation to take it). Shopping tips specific to particular species are included in the field guide below. But first, a few more thoughts on how you might acquire your shellfish for free.

gathering your own shellfish

The tidal zone is a rich haven of life, a substantial proportion of which is both bountiful and edible – making a good beach both fascinating from the point of view of the amateur naturalist and highly productive from the point of view of the chef. I like foraging for free food in all manner of places, but I'm simply never happier than when doing it on a beach.

Between the tides on a good beach, there may be half a dozen seriously worthwhile shellfish to be gathered, with no more specialized apparatus than a net, a rake, or a good right hand. For those prepared to go a little beyond the beach, either with mask or snorkel or by taking to a boat and putting out pots, another dozen species come into play.

The field guide on page 291 lists the most worthwhile shellfish species that are to be found on and just off the seashore, with specific tips on how best to acquire, prepare, and cook them. But first, I will describe in general terms the basic methods of catching and gathering these goodies.

beachcombing

I think we have a natural instinct for beachcombing. Put any child of toddling age on a beach at low tide, and pretty soon they will be scrambling over the barnacled boulders, probing and peering through the seaweed, dabbling in pools, and prodding the flotsam and jetsam. After a while they begin to specialize: some collect empty shells, others driftwood or pebbles; and many young kids, like me in the Fairy Ring Pool, need no encouragement to set about creating an aquarium in a bucket.

Sadly, many people seem to lose their beachcombing instincts as they head toward adulthood. Those who do are missing out – not only on the charmed and innocent joy of chuckling at the sideways gait of the claw-waving shore crab and marveling at the symmetry of the Medusa-like sea anemone, but also on the very real possibility of returning home at the end of the adventure with the ingredients for a fabulous seafood feast. If your beachcombing skills are a bit rusty, then it's high time you held a bucket in your hand and got some saltwater between your toes.

the best shellfish beaches

There are many different kinds of beaches, providing many different habitats for sea creatures and seaweeds, edible or otherwise. Very few beaches are barren of life, but the least rich hunting grounds are certainly long stretches of beach comprised of smooth pebbles gradating to loose shingle at the low tide mark. Without permanently anchored rocks for weed to cling to, and without fine sand to provide the organic base from which the whole food chain spirals upward, pebbly beaches have little to offer the forager in search of a free meal. Be aware, however, that what appears to be a barren, pebbly beach at high tide may, at low tide, reveal rocky reefs, sandy patches, and all kinds of opportunities for the beachcomber.

Beaches of pure sand at first appear to be unpromising flat deserts, but sand can often be rich in planktonic foods, especially if mixed with a little mud, and there may be rich pickings lurking beneath the surface. Worm casts are a sure sign that there is life a few inches down, and an indication that more palatable sand-dwellers may not be far away. Muddy, slightly pebbly sand is a likely habitat for cockles, razorfish, and other clam species, especially when fringed by weedy rocks, whereas cleaner "yellow" sand may harbor shrimp.

The biggest variety of habitats, and therefore potential food, is provided by classic rocky beaches of sandstone or granite reefs or broken rock, gently gradating toward the low tide mark, with plenty of weed-fringed rocks and rock pools, ideally interspersed with or edged by patches of sand. Here you will find all kinds of edible shellfish and crustacea, from shrimp and small crabs to mussels, periwinkles, and limpets – not to mention a whole variety of edible seaweeds. You may even be lucky enough to find a lobster lurking in a hole. (This happened to me once, on another great Dorset rocky beach at Osmington Mills, but it wedged itself so firmly under a rock that I eventually broke the handle of my shrimping net trying to pry it out.)

It goes without saying that the time for beachcombing is at low tide, and a tide chart is the first vital piece of equipment for anyone planning to make any kind of harvest from the sea. Two hours either side of the low tide will give you a good four hours' foraging, and if you want to spend maximum time at the lowest possible mark, it helps to know exactly when the tide will turn (usually about twenty minutes after the given time for low tide). Habitually, the bigger mussels, periwinkles, and limpets seem to be found nearer the low tide mark. I have always assumed that this is because they spend more time underwater, and therefore feeding.

Remember that the height of tides varies greatly throughout the year – the biggest (i.e., highest and lowest) spring tides occurring when the moon is either full or new; the smaller neap tides occurring in the middle of the lunar cycle. Some beaches – for example, those where rocky reefs are usually below the low tide mark – only come into their own as gathering beaches during spring tides. Razor clams and some of the best cockle beds will often only be fishable on the springs.

There is, unfortunately, a health issue when gathering shellfish from the beach. Our shores are by no means free of pollution, especially in populated areas of the coast where sewage is still, in some places, pumped out into the seas fairly close to the shore. Local authorities (and local fishermen) should be able to tell you which beaches are considered clean, but as a general rule sheltered bays near houses, enclosed harbors, and populated estuaries are likely to experience and retain contaminants, whereas remote and exposed beaches will be a safer bet. Cooking will take care of many harmful bacteria, but not all – especially since good cooks like to err on the side of underdone with shellfish, particularly mussels. It is therefore worth making inquiries to establish the hygiene credentials of your chosen beach. If you want to eat your shellfish raw (and why shouldn't you?), such inquiries are essential.

snorkeling

Many Britons only bother to put on a mask and snorkel on foreign holidays, in the assumption that the British coast doesn't have much to offer the snorkeler. Big mistake. I have had as much fun snorkeling in Britain (particularly in Dorset and on the west coast of Scotland) as anywhere else in the world. The visibility here, particularly in sheltered bays during late summer and autumn, can be absolutely superb, and the rocky reefs, especially those just below the low tide mark, are often teeming with life.

Of course, the downside of snorkeling in the U.K. is the water temperature (almost never more than about 64°F). Such are the distractions of the undersea world that cold and fatigue can creep up almost unnoticed on the snorkeler, so that suddenly you may find yourself chilled to the marrow, exhausted, and some distance offshore – a dangerous situation for even a strong swimmer to be in. So if you are planning to go snorkeling for more than just a few minutes, you should consider wearing a thick wet suit.

Most of my snorkeling forays are "just for fun" – to look rather than hunt – but there are some species that usually elude the beachcomber but regularly fall to the snorkeler. Razor clams are a case in point, since they are rarely found above the low tide mark except on the lowest tides. Similarly, crustaceans, most of which do everything within their power to conceal themselves from predators when exposed at low tide, will venture out with more confidence when they have a few feet of water over their heads. Consequently, spider crabs, shore crabs, velvet swimming crabs, and even the occasional lobster can be taken by sharp-eyed British snorkelers.

diving

Scuba diving is a specialized sport that requires expert tuition. The two best ways to learn are either to join a local club – in the U.S., most are affiliated with the American Canadian Underwater Certifications Inc. (ACUC) – or to take the basic Professional Association of Diving Instructors (PADI) Open Water Diver course, which can usually be done in about five days of intensive tuition, either in your home country or on holiday abroad.

Few sports divers plan dives specifically around the acquisition of food, but if you dive regularly you will come across many edible creatures on your adventures. As a general rule, it is considered perfectly acceptable for divers to remove the odd lobster, crab, or a dozen or so scallops that they might encounter during a dive, to take home and eat. And certainly no one should begrudge you any number of whelks and large hermit crabs.

However, on some well-known dive sites, wrecks, and the like, divers are requested to observe a voluntary "no goodies" policy, which means not removing anything, alive or dead, from the water. Such policies, however unofficial, are intended to maintain the quality of diving for everyone, and should be respected. Some "residents" on such wrecks – conger eels, large wrasse, lobsters even – are well known to regular divers and practically have the status of pets. You would not be well regarded if you swiped them!

If you can find a like-minded dive buddy (diving alone is not countenanced by either the ACUC or PADI, and is not advisable under any circumstances for nonprofessional divers), there is no reason why you cannot plan "foraging dives" in pursuit of lobsters, scallops, and the like, over ground where you think they may be found. As with putting out pots (see opposite), it is as well not to cross swords with others involved in such activities on a commercial basis. If you think you may be infringing on somebody's patch, make inquiries first, and don't take more than you need for your own consumption.

Incidentally, spear-fishing with scuba apparatus is illegal in the U.K. and U.S., as in most countries.

putting out pots

If you live near the sea, or holiday regularly on the coast, a couple of lobster pots and/or a string of shrimp pots can be great fun to work and can supply you with a surprising array of crustacea and other shellfish – unbeatably fresh, and free to boot.

The fruits of the sea are available to everyone and, contrary to what you might hear in some areas, in Britain you do not need a license to put out lobster pots, provided the catch is strictly for your own consumption.[20] But if you are going to give potting a whirl, it is important to bear in mind that there are others who are struggling to make a living at the same game. The chances are that locals have already established an unwritten agreement about who will throw their pots where, and before you throw your own pots, you should take steps to ensure you will not further complicate the local fishing politics (which may already be sensitive enough).

There is certainly no point in making enemies by being defiant about your right to throw pots: in any contretemps with the local fishermen it is you, the "tourist," who is sure to come off worst. If you do put your pots where they are not welcome, you are likely to find out about it pretty soon. Chances are the locals will be up and out on the water well before you are; if you are experiencing a mysterious lack of success, it may well be because they are generously "checking" your catch for you. And if your pots simply disappear – well, then you really have managed to piss somebody off!

The best thing you can do, therefore, is go to the port nearest to where you are thinking of throwing your pots and make direct contact with the local fishermen themselves (it is the lobster and shrimp fishermen whose territory you are most likely to impinge on, as most of the serious crabbers now fish on deep reefs a long way offshore). Explain exactly what it is you want to do, and ask them if they can suggest an inshore reef or piece of rocky ground where you might pick up the odd lobster and spider crab, or a few shrimp, without annoying anyone. If you are only throwing a few pots (no more than four lobster pots, I would suggest, or half a dozen shrimp pots) and are seen to be taking the trouble to bait and check your pots daily, they shouldn't begrudge you a modest catch. It might be a smart move to buy some bait off them as well.

Alternatively, you could have a chat with the local harbormaster, who will know all the local fishermen and should be able to advise you on the best way to get your pots in the water without antagonizing anyone.

buying pots

There are only a few places where you can buy lobster pots new, and they are expensive. However, if you think you will be able to use them for at least several weeks a year, for many years to come, it may be worth investing in a few new pots.

The obvious choice is to buy second-hand pots – which turns out to be harder than you might think. First, and understandably, a working potsman will want to throw and maintain as many pots as possible – and will generally keep any spares to cover for losses. Second, the innumerable spare pots one does see lying around (apparently discarded) in fishing ports and harbors often turn out to be not so "spare" after all. They always seem to belong to someone who's "not yet in the water," but apparently coming back for them in some unspecified number of days, weeks, or years. I have found, however, that persistence may be rewarded in the end. If you keep going down to the boats and chatting with the fishermen, you may finally find yourself introduced to someone who's not entirely averse to the idea of selling you a pot or two. Snap them up – and whatever you do, don't ask them if they'll take a check.

baiting your pots

You can bait lobster and shrimp pots with just about anything, from a scrap of bacon to a lump of catfood tied up in the foot of a pair of tights, but the preference of all commercial potsmen is for fish baits. Some fishing ports have a shared bait pool for the potsmen, consisting of fish skeletons (usually flatfish that have been filleted) and unsaleable fish like small dogfish, which have turned up in nets (or indeed, pots). You may be able to buy a supply of bait from such a pool, or ask for rejects and skeletons from a fishmonger. If you are an angler as well, it is worth keeping any small pollack that you catch as pot baits. A rather gruesome but, I have to say, effective emergency pot bait is the contents of a tin of catfood emptied into an old sock.

Brown crabs are said to prefer fresher bait than lobsters do, but that doesn't mean you won't get lobsters on a fresh bait or crabs on a smelly one. You should always rebait a pot every time you haul it, even if the old bait appears to be intact. A new bait will create a fresh scent trail, which is essential to lure a good catch to your pot.

throwing pots

Before throwing your pots for the first time, make sure each is securely attached by a good strong line (at least 3⁄8-inch thick for comfortable pulling) to an easily visible floating marker – this can be anything (a white plastic container, for example) provided it is strong, buoyant, and doesn't leak. The line should be long enough to show on the surface in the depth of water you expect to throw your pots in – bearing in mind that the tide can rise as much as 12 yards from low to high – but not so long as to drift too far off the mark. About 25 yards is usually ample for most inshore work.

You don't need a great big motor launch to throw and maintain a few lobster pots – though if you are a "boat person" with your own craft, you will obviously have the advantage of range and a bit of seamanship. But provided the weather is reasonable, you can throw your pots from the most modest vessel. I have even used a giant inflated tractor tire inner tube to paddle my cuttlefish trap a couple of hundred yards off the beach – it worked, to the tune of four of these fabulous cephalopods. In some places it is quite possible, and worthwhile, to throw pots directly off the shore, by walking out onto a reef at low tide and dropping your pots off the end. This can be particularly effective for catching shrimp and spider crabs – and even the odd lobster.

In terms of choosing where to throw your pots, the only essential is that it should be on, or at least very close to, rough or rocky ground – ideally a reef (this does not apply to langoustine pots, as these crustacea prefer muddy sand – see page 296). Generally, rocky reefs are the natural habitat of the crustacea you are hoping to tempt into your pot. To this end, there is an advantage in throwing your pots for the first time at low tide: in shallower water it will be easier to see what kind of bottom you are over. If the ground looks good, there is no reason not to throw your pots very close to the shore, or only just below the low tide mark, in just a few yards of water.

Pots are best left for twenty-four hours, then checked and rebaited. Whether and how far you move them each day will depend largely on how well, and what, they are catching. The casual enthusiast doing it for fun need not be so fussy as the commercial fisherman – I know that a few velvets and a spider crab will give me a fine meal (at least a great soup), so if that's all I'm catching, I won't feel bound to move my pot in search of the big lobster. Besides, lobsters are wanderers by nature, and you never know when one might turn up. Eventually, however, you will want to vary the ground over which you throw your pots, even if only by 50 yards at a time.

favorite shellfish and how to catch them

Like angling, setting out to catch shellfish is something that will either interest you or not. But don't assume you need a lot of expensive tools. In some cases – cockles and mussels, to name but two – your bare hands will suffice.

BROWN (EDIBLE) CRAB The brown, or edible, crab is, commercially speaking, one of the most important crustaceans harvested in our waters, and it is taken by potsmen (in boats known as "crabbers") in vast quantities. These days, the best catches are mostly made over deep reefs a long way offshore, but they do occur on inshore reefs, and can be taken in pots placed beyond the low tide mark, and even occasionally by beachcombing. The U.S. equivalent is the Dungeness crab, which has all white meat.

Crabs do not enjoy the same culinary status as lobsters, but only, I suspect, because of the relatively portionable meatiness of the lobster's fat tail. Being a great fan of the brown meat (inside the carapace), which others scorn, if anything I prefer crabs.

There is a minimum keeping size for brown crabs in Britain – 12cm (not quite 5 inches) across the widest part of the shell. This doesn't strictly apply if you are not offering them for sale, but it is good to observe this minimum for conservation reasons in areas where crabs are regularly fished. Females carrying eggs should always be returned.

For information on catching crabs in pots, see principally the section on throwing pots, opposite. The brown crab does not share an identical habitat to the lobster, though they certainly overlap. As well as on reefs, brown crabs can be caught on a "mixed" bottom of muddy sand, rough ground, and shingle. They will come to just about any bait, but are said by some fishermen to prefer white fish to oily (such as mackerel) and fresh to smelly.

Buying Despite the massive quantities in which brown crabs are taken from British waters, they seem to remain plentiful and therefore relatively cheap. The best and cheapest way to buy them is alive and intact – preferably still waving their claws defiantly at you and blowing indignant bubbles. You can buy crabs ready-boiled, or boiled and dressed, but why pay the fishmonger to cook and dress them for you when it is so easy, and satisfying, to do it yourself? In my experience, a lot of fishmongers tend to overboil their crabs anyway. Never buy an uncooked dead crab: the flesh deteriorates within hours, and they are likely to be tainted in flavor, if not a positive health hazard.

Killing There is an officially sanctioned technique for humanely killing crabs: a sharp spike or small screwdriver is pushed through the mouth, between the eyes, and into the head at the top of the carapace. A second point, which should also be spiked, is the ventral nervous center. Lifting the tail flap of the crab reveals a cone-shaped patch – the spike should be driven into the center of this. It is also, in my view, quite humane to immerse a crab quickly in a large pan of rapidly boiling water, which will kill it almost instantly. The main reason this is not the commercial practice is because the crab will tend to shed its legs and claws. This may make them harder for a fishmonger to sell, but for those that are going to be eaten at home it really doesn't matter.

Cooking Crabs should be plunged into a large pan of rapidly boiling seawater (alternatively, add 2 tablespoons salt to every 4 cups of fresh water). After the water comes back to a boil, allow twelve to fifteen minutes for crabs weighing up to about 2 pounds; for larger crabs, add four or five minutes per extra pound.

There is no reason not to eat just-boiled crabs still hot (but just cool enough to be handled for cracking), either with homemade mayonnaise, garlic butter, or just plain melted butter with a little squeeze of lemon. Boiled crabs that you want to eat cold and dressed should be left to cool naturally in a cool, well-ventilated place. Most recipes for crab begin with cold cooked crab.

There are a few bits of the crab – the shell, for starters – that you shouldn't eat, though it is an exaggeration to say that any of it is poisonous. Once you have pulled the carapace away from the main body of the crab, the most obviously dodgy bits are revealed at once: the gills (or "dead men's fingers"), which are the gray spongy bits clinging to the main body. Pull them off and discard them. In the center of the carapace itself, attached to the mouth parts, is the stomach and connected organs: break off the mouth part, and the stomach will come away with it. Throw this away. All the meat that is left – the rich, creamy brown meat inside the carapace, the fine-grained white meat inside the legs, claws, and body, and any other pink bits of coral or brown soupy bits – is edible, so waste nothing!

Once you know what not to eat, it's really up to you to choose any method that appeals, brutal or subtle, to pry out all the meat. My own preferred tools are a hammer and a chopstick.

There are many ways to dress cold crab, but my favorite is to mix the brown meat with a good blob of mayonnaise, a little mustard and black pepper, and a chopped hard-boiled egg, and serve it next to a pile of the

white meat, absolutely plain. The only other accompaniments are buttered brown bread and a wedge of lemon (which I use only extremely sparingly).

Other good crab dishes are Crab Linguine (see page 336) and Crustacea Soup (see page 337).

SHORE CRABS It is widely thought in Britain that the common shore crab (sometimes called the green crab, although the color varies widely) is not edible. This is not true, and in fact it is exactly this species of crab that is prized in Italy (Venice in particular) in its soft-shell state (immediately after shedding its carapace – a necessary molting that allows the crab to grow). In the U.S., soft-shell blue crabs are the equivalent.

There is no theoretical reason why British soft-shelled shore crabs of a decent size cannot be prepared in either the Venetian (stuffed and baked) or American (floured and deep-fried) manner, but to do so would require some dedication. The crabs are truly "soft shelled" for only a matter of hours before the shell starts to harden (as opposed to the bait collectors' "softies," checked only once a day, whose new shell, though still flexible, is usually already too hard for gastronomic purposes). This means that for a decent supply you need to keep a lot of crabs in a well-maintained cold-water marine tank, and catch them just after they molt. I've never attempted to harvest British soft-shelled crabs in this way, but I'd love to hear from someone who has – I suspect there may be commercial possibilities.

When in the normal hard-shell state, shore crabs are also quite edible. Whether or not they are worthwhile depends on their size and your own patience. But you shouldn't dismiss them till you've tried them. They can certainly be usefully included in my Crustacea Soup on page 337.

Shore crabs can be found at low tide hiding in seaweed and under rocks and can be gathered by hand – but watch out for the pincers. Larger shore crabs often congregate in harbors, at the bottom of sea walls, and around the concrete piles under jetties. They are easily caught by lowering a decent bit of bait (squid or bacon is always a good bet) on a weighted hand-line to the bottom and waiting till you feel an aggressive tug. These feisty crabs are usually so reluctant to let go of the bait that they can easily be pulled to the surface and dropped in a bucket. A net is useful if you need to hoist them any distance through the air, as once they leave the water they are inclined to drop off.

Shore crabs will often turn up in pots, and those that do will tend to be of reasonable size, so may be worth keeping. They can be killed in the same way as brown crabs and need just five minutes in salted water to cook through. As with the brown crab, remove and discard the stomach and gills (dead men's fingers).

SPIDER CRABS In Dorset spider crabs are plentiful and relatively cheap. I catch more of them than anything else in my pots, and when I can't get out to sea myself I buy them off the boats for a couple of quid apiece.

These extraordinary-looking, spiky-shelled creatures are often covered in barnacles, and sometimes even sport seaweed and anemones (self-planted, according to some authorities, to create a good camouflage for their winter hibernation). With their distinctly arachnid and rather hairy legs they are not, in appearance, the most appetizing of creatures. But crustaceans are not to be judged by their covers. The meat is sweet and beautifully textured, which is why the Spanish, who appreciate such things, will pay more for a large spider crab than a lobster of the same weight. I am a total convert, and rate them as even better than brown crabs.

Spider crabs have a preference for warmer water (they are particularly prevalent on the French and Spanish Atlantic coasts), so in Britain they are far more common in the south than the north, and are only very rarely encountered in Scotland. From May to December, they can be caught in large numbers in pots fished off the south coast, particularly inshore on reefs and rocky ground.

While beach foraging, you may occasionally encounter a spider crab hiding in a hole on a reef at low tide. But apart from putting out pots, your best chance of acquiring a spider or two is by snorkeling or diving over rocky, weedy reefs and rough ground. Swim slowly and look carefully, or you may mistake your potential supper for a lifeless rock. Here in Dorset, there is an annual spider crab migration – vast numbers congregate on Chesil Beach, usually in July or early August. Local marine biologists are still unclear whether this is a "mating thing" or some other phenomenon, but whatever it is, when the water is clear, snorkelers can pluck them by the dozen.

There is no official minimum taking size for spider crabs, but as all the sweet white meat is in the claws and legs, the smaller ones are best left unmolested to grow. I don't bother with any spider crab whose claws are not at least as thick as my index finger – which generally rules out any crabs of under about 2 pounds in weight.

Buying spider crabs is not as easy as it ought to be, but I have a hunch they will become more readily available as more people appreciate their qualities. I have already seen excellent-looking spider crabs on sale alive at London's Borough Market. At the moment though, due to the Continental demand for spider crabs, and our own ignorance, most of these fine crustacea still go for export. Near the coast where they are caught, however, you should be able to order them from a local fishmonger or fish merchant. Better still, try buying directly from the boats as they come into port. For preference, choose the largest crabs you can get, as the smaller ones are difficult to deal with.

Spider crabs should be killed and cooked exactly as for brown crabs, in a large pan of boiling seawater (or salted freshwater). The timing, by weight, is the same (see page 291). When the cooked crab is cool enough to handle, the carapace can be removed, and the stomach and dead men's fingers discarded, in the same way.

In my view, the large amount of brown meat inside the carapace of the spider crab is better even than that of the brown crab. Cold, it can be served as for dressed brown crab on page 292, with the legs and claws, and something to crack them with, served on the side. But it is the white meat that is really outstanding: very succulent, sweet, and delicious. It is worth taking the trouble to crack all the legs as well as the claws. There is also good white meat in the body of the crab: the bit to which all the legs and claws are attached. It's hard to remove but worth every morsel.

You'll want as much white meat as you can muster for Crab Linguine on page 336.

VELVET SWIMMING CRABS With their purplish color, flat, paddle-shaped legs, and the fine velvety covering on their shells, these are an unusual, and I think rather beautiful, species of crab. They are by no means uncommon, and are often caught by the dozen in lobster pots. Being in the same size range as the shore crab, they have been of little commercial interest – until recently. Whereas they were once either thrown back or killed for shrimp pot bait, velvets are now an important constituent of the crustacea export market. Most go to the south of France, where they are a principal ingredient of Provençal fish soup, produced in increasingly huge quantities. Their merits are beginning to be recognized over here, and they can now occasionally be found at more adventurous fishmongers.

Since they tend to live below the low tide mark, velvet crabs are rarely found on the beach, though they frequently turn up in pots and are likely to be seen if you are snorkeling or diving. They can also be caught occasionally on a baited crab line lowered from a pier, sea wall, or jetty (as for shore crabs, page 293).

These pretty crabs, a very bright orange when cooked, look good on a seafood platter, and their fine flavor repays the effort of picking out the white meat from the little claws. Crabs of this size are, of course, hard to pick, but the upside is that once you have removed the legs and carapace and taken off the gills, the main inside body of the crab can be eaten up, shell and all, if you don't mind spitting out a few little splinters. Five or six minutes in boiling seawater is sufficient to cook an average-sized velvet, and any extra-large ones could be left in for another minute or so.

LOBSTERS For a long time now, the lobster has been the king of crustacea, symbolizing, along with oysters perhaps, the sheer luxury and indulgence of seafood gourmandising. They are notoriously expensive, which means that getting one for nothing is a particularly good cause for celebration. Why not spend the $40 you saved on a nice bottle of white Burgundy?

Actually, a number of tiresome individuals have pointed out to me that by the time you have bought a few pots and kitted out a seaworthy vessel to throw them from, just about anything you catch in them is probably costing you about $100 a pound minimum. I refer these spoilsports to my paragraphs above on throwing pots: you really don't even need a boat to do this.

Those who regularly scour beaches for crabs, shrimp, periwinkles, and other edible quarry will, once in a blue moon, happen on a tide-stranded lobster – and what a thrill that will be. Divers and snorkelers stand a rather better chance of encountering lobsters, especially if they dive at night. But by far the best chance of landing a lobster belongs to those who throw pots. See pages 289–290 for tips on how to get started in this game.

Buying I would only ever buy live lobster. As I'm likely to be paying a fairly hefty sum, I like to be sure that it's completely fresh and then take full responsibility for the cooking of it – many fishmongers overboil their lobsters.

Most good fishmongers will sell you a live lobster but charge the earth for it. Better to find a fish wholesaler to get a good price. Better still, go straight to the source and buy from the fisherman.

Cooking Lobsters are primitive beasts, with nothing in their heads that could be reasonably described as a brain. Their nervous system runs in a lateral line from head to tail. This means there is no specialized manner of delivering a swift dispatch. The officially sanctioned method of killing them is to put them in the freezer for about two hours to reduce them to a torpid state, then put them straight into a large pan of rapidly boiling water (from the cook's point of view, ideally seawater, but alternatively freshwater with salt added in the ratio of 2 tablespoons per 4 cups). Cooking times are, by weight, just a little longer than those for crab: twelve minutes for a minimum-size lobster of 1 pound, fifteen minutes for anything up to 1½ pounds, and an extra five minutes for every pound after that.

There are many ways to enjoy lobster, some romantic, some classic, and some deeply indulgent. Cold lobster with a good mayonnaise is hard to tire of. But in fact, the white meat is so rich and robust that it stands up to all manner of spicing and sophisticated sauces – so much so that I have rather a soft spot for lobster curry. Many lobster eaters make the mistake of eating only the white meat, from claws and tail. There are plenty of other goodies: the creamy meat inside the head, the browny-green liver inside the body, and the pink coral that often lines the shell of a female lobster. The only bits you can't eat are the dark gut that runs along the top of the tail (and is easily removed), the small gritty sac just behind the mouth, and the gills (similar to dead men's fingers in a crab, but smaller).

As long as it is very fresh, and not overcooked, I enjoy lobster just about however it comes. But when I cook it myself I tend to make that magnificently indulgent classic, Lobster Thermidor (see page 338).

DUBLIN BAY PRAWNS Also called the Norway lobster, and commonly known in the restaurant trade as langoustine, the Dublin Bay prawn is very much between the lobster and the shrimp both in terms of size and armor plating. On average 4 to 8 inches long (not including the claws), the Dublin Bay prawn has a hard shell of a pretty orange color that, unlike that of so many other crustacea, scarcely changes when the creature is cooked. The shelled tails of Dublin Bay prawns, often crumbed or battered and deep-fried, are what traditionally go by the name of scampi – though in recent years a lot of other less worthwhile things have gone by that name, including, I suspect, processed white fish. Incidentally, the name comes not from the fact that Dublin Bay has a population of the prawns, but because they first became known in this country from the fishing boats of Dublin Bay, which often caught them while trawling for other species.

They live on a muddy, sandy sea bottom, or on rougher ground provided there are sandy patches to burrow in. They spend daylight hours buried in the mud with just their antennae protruding, and emerge at night to feed. These nocturnal habits mean that the only practical way to catch Dublin Bay prawns is to throw pots for them.

The distribution of Dublin Bay prawns is in the northeastern Atlantic, from Iceland all the way to Morocco, and in the Mediterranean, but in the U.K. the best catches are made off the coasts of Scotland and Ireland. I have never encountered them here off the Dorset coast, but have had great success on Scottish holidays by the Sound of Mull. I believe they are caught sometimes off Cornwall and the Scilly Isles.

For those who live or holiday near waters where the Dublin Bay prawn is found, casual potting can be great fun. The pots specially designed to catch these prawns are relatively light and can easily be pulled by one person in strings of three or six. In Scotland, I used to shoot them from a small inflatable dinghy, rowed just a hundred yards offshore. I suspect there are many sea lochs and calm bays on the west coast of Scotland where fair catches of prawns could be made by throwing a few pots. The important thing is to be sure you are on the right kind of bottom: if you are catching a lot of small, flat-tailed, spiny squat lobsters, it is a sure sign that you are on rough or rocky ground. Once you get bored of eating squat lobsters, you can throw your pots over fresh ground.

Buying The merits of Dublin Bay prawns have only relatively recently been recognized in our gastronomy. Before the 1950s, they were barely known in Britain. Now they are among the most sought after, and expensive, of all our crustacea. They can be bought fresh (preferably alive) or frozen at many good fishmongers, but if you want to avoid paying punitive money for them, try to get them wholesale. As suggested on page 286, a good local restaurant that regularly serves langoustines might be able to help you out with this mission.

Cooking When it comes to eating your Dublin Bay prawns, the simplest preparations are the best. Plunged alive into rapidly boiling seawater, or freshwater salted with 2 tablespoons of salt per quart, Dublin Bay prawns will take between three and five minutes after coming back to a boil, depending on size. They can then be eaten hot or cold, with melted butter, mayonnaise or, better still, good olive oil with a little finely chopped chile, lemon juice, parsley, and garlic.

My favorite way to cook Dublin Bay prawns is over a beach fire or grill. Turn them frequently, and over hot embers they will take about ten minutes. They are done when the bend in the tail has stiffened.

SHRIMP The common shrimp of inshore waters (called *prawns* in the U.K.) is a fabulous little creature for which I have had a large and enduring soft spot ever since paddling in the Fairy Ring Pool with my little net thirty years ago.

But despite my enthusiasm for shrimping, I've never been able to work out exactly what it is that makes some rocky beaches prime shrimp-hunting territory and others relatively shrimp-free. I have known beaches scattered with hundreds of shrimpy-looking, weed-fringed rock pools – from which I have drawn a complete blank; others where just a few shallow pools have yielded a fine harvest. A combination of rocks, muddy sand, and plenty of seaweed seems to be productive, but I have also had success in rock pools that appear on sand- and mud-free limestone reefs exposed at low tide. I suspect there are good shrimp beaches all around the coast of England, but I have had my most productive hunting in the south and southwest – particularly on the coast of South Wales, Dorset, and Devon. Common shrimp seem to be very scarce in Scotland.

When you arrive at a new hunting ground, one fairly quick way to ascertain how good the sport is likely to be is to knock a few limpets off the rocks, mash them up with a stone, and throw the juicy mess into a likely-looking rock pool. Blennies, gobies, and small crabs will certainly go for them, but within a couple of minutes shrimp, if there are any in the vicinity, should arrive to investigate the smell.

On a good shrimpy beach, you will catch shrimp by wading through rock pools and simply running a fine-meshed net along the edges of weed-fringed rocks and beneath little underwater overhangs. The choice of net is important: shrimping nets with a wooden bar at the front for pushing through the sand are not suitable for rock pool work. The best shrimp net I ever owned had a diamond-shaped opening, the pointed end of which was ideal for poking into little corners. I wonder what happened to it.

Another effective rock pool technique, however, is to stalk individual shrimp, again using the ubiquitous limpet as bait (or a small shore crab with the carapace ripped off). Place the bait in your net and sink it in the bottom of a rock pool. Any shrimp will soon start to approach. When a decent specimen is right in, or over, your net, lift it up smoothly and quickly. Should you twitch the net prematurely, your shrimp will shoot backward out of range, but let it settle and they'll soon creep cautiously back. If you are patient and efficient, you can often get two or three at a time. Using this method, it may take all the time that the tide allows to catch enough shrimp for tea for two, but it's hard to imagine how to have more fun on a beach.

There are various nets and traps especially designed for catching common shrimp. It seems they are mostly used by anglers collecting shrimp to use as bait (live shrimp are deadly for pollack and bass), but there is no reason why they should not be deployed by those with culinary motives. Most useful is a circular drop net, with either a nylon or collapsible wire mesh, which is baited and then lowered on a line into deep rock pools, off the end of reefs, or from jetties and harbor walls where shrimp are known to congregate, until it touches the bottom. Every few minutes, the net is pulled up, swiftly and smoothly so the shrimp do not have time to swim up and out. You can buy a drop net from most seaside tackle shops or make your own from the rim of an old bicycle wheel.

Common shrimp are also caught commercially on strings of shrimp pots, which are baited with crab or fish and thrown, like lobster pots, on inshore reefs. It was on holidays in Dorset as a child that I first encountered this highly effective technique, as practiced by Weymouth schoolteacher and part-time potsman, Dennis Cheeseman. Dennis used to take me and my friend Charlie out on his little skiff to pull the pots, and our job was to sift through their contents, throwing back all the periwinkles, whelks, and blennies and keeping all the shrimp. It was sheer bliss for a seven-year-old, who found every single critter that appeared in the pot (including, on occasion, pipefish, small conger eels, and brightly colored cuckoo wrasse) an object of deep fascination.

If you can get hold of two or three shrimp pots, they can usefully extend the range of your shrimp hunting: marked with a buoy on a line, they can either be dropped from a boat or thrown from the end of a reef. They should be checked every day or every low tide. Small collapsible shrimp traps, built on the same "they can check in but they can't check out" principle, can also be bought from some tackle shops, and can be fished in strings if weighted with an anchor and marked by a buoy, or simply anchored in a good rock pool for the duration of a tide. Pots and traps dropped below the low tide mark often tend to catch the larger shrimp.

Buying Buying shrimp is not nearly as much fun as catching them, but there is a sensible and not-so-sensible way to do it. At fishmongers, the "shell-on" cooked shrimp you see have been bought frozen in large catering packs and dished out, a few handfuls at a time, onto the counter. Cooked shrimp freeze well, so this isn't the end of the world. But these defrosted shrimp may sit around for a while, losing condition, before you buy them. And some of our less scrupulous fishmongers have a naughty habit of popping any unsold shrimp back in the freezer at the end of the day and bringing them out again the next. They end up mushy and stale. The obvious answer is to buy your own catering pack of frozen shell-on shrimp and dispense and defrost them as and when you need them. They will be as good as, or better than, anything you can buy at the fishmonger's, and you will be master of their quality.

Shrimp are now imported from all over the world, and all sorts of them turn up on the fishmonger's counter. Whether raw or cooked, most of these have been previously frozen, but occasionally you will find giant shrimp such as tiger shrimp that have been airfreighted in fresh and still uncooked. At their best, they can be very good, but they are always extremely expensive. With the frozen alternatives, quality is variable. If you find something you like, it may again be worthwhile buying the frozen product in bulk and defrosting as needed.

Cooking I rarely cook shrimp in an elaborate way. Live shrimp should be dropped in boiling seawater (or freshwater salted at the rate of 2 tablespoons per quart). Two minutes is all that is required to turn them pink and cook them through, unless they are unusually large, when three minutes may be allowed. I like to eat them as soon as they are cool enough to peel without burning my fingers. The tails are obviously where the meat is, but the heads are definitely worth a suck. Freshly boiled shrimp really need no accompaniment, but if you want a little extra something, then a homemade mayonnaise, melted butter, or a dipping pool of olive oil can be nice, especially if flavored with a little chopped garlic and black pepper.

The exception that proves my simplicity rule for shrimp is the Shrimp and Sea Lettuce Tempura on page 340.

BROWN SHRIMP Although superficially similar to common shrimp, the lifestyle and habitat of the brown shrimp are distinctly different. While the common shrimp swims freely over and around rocky reefs, the brown shrimp spends most of its life either on, or just under, the sand. Likewise, in a curious way, the taste is somehow similar but different. I couldn't tell you which I prefer, only that I like eating both of them very much indeed.

There is no shortage of sand around our coast, but to support a large population of shrimp the sand has to be of just the right quality – a little bit muddy, but not too much – and also have the right relationship with the tide and currents. For this reason, the presence of shrimp in inshore waters is fairly localized. I know of no good shrimping grounds in Dorset, but a few in Cornwall and Norfolk. The beaches and bays of the Severn Estuary and Morecambe Bay have, at one time or another, all been known for the quality and abundance of their shrimp, but both these shrimping grounds are now in decline thanks to overfishing, and perhaps also pollution. Nonetheless, there are many sandy beaches that are never fished commercially that have resident populations of shrimp, which can be caught at low tide in sand pools, and occasionally in the shallows on the shoreline (provided there is very little surf). It never hurts to have a go.

Commercial shrimp fishermen use various customized dragnets, all of which operate on exactly the same principle as your common or garden shrimping net: a heavy pole or bar is pushed (or dragged) through the sand, forcing the shrimp out of the sand so they can be scooped up by the net that comes behind. Some use large scaffold poles on a chain, dragged behind a special boat that, drawing only 1 foot or so, can be used in very shallow waters. Others drag their shrimp nets behind tractors that are specially adapted to drive through a yard of water. And until fairly recently, horses were also used to trawl for shrimp.

Casual but "serious" shrimpers also pull customized dragnets (usually fronted by a short length of scaffold pole) over their shoulders. It's very hard work, but productive when the shrimp are in. You could, if you are good at that sort of thing, make your own dragnet.

The rest of us will have to content ourselves with a good old-fashioned shrimping net mounted on a stout pole. I suggest you buy the largest (i.e., widest) and strongest you can find. Shrimp can be fished in sand pools (as opposed to rock pools) left by the tide, and also on sand flats in a yard or so of water, at any stage of the tide, but especially on a rising tide. Simply push your shrimping net through the water, with the bar a couple of inches under the sand, checking every few yards to see if you have caught anything. You should not expect to see your quarry before it ends up in your net.

Buying Freshly cooked brown shrimp (*crevettes grises* to the French) are frustratingly hard to come by in the shops, though posh London fishmongers sometimes have them. Acquiring them regularly is another problem that a good fish wholesaler might be able to help you with. Already prepared potted shrimp may be easier to find, and at their best they are well worth seeking out. I keep a small stack of James Baxter's finest, from Morecambe Bay, on permanent stand-by in the freezer. They are what I use for my one and only "fancy" shrimp dish – as a dressing/sauce for purple sprouting broccoli (see page 97).

Cooking The sandy-gray, semitranslucent brown shrimp turns pinky-brown when cooked. As with regular shrimp, seawater is best, and it should be boiling when the shrimps are thrown in. They will be cooked just two or three minutes after the water comes back to a boil.

Like prawns, freshly boiled shrimp need little accompaniment, but it would be a sin not to mention their amazing affinity with butter. Peeled shrimp can be tossed in melted butter, to which has been added a pinch each of mace, nutmeg, and cayenne pepper. They can then be eaten straight away, or potted in butter and refrigerated for later consumption, either hot or cold.

favorite mollusks

Before describing what I consider to be the most worthwhile edible mollusks, it seems in order to issue a mild warning about the small risk of food poisoning that consuming them may entail. It has long been said that shellfish, particularly oysters and mussels, should not be harvested and eaten unless there is an "r" in the month – thereby excluding the summer months between May and August. There is a certain logic to this guideline, but not one widely understood. There is no mysterious poison that arises seasonally in these organisms. It is rather that, in the summer months, when the waters are warm, most mollusks have their breeding season, which already puts them partly out of condition. This is also a time when, due to the higher water temperature, naturally occurring bacteria are greatly on the increase and are also introduced by organic pollutants such as sewage. Under this combination of conditions, the ability of some shellfish (cockles, mussels, and other bivalves in particular) to filter out dangerous toxins may be impaired.

But provided you take your shellfish from clean waters and follow a few simple rules in their preparation, you can safely eat mollusks all year round. (Having said that, you might like to try, for considerations of conservation rather than safety, not knocking them too hard when the poor little blighters are trying to make babies.) So the full set of safety rules is as follows:

- Never collect shellfish (bivalves especially) close to human habitation, near busy ports and harbors, or near a sewage outlet.
- Always rinse shellfish well in clean water before cooking.
- Always check that your shellfish are alive immediately before cooking. Bivalves should close tightly shut when tapped with a finger or run under cold water.
- You should not eat any shellfish raw unless you are 100 percent confident that it is not contaminated.

CLAMS There are almost twenty species of clams found around the British coast, some more easily encountered than others, depending on their habits. All are edible, and many are delicious, though some, like the little pink tellin, are often too tiny to be viable. Perhaps the best find is the carpet shell clam (which the French call *palourde*), which can be raked from gravelly sand at low tide, sometimes rather closer to the high tide mark. Their presence is indicated by two little dimples in the sand, ⅜ to 1¼ inches apart. They are outstandingly good.

Another lovely clam is the enormous American hard clam, or quahog – almost the size of a scallop. It is not native to our waters but has been introduced here either deliberately or by accident, according to the theory you choose to believe. The story I like is that the quahogs on the south coast are descendants of clams flung out of the galley portholes of American cruise ships as they came into port at Southampton – the clams being discarded, as they would not stay fresh for the return journey.

Also worthwhile, though on the small side, is the wedge shell, or bean clam. These have a triangular but not quite symmetrical shell, and are found right at the low water mark: their patches are often only rakeable at the lowest low water marks, during spring tides. The meat is a little chewy but very pleasantly sweet.

Buying The clams you are most likely to find on sale in fishmongers in Britain are carpet shells. They are very popular with the restaurant trade and therefore becoming increasingly expensive. If you want to buy them in any quantity, try to go direct to a fish wholesaler.

Cooking Clams are usually fairly clean, but, to remove any loose grit, they should be briefly scrubbed under cold running water before cooking. All clams can be steamed open, like mussels, in a court-bouillon of wine and/or water, butter, herbs, and, optionally (but highly recommended), garlic. They are ready when all, or at least the vast majority, are open.

Small clams such as the wedge shell, steamed open and mixed with a piquant tomato sauce, make a classic vongole sauce for spaghetti.

RAZOR CLAMS Anyone who has kept their eyes open on a beach will have seen the long, empty shells of this creature, so resembling the eponymous cut-throat razor, but few have ever seen one alive. Still fewer have had the distinct pleasure of eating them. This lovely clam deserves, I think, its own entry in this chapter, partly because it is very underrated, and partly because there is a specialized and highly effective technique for gathering them. I have deployed it successfully in Dorset, Norfolk, and Scotland, so take it from me – it works.

Razor clams are found on sandy beaches at, and just below, the low tide mark. Generally, it is only practical to gather them on the lowest spring tides. But when conditions are right, and provided you have the tools for the job, a good number can be collected in a fairly short time.

Like most species of clam, the razor lives a few inches below the surface of the sand, but if disturbed, or sensing danger, the powerful muscular foot of this species can quickly pull it almost a yard under. The secret of luring it out is to irritate it, and the best way to do this is to pour salt down its burrow. A particularly effective technique is to put a very strong warm saline solution in a gardener's backpack-mounted weedkiller spray can. The razor clam reveals its place in the sand by a single dimple, about ¾ inch wide, in the center of which is its blow hole. Into this hole, you insert the nozzle of the spray can and give a good squirt of very salty water. Within a minute or two (sometimes longer, and occasionally not at all) the razor clam will shoot to the surface, sometimes with impressive speed, and usually protruding by a good few inches, allowing you to pluck it easily from the sand. In areas where razor clams are plentiful, you can walk along the low tide mark, squirting a couple of dozen holes, then turn back on yourself to pick up the razor clams that have emerged.

A slosh of neat table salt also works well, and is even more effective if swiftly followed by a squirt of water to wash it down the hole: an old liquid dish soap bottle does the trick nicely.

Buying The restaurant trade is starting to use razor clams, and I predict we shall be seeing a lot more of them. At the moment, they crop up in some good fishmongers and are not that expensive. Any decent fishmonger, or fish wholesaler, should be able to order them for you.

Cooking Razor clams can be a bit sandy, so it is a good idea to purge them – just rinse well and then leave them in a bucket of clean seawater for a few hours. Rinse again in freshwater before cooking. Thus purged, the entire contents of the razor shell can be eaten, though the muscular foot is the sweetest morsel. Pulled away from the rest of the meat, this little chunk can be eaten raw, and makes excellent sushi.

Otherwise, their elongated shape notwithstanding, razor clams are prepared much as any other clams: steamed open in a shallow court bouillon of water, wine, butter, herbs – and, of course, garlic. Their size and shape also make them well suited to a beach fire or barbecue: lay them on a wire rack above the hot coals and cook until tender and bubbling in their own juices.

See also Clams with Pork Tenderloin and Chorizo (page 341).

COCKLES The cockle doesn't have the sweetness of the mussel or the subtlety of the scallop, but these plump, heart-shaped shells provide a tasty morsel of meat all the same. Populations are found all around the British Isles, but are localized where conditions are just right: cockles prefer a mixture of sand, mud, and sometimes fine gravel. Wide, flat beaches around tidal estuaries are a good bet. My own most productive patch is an hour's drive from River Cottage, to the east. I'm afraid I'm not going to tell you exactly where! They are found on the Pacific coast in the U.S.

Generally, local knowledge may point you in the right direction, but finding a new cockling patch is a cause for great satisfaction, so always be on the lookout for a profusion of empty cockle shells – a natural sign that living progeny may not be far away. Cockles occur usually between the mid- and low water marks, but some cockling patches are revealed only at the lowest tides (during full and new moons), so this may be the best time to try out new hunting grounds.

You will occasionally encounter cockles just sitting on the sand waiting to be plucked, but most will be found a few inches under the surface. The essential tool for exposing them is an ordinary garden rake – or a customized cockler made by banging a few 4-inch nails through a bit of wood and fixing a handle to it. Rake backward and forward over the sand and see what comes up. Where cockles are regularly raked, you may have to work hard for every shell, but if you are lucky enough to find a new patch, you can often fill a bucket in half an hour.

Buying Cockles are still plentiful in Britain and therefore fairly cheap. Good fishmongers sell them alive and in the shell – to make sure they really are alive, check that all, or almost all, of the shells are tightly closed. You can also buy fresh or frozen cockle meat, out of the shell, but in my experience this has lost all the sea-fresh flavor of the live cockle and is not worthwhile. Nor am I a fan of cockles pickled in vinegar.

Cooking Cockles can contain quite a lot of sand. The best way to purge them of it is to rinse them well, then leave them in a large bucket of clean seawater in a cool place for several hours. Rinse again in clean freshwater before cooking.

One of the best and simplest ways of cooking cockles is to steam them open in a shallow court-bouillon of wine brought to a boil with butter, garlic, and a few herbs. Throw in the cockles, in batches if you have a lot of them, and remove each batch with a slotted spoon when they have opened. If you want to serve the liquor with cockles (and you should; it's delicious), then it is a good idea to strain it through a cloth to filter out any sand that may have remained. You can enrich it with a spoonful of cream and flavor it with a little chopped parsley just before serving.

MUSSELS Although mussels are one of the most prolific of the bivalve species, and one of the best distributed, I have yet to find really good mussel beds that are within easy striking distance of River Cottage. It's a disappointment, as I'm mad about mussels – so any inside information will be gratefully (and discreetly) received.

All wild mussels growing in clean water taste good, so as far as I'm concerned the main issue for the mussel hunter is size – the bigger the better. The enthusiast is ever in search of new pastures, where bigger, fatter mussels may be found. Mussels will grow on just about anything (as mussel farmers have demonstrated, rearing seed mussels on wooden stakes, scaffold poles, and heavy ropes). Experience shows that larger mussels are often found nearer the low tide mark, and logic suggests that this may be because they are submerged for longer and so spend more time feeding. There are anomalous exceptions, and occasionally you will find a lush clutch of plump mussels growing near the high tide mark, sometimes among a bed of their rather tiny cousins.

Mussels can simply be pulled from the rocks or other obstacles to which they have anchored themselves. If you are collecting a large number, a stout gardening glove (or similar) is a distinct advantage, since the shells can be sharp, as can the barnacles that cling to them.

Some mussels, and sometimes whole colonies of mussels (mainly those that have to filter a lot of sand), can be gritty, as they contain tiny pearls spun around irritant particles to protect their sensitive gut. This does not make them inedible, but it can be a bore spitting out the little pearls. If you can't hack it, it's time to move on to a fresh, pearl-free hunting ground.

Buying The mussels you buy are almost always farmed these days, and some are a lot better than others, so be ready to shop around. I have had too many small, anemic mussels of indifferent flavor in restaurants and from fishmongers. Mussels are still fairly cheap, but if you want to buy a lot, for a party perhaps, go direct to wholesalers. Increasingly popular are those giant greenlip mussels imported from New Zealand and elsewhere. In the U.S., Prince Edward Island (PEI) mussels are prized.

Cooking Before cooking, mussels should be well rinsed in freshwater and scrubbed if they are very dirty. The "beards" (those wiry hairs that hold the mussels to the rocks – and often to each other) should also be removed. They are easily torn away either with a light pair of pliers or if gripped between your thumb and a blunt knife.

If your mussels are going to be presented in their shells, it is particularly important to clean them thoroughly and scrape off the barnacles. But if you are planning to remove the meat from the shells and present it in some other way (see Mussel and Sea Beet Gratin on page 343), then as long as mud and loose dirt are removed, you don't need to scrape or debeard them. The beards can be easily removed from cooked mussels, and if you want to use the liquor as a basis of a sauce, just strain it through cheesecloth or a cotton cloth to filter out any loose grit.

The simplest way to cook mussels is to throw a glass of wine, a glass of water, and a good tablespoon of butter into a large pan, add two crushed cloves of garlic, and bring to a fierce boil. Add the mussels, put on a lid, and shake the pan well every minute or so. Check progress after about three minutes. Mussels should be cooked as lightly as possible: remove them from the heat as soon as a good three-quarters of them are wide open, and discard any that fail to open. Never overcrowd the pan (not more than three mussels deep, I always say), and if you have a lot of mussels, cook them in batches: each batch can be removed with a slotted spoon and the liquor brought back to a boil before the next batch is added.

The cooking liquor is too delicious not to serve with the mussels, but it may need to be strained through a cloth if it looks a bit sandy. You can enrich it with a spoonful of cream and a pinch of saffron.

It can be very satisfying to cook up a few mussels right where you find them. Good-sized specimens can be grilled on a barbecue, a rack over a beach fire, or in hot ashes until the shells open. Mussels from very clean water are delicious raw: a little less meaty, but much sweeter, than oysters. Try dressing them with just a few drops of very good olive oil, a twist of black pepper, and the tiniest squeeze of lemon.

SCALLOPS The inshore waters off the Dorset coast have long supported excellent and productive scallop beds. They may not for long, as the dredgers are hard at work dragging them up, along with anything else that gets in their way. I have seen with my own eyes, while diving, that dredging has rendered whole areas of seafloor into near deserts. It is ecologically disastrous and should be banned. Diving for scallops is the sound alternative: it is selective, in that no other species are molested, and sustainable, in that undersized scallops are left on the seabed to grow on.

Scallops are widespread all around the British coastline and are found on the U.S. Atlantic coast. Gregarious creatures, they live in beds on firm mud, sand, and gravel, often close to kelp forests (which provide the necessary cover for tiny young scallops). Dedicated snorkelers may find a few scallops in water shallow enough to duck-dive for them, but their usual range is 10 to 40 yards, and only qualified divers will regularly enjoy the privilege of a free scallop feast.

Buying Nondivers will have to pay (or barter) for their scallops: if you want a decent number, you will get a far better price if you can buy direct from a scallop diver than you ever will from a fishmonger. I always like to buy my scallops alive and in the shell, as a guarantee of freshness. When touched or prodded, a live scallop should snap shut.

Preparation The scallop contains a really exquisite disk of sweet white meat (the adductor muscle), but it is wrong to think that this is the only worthwhile part. In fact, the only part of it that *must* be discarded is the black sac near the hinge of the shell, which contains the waste from feeding. Get rid of this, and everything else is edible – including the juices, the coral, and the ribbonlike "fringe" (which is actually a string of eyes!) that runs around the inside of the shell. My recipe for Fennel Risotto with Scallops (see page 348) is especially designed to make the best use of all these goodies, while still presenting the muscle meat center stage.

To open a scallop, hold it vertically on a board, hinge end up, with the flat side of the shell facing toward you. Insert a knife blade into the gap in the shell just below the hinge and slice down, as close as possible to the flat side of the shell. The shell will spring open, and you can snap off the flat side at the hinge: all the meat and organs will be left sitting in the deep side of the shell. Then run a sharp, flexible blade around the offending black sac; remove and discard it. If you just want the main muscle for your meat, scrape everything else away – ideally into a small pan to make a lovely sweet stock (see page 348). The muscle can then be released by running the flexible blade between it and the shell.

The muscle from very large, fat scallops can be sliced horizontally in half to create two disks of meat that will cook through in a matter of seconds.

Cooking There are dozens of ways to cook a scallop and dozens of ways to overcook them – this is a great mistake, as it quickly renders one of the sweetest and most pleasant-textured of all shellfish rubbery and bland. I don't like elaborate scallop dishes, both because of the danger of overcooking and because I don't find them conducive to enjoying fresh scallops at their best.

One good way to be absolutely sure you don't overcook scallops is to eat them raw, as sashimi. Prepare this dish with only the freshest scallops and use only the white adductor muscle, not the pink coral. Slice them as thinly as possible and arrange on a plate. Dress with just a trickle of toasted sesame oil, a few drops of light soy sauce, and a bit of wasabi mustard on the side. Serve with thin strips of cucumber marinated with rice wine vinegar.

When I cook scallops, they tend to get between thirty seconds and a minute either side, on a hot griddle, a heavy frying pan, or a grill. I prefer piquant dressings and salsas to creamy sauces. See page 344 for a super and simple scallop dish that you can eat with your hands on the beach.

WHELKS Whelks are one of the larger species of sea snail in our waters and are extremely widespread, living on carrion on mud, sand, and rocks all around the British coast. They seem to divide seafood enthusiasts: some dismiss them as uninteresting, rubbery lumps; others rave about their chewy texture and a flavor that has been described as "between lobster and chicken." Once siding with the skeptics, I am now a recent convert – to whelks that have been properly prepared. I mostly get mine from Jack; he doesn't fish for them, but a fair few always end up in his net. He'll usually add a few in with the rest of my fish at no extra charge.

The common whelk lives mainly below the low tide mark, but smaller ones can be found in (and gathered from) rock pools near the low tide mark. A smaller species of whelk, known as the dog whelk, with a whitish, yellow-, or brown-banded shell, feeds on mussels and barnacles and is often found among them on rocky beaches at low tide. It is also edible. Knobbed whelks are found on the U.S. Atlantic coast, and lightning whelks in Gulf waters.

Larger whelks are easily caught in baited traps dropped on the bottom below the low tide mark and marked with a buoy. Traditionally, large wicker baskets with simple lobster-pot-style entries were used, especially on the prolific whelk fisheries off Grimsby, East Anglia, and Whitstable. Now nylon and wire mesh traps are more common. You can easily fashion your own whelk trap from fine-mesh chicken wire wrapped in a tube shape and sealed at one end, with a crude, inward-pointing entrance at the other. Lash it securely to a couple of bricks to anchor it to the seafloor.

Whelks have a tendency to concentrate toxins in their gut and should only be taken from waters in whose cleanliness you have complete confidence.

Buying Whelks should never be expensive to buy, but those you find at the fishmonger's are rarely as fresh as you would ideally like them – i.e., alive. Mostly they've been boiled and shelled. They're not as tasty as if you'd done them yourself – with a few herbs and spices and a little wine or vinegar in the cooking liquid.

Cooking Whelk shells can be very dirty and silty, and the whelks have a tendency to exude slime. To minimize both problems, they should be well scrubbed, placed in a bucket of cold freshwater for a few hours, then scrubbed again. They can then be boiled in clean seawater or well-salted freshwater, to which you have added plenty of black pepper, a halved onion, two bay leaves, a large carrot, sliced, and a glass of wine or tablespoon of wine vinegar. These flavorings will help bring out the whelks' unusual savory taste. They take about ten minutes to cook at a merry simmer – traditionally, they are ready when the "operculum," a scaly disk that seals the creature in its shell, comes away from the meat of the foot.

I like to eat just-boiled whelks still warm with a good homemade mayonnaise, to which I sometimes add chopped chives. Pull them out with a pin and dip them in. As with periwinkles, the last part to emerge from the shell, though it is edible, can be separated from the firm meat of the foot and discarded.

PERIWINKLES You've got to hand it to a sea snail that in Britain has lent its name not only to an item of fashion footwear but also, as affectionate slang, to a vital part of a small boy's anatomy. Apart from this claim to fame, periwinkles are the beach forager's favorite stand-by – not the most subtle or sophisticated of seafoods, but dead easy to collect and fun to eat all the same. On almost every rocky beach, you will find them in rock pools, on and under rocks, and especially underneath the seaweed. In the U.S., they are known as sea snails.

If you can't find a periwinkle on a rocky beach in the U.K., then I can only assume that you are extremely short-sighted and have forgotten your glasses – or that there has been a nuclear catastrophe. You should be able to gather dozens of them at low tide in a matter of minutes. Having said that, it is worth a little wander to find an area where all the periwinkles seem to be of a good size – normally near the low tide mark.

Buying Periwinkles can occasionally be bought alive from fishmongers or fish wholesalers. You are more likely to encounter them cooked – in which case, if at all possible, sniff before you buy to make sure they are cooked.

Cooking Live periwinkles are usually fairly clean, needing only a thorough rinse under the tap or in clean seawater. From some sandy localities, however, they may be a little gritty: they can be improved by soaking in cold freshwater overnight.

Like whelks, their flavor is improved if they are cooked in salted water with a few aromatic additions: try a bay leaf, quartered onion, large carrot, a few parsley stalks, and *a lot* of black pepper. Simmer this little stock together for at least ten minutes before adding the periwinkles. Once they have come back to a boil, give them five minutes.

Warm or cold, the periwinkles thus cooked are removed from their shells with a pin (the original winkle-picker) and eaten plain, or dipped in shallot vinegar or mayonnaise. The only nonedible bit is the scaly "door" to the shell – easily removed with your pin – though some people also like to discard the "trail" (the last 3/8 inch or so that emerges from the shell), as it can be a little gritty.

Finally, a subsection of the family of mollusks, the cephalopods:

CUTTLEFISH Cuttlefish are not much explored in British kitchens, which is a pity because they make very fine eating. Basically, you're sure to like cuttlefish if you like squid, which they resemble closely and for which they can be substituted in any recipe. You may even prefer them to squid. They are not found on U.S. coasts, however.

I didn't realize until I came to Dorset that cuttlefish are taken in considerable quantities here on the south coast, and close inshore too. Sometime in early summer – May, usually – the first cuttlefish start coming into the bottom nets a few miles offshore. Often within a week or two, large numbers come within a few hundred yards of the beach, and a few of the local fishermen start to go for them in earnest. The cuttlefish have usually disappeared by early July.

They are caught in a trap not unlike a lobster pot, but larger and with two or more entrances. Instead of being tempted with fish bait, the cuttlefish are lured in with an attractor that's supposed to look like another cuttlefish. These creatures must be easily fooled, because most cuttlefish attractors are nothing more than a wedge of white polystyrene or plastic. This year, I finally acquired a cuttlefish trap of my own, and furnished it with my own homemade attractor – a sophisticated imitation guaranteed to drive the visiting cephalopods into paroxysms of sexual excitement. I can't actually prove that my lure worked any better than the traditional plastic wedge, but it did work – to the tune of four fat cuttlefish.

If you want to catch cuttlefish, you too will need a trap, and you will probably have to make it yourself. It doesn't have to be sophisticated to be successful – basically a robust metal framework stretched with a strong nylon mesh and a couple of funnel entrances fashioned from chicken wire should produce results. Don't forget the lure, or flapper.

A boat is not essential: I dropped my trap from an inflatable tractor tire, having paddled out in my wet suit. Pulling it up again is a bit difficult, but it can be done. Lie over the inflatable to maximize your buoyancy as you pull up the trap. When it comes to the surface, roll the trap over the edge of the tire, so it sits up in the middle.

Cuttlefish really come very close to shore, so an alternative to the inflatable tire technique would be simply to wade out with your trap at low tide and drop it in a few feet of water. At high tide, a few feet will become a few yards, and the cuttlefish should come to explore. But they will only come close inshore during calm weather – don't bother putting your trap out if the sea is rough.

However you catch your cuttlefish, don't be alarmed by its spectacular defense. They can squirt remarkable amounts of ink, both in the water and at you as you take them out of the traps. It is a good idea to have a dedicated cuttlefish T-shirt, rather than ruin another one every time you go fishing.

There is no officially sanctioned way to dispatch a cuttlefish, but personally I don't like to let them suffocate in the air. So I give them a firm smack between the eyes with a stick or stone, and that seems to do the trick.

Buying When it comes to buying cuttlefish, they should not be too expensive, but a little caution is in order to ensure you get a good specimen: stale cuttlefish, or defrosted frozen ones, are really of no interest.

Cuttlefish will either be on sale whole and unprepared or all scrubbed up, gutted, skinned, and ready to cook. Either way, it may be fresh or it may be grim. To find out which, you really need to get your hands on it: slip a finger just inside the body cavity and pinch the flesh between finger and thumb. It should be firm, rubbery, and resistant. If it is at all soft and gives to pressure, it's past its best.

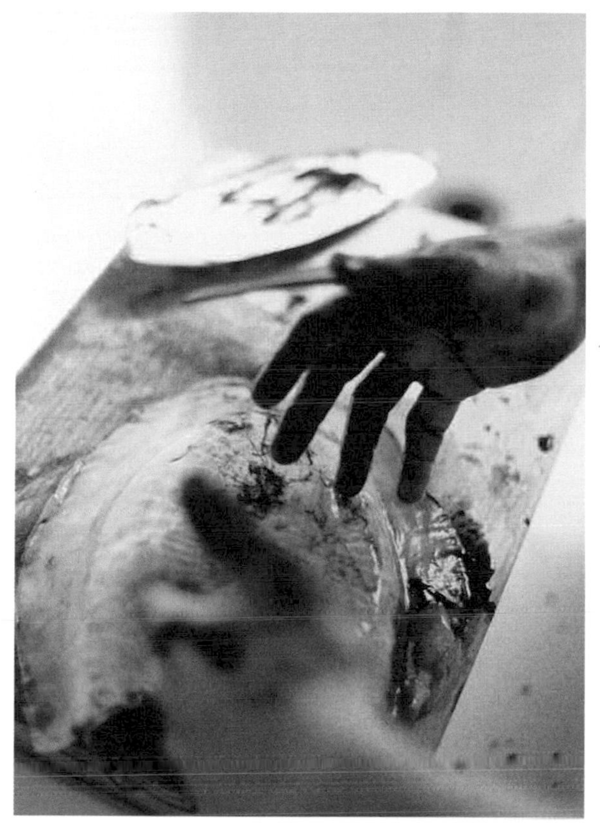

Preparation The first time I prepared a just-landed cuttlefish I did so in the kitchen sink. Three years later, the ink stains on the wall are still there. These days, I do the job in the bath. The problem is, the ink gets *everywhere*!

The first thing to do when cleaning a cuttlefish is to separate the head and tentacles from the body. This can be done with a good firm pull, and with a bit of luck you will find that most of the intestines come away with the head. Put the head to one side for the moment, but do not discard it: bits of it are edible.

At this point, it's worth trying to save the ink, especially if you want to make the delicious cuttlefish/squid recipe on page 346. Theoretically, it is possible to locate the ink sac inside the body cavity of the cuttlefish and remove it unpunctured. Practically, it is just one big black inky mess in there. I just scoop the inky contents of the cavity into a bowl, stir it to release as much ink as possible, then discard any "bits" (which may include egg or sperm sacs and the membrane from the ink sac). What's left, as far as I'm concerned, is all usable ink. If this all sounds like too much trouble, you can simply clean your cuttlefish under constantly running cold water, so that all the ink washes down the drain; as you proceed, general visibility will improve.

Next, take the body cavity and feel for the bony structure that keeps it rigid: this can be gripped between finger and thumb and pulled out. This is what they sell for budgies at the pet shop. Pull off the short, bony wings from the outside of the body, taking much of the skin with them. Peel off the rest of the skin with your fingers. What's left, when thoroughly rinsed, is the clean and empty body of the cuttlefish. It's all edible.

Now, return to the head. Squeezing the head just in front of the eyes, cut off the tentacles so that they remain attached to a small ring of flesh at the front of the head. Discard the rest of the head, including the eyes and any intestines attached to it.

You now have possession of the prime edible meat of the cuttlefish, that is, the body and the tentacles. In a good fresh specimen, you could eat it raw, as sushi.

Cooking If you're going to resist the sushi option and cook your cuttlefish, you have, in my opinion, two sensible choices: cook it very fast, in a very hot frying pan, griddle, or grill; or very slowly and gently in a stew. Either way, slit the body cone down one side and open it out so that you have a big flat triangle of cuttlefish meat. Cut it into slices 3/8 inch thick.

Cooked fast, the cuttlefish will be firm – gently resistant to the bite – but still tender enough for you to enjoy its delicious, sea-fresh flavor. Cooked slowly, it should simmer until it is completely tender – almost like soft cheese. Anything in between and you are likely to find yourself in the realms of rubber.

Good flavorings for the fast version are chile and garlic, which can be thrown on the cuttlefish, previously brushed with olive oil, as it fries or grills. The best slow version I know is described in full on page 346.

SQUID Squid, one of my favorite seafoods, can also be caught by the resourceful amateur, but you will need to go out on a boat. Here on the south coast, October and November is the season, and after dark the best time. The squid are caught on a special luminous lure with a crown of hooks called a jig, which is lowered over the side of the boat and lifted up and down until an excited squid throws out a tentacle and gets hooked up. I haven't done it yet, but plan to do so this autumn. I'll let you know how I get on.

Sometimes squid will be encountered in late summer and autumn when you are out fishing from a boat. They occasionally attach themselves to passing lures or feathers, but if you have a jig handy you have a much better chance of catching one.

freshwater fish

The river from which River Cottage gets its name is the Brit. It rises only about ten miles upstream from the cottage in the hills above Beaminster, and enters the sea at West Bay, some seven miles down river. So, not the grandest of south-coast rivers then – but to my mind there's none finer. Just about the first thing I did on arriving at River Cottage was string up my hammock between two trees beside the river at the bottom of the garden. It's a perfect vantage point for watching the wild brown trout nibbling sedges off the surface – for as long as you can keep your eyes open. I haven't spent as much time in the hammock as I'd have liked over the last four years but it's still there, albeit with a few holes in it now, and even just to look at it is a kind of therapy.

I probably spend more time actually in the river than in the hammock – setting or checking my eel trap, looking for crayfish, or flicking a fly or spinner in pursuit of the aforementioned trout. Those are the three species I occasionally take from the river to the kitchen – with not a little satisfaction and relish. But my harvest is a light one. I don't suppose I take more than a couple of dozen eels, a similar number of crayfish, and three or four brownies in an average summer.

But in another way the river sustains me on a daily basis. About fifty yards upstream from the cottage is a weir, a relic of the time when there was a small flax mill on the site (I suspect River Cottage was originally built for the mill keeper). The weir still functions, and the water that comes through it drops four or five feet as it rushes through, producing that constant stream of white noise that only water does so well. Wherever I am around the cottage – in the field, garden, or kitchen – the background hum of the weir is a constant presence. I barely notice it until I climb into bed at night, when it becomes the kind of soothing noise that isn't really noise, but silence you can listen to. If anything's bothering me, and I can't sleep, I open the window and the silence gets louder. Increasing the volume increases the sense of calm, and pretty soon I'm drifting off and dreaming.

When I say goodbye to River Cottage, as eventually I must, the soothing sound of the eponymous river is one of the things I will miss most.

the freshwater harvest

As I have said, there are only three species I take for the pot from the humble Brit. But farther afield, in some of Dorset's more substantial rivers, are more varied piscine quarry: pike, grayling, sea trout, and even the occasional salmon. There are also a number of angling sites near here, containing such underrated eaters as carp, perch, and roach. I have enjoyed experimenting with freshwater fish in the kitchen, and in so doing have proved – to my own satisfaction at least – something that I long suspected was the case: that the suitability of line-caught fish for eating is not simply a question of species. At least as important is where it came from, and the key question is, was it still or running water? The bottom line is that fish from clear running water will taste "fresher" and cleaner than fish from lakes, ponds, and gravel pits, which may have a tendency to muddiness. Generally speaking, here in Dorset I am spoiled for water quality. The pike in the photos illustrating the recipe on page 349 was caught in a weir pool on the River Frome, just outside Dorchester. The clear waters of this famous Dorset chalk stream maintain a healthy population of wild brown trout, for whom the pike is the most persistently threatening predator. What the water does for the flesh of these opportunistic aggressors is put it instantly in the seriously delicious category: anyone who enjoys eating wild trout and salmon will find a sweetwater pike a revelation.

In still waters, one can never be sure how bad the muddiness problem is going to be – although it is a pretty fair bet that a carp from a small pond that is not fed by freshwater will be distinctly earthy. Larger lakes, particularly those that are fed by rivers and streams, will not be so bad (I have never caught a pike in Loch Lomond, but when I do I'm sure it will be delicious). The quality of water in canals, the way they are fed, and the flow of the water vary considerably: some canals have the constitution of a stagnant pond, others of clean and gently flowing rivers, and the taste of the fish that you catch in them will vary accordingly. Obviously, you can make a rough visual assessment of any water you are fishing in, but the real proof of the pudding will only come with the eating. Those that feed you well will be worth revisiting.

favorite freshwater fish

The following guide to my own favorite edible freshwater fish assumes a basic knowledge of fishing techniques – and doesn't attempt to add much to it, either! An exhaustive guide to angling seriously for the seven species listed below could fill a larger book than this – and I am certainly not a good enough angler to write such a volume. What I have done is to outline in brief the accepted wisdom on basic tackle and technique for each species, plus a few little tips of my own (which may or may not stand you in good stead).

If fishing leaves you cold, but a sense of gastronomic inquiry moves you to experiment with some of the more unusual fish described below, talk to your fishmonger, who may be able to acquire them for you. If it's pike you want, talk to local fishermen. In many places they are systematically removed from the waters to help ease the pressure on trout.

CARP Originally from central Asia, most of the species of carp found in British waters were probably introduced by the Romans, who certainly appreciated the carp as food. There are several different species regularly taken by anglers, including the common, leather, mirror, crucian, koi, golden, grass, and ghost. There are also innumerable hybrids, since most species happily interbreed. All are edible, but the common, leather, mirror, and grass carp (and the hybrids closest to them) are the best eating. Best of all are the true common carp – relatively small fish that are only found in waters where no other types of carp have been introduced.

Carp have now colonized, or been introduced to, waters all over Britain. Many still waters are now managed specifically with the carp angler in mind – which means you will probably not be allowed to kill any carp that you catch. However, they can also be caught in canals, and in the stiller, deeper parts of our larger rivers – and these are likely to be less muddy-tasting than pond carp anyway.

At River Cottage, I devised a special "carp-cleaning" system, made from an old loft water tank, which fed a constant supply of fresh, flowing water from the River Brit through an old scaffold pole lowered into the middle of the weir. I kept a grass carp caught in my landlord's lake in it for a week. It came up tasting pretty clean – at least, the hint of muddiness that remained was quite acceptable, like freshly dug potatoes.

The easiest way to catch carp is bottom fishing, with a float or leger, with almost any bait, but especially lunch meat or corn. The larger carp are shy fish and fussy feeders, and the pursuit of such specimens has

become one of the most obsessive and highly specialized forms of angling. If you are interested, there is endless literature on carp fishing, and the angling press is always packed with articles about the latest techniques, gizmos, and gadgets designed to help you catch more and bigger carp. But don't expect much sympathy from the carp fraternity if you express an interest in cooking your catch.

I particularly like fishing for carp in hot weather, when you can actually see the big ones basking on the surface. They can often be tempted by a dog biscuit Super-Glued (or rubber-banded) to a size-eight hook and floated on the surface with a controller or bubble float.

Carp of between 1 and 4 pounds make the best eating. Specimens over 10 pounds are highly prized by anglers, and unless you know twenty people who would like to sit down and eat a carp, it would be a kindness to return such fine specimens to the water for other fishermen to enjoy.

Buying Nonanglers should not find it too difficult to buy carp: they are one of the few line-caught fish that are available from more enterprising fishmongers. This is because they have a small but faithful following, particularly in Chinese and Eastern European communities. So if you are curious to try this greatly underrated fish, your fishmonger should be able to get you one without too much trouble. Londoners need look no further than Soho's Chinatown; the fishmonger at the end of Gerrard Street sells live carp all year round – and live eels, too, for that matter. The problem with bought (as opposed to caught) carp is that they are pretty much certain to be farmed fish from still-water fisheries and therefore will probably taste muddy.

Cooking All carp should be gutted, de-scaled (except for leather carp, which have no scales), and thoroughly wiped of their slimy coating before cooking. As to the muddiness problem, it can certainly be partially alleviated by using only boneless, skinless fillets in your recipe. However, most traditional recipes for carp involve baking them whole in the oven, and though I have tried frying and grilling them with moderate success, I side with tradition on the whole. A foil packet, or appropriate oven pot with a lid, is the best receptacle, and the carp may be flavored with butter, sliced onions, wine, and herbs (particularly bay leaf and fennel) and, of course, seasoned with salt and pepper. For a fish of, say, 2 to 4 pounds, bake in a fairly hot oven (375°F) for thirty to forty minutes. A strongly flavored sauce complements this meaty fish, so strain off the cooking juices and whisk in a little butter or cream, then add a few drops of lemon juice or vinegar and a decisive pinch of paprika.

EELS I love eels. Not just to eat, but to wonder at. And I consider it an enormous privilege that I can catch them right here in the river at the bottom of the garden. They are an extraordinary species: immensely successful and highly adaptable. They have been fished for, farmed, and eaten in Europe for hundreds of years, yet many aspects of their natural history remain a mystery. Their migratory life cycle is the inverse of that of the salmon: they live in freshwater and migrate to the sea to breed. It is widely believed (but by no means proved) that *all* Northern Hemisphere eels breed in the Sargasso Sea (in the Atlantic, between Bermuda and the Leeward Islands), which is pretty extraordinary when you think that the adults are distributed all over Europe and on the east coast of the U.S.

Adult eels are believed to die after breeding, but the eggs, and subsequently the leaf-shaped larvae called *leptocephalus*, are borne toward Europe in the surface current known as the North Atlantic Drift. By the time they reach our shores, in late February and March, they are free-swimming elvers, and every effort of their 3-inch long transparent bodies is directed at getting into freshwater. In estuaries like the Severn, and even here in the Brit, they swim upstream with the incoming tide, especially at night, and when the tide turns, they hug the bank to avoid being swept back out to sea. And that's when the elver fishermen get their chance.

Elvers are traditionally caught in a fine-meshed rectangular net, over a yard long, mounted on the end of a pole, and set up to cover the edge of the river where the elvers are expected to be swimming. Escape routes under or around the net are blocked by piles of mud, and the net is checked every few minutes.

On a good night, an elverman on the Severn or Thames can still net up to 40 pounds of elvers. But more often he will draw a complete blank, or net only a few stragglers. Here in Dorset, the professional elvermen have long since given up the game. The catch is too unpredictable and the market too volatile – although they can fetch up to £160 (about $320) per kilo! The reason for this is that live elvers are increasingly in demand for stocking eel farms: because of their life cycle, eels cannot be bred in captivity, but elvers can be raised in ponds, where they grow rapidly to a market weight of around 2 pounds. The Japanese in particular are paying bigger and bigger sums for live elvers, which they fly to Japan and raise in massive eel farms. Eels are much in demand there, both for sushi and for a delicious traditional dish called *unagi* – grilled eels glazed with sweet soy sauce.

Because of these crazy prices, the traditional West Country elver feast is a thing of the past. Having once tasted elvers myself, with a notorious Severn elverman named Hartley Everett, I think this is a great shame. They are sensational, both his way – fried in bacon fat with a fried egg on the side – and mine (the Spanish way) – fried in olive oil with red chiles, garlic, and salt. If you ever get a chance to try them, grab it!

Here in Dorset, it is the adult eels that are of serious interest, and fortunately they are not so hard to come by. They are found in almost every conceivable kind of water, from the harbor estuary to the tiniest stream, from

the lowliest ditch to the biggest lake. And they can be caught in all of these places by a wide range of methods. Eels are largely nocturnal creatures, and whatever method you employ to catch them, success is most likely to be had at night. They can be caught the year round but are at their best for eating in the autumn, when "silvered up" in preparation for their journey back to sea.

One traditional West Country method of catching eels is called "babbing," or "ray-balling." This requires a rod (a long bamboo pole will do) and line, but no hook, and relies on the eel's penchant for earthworms. Up to a dozen worms (the larger the better) are threaded onto a length of worsted wool, using a darning needle, so that the wool passes right through the middle of their body. The threaded worms are gathered into a ball and tied to the end of the line. The ball of wool-mounted worms is then lowered into an eely stretch of water, until the first bite is felt. Then the clever bit happens: the eel, whose mouth is lined with tiny backward-pointing teeth, bites through the worm and into the wool, the fine fibers of which, in accordance with the Velcro principle, catch onto its teeth. A skilled practitioner (which I am not) then draws the eel smoothly out of the water, and with one firm shake drops it into a waiting receptacle – traditionally, an upturned umbrella.

I have had more success with eel traps. They come in various shapes and sizes, but the general principle is the same and a variation on the lobster pot idea: it's a lot easier to find your way in than out. My own trap is a classic Dutch fyke net designed for use on streams and small rivers, or ponds and small lakes. It doesn't need to be baited but relies on the eel's natural restlessness, moving around in pursuit of food and new territory, to get it into trouble. In a stream or river, the net is set parallel to the bank, and the long guide net that leads to the trap section acts as a false bank, guiding the eel into the trap. Stretched across the floor of a lake or pond, the same principle will guide any eel that wanders into the net to one of the trap ends. Last October, I went with a river-keeper friend of mine, who has a sideline in eel trapping, to net a half-acre pond. He threw a dozen or so double fyke nets randomly around the pond, and in one night we netted over 60 pounds of eels. You can see my fyke net in operation in the photograph on page 315. If you have access to a stretch of water where you suspect an eel trap might be effective, it's well worth investing in one. Try contacting a local fishing tackle shop: they may be able to order one for you.

Alternatively, catching eels on a rod and line is not difficult, provided you are prepared to be nocturnal. Fairly strong tackle is required (especially when fishing in tidal estuaries and fast water, where you will need some weight to hold the bottom). Weighting a small dead fish, or a strip of liver or bacon, is a good method. The Thames is full of eels, as are most of our major rivers. Fishing the tidal zone of such rivers can often be productive, especially when a high tide coincides with darkness. On such occasions, I used to fish eels from the towpath near Hammersmith Bridge – and I rarely came away empty-handed.

Buying Fresh eels can be bought at some of the better fishmongers, and some, especially ones that serve Asian communities in large cities, may keep live eels in special tanks. There is nothing wrong with a dead eel (except, I suppose, from its own personal perspective, or that of a veterinarian) if it is really fresh, but they do not keep well and I prefer to take mine alive, which of course guarantees freshness. Traditional eel and pie shops will also sometimes sell live eels.

Muddy-tasting eels from still ponds and lakes can be cleaned by keeping them in fresh, flowing water for about a week (any more and the eel will start to lose condition). I clean pond-caught eels here in the Brit in an old water trough with a few holes in it sunk into the river. Or at least, I did last year, until a raging torrent after a storm washed the trough downstream, taking half a dozen fat eels with it.

Killing If you are going to eat an eel, you may as well kill it as soon as you have caught it: a live eel of any size is a difficult beast to handle, and a quick dispatch will save you a lot of grief and sometimes a very bad tangle. The first rule is to use a dry cloth for handling an eel, and if possible to lay it on a bit of newspaper: the dry surface tends to stop them wriggling. Unhooking eels can be extremely difficult, especially if they have swallowed the hook. In such cases, the sensible thing is to cut the line straight away – you can retrieve your hook when you skin and gut your eel. In order to subdue an eel, the best thing to do is to whack it, not on the head but on the tail: hold it firmly with a cloth or gloved hand at the head end, and bring the tail down sharply on a heavy object, such as a log or stone. This should stun it. Then give it a sharp blow on the head. The next best step is a gory but effective one: cut its head off, just behind the gills. Unfortunately, eels being the remarkable creatures they are, it may continue to exhibit apparent signs of life long after your dispatch blow. Don't be distressed: the eel really is dead; it's just that its nervous system doesn't quite know it yet. Just cover it and go back to your fishing. It should be quite still by the time you get it home.

Skinning Unless they are going to be smoked, eels should be skinned before cooking. The vital tool for this job is a pair of pliers: the skin is tough, and clings hard to the body, so good leverage and a strong pull are essential. Use a sharp knife to release a flap of skin at the (severed) head end of the eel. Gripping the body hard with a cloth, use the pliers to work the skin back down the body toward your gripping hand. When you have skinned enough of the eel to get a grip on the skinned head end (i.e., a few inches), move your grip to this end and, pulling your two hands away from each other, peel the skin off the middle and tail: it should come off in one tubular piece. The whole process can be made easier by nailing your eel's head end to a stump or post – that way you can get two hands on the pliers.

My favorite way to cook eels is to smoke them, either hot or cold. For more details on that procedure, see the Smoking section (as opposed to the nonsmoking section) starting on page 273 of the Sea Fish chapter.

Although most of my eels go up the chimney, I ring the changes with a couple of other favorite recipes. Chinese-style eel is prepared by tossing fillets of skinned eel in finely chopped garlic and red pepper flakes, then dipping them in batter (such as the All-Purpose Fish Batter on page 345) and deep-frying them. Serve with a sweet and hot dipping sauce – either the one on page 103 or a commercial brand. My other favorite eel recipe, Eels in Green Herb Sauce, is on page 353.

PERCH Perch are beautiful fish, fun to catch (putting up, ounce for ounce, a fine fight), and very good to eat – though I must confess a prejudice, as the first fish I ever caught and ate, aged six, was a magnificent 2½-pound perch, caught in Lough Corrib, near Galway, in Ireland. It probably remains my single most impressive fishing feat – a perch of that size is really a specimen fish. It also instilled in me at an early age the pleasure and satisfaction of eating a self-caught fish.

Perch are found in a great variety of waters, but particularly in lowland lakes and ponds, and larger, slow-flowing rivers. They were all but wiped out in Britain in the 1970s by a mysterious "ulcer disease." Happily, the disease seems to have run its course and perch are bouncing back, though bigger fish are still hard to come by.

They are greedy fish, and can be caught by a variety of methods. They often gather in shoals around underwater obstacles, walls, and canal lock gates, and these are the places to try first. The depth at which they feed varies, so float fishing is probably the best bet. Maggots and worms are the standard bait, and hard to improve on, though small minnows, dead or alive, and spinners will catch the larger fish, if there are any about.

Perch scales are big and hard, and must be removed before the fish can be cooked. The fish should then be gutted – and the spiny dorsal fin can be cut off with scissors.

Buying and cooking I have never seen perch for sale in a fishmonger's in Britain, which is a pity. They have nice firm curds of tasty white meat that stand up to all kinds of cooking methods. Very small fish are good simply fried or grilled. But if ever I get one of any size (more than 1 pound), I like to bake it in a foil packet with butter, fresh herbs, and a trickle of wine, using the cooking juices as the base for a simple sauce (see Carp, page 314, for more detailed instructions).

PIKE Pike is the king predator in freshwater, and has a large mouth of viciously sharp teeth to make the point. When hungry, they will tackle any fish that come their way, as well as ducklings, frogs, and water rodents. From the angler's point of view, their aggression is their downfall. Where pike are plentiful, they are relatively easy to catch, as they can barely resist the flash of an artificial lure. Wobbling spoons, spinners, and plugs take a good number of fish, and this is certainly the most active way of fishing for them. Strong line, a reasonably stout spinning rod, and a robust fixed spool reel is the best outfit for lure fishing.

But in winter, my tried-and-true method of catching pike is what I call the stake-out: a whole dead fish, usually a sardine, small mackerel, or herring, is tossed out with a couple of treble hooks in it and a lead to keep it on the bottom, and the waiting game begins. I sometimes stick a polystyrene float inside the dead bait, to lift it off the bottom. Livebaiting, with roach, gudgeon, dace, or other small fish, can be deadly, but it is not allowed in some waters: and those that do allow it usually specify that the bait must be caught in the same water you are fishing in. Fly-fishing for pike, with large sparkling streamer flies, is a relatively new technique but is proving deadly – particularly in the hands of those with local knowledge, who know where the fish are likely to be lying.

Pike are found in rivers, lakes, and canals: most waters, in fact, from which they have not been deliberately excluded. River pike tend to make better eating than lake or pond pike, owing to the muddiness factor (see pages 311–312). On the other hand, pike from larger expanses of clean freshwater – particularly the Scottish and Irish lochs and, indeed, the great Cumbrian lakes – should certainly taste clean.

Buying Once in a blue moon, you will see a pike on a fishmonger's counter, suggesting that the more resourceful and dedicated retailer might be able to find one for you if you order it well in advance. If your fishmonger cannot oblige, and you have neither the time nor the inclination to try to catch a pike of your own, try contacting local anglers or river keepers – first stop, your local tackle shop.

Cooking Pike's great virtue as an eating fish is its flavor, which is excellent and quite distinctive. Its downside is its bones: between every flake of flesh on its back fillet is a nasty little bone shaped like a pitchfork. Forewarned, however, is forearmed, and once you know where to find these bones, you can tackle a pike without fear. Incidentally, the larger the fish, the less difficult the business of finding and removing the bones.

For those who prefer not to take their chances with bones, the solution lies in a number of preparations that have become classic for pike: mousses, quenelles, and fish cakes (see the recipe for Pike Fish Cakes on page 352). In such dishes, the flesh is mashed to a pulp (easily done in a food processor) and then rubbed through a sieve, which breaks down the smaller bones and catches the larger ones.

I have devised a special pike terrine, which I think presents the meat of this much underrated fish to its best advantage. For those ready to take up the pike challenge, you will find the recipe on page 349. Before cooking, any pike should be gutted and descaled, washed well of any slime, and patted dry.

SALMON I have never caught a salmon in Dorset, and unless stocks improve greatly I don't suppose I ever will. Barely a dozen are caught each year, mostly on the Frome. I have enough trouble pulling fish out of the (relatively) salmon-rich River Findhorn near Inverness in Scotland, where I go most years. My tally to date is four fish in fifteen years – each of which has been worth every minute of the several dozen hours' fishing it's cost me. The reason I keep going back, though, is not just for the slim chance of making contact with one of these beautiful wild fish. The process of generally not catching fish has been honed into a fine art: long days on the river are punctuated with frequent breaks for picking mushrooms, gathering bilberries, and watching the ospreys catch the fish that we can't move. Heaven.

Salmon fishing is always going to be a rather specialized pursuit, but if you want to discover whether it may be for you, one of the best places for British beginners to go is Ireland. Fishing rights on all but a few of the major salmon rivers are not privately owned, and access to genuinely good sport can often be had by just paying a few pounds at the local post office. Salmon are also found from northern California to Alaska on the Pacific coast.

Buying Wild salmon is available seasonally in fishmonger's shops – usually from early March until October – but it is often outrageously expensive. If you want to buy a whole large fish to cook for a party, your best bet might be to try to contact a wholesaler and see if they can include you in their round of deliveries. Or go for sea trout, which is always wild, every bit as good, and usually much cheaper.

Of course, the vast majority of salmon eaten in Britain is farmed. And the vast majority of farmed salmon is, in my opinion, rubbish – not least because it is fed rubbish (almost literally, in some cases) and rubbish laced with chemicals at that. On the cooking courses I sometimes give in Scotland, my first demonstration on day one is to show my course guests the difference between a wild and a farmed fish. They actually look like different species. Everything about a farmed fish looks fat, lazy, and sluggish. Its fins and tail are worn to blunt stumps by constant rubbing against the walls of its cage. By contrast, the wild fish looks sleek and bulletlike. Its fins and tail are sharp edged and keen. Once the fish are cut, the differences are even more plain to see: the exposed flesh of the farmed fish looks flabby and greasy and is dyed an unnatural orange. The wild fish is a proper salmon pink, and its flesh is firm, tight, and almost dry to the touch.

A comparative tasting of homemade gravlax, one farmed, one wild, revealed that my guests' taste buds in every case discerned the difference, and in every case preferred the wild fish.

To add to this depressing tale of taste is a huge environmental question mark over the whole business of salmon farming. Or perhaps that should be an exclamation mark, with several expletives before it. It is beyond dispute that the waste from huge numbers of caged fish is contaminating lakes. Less clear, but even more alarming, are the potential long-term effects of the massive chemical doses that are necessary to prevent mass disease wiping out whole farms of fish herded together at such unnatural stocking rates. The chemicals, of course, don't always work, and mass expiries of stocks – hundreds of thousands of fish at a time – are commonplace.

Whether pollution from fish farms is directly or indirectly responsible for the recent outbreak of amnesic shellfish poisoning (a disease that has rendered scallops, mussels, and other shellfish too dangerous for human consumption in many Scottish waters for the last two years) is a matter of vigorous dispute. But there can be little doubt that, due to overproduction and a downward price war, the industry is spiraling out of control. Let's not forget that it was the pursuit of ever-cheaper beef that produced the greatest food disaster of our age, mad cow disease. The recklessness of the salmon farming industry seems well on course to produce a similar (or perhaps frighteningly dissimilar) disaster.

Having said all that, I believe that salmon farming could and should be a completely legitimate and worthwhile activity. The best farmed salmon is really pretty good. I know that many Scottish fish farmers are working to improve their industry standards. The Soil Association has recently approved the use of the term *organic* to describe farmed salmon produced according to a more reasonable set of strictures, placing specific limits on stocking density, types of feed, and the use of chemicals. One could argue over whether *organic* is the right word to describe these fish, but if they are produced on a sustainable and nondamaging basis, then they certainly deserve recognition in the marketplace.

Cooking There must be thousands of recipes for salmon, and I suppose that now there is so much cheap farmed salmon on the market there might be an argument for getting a bit experimental with this fish. But I've said my bit about the farmed product, and I can't say I'm much inclined to expand my limited repertoire for preparing the wild fish. A fresh wild salmon is such a beautiful raw ingredient that it hardly requires any fancy preparation. If I catch one (and I am not faced with this dilemma as often as I would like), there are only four options for me: sushi (or sashimi), gravlax, smoking (see page 273), or the very simplest of cooking methods (usually a foil packet or a frying pan).

The last salmon I caught was a beautiful fresh fish, weighing just under 10 pounds. I split it into two large fillets, and on the evening of the day it was landed served up sushi and sashimi made with thin strips of fillet from the naturally fatty belly and some leaner meat from the head end. I cut two small fillets from the tail end, which I fried up for supper for Marie and myself, and served with French lentils tossed with chopped fresh parsley and a mildly mustardy dressing. What remained was two beautiful fillets from the middle of the fish, weighing about 3 pounds each. These I turned into gravlax (see page 329), which I cured for exactly a week – which just happened to coincide with my father's sixty-fifth birthday party. All highly satisfactory.

In the past, I have also dedicated my rare salmon catches to the instant gratification of my fellow houseguests. One of the factors in making this decision is how "fresh" the fish is – not in the sense of hours since death, but rather time spent in the river. Running fish just in from the sea may be identified by their fresh silvery color, full plump bodies, and the possible presence of sea lice. Fish in such good condition are likely to be full of shrimpy flavor and nicely barded with a natural layer of fat. This is wild salmon at its sea-fresh best, and any such fish of, say, 4 to 8 pounds is a prime candidate for baking in a simple foil packet.

To do this, lay the fish on a generously buttered double layer of foil and place in the cavity a bay leaf, a few parsley stalks, maybe a sprig of fennel, and a tablespoon of butter. Season the fish inside and out with salt and black pepper. Dot with more butter and, just before sealing up the parcel, trickle over a tablespoon of white wine. Always wrap a fish loosely to allow hot air to circulate around it. Bake in a very hot oven (425°F) for about fifteen minutes per pound – but start testing any fish of 4 pounds or more after thirty-five minutes. Test the fish by pushing a thin blade into it along the lateral line to the bone at the thickest part of the fish. It is done when the flesh is opaque right through to the bone – but err on the side of underdone. Serve with the juices reserved from the packet, with perhaps a little chopped chervil, chives, or fennel.

TROUT Trout, both rainbow and brown, are great sportfish, and trout fishing has understandably become an immensely popular, and highly commercial, sport. Many fisheries have been set up with the trout fisherman in mind, and lakes, ponds, and gravel pits have been stocked to the brim with farmed rainbow trout, providing easy and accessible sport. I would hazard a guess that there are now few places in Britain where you are more than an hour away from a trout farm. However, what is good for the fisherman is not necessarily good for the gourmet. Many, probably most, still-water trout fisheries are overstocked with fish that adapt only slowly (if at all) to a natural diet and, without the benefit of flowing freshwater, retain the unpleasant, dull, and muddy taste that characterizes farmed fish. I really hate catching trout that turn out to be almost inedibly muddy, and for this reason I restrict my stillwater trout fishing to a few fisheries where the eating quality is consistently good – or to larger lochs and lakes, usually river or stream fed, that sustain a healthy resident population of trout.

Fishing for trout in rivers and streams is an entirely different matter. Rivers like the Brit, and a dozen others in West Dorset, where wild brown trout thrive, come with their own guarantee: if they weren't clean and fairly fast flowing, the brown trout would not tolerate them. Such rivers are often also stocked with farmed rainbows. But they, too, will thrive in the clean, well-oxygenated water, adapting quickly to a natural diet of insects, small fish, and larvae. And their succulent, clean-tasting flesh will bear witness to their much-improved lifestyle.

Fly-fishing, with a rod, reel, and line specially designed for the purpose, is still the most popular, most exciting, and often most effective way to catch trout. Casting a fly is an acquired skill, and before you attempt to deploy the technique in a potentially fish-catching situation, it is good to take a lesson or two – either from a professional or from an experienced friend. The first time you feel the determined tug of a feeding trout on your line is a moment to cherish: if that doesn't get you hooked on fishing, nothing will.

In most British trout rivers, fly-fishing is the only method allowed. But in some trout farms, and a few of the larger lakes where other species are also fished, controlling authorities operate an any-method policy. Under such circumstances, artificial lures, such as plugs and spinners, can be effective, as can float fishing or legering with maggots and worms. Large rainbows, and the great cannibal brown trout (known as *ferox*) of the northern lakes and some Scottish sea lochs, may fall to small trout, used as live or dead bait, and slowly trolled at some depth behind a boat.

The sea trout is a brown trout that has decided, for reasons best known to itself, to go to sea. It has always struck me as an eminently sensible thing for a brown trout to do. They come back to the river a little older, a little wiser, and a whole lot tastier – as good, or better, than either salmon or trout. They can be caught, on fly or spinner (where allowed), in estuaries, rivers, and lochs that empty into the sea. Keen sea trout enthusiasts cast their fly after dark, when the sea trout run upriver and are most inclined to take.

Buying The wild sea trout excepted, when it comes to buying trout, I have one simple piece of advice: don't. You simply will not find wild (or river-dwelling) rainbows or brownies on sale at the fishmonger's. Farmed trout, which are sure to be rainbows, are almost without exception disappointingly insipid and unpleasantly muddy.

The wild sea trout, on the other hand – now there's a fish. In prime season (from late spring to late summer), it is both reasonably priced and unreasonably delicious – making it one of the great bargains of the fishmonger's counter. The best, freshest fish will be plump but sleek and very firm to the touch – look for a nice red color in the gills, and also the odd still-wriggling sea lice attached to the scales.

Incidentally, beware of a strange creature, sometimes misleadingly called a sea trout or salmon trout, that looks exactly like a giant farmed rainbow trout, often around 4 to 6 pounds. These are, in fact . . . giant farmed rainbow trout! They have been farmed at sea, which means they may be a marginal improvement (less muddy, for example) over freshwater-farmed rainbow, but they are pretty flabby and uninteresting all the same.

Cooking When it comes to cooking, trout and sea trout should be approached in pretty much the same way as their relative, the salmon – except that wild brownies will often be under 1 pound in weight, making them well suited to a quick grilling or frying on an impromptu river- or lakeside grill or campfire. For just such an eventuality, a small frying pan or wire grill, plus salt, pepper, and a bit of butter, can be useful kit in the tackle bag. And some fire lighters.

The classic French treatment for a very fresh wild river trout (brown, rainbow, or small sea trout) is also well worth your consideration. It's called *truite au bleu*, and only works really well with smallish fish (max 1 pound) that are only a few hours' dead. The fish should be gutted but not wiped, and dropped straight into a rapidly boiling court-bouillon (water flavored with wine, a splash of vinegar, peppercorns, and bay leaves). Simmer gently for six to ten minutes (for fish of 8 ounces to 1 pound, respectively). Drain and serve with melted butter, black pepper, and a squeeze of lemon.

In my kitchen, all larger trout (over, say, 3 pounds) tend to get the salmon treatment: either baked in foil (see page 321) or dill-pickled as for gravlax (see page 329). Large clean-river rainbows grav as well as any salmon.

CRAYFISH The native freshwater crayfish is a relative of the marine lobster (which it closely resembles), and its typical habitat is the shallower reaches of clean, fairly fast-flowing rivers and streams. They live under stones, in holes in the bank, and among the submerged root systems of waterside trees. They are only found in hard water, as soft water lacks the calcium and other minerals necessary to build the creatures' protective shells.

The native crayfish was once prolific, and remains so very locally in well-maintained clean rivers. But in its general distribution it has declined greatly this century, owing to pollution and the overzealous dredging and bank-clearing of many of our rivers and streams.

As water quality has improved in recent years, one might have expected an increase in craytish numbers. But in many areas they now have a new menace to contend with: their own kind. For some time, the American signal crayfish, larger, more adaptable, and more voracious than its English cousin, has been farmed in Britain to supply the restaurant trade. Escapees have begun to colonize our river system, and in certain areas – including the River Brit – they are rife. They are ruthlessly efficient predators, making a quick meal of any natives they encounter and soon supplanting them from the habitat. The wisdom is that if you find a signal in any given stretch of water, you may as well forget about looking for natives nearby. They'll be as good as gone.

The environmental impact does not end there, either. Signals are a predator out of tune with the species they prey on. Their favorite food, once the native crayfish have been wiped out, is fish eggs. Angling clubs in areas under invasion by the signal are complaining of decimated fish stocks.

Native British crayfish are now officially protected under schedule five of the Wildlife and Countryside Act. It is therefore illegal to move them, sell them, or eat them. Catching a few American signals, on the other hand, as I do from time to time in the Brit, can only be an environmental good turn. The fact that they are excellent eating, and carry considerably more meat than their diminutive English cousins, provides further incentive for the mission. Of course, you will need to be able to make the distinction with some confidence. It isn't hard. The giveaway is the claws. American signals wave theirs in a most aggressive manner, revealing a distinct reddish-brown color on the underside of the claw. They also have one claw noticeably fatter than the other. The English crayfish is smaller, less inclined to display, has two nearly equal claws, and is rarely longer than 4½ inches. Signals may be up to 1 foot, weighing almost a pound in exceptional circumstances.

In Britain, all crayfish hibernate, and though they can occasionally be lured out of their hole to investigate a bait during winter months, you will catch them in far greater numbers from April onward.

When the water is warm and crayfish are on the hunt, they are so voracious that they are not difficult to catch. Where signal crayfish are present in large numbers, one effective technique is much as for catching crabs off a harbor wall. The preferred bait is a chicken carcass, the smellier the better. Tie it to a piece of string, lower it into the water to the riverbed (right under the bank, by a tree, is often a good spot), and wait for a crayfish to grab hold. And grab hold they do – so forcefully that you can actually feel them tugging and trying to make off with the meat. They can then be hauled up onto the bank – though some kind of landing net is a useful extra, as they will occasionally drop off as you lift them out of the water.

Crude traps can also work well, and mean that you don't have to be permanently attached to the other end of your string. A square or circle of chicken wire can be attached by three or four strings at the edges to a stout cord in the middle. Tie a bait (a chicken carcass, piece of bacon, or fish skeleton) in the middle, and lower the trap into the water. Check the trap every fifteen minutes or so: haul it up smoothly and swiftly, and any crayfish feeding on the bait will not have time to jump off. If you want to catch crayfish in some numbers, several traps, placed at intervals along a riverbank and checked regularly over the course of a few hours, can produce good results.

Dedicated crayfish traps made of plastic are available in kit form, and work according to the lobster pot principle: the crayfish check in but they can't check out. Baited, and tied with a strong cord to a peg or the branch of a tree, they can be checked every few hours, or left overnight. More substantial seaworthy pots of the kind used for Dublin Bay prawns (see page 296) are also extremely effective.

Signal crayfish are as happy in still water as running, and can even be kept alive for a week or two in a small garden pond. But as with other stillwater fish, there is a danger of muddiness if they spend any length of time in still water. When I am planning a crayfish cook-up, I fish half a dozen traps up and down the river for a few days, and transfer any catch every morning to a holding cage that I keep in the river, until I have enough for my purposes. Out of water, crayfish can be kept alive in a well-ventilated box in a cool place for about forty-eight hours. A dead crayfish should be thrown away, never cooked.

Buying Crayfish can be ordered in advance from good fishmongers, but will be considerably cheaper if you buy direct from the source – i.e., fish farms or hobbyists who breed a few in their lake or pond.

Cooking Like lobsters and shrimp, crayfish should be cooked alive. The recommended technique for humane killing involves putting them in the deep-freeze before boiling to reduce them to a torpid state. I have found that about half an hour at -0.4°F achieves this without freezing them solid. They should then be dropped straight into a large pan of rapidly boiling, well-salted water. Average-sized crayfish (4 to 6 inches) will be ready in five minutes, though exceptionally large ones might take eight to ten minutes, in which case put them into the water a few minutes before the rest of the batch.

Freshly boiled crayfish can be peeled and eaten as soon as they are cool enough to handle. As with larger shrimp, remove the dark vein than runs along the back of the tail. Compared to, say, langoustines or shrimp, the flavor is subtle, so a good way to perk them up is to dip the tails in chive or garlic butter, or a good homemade mayonnaise spiked with herbs or garlic. My own Crayfish Cocktail (see page 352) is a more glorified version of this. Don't forget the claws – they contain a good little morsel of meat that is well worth extracting.

Aside from that rather fancy presentation, there is probably no more satisfying way to cook crayfish than over hot coals – but you should give them the freezer treatment first, then plunge them into boiling water for one minute to kill them. After that, on a wire rack, over charcoal or wood embers, crayfish will take between five and fifteen minutes, depending on heat and size. Garlic butter or a spiked mayonnaise makes a nice accompaniment.

fish

recipes

DOW'S
VTG1986BF

gravmax

The Scandinavian cure for salmon of dill, sugar, and salt is now almost as well known to us in Britain as smoked salmon. Less well known is just how good it is with other oily fish, particularly mackerel. Mackerel is a cheap fish at any time of year, but in harbor towns in the summer months the fishermen, and even the fishmongers, are often practically giving it away. That's a good time to make a large batch of gravad lax (which, incidentally, freezes well when finished).

I have read many recipes for the cure, and the ratios of sugar, salt, and pepper vary hugely – from twice as much sugar as salt to twice as much salt as sugar. I tend to use a bit more sugar than salt, but I don't usually measure accurately. The quantity of coarsely ground white and/or black pepper, on the other hand, is fairly consistent: about one-tenth the combined weight of salt and sugar. As for the dill, I simply pile in as much of the finely chopped fresh herb as I can lay my hands on – usually between a fifth and a third in volume. The quality of the dill is more important than the quantity. I find the potted dill plants in the supermarket have been forced too hard in heated greenhouses, and have a very feeble flavor. If you don't have a good herb supplier, it's well worth growing your own dill. Dried dill can be used in emergencies.

A grav kit I now have a dedicated "grav kit," which I use for salmon, large trout, and mackerel. It's basically just an old half-bottle wooden wine crate, with a chopping board that happens to fit neatly inside, which I put the weight on. A wooden box like this has a natural leakage, which is important, as you don't want the fish to stew in its own juice, so to speak (a regular trickle through is preferable – see below). I like to tell myself that the flavor of each batch improves as the wood becomes impregnated with the cure, but that may be a romantic notion. If you use a plastic container (which is fine), just take a skewer or knitting needle and pierce a couple of holes at either end, flush with the base, to let the liquid run out. The weighting board can be wood or plastic; it should be stiff, not flexible, and should fit fairly neatly.

Never use metal containers for gravlax or any other salt-based cure, or let metal weights touch the cure or fish directly. The metal will start to corrode and ruin the dish.

About 10 very fresh mackerel

FOR THE CURE
About ½ cup superfine sugar
About 5 tablespoons coarse salt
About 1 tablespoon coarsely ground black or white pepper, or a mixture
A large bunch of dill, coarse stalks removed, finely chopped

FOR THE ACCOMPANYING SAUCE
4 teaspoons English mustard
4 teaspoons light brown sugar
2 teaspoons wine vinegar
6 tablespoons crème fraîche
2 to 4 tablespoons chopped dill

The quickest way to prepare the mackerel is simply to take one fillet from either side of an ungutted fish, slicing from head to tail as close as possible to the backbone, piling up the fillets on a plate as you go and discarding the heads, guts, and skeletons. A slightly more skillful and less wasteful procedure is to cut off the head and slit the cavity to remove the guts. Then run the knife in a continuation of the belly slit to the tail of the fish. Turn the fish belly down on a board and press firmly on the backbone with the base of your palm, flattening out the fish. Turn it over again, so the skin is facing down, and carefully tease out the whole backbone with your fingers, using the point of the knife to cut away the flesh should it start to tear away with the bones. This technique needs practice, and is almost impossible with very fresh fish, as the backbone is exceedingly reluctant to leave the flesh. Successfully executed, however, it does leave you with very neat double fillets, and almost no waste. Anyway, the filleting is the hard part; the rest is easy.

In a nonmetallic bowl, thoroughly mix together all the ingredients for the cure. Sprinkle some of the cure lightly over the base of your chosen box and place the first layer of fillets (single or double), skin side down, with the thin edges just overlapping. Then sprinkle another layer of cure over, slightly heavier this time. Place the next layer of mackerel skin side up and sprinkle over another layer of cure, then place the next layer skin side down, etc. The final number of layers depends on the size and shape of your box. It feels tidy to finish on a layer skin side up, but it really doesn't matter.

Place a board inside the box on top of the final layer and weight it down with a couple of bricks, storage jars, or whatever comes to hand. Remember that the box is going to leak, and you want to catch the leakage, so place it on a nonmetallic tray. Leave in a cool place, such as a cellar, pantry, or fridge. Once a day, baste the mackerel by removing the weights and board and spooning over the liquid that has accumulated in the bottom of the tray. Then replace the board and weights.

You can eat the gravmax after 24 hours, but 72 is best. Remove the board and lift out the fillets carefully, one at a time. There is no need to scrape off the sticky dill fronds. Place each fillet skin side down and cut into 3 or 4 slices with a sharp knife; with the blade at an angle, you should be able to lift each piece away from the skin beneath.

To make the sauce, mix the mustard, sugar, and vinegar together until thoroughly blended, then mix in the crème fraîche, followed by the dill.

Serve the mackerel pieces piled roughly in the center of a plate, surrounded by a few dressed salad leaves. Pass the sauce around and have plenty of brown bread and butter, or rye bread, at hand.

variation traditional gravlax

Traditional Scandinavian gravlax using salmon, sea trout, or large trout is made in exactly the same way, except that instead of layers of fillets you use 2 large fillets, ideally from a single fish of at least 4 pounds, skin side out, cut side in, to make a sandwich, with plenty of cure underneath, in the middle and on top. Press under a weighted board and baste in the same way, but leave longer: 5 to 7 days is ideal, 3 days an absolute minimum. Serve in the same way as gravmax.

grilled sprats with mustard sauce

serves 4 as a starter, 2 as a main course

On a windy September day last summer, I was walking on the beach at West Bay when I noticed a large flock of gulls diving into the water about 500 yards offshore. They got closer and closer to the beach until the noise was deafening and you could almost feel the beat of their wings. You could see the bright-silver panicking sprats they were hunting flashing in the surf. Then, one particularly big wave came inshore, then retreated, leaving behind on the shingle a few dozen flapping little sprats. This happened several times in the next half hour, and once I'd filled my pockets I decided to take off a gumboot and start filling that. I hobbled back to the car with over two pounds of sprats in my boot. When I got home, I cooked them, as I usually do with sprats, according to the procedure below.

If you are buying sprats, make sure they are firm, shiny bright, and not at all sunken in the eye. The season in Britain is from early autumn till around Christmas. In the U.S., this recipe would use fresh sardines.

FOR THE MUSTARD SAUCE
2 anchovy fillets
½ teaspoon coarsely ground black pepper
½ teaspoon brown sugar
4 teaspoons English mustard
¼ cup crème fraîche

1 pound fresh and shiny-bright sprats or sardines
Olive oil
Sea salt and freshly ground black pepper
Chopped parsley, to garnish

First, make the sauce: on a cutting board, mash the anchovies with the black pepper and sugar, using a fork, until you have a coarse paste. Scrape this paste into a small bowl, then stir in the mustard followed by the crème fraîche. Cover until ready to serve.

Now prepare the sprats: they don't need to be gutted but should be well rinsed and patted dry with a tea towel. Then place a piece of foil on a broiler pan, brush thoroughly with olive oil, and sprinkle with black pepper. Lay the sprats on the foil and cook under a very hot broiler until they start to brown and blister. Turn over and cook until the heads and tails are crispy and the skin is golden brown.

You can serve the sprats on a warmed round plate arranged like the spokes of a wheel, tails to the center. Sprinkle with sea salt and chopped parsley and place the sauce in its bowl in the center of the plate for communal dipping. Alternatively, divide the sprats between warmed plates and spoon the sauce over them.

Real sprat enthusiasts eat the fish whole, heads and all. More squeamish diners may prefer to nibble around the backbone and leave the heads and tails. Either way, they are most easily eaten with the fingers. Serve with buttered brown bread and plenty of napkins.

Gary Fooks' Chinese sea bass

serves 1 to 2

This is a simple and excellent recipe. Gary, an accomplished spear fisherman, cooked it for me on the rocks on the beach, in a wok on his pot-bellied grill. When I ribbed him about using bottled oyster sauce, he replied, "So you know how to make an authentic Chinese oyster sauce, do you?" Point taken.

1 or 2 sea bass that will fit inside a large wok
Fresh ginger, peeled and sliced into fine disks
2 tablespoons peanut oil
3 to 4 green onions, sliced into 2-inch pieces
A small bunch of cilantro, coarsely chopped
Good-quality oyster sauce

Gut and scale the bass (or ask your fishmonger to do this), leaving the head and tail on. Place a dozen or so pieces of ginger on a heatproof plate and place the bass on top. Insert 2 or 3 pieces of ginger in its belly.

Make a grid with 4 chopsticks in the bottom of a wok (or use a wok steaming lattice), then fill the wok with water until the water level is just below the chopsticks. Place the wok in the glowing embers of a very hot grill, or over a gas ring on a wok support. When the water is boiling, place the plate of bass on the chopsticks and put the lid on the wok. Steam the bass for 6 to 8 minutes, depending on size. Remove the bass on the plate from the wok and cover it with the wok lid to keep it hot.

Empty the wok of water and chopsticks, add the oil, and return to the heat. Sprinkle the green onions and cilantro over the bass and pour on a good measure of oyster sauce. When, and only when, the oil is smoking hot, pour it over the bass and serve immediately, still crackling.

Hugh's gray mullet grilled over fennel stalks

serves 1 to 2

This was my answer to Gary's bass (see above). Not that it was a competition or anything.

A little oil
1 gray mullet or red snapper, cleaned and scaled
Salt and freshly ground black pepper
A large bundle of fennel stalks

TO SERVE
Mayonnaise
Chopped fennel fronds
Chopped chives
Lemon juice

Light a grill and wait until it has died down to red-hot coals. Lightly oil the fish and season it with salt and pepper. Lay the fennel stalks over the coals and, as they begin to smoulder, place your fish over the fire. Grill, turning once, until cooked through (the time will vary according to the size of the fish and the heat of the fire). Continue to stoke the fire with fennel stalks as you cook.

Serve the fish with mayonnaise (preferably homemade) flavored with chopped fresh fennel and/or chives and lemon juice.

taramasalata

serves 6 generously

In the winter months when the biggest cod are caught, you can often buy fresh cod roe very cheaply: I get it straight off the boat in West Bay. It's fantastic stuff for home smoking (see page 278), and taramasalata made with your own home-smoked roe is a world apart from the fluorescent pink version so ubiquitous these days in delicatessens and supermarkets.

If buying cod roe, choose a whole piece, still in its tough outer membrane. If it weighs more or less than the amount specified in the recipe below, you can adapt the quantities accordingly, but don't worry too much, as it's a forgiving recipe.

Bulk quantities can easily be made in a food processor, but preparing it by hand produces a nice grainy texture, which I slightly prefer.

8 ounces cod roe, smoked (see page 278)
1 garlic clove, peeled
3 to 4 thick slices of stale white bread, crusts removed
⅔ cup milk
7 tablespoons good olive oil
⅞ cup sunflower oil
2 tablespoons lemon juice
1 tablespoon finely chopped parsley
1 tablespoon finely chopped chives
Freshly ground black pepper

With a spoon, scrape the smoked cod roe out of its skin and put it in a mixing bowl. Mash the garlic clove with a fork and mix with the roe. Soak the bread in the milk for a couple of minutes, then squeeze to extract most of the milk. Add the squeezed bread to the cod roe and mix thoroughly.

Stir the olive and sunflower oil together in a small bowl, then beat them into the bread mixture a tablespoon at a time with a heavy wire whisk. After you have added about half the olive oil, start adding the lemon juice, also a little at a time, alternating with the remaining oil. (This is heavy work and you may prefer to use a food processor, in which case trickle the oil slowly into the bread and roe through the funnel of the working machine. Alternate oil and lemon juice after the first tablespoon of oil has been incorporated.)

Finally, mix in the parsley, chives, and a few twists of freshly ground pepper. Spoon into a pot and refrigerate until required. Serve with hot buttered toast, black olives (ideally, kalamata), and radishes.

Provençal marinated salt cod

serves 4 to 6 as a starter

In this dish, which was first prepared for me by the chef Adam Robinson, the humble cod is elevated to new heights of luxury. It is best made with prime cuts of lightly salted, homemade "wet" salt cod (see page 272), as the dried version does not reconstitute well enough to serve raw in this way.

8 ounces "wet" salt cod (see page 272)
6 good, flavorful plum tomatoes
Olive oil
3 large red bell peppers
Salt and freshly ground black pepper

FOR THE MARINADE
1 small red onion or 2 shallots, finely chopped
1 large garlic clove, finely chopped
1 tablespoon white wine vinegar
5 tablespoons good olive oil

Prepare the salt cod for use by soaking and rinsing, as described on page 272. Mix together all the ingredients for the marinade. Cut the salt cod into thin strips, toss well with the marinade, then cover and let sit for at least 6 hours.

Cut the tomatoes in half and scoop out the seeds. Place the tomato halves, cut side up, in a baking dish, sprinkle with a little salt, and drizzle with olive oil. Roast gently in a preheated 300°F oven for an hour, so they are half-dried, half-roasted, and nice and sweet. Remove from the oven.

Turn the oven up to 400°F and roast the peppers whole until they are nicely blackened all over. Place in a bowl and let sit until cool enough to handle, then peel, discarding the seeds and skin and retaining the flesh and the juices. Cut the flesh into thick strips.

Gently toss the salt cod strips in their marinade with the tomatoes, strips of red pepper, and any juice saved from either. Season with black pepper, then refrigerate for at least 6 hours or overnight. Serve with hot pita breads to mop up the juices.

crab linguine

serves 5 to 6 as a main course

I buy spider crabs straight off the boat of my fishmonger friend, Jack, in West Bay harbor. They are ridiculously cheap. I predict that in the coming years spider crabs will become more and more commonplace in British fishmonger's shops and restaurants. A large spider crab has plenty of good white meat in the legs and claws and, if anything, the flavor is better, and sweeter, than the more familiar brown crab. In the States, the crab to use would be the Dungeness. Linguine, which is like a rather thick, slightly flat spaghetti, is one of my favorite pastas, but you can use anything you like.

2 large live spider crabs, brown crabs, or Dungeness crabs (about 1 pound white crabmeat in total)
1 pound linguine or other favorite pasta
3 garlic cloves, chopped
2 tablespoons olive oil
1 to 2 small red chiles (according to heat), deseeded and finely sliced
2 pounds best ripe tomatoes, such as Sungold, skinned, deseeded, and coarsely chopped
Salt and freshly ground black pepper
Chopped chives

Humanely kill and cook your crabs as described on page 291. Crack open the claws and legs to retrieve all the white meat. (Collect any brown meat too, and reserve it for another dish, such as fish soup, or for crab sandwiches.)

Bring a large pan of lightly salted water (at least 3 quarts) to a boil, add the linguine, and cook, uncovered, for 10 to 12 minutes, until al dente. Meanwhile, prepare the sauce: cook the garlic in the olive oil until softened, then throw in the red chile (check for heat and use sparingly). Add the chopped tomatoes before the garlic colors. Simmer for 5 to 6 minutes, until soft and pulpy, then add the crabmeat and heat through. Season to taste, adding more chile if you like. Add some chives at the last moment. Serve tossed with the drained linguine.

crustacea soup

serves 4 to 6

Like all good fish soups, this recipe is infinitely variable. You can add fish bones or whole fish to the stock. You can make it with or without shrimp and with just about any species of crab. I like to include velvets if at all possible, as they have such a wonderful sweet flavor. The following list of ingredients should be taken merely as a guide.

1 large or 2 medium brown crabs, spider crabs, or Dungeness crabs
About 8 velvet or blue crabs, and/or large shore crabs
3 or 4 large langoustines (Dublin Bay prawns), or 4 ounces large shrimp, or squat lobsters
1 whole fresh white fish, such as a plaice, wrasse, or red snapper, skinned, gutted, and cut into chunks (optional)
2 tablespoons olive oil
1 onion, chopped
1 carrot, chopped
1 large or 2 small tomatoes, chopped
4 garlic cloves, crushed
A few sprigs each of wild fennel and wild chervil, if available
A few parsley stalks or cleaned leek tops (optional)
Salt and freshly ground black pepper
A pinch of cayenne pepper

Humanely kill and cook all the crabs as described on page 291. Cook the shrimp (see pages 296–298). Leave everything until cool enough to handle, then discard the dead men's fingers and stomachs of the crabs and remove as much of any brown meat as you can from the carapaces, and white meat from the larger claws. Set the meat aside. Shell the langoustines and shrimp and set the tail meat aside, separately from the crabmeat.

Discard only the main carapace of the brown crabs. All other heads, legs, and shells of the crabs, langoustines, and shrimp should be placed in a large bowl or heavy saucepan and pounded with a hammer or rolling pin.

In a large clean pan, heat the olive oil and add the onion, carrot, tomato, and garlic, plus the wild herbs and parsley stalks or leek tops if you have any. Fry gently for a few minutes to soften. Add the hammered shellfish, and the fresh fish, if you have one. Pour over enough water just to cover everything and bring to a boil. Simmer gently for just 20 minutes (no more), then remove from the heat.

This shellfish stock can then be processed in a number of ways. Either strain it through a heavy-duty conical sieve, pressing hard with the back of a ladle to extract as much fishy juice as possible. Or put everything in a heavy-duty blender, whiz it up, and then pass through the sieve.

When you have extracted the best from the stock (or excluded the worst of the shells, depending on how you look at it), put it back in a clean pan over a low heat and stir in all the white and any brown meat you originally saved from the crabs. Heat through but do not let it boil.

Season to taste with salt, pepper, and cayenne, then divide among warm bowls. Garnish with the tail meat from the shrimp or squat lobsters.

lobster thermidor

serves 2

This is a classic dish and an unbeatable one. One good-sized lobster serves two people to make one of the finest special-occasion dishes I can think of. Ideally, the lobster flesh, smothered in the finished sauce, is piled back into the two half shells and finished under the broiler. If you should happen to make a mess of splitting the lobster (I often do) and thereby spoil the shell, you can pile the filling into one or two individual ovenproof dishes. It may look slightly less spectacular, but it will taste every bit as good.

Most recipes stipulate heavy cream for the sauce, but I find it almost too rich, so I prefer to use béchamel sauce.

1 live lobster, weighing 2 to 3 pounds
2 shallots, finely chopped
2 tablespoons butter
A small glass of white wine
¾ cup thick béchamel sauce (made as for Real Parsley Sauce on page 119)
1 tablespoon heavy cream (optional)
1 teaspoon strong English mustard
Leaves from a sprig of tarragon, finely chopped
½ cup shredded Gruyère cheese
A good pinch of cayenne pepper
Salt and freshly ground black pepper

Kill and cook your lobster as described on page 295, then let cool. Twist off the claws, crack them with a hammer or nutcracker, and remove all the meat. Set this aside. The body of the lobster should be split lengthwise along the lateral line with a large, heavy, and very sharp knife. This is most easily done if you lay the lobster on its back on a large wooden board, press the point of the knife into the tip of the tail, and bring the knife down the length of the lobster, bisecting it evenly between the two sets of legs – do this carefully so as not to damage the shell. Once you are through the flesh to the shell at the back of the lobster, press hard on the knife with your free hand to cut through the shell. You may want to use a pair of kitchen scissors to snip through any bits of shell that are not quite cut through.

Carefully remove the tail meat from each half of the lobster, chop coarsely, and add to the claw meat. Scrape out any brown meat from the head, along with any pink coral, and add that to the white meat from the claws and tail. Remove the nasty bits (see page 295) and discard. You should be left with 2 empty shell halves, with plenty of space in the head and tail cavities to replace the finished meat.

In a frying pan, cook the shallots in the butter over medium heat until soft and lightly browned. Add the white wine and simmer until reduced to a scant tablespoon of liquid. Stir in the béchamel sauce and the cream, if using, plus the mustard and tarragon, and allow to bubble in the pan for just a minute. Remove from the heat and stir in three-quarters of the cheese and the cayenne pepper. Then mix in all the meat from the lobster until it is well coated in the sauce. Season to taste with salt and black pepper.

Pile the meat back in the shell, sprinkle over the remaining cheese, and place under a hot broiler for 5 to 10 minutes, until brown and bubbling. Serve at once.

shrimp and sea lettuce tempura

serves 4

This recipe was devised to challenge the palate of my friend, Dennis Cheeseman, a schoolmaster and fisherman who first took me out to pull his pots off Ringstead Bay in 1971, when I was only seven years old. In 30-odd years, he's always cooked shrimp the same way: boiled and salted, then served with brown bread and butter. It has to be said that they are very good like that, but I thought it was time for a change. "Surprisingly good," was his verdict on this dish, with much emphasis on "surprisingly."

Sea lettuce can be found all around the British coast on rocks and in rock pools. If the edges of the bright-green, papery fronds are bleached or ragged they can be trimmed. Sea lettuce can be eaten raw, but is delicious combined with the shrimp and Japanese tempura batter. In the States, you can use escarole or chard.

3 to 4 dozen large fresh shrimp
A bag of freshly collected sea lettuce, rinsed in fresh water and trimmed, or escarole or chard leaves, stemmed
Oil for deep-frying
A small bunch of green onions, cut into 2-inch lengths
Salt

FOR THE TEMPURA BATTER
1½ cups all-purpose flour
1 large or 2 small egg yolks
1½ cups water
A pinch of salt

FOR THE DIPPING SAUCE
2 tablespoons soy sauce
1 tablespoon rice wine vinegar
2 green onions, finely sliced

Bring a pan of well-salted water – or seawater – to a boil and blanch the shrimp in it for about 30 seconds. Drain and let cool, then shell. Wrap each shrimp in a piece of sea lettuce or escarole or chard leaf and thread onto short bamboo skewers, interspersed with pieces of green onion. Aim for 3 medium or 2 large shrimp per skewer.

Make the batter by quickly mixing all the ingredients together, adding more water if necessary to bring it to the consistency of thick paint. Don't overmix the batter or it won't have the light texture you want – don't worry if it has a few lumps in it.

Make the dipping sauce by mixing the soy sauce and rice wine vinegar together and then adding the finely chopped green onions.

Heat some oil for deep-frying in a large pan, then dip the skewers 3 or 4 at a time in the batter and drop straight into the oil. Fry for about 1 minute, until crisp and golden.

Remove the tempura with a slotted spoon, drain briefly on paper towels, sprinkle with salt, and serve immediately. Eat by picking up the sticks by the long end, dipping them in the sauce, and eating the shrimp off the stick.

clams with pork tenderloin and chorizo

serves 6 as a starter

The combination of pork and/or charcuterie with shellfish is explored in all kinds of ways in Portuguese cooking, and rarely fails to please. This dish, known as *porco alentejana*, is a particularly delightful example, which I first made using razor clams gathered in Studland Bay. I have since tried it using ordinary clams (*palourdes*) and, in Scotland, large cockles. It worked well in every case. This dish makes a good main course for 4 people when served with a green salad and boiled rice.

1 pork tenderloin (about 1 pound), diced into ½-inch cubes
1 to 2 teaspoons freshly ground black pepper, to taste
2 garlic cloves, chopped
About 2 pounds clams, razor clams, or cockles
A glass of white wine
A glass of water
Olive oil for frying
8 ounces Spanish chorizo (or other spicy sausage), sliced
A handful of parsley, chopped
½ to 1 red chile, deseeded and finely chopped (optional)

Mix the diced pork with the black pepper and garlic and let sit for at least 30 minutes in a cool place.

Wash the clams thoroughly in cold water and leave in a colander for 30 minutes. (If using cockles gathered by hand, follow the de-gritting procedure on page 302.) Put the white wine and water in a large, heavy pan and bring to a boil, then throw in the clams and cover the pan. Check after 2 minutes whether the shells have opened. If not, give them another 30 seconds or so with the lid on. Once the shells are almost all open, take the clams out of the cooking liquor with a slotted spoon and remove the flesh from half of them. Discard any clams that do not open. Set the shelled and unshelled clams aside (if using razor clams, cut them into 1-inch lengths).

Heat a little olive oil in a frying pan and fry the seasoned pork until golden brown. Add the chorizo, then the clams, with a ladleful or two of their cooking liquor to moisten.

When all is heated through, toss together with the chopped parsley and chile to taste (depending on the heat of the chorizo, extra chile may not be necessary at all). Check for seasoning – it probably won't need any – and serve at once.

rappie pie

serves 6

This recipe is adapted from *North Atlantic Seafood*, that great treatise by seafood guru Alan Davidson. Alan's recipe uses softshell clams. This version uses the relatively humble, but easier to gather, cockle. The results are excellent, although I once tried another version using limpets, which I can't recommend with quite the same level of enthusiasm! Littlenecks, which are a hardshell clam, can be substituted.

The cream is my addition. It mollifies what can otherwise be a rather harsh and salty dish. *Rappie*, by the way, is short for rapture.

3 pounds potatoes
A glass of white wine
A glass of water
2 garlic cloves, crushed
3 tablespoons butter
2 pounds cockles, cleaned (see page 302), or littleneck clams, scrubbed
8 ounces pancetta or salt pork, diced
1 tablespoon heavy cream
Freshly ground black pepper

Peel the potatoes and shred them on the coarse side of a cheese grater. Take a cupful of potato at a time and place in a cotton cloth, which then must be twisted to wring out as much liquid as possible. Collect the liquid in a bowl, so that you can measure it; you will later need twice that quantity of cockle juices. Put the wrung-out potatoes into a clean bowl.

In a large pan, bring the wine, water, garlic, and most of the butter to a boil, then add the cockles. Cover and steam for a few minutes, stirring occasionally or shaking the pan, until most of the cockles have opened. Remove the cockles from the pan with a slotted spoon. Strain the cooking juices through a cloth or cheesecloth into a large glass measuring cup. Take the cockle meat out of the shells and set aside.

Fry the pancetta or salt pork in a heavy-based frying pan so the fat runs and the meat crisps up a little. Take off the heat but keep warm.

Measure out enough of the cockle cooking juices to bring the volume up to twice that of the liquid extracted from the potatoes (top up with water if necessary) and then add the cream. Bring this mixture to a boil, then add the wrung-out potatoes to it, little by little. The potatoes will swell up as they absorb the new liquid. Stir carefully until full absorption has occurred.

When this operation has been completed and almost all the liquid has been absorbed by the potatoes, strain the pancetta fat into an ovenproof dish, holding back the meat. Place a layer of potatoes in the bottom of the dish, cover this with a layer of cockles and some of the pancetta, and season with a few twists of pepper. Then make another layer of potato and so on – the pie can have 3 layers or 5.

Season with pepper to taste, and dot with the remaining butter, cut into little pieces. Bake in a preheated 375°F oven for 20 minutes, then reduce the temperature to 350°F and continue to bake for another hour or so, until the top of the pie is brown and crusty.

mussel and sea beet gratin

serves 6 as a starter, 4 as a main course

I love this simple mixture of creamed spinach mixed with mussels and finished with a crispy bread crumb top, and if it is made with wild sea beet, I love it even more. Spinach makes a good substitute.

1 tablespoon butter for cooking the mussels, plus 3 tablespoons for the sauce
2 garlic cloves, crushed
A glass of white wine
2 pounds mussels, cleaned (see page 303)
⅔ cup milk
3 tablespoons plain flour
About ½ carrier bag of sea beets (or 2 pounds fresh spinach), blanched, squeezed dry, and coarsely chopped
2 tablespoons freshly grated Parmesan cheese
A pinch of grated nutmeg
Salt and freshly ground black pepper
⅞ cup fresh white bread crumbs

Melt 1 tablespoon of butter in a large pan, fry the garlic in it for just a minute, then add the wine and a little water. When this mixture is boiling rapidly, add the mussels. Cover and cook for a few minutes over fairly high heat until open (you may have to do this in two or more batches). Remove all the mussels from the pan with a slotted spoon and let cool enough to handle, then take the mussels out of their shells and set aside. Discard any unopened mussels. Strain the cooking liquid and add enough of it to the milk to yield 1⅔ cups.

Next, make a béchamel sauce: melt the 3 tablespoons butter in a pan, stir in the flour to make a roux, then cook for a few minutes, gently browning it. Gradually add the hot milk/liquid mixture by degrees, stirring all the time, to get a smooth, thick sauce (you may not need all the liquid). Stir in the chopped sea beets or spinach, along with half the Parmesan and the nutmeg. Season with black pepper, but add salt only if necessary. Stir in the mussels gently, so as not to break them up.

Spread the mixture in an ovenproof dish (ideally, a shallow gratin dish). Mix the bread crumbs with the rest of the Parmesan and sprinkle them over the top. Bake in a preheated 400°F oven for just 10 minutes, to heat through and brown the top.

scallop tacos with red salsa and guacamole

serves 6

This is perfect beach food, requiring no cutlery, only hands. I got the idea from a holiday in Baja California, Mexico, where they often eat deep-fried fish rolled in soft tortillas (see variation, opposite). You don't have to use any fat in the tortillas, but it does make them softer and easier to roll.

A dozen (or more) scallops, white muscle and coral only (see pages 303–304)
Olive oil
Salt and freshly ground black pepper

FOR THE TORTILLAS
1¾ cups masa harina (Mexican corn flour) or all-purpose flour
1 teaspoon salt
3 tablespoons lard
Up to ½ cup warm water
1 teaspoon sunflower oil (if needed)

FOR THE RED SALSA
2 large red bell peppers
1 pound ripe tomatoes
½ red onion, finely chopped
1 garlic clove, finely chopped
1 to 2 green chiles, deseeded and finely chopped (to taste and according to strength)
Juice of ½ orange
Juice of ½ lime
1 teaspoon sugar
¼ cup chopped fresh cilantro

FOR THE GUACAMOLE
2 avocados, peeled and pitted
2 tablespoons lime juice (or lemon, if pushed)
½ teaspoon superfine sugar
1 garlic clove, crushed with a little salt
A drizzle of olive oil
About 1 teaspoon chile sauce, or about ½ small red chile, finely chopped

For the tortillas, sift the flour and salt into a bowl, then rub in the lard. Stir in enough water to form a soft but not sticky dough (you probably won't need all the water). Knead the dough well on a floured surface for about 10 minutes or until smooth and elastic. Put the dough into a clean bowl, cover, and set aside to rest for 1 hour.

Meanwhile, make the salsa and the guacamole. For the salsa, roast the peppers whole in a preheated 400°F oven, until blackened all over. Place in a bowl, cover with a plate, and let sit until cool enough to handle. Pick off the charred skin and discard, along with the seeds. Coarsely chop the flesh. Pour boiling water over the tomatoes and leave for 30 seconds. Peel off the skin with the point of a sharp knife and scoop out the seeds. Finely chop the seedless, skinless tomato flesh and mix well with the chopped red pepper flesh. Add all the other ingredients and mix well together, being careful to use only enough chile to achieve the heat level you like. Season with salt and pepper, then chill the salsa in the fridge until needed.

For the guacamole, put the avocado flesh in a bowl with the lime juice, sugar, and garlic and mash together with a fork. Drizzle in some olive oil and beat until you get a smooth, thick, not quite pourable consistency. Season to taste with the chile and some salt and black pepper. Cover and refrigerate until needed.

Divide the tortilla dough into 12 equal pieces and form into balls. Roll out each piece on a lightly floured surface until about 8 inches in diameter (alternatively, you can press the balls in a lightly floured tortilla press – a tool designed specially for the job). Cook the tortillas one at a time on a preheated dry heavy frying pan until the underside is flecked with brown and bubbles appear on the surface. Turn the tortilla and cook the other side, pressing the bubbles with a rolled-up tea towel. If the tortillas are sticking, you can grease the pan very lightly with the sunflower oil. Keep the tortillas warm by wrapping them in a clean cloth when they are cooked.

Finally, cook the scallops. Heat a heavy pan or griddle (over your beach fire, if appropriate) and drizzle a bit of olive oil onto the surface. Flash fry the scallops for just a minute on each side.

To serve, place 2 or 3 scallops in a warm tortilla with a generous spoonful of guacamole and a more modest one of salsa. Roll up and eat at once.

variation fish taco party

This is a really fun dish and great party food. All sorts of other seafood is eaten this way in Mexico, especially squid, large shrimp, and strips of snapper and king mackerel fillet. These can be deep-fried in my favorite All-Purpose Fish Batter, made from flour, beer, and egg white: mix a scant $^{2}/_{3}$ cup all-pupose flour with 1 tablespoon olive oil and then thin it to the consistency of thick paint with beer. Leave at room temperature for at least an hour, then fold in a whisked egg white just before the fish are coated and deep-fried. Alternatively, you could use the tempura batter on page 340.

As well as the red salsa and guacamole, a simple mixture of chopped green onions and fresh cilantro can be served with the tortillas and fried fish.

For a simplified version for kids, just use frozen fish fingers in bread crumbs.

cuttlefish (or squid) in the Greek style

serves 4 to 6

The danger of rubberiness when cooking cuttlefish or squid is well known. The secret of avoiding this tragedy is either to cook them fast and short, for just a few minutes, or long and slow, for at least $1^1/_2$ hours. This dish can be done either way. The fast option is to cook the sauce without the cuttlefish, then flash-fry the cuttlefish and add it at the end. For the long, slow option, all the ingredients go in together and are gently simmered until the sauce is thick and rich and the cuttlefish as tender as soft cheese. The slower-cooked dish has a more fully developed flavor. The quick version works best when the cuttlefish is exquisitely fresh – the meat is more bite resistant but has a wonderful sea-fresh flavor.

In either case, any ink saved from cleaning the squid or cuttlefish can be included in the sauce. It acts as a mild flavoring and a dramatic colorant, turning the entire dish a stunning inky black.

In the Mediterranean, a dish like this would be served with bread and/or plain steamed rice. It's also rather lovely served with creamy mashed potatoes.

4 tablespoons olive oil
1 large or 2 medium onions, finely sliced
2 large garlic cloves, crushed
2 pounds ripe tomatoes, skinned, deseeded, and coarsely chopped, or two 14½-ounce cans of best Italian plum tomatoes
About 2 pounds cuttlefish or squid (i.e., 2 large cuttlefish or 4 to 5 medium squid), cleaned (see page 308) and cut into ½-inch-thick strips, with tentacles
A few fennel sprigs or stalks
2 bay leaves
2 to 3 strips of thinly pared lemon zest (strictly no pith)
A glass of red wine
Salt and freshly ground black pepper
A squeeze of lemon juice

Heat half the oil in a large, heavy saucepan and cook the onion gently until softened. Add the garlic and cook for a minute or two. Add the fresh or canned tomatoes, turn up the heat a little, and simmer gently until you have a nice, pulpy sauce.

Slow-cooked version: in a separate pan such as a heavy frying pan, heat the rest of the oil. Add the cuttlefish/squid and stir-fry over high heat for just a few minutes until lightly browned. Then add to the tomato sauce with all its juices and the oil. Add the fennel, bay leaves, lemon zest, and wine (and the ink from the cuttlefish or squid, if you have it) and season with black pepper, plus just a little salt at this stage. Bring to a very gentle simmer and cook, uncovered, until the fish is completely soft and tender, almost melting in the mouth; $1^1/_2$ to 2 hours usually does it for me. Stir occasionally to make sure the sauce is not sticking to the bottom of the pan, and add just a dribble of water if it seems to be getting too thick.

Adjust the seasoning to taste, adding a few drops of lemon juice if you like.

Quick version: proceed as above, omitting the cuttlefish or squid. You can let the sauce cook rather quicker than it would if it had the fish in it. After half an hour of merry simmering, it should be done. Then stir-fry the fish as above, add to the sauce, and heat through for just a couple more minutes before serving.

variation The juices of the nearly finished dish are such a fine blend of flavors that they will complement all kinds of other fish. Occasionally, to make this an even more spectacular and generous dish, I add other seafood toward the end of cooking: strips of well-soaked salt cod (see page 272) or cutlets of meaty white fish such as monkfish, gurnard, or brill, for the last 10 minutes; cooked crab claws or whole large shrimp for the last 5; just-steamed mussels or sliced raw scallops at the very last moment. Any or all of these additions make for a really dramatic, intensely flavored fish stew.

fennel risotto with scallops

serves 4 as a starter, 2 as a main course

This is a hugely satisfying dish for me, as it uses all the bits of the scallop that normally get thrown away, and the fennel trimmings go in, too. It may look dauntingly long, but it is not really a complicated recipe. If you can't get scallops in the shell, it's still a worthwhile dish – just use a good fish stock to make the risotto instead of making a stock from the scallop trimmings.

6 large scallops in the shell
2 to 3 fennel bulbs (about 1 pound total before trimming)
2 small onions – 1 sliced for the stock; 1 finely chopped for the risotto
1 bay leaf
A small wineglass of white wine
1 garlic clove, finely chopped
2 tablespoons good olive oil
¾ cup Arborio rice
A dash of Pernod (optional)
Salt and freshly ground black pepper

Prepare the scallops as described on pages 303–304, scraping into a small pan the coral, the juices, the fleshy fringe around the edges, and any meat left clinging to either the deep or the flat half of the shell.

Prepare the fennel by cutting off the fingerlike tops and the coarse outer layer(s) – one or two layers, depending on size and freshness. Finely slice the clean, firm hearts of the bulbs and set aside for the risotto. Holding back a few of the frondy leaves for the risotto, coarsely chop the rest of the fennel trimmings and add to the scallop trimmings and juices in the pan. Also add the sliced onion and bay leaf and the glass of wine. Pour over about 2 cups water to cover the contents of the pan generously. Bring to a boil and simmer gently for no more than 20 minutes, then strain through a fine sieve; if the scallops look sandy or gritty, strain the stock through cotton or cheesecloth. Return to a clean pan and keep warm over very low heat.

To make the risotto, cook the second onion and the garlic in the oil in a heavy saucepan for a few minutes, until softened. Add the sliced fennel and cook gently until softened. Add the rice and stir to coat the grains in the oil, then add a third of the stock and bring to a gentle simmer. Cook gently, adding more stock whenever the liquid in the pan has been almost absorbed. If you run out of stock before the rice is done, use boiling water instead. The final result should be smooth and creamy, with the rice still a little al dente.

Prepare the scallops while the risotto is cooking. Rinse them in cold water and pat dry with paper towels, then cut each scallop in half horizontally to make 12 thinner scallops, as it were. When the risotto is almost done, "dry" heat (i.e., without oil) a heavy, nonstick frying pan, or a cast-iron skillet or griddle pan, until very hot. Brush both sides of each scallop with a little olive oil and place on the pan. They really take no more than 30 seconds on each side, so as soon as you have laid the last one down you should turn over the first one.

Finish the risotto by stirring in the finely chopped fennel leaves and the Pernod if you are using it, then check the seasoning. Divide the risotto among warmed plates, arranging the griddled scallops on or around each portion.

little pike terrines

serves 10 as a starter

The pike is a much-underrated eating fish, and one from a clean, fast-flowing river (such as the Piddle, near River Cottage) ranks up there with wild salmon. The bones are the only problem, and this recipe deals with them by serving the fish cold after they have been removed. A large pike will comfortably serve 10 people as a starter in this way, with meat to spare. Use the leftover meat to make fish cakes (see page 352).

1 pike, ideally 4 to 7 pounds, or the head end of a larger fish, cut to fit snugly in the fish poacher
Bay leaves
Sprigs of fennel
Parsley
1 onion, sliced
A few black peppercorns
1 bottle of white wine
1 level teaspoon plain gelatin (if needed)
Salt and freshly ground black pepper
Lightly dressed green leaves, such as mâche, watercress, or baby spinach, to garnish

Clean the pike and lay it in a fish poacher. Cover with the herbs, onion, and peppercorns, putting some inside the belly of the fish, too. Add a sprinkling of salt, but not much or the stock will be too salty when reduced. Pour the white wine over the pike and add enough water to almost cover it. Cover the fish poacher, put it on the stove, and bring to a boil. Let it boil for 2 to 3 minutes, then turn off the heat. Leave the lid on and allow the fish to cool slowly in the stock – ideally, overnight, and certainly for at least a couple of hours. The residual heat will be enough to cook the fish through.

Take the cooled pike from the fish poacher and remove the head, tail, and skin. Take off the fillets and flake the flesh, being careful to extract all the pitchfork-shaped bones from between the flakes. Season the pike meat with black pepper and some finely chopped parsley.

Strain the liquid that the pike was poached in through cheesecloth or a cotton cloth. Boil in a clean pan until reduced to a scant 2 cups. Test for setting ability by pouring a little of the stock into a shallow saucer and letting it chill in the fridge. If it is not set in 30 minutes, add the gelatin to the remaining hot stock and stir until dissolved.

Lay a sprig of fennel in the bottom of each of your chosen molds (custard cups, teacups, or miniature pie dishes could all be used). Pile the seasoned pike meat loosely into each mold. Pour in enough stock just to cover the fish and transfer the molds to the refrigerator to set firm, which may take up to 3 hours.

To turn out the terrines, dip each mold in warm water for a moment, then cover with a small serving plate and flip over. Garnish each one with lightly dressed green leaves to serve.

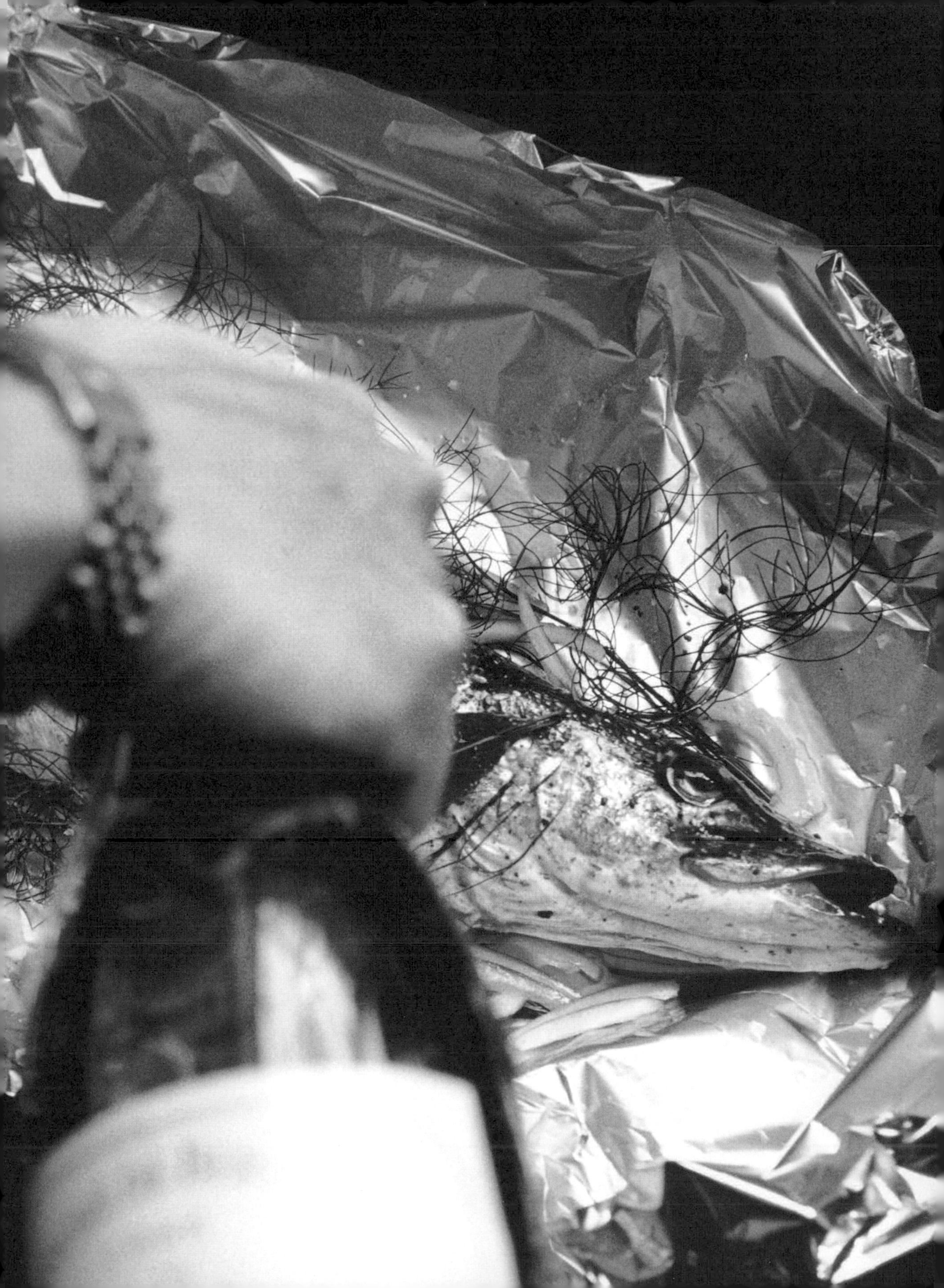

pike fish cakes

Pike has a very distinctive flavor, which makes these fish cakes a cut above the average. You can make fish cakes from other freshwater fish, such as trout or perch, in exactly the same way.

Boneless cooked pike meat
A roughly equal quantity of mashed potatoes
Beaten egg (about 1 egg per 1 pound pike meat)
Sifted flour (about 2 teaspoons per 1 pound pike meat)
Chopped chives
Chopped parsley
Cayenne pepper
Oil for frying
Salt and freshly ground black pepper

TO COAT THE FISH CAKES (OPTIONAL)
More beaten egg
Dried bread crumbs

Mash the pike meat with a fork, checking it again for bones, and mix thoroughly with the mashed potatoes, beaten egg, flour, and herbs. Season to taste with cayenne, salt, and pepper. Using floured hands, form the mixture into small cakes, not more than 1 inch thick. Either fry them gently as they are or, for a nice crunchy outside, dip in beaten egg and coat in the bread crumbs first. Either way, fry fairly gently in hot oil until nicely browned – 4 to 5 minutes on each side.

Drain on paper towels and serve at once, either with homemade tartar sauce (see page 233) or my homemade Tomato Ketchup (see page 105).

crayfish cocktail

serves 3 to 4

For those who can lay their hands on wild crayfish (see page 323), here is a freshwater alternative to that seafood classic, the shrimp cocktail. For those who can't, the very homemade version of the cocktail sauce also makes an excellent dressing for cold shrimp, crab, and lobster.

At least 20 live crayfish (unless they are very large, you will need at least 7 to 8 per person)
Lettuce leaves, to serve
Lemon slices

FOR HUGH'S COCKTAIL SAUCE
1 pound Sungold or other cherry tomatoes, cut in half
1 tablespoon olive oil
2 garlic cloves, finely chopped
⅔ cup mayonnaise, preferably homemade
Lemon juice
Cayenne pepper or red pepper flakes

Put the crayfish in the freezer for about an hour, until completely torpid but not frozen solid. Then transfer them to a very large pan of rapidly boiling, salted water (this is the most humane way to kill them). When the water returns to a boil, boil the crayfish for 5 minutes. Drain and let cool.

To make the cocktail sauce, put the tomato halves in an ovenproof dish, sprinkle over the olive oil and garlic, and roast in a preheated 325°F oven for 45 minutes. Let cool, then rub through a sieve to make a rich, pulpy sauce.

Add the tomato sauce to the mayonnaise 1 tablespoon at a time until you get a taste and consistency you like (2½ tablespoons about does it for me). Sharpen with a little lemon juice and pep up with a pinch of cayenne pepper or pepper flakes. Chill in the fridge until ready to serve.

Shell the cold crayfish, carefully extracting the meat from the tail and the larger claws. Reserve 6 or 8 whole heads with claws attached and set aside. Mix the flesh with enough of the sauce to coat it generously. (The rest of the sauce will keep for a week in the fridge and can be used with other seafood – try mixing it with canned tuna for a sandwich filling!)

Serve the dressed crayfish on a bed of lettuce, garnished with 2 whole crayfish heads and 2 lemon slices on each plate. Finish with another pinch of cayenne or pepper flakes over the dressed meat.

eels in green herb sauce

serves 4

In my second summer at River Cottage, I once made this dish on a portable stove in the garden, with a fat eel straight from my trap in the river below me and herbs and spinach from the garden at my feet. The finished dish was pretty good, even though I say so myself. But what was unforgettable was the sense of profound satisfaction at putting together a meal from ingredients within grabbing distance. It was River Cottage on a plate.

2 tablespoons olive oil
4 slices of slightly stale baguette or white bread, cut 1 inch thick
5 tablespoons unsalted butter
1 pound eel fillets (see page 318 for eel preparation)
A fistful of spinach leaves, lightly blanched, squeezed dry, and finely chopped
A fistful of sorrel leaves, finely shredded
½ tablespoon finely chopped parsley
¾ cup dry white wine
Juice of ¼ lemon
1 large egg yolk, beaten with 1 tablespoon water
Salt and freshly ground black pepper

Heat the oil in a heavy frying pan, add the bread slices, and fry very gently until golden brown on both sides. Drain on paper towels and keep warm.

Pour off some of the oil and add half the butter. Fry the eel fillets for 2 to 3 minutes or until lightly browned, then remove from the pan and keep warm. Melt the remaining butter in the pan and add the spinach, sorrel, parsley, wine, and lemon juice. Bring to a simmer and cook until most of the liquid has evaporated. Season with salt and pepper.

Take the pan off the heat and let cool a little. Stir in the beaten egg yolk and heat very gently until the sauce thickens. To serve, arrange the eel fillets on the slices of bread and spoon generous amounts of the sauce over them.

variation If you haven't got an eel handy, fresh mackerel fillets make an excellent substitute. It's also worth making the sauce to serve over a poached egg on toast.

hedgerow

The sense of creativity, anticipation, and reward that comes from growing your own vegetables and raising your own animals for meat has to be experienced to be fully understood. But there is another whole dimension of pleasure, comparable yet different, to be had for the adventurous cook who learns to harvest truly wild food. If growing your own affords the deep and lasting satisfaction of hard work rewarded, gleaning the hedgerow, or field and forest, provides a thrill that's more primordial: you're not just out of the supermarket, you're back to being a hunter-gatherer.

At River Cottage, I have found that the one thing guaranteed to raise my spirits (especially, in fact, when some garden disaster or livestock anxiety is getting me down) is a walk into the surrounding hills and hedgerows in pursuit of some free food. Not everyone understands this. Many regard eating nettles as downright eccentric – and killing rabbits or squirrels for the pot as simply appalling. Why, they are inclined to argue, in a country where there are no significant shortages of food, need anyone resort to such primitive behavior? While some regard my enthusiasm for the wild pantry as barbaric, others seem to think its only value is in knowing how to look after yourself in some bleak, post-holocaust scenario. "Do you reckon you could survive," a taxi driver recently asked me, "if you were dumped in the middle of the countryside with just your Swiss Army knife?" Yes, is the answer – provided the nearest pub wasn't too far away, and the landlord was prepared to take the knife in lieu of cash.

For me, learning how to glean the wild pantry has never been an exercise in survivalism, and this section is not intended as a survival manual. The shortages I mean to address are not the urgent ones of nutrition and shelter. We are largely spared these anxieties in Britain. However, we have another modern social famine to contend with – in quality of life. I happen to believe that our lives will be better if we can achieve some closeness to the natural environment, and some understanding of the nature and origins of what we eat. Growing your own food fosters these aims to a considerable degree. But a knowledge and appreciation of the wild pantry completes the picture.

Remember that every single plant and animal that is used for food is descended from a wild ancestor – and many of those wild ancestors are alive and well in our fields, forests, and hedgerows. Wild food also comes with a unique guarantee: unlike almost every kind of cultivated food, it has not been messed with by people. It is pure, natural, and untampered with. An understanding of wild food is therefore, in part at least, an education about food history, and food safety. Best of all, it is not a force-fed education but one that both taps and nourishes inquisitiveness, a delight in the natural world, and a sense of adventure – three things that I happen to believe can do the human soul a power of good.

One thing, however, that you will definitely need to reap the benefits of the wild pantry is a little time. And perhaps it is the time famine that is the greatest blight of our age. But as we strike out into a new millennium, many of us are growing discontented with the questions that sustained us through the decades of greed: "How long have I got?" "How much can I have?" and "How fast can I get it?" Some of us are beginning to ask new questions – about how our quality of life might be improved by a more fulfilling relationship with the land around us. Gentle answers to these questions, or hints at them, can occasionally be found, I feel, while gathering our own food in wild places. For this is an activity that not only demands a little time, it gives a little back: time spent in pursuit of wild food – walking, picking, diving, fishing, hunting – is *your* time.

Ironically, though, gathering wild food is something that can still be enjoyed by people who don't have the time – or space – for the more high-maintenance pursuits of gardening and animal husbandry. You may live in the town – even more reason to make a break for the country. You only need a couple of hours to go blackberrying or mushrooming. And if your life is busy and stressful, that may be just the couple of hours you need to save your sanity.

More therapy for the beleaguered is on offer back in the kitchen, when you prepare a meal, a free meal, with the fruits of your foraging. Here, there is time to be creative, to make something special out of something commonplace, which costs you nothing. And with any luck, there is also time to spread the enjoyment to others. I have always found sharing food with friends to be among the highest of pleasures. Sharing wild food is particularly satisfying: I see those who partake in it sharing an unsung communion, ingesting a little of the wilderness spirit into themselves. And it reminds me that wild food is more than just something for nothing. It's something for everyone.

hedgerow | wild meat

Although the field and the freezer at River Cottage mean that I am now pretty much self-sufficient in pork, beef, and lamb, I still like to top up my meat supply with flesh garnered from the wild. And I have found, over the years, that some of the carnivorous dishes I have enjoyed the most have been made from animals and birds I have killed and cooked myself.

Why should this be? Perhaps because the finding, killing, preparation, and eating of a wild animal (or, indeed, a plant or fish) is, in a society increasingly obsessed with quick fixes and instant gratification, an unusually holistic procedure. It begins, more often than not, with a solitary walk in a wild place and a rare chance for quiet reflection. There is a tremendous weight of history behind this act – not just social history but evolutionary history.[21] And as I walk up the edge of a wood with my gun, hoping to bag a swooping wood pigeon or a scurrying rabbit, I am aware that my motivation, like that of all our hunting ancestors, is largely connected with my stomach.

Then comes the sighting of the quarry, and in an instant the mind becomes entirely focused on the movement of the animal, the zig zag of its run, or the arc of its flight. Perhaps there is a bit of stalking to be done – our attempts to regain the stealth and cunning of our ancestors may be pretty hopeless, but it always feels good to discover that the instinct is still there.

As you pull the trigger, the gap between you and the seemingly unreachable quarry is closed in an instant. The moment of death, as beast tumbles or bird crashes to the ground, is an emotional one that combines the triumph of possession and power with contradictory feelings of respect and regret. Then comes a period of contemplation, almost mourning, as the corpse is carried home, a pang that slowly subsides, giving way to anticipation of the feast to come.

But first, the animal must be plucked or skinned, then gutted. This is a messy, visceral task that many would find unpleasant but, I must admit, I find rather satisfying, even educational. Opening, for example, the crop of a dead pigeon, I can find out whether it has been fattening itself on corn, clover, elderberries, or peas, and wonder how this might affect the flavor of the meat.

Then comes restoration: the transformation of the cold, lifeless corpse, with wine, herbs, and the magic of the oven, into something delicious, either to be savored in a solitary session or shared with friends. By the time it is served up, the hunter-cook has achieved a uniquely close relationship with his quarry: observing it in the wild, taking its life, handling it, preparing it, and then, the ultimate act of intimacy, devouring it. And for me that is something very special.

No doubt some people would find the above sentiments unsympathetic, or even incomprehensible. Without doubt the most controversial scenes in the *River Cottage* television series were those in which I went in pursuit of wild meat – stalking roe deer, shooting rabbits by spotlight, and culling my neighbor's white pigeons from his roof. As I expected, I received a certain amount of hostile mail about this. But I have also received supportive letters, congratulating me for having the guts to show what other programs would have left out.

I think it is important that those of us who choose to kill fish, birds, and mammals for the pot are ready to explain to others why we do what we do. This is a responsibility I have always tried to meet, as a journalist and a broadcaster. I do not argue that we have an inalienable right to eat meat. I do say, however, that if we are going to make meat part of our diet, then wild meat is, for me, the least morally problematic of all. All meat is the product of a killing, and those of us who kill for the pot are merely taking responsibility for the manner of that killing. A squirrel may have a cuteness factor that makes some people shudder at the sight of its back legs crackling on a grill. But if those people have ever seen young calves and lambs playing in the fields, then why have they not applied the cuteness argument to their own carnivorous habits? For I have found that most of the people who seem to be upset by the eating of rabbits, squirrels, and the like are not vegetarians but town-dwelling carnivores. Most vegetarians I know are far more sympathetic to the eating of game and other wild meat than they are to the consumption of meat produced by modern farming practices.

And this brings me to the second vital point about wild protein: all wild meat comes with a unique and invaluable guarantee of quality. First, it has been fed on an entirely natural diet, selected, as nature intended, not by man but by the animal itself – no hormones, no chemicals, and no revolting and dangerous feeds made from other ground-up animals. Second, it has lived a life, however short, as nature intended, free of the many stresses that give so much cause for concern about the welfare of our farm animals. Third, if the killer is also going to be the butcher and the cook, he or she has complete control over how the meat is stored, butchered, and otherwise prepared before cooking.

Remember that every time you go to the butcher's for a chicken or a steak, or buy meat from a supermarket, you are at the mercy of a whole chain of intermediaries: the farmer, the slaughterhouse, and the butcher himself. You have to take it on trust that all three links in the chain have done their jobs as well as you would like them to. If you buy wild meat, you can eliminate the first two links in the chain, and if you kill it yourself, you can eliminate all three. And that's satisfying.

what is wild meat?

Having sung the praises of wild meat, both as a quarry and as an ingredient, it's time to make some clear distinctions, both generally and for the purposes of this chapter.

Wild meat can be fairly simply defined as meat from any animal or bird that is not bred and fed by man. But there are a few gray areas. Some species of game birds – notably most pheasants, some partridges, and ducks, particularly mallards – are reared specifically for sport. They are therefore not, strictly speaking, wild. And while a shot pheasant is at least in some sense "free range," it would be a mistake to think of it as organic. The feeds given to some pheasants are at least as high in additives as those given to some commercially farmed poultry. And there is nothing one can do to identify the dosed birds either. I would still consider a reared pheasant infinitely preferable to an intensively farmed broiler, but increasingly I find I am encountering disappointing birds.

An even more abused bird is the quail. Contrary to the implication on some packaging, quails that you find in Britain are never wild: they are always farmed, sometimes as intensively and unpleasantly as battery chickens.[22] I tend not to buy quails unless I know they have been humanely reared and naturally fed. Unfortunately, since they are technically classed as game, there is no statutory labeling legislation governing the use of the term *free range*, so if you want to get hold of decent quail you will have to do some homework. Truly wild quail are native to the flat plains of eastern Europe. No doubt they are delicious, but unfortunately I have never seen them on sale in the U.K.

The British game birds that are pretty much guaranteed to be truly wild (and, in the hands of a good cook, pretty much guaranteed to be delicious) are wild ducks (other than mallard, but including widgeon, teal, and pintail), wild geese (including greylag, pink-footed, and white-fronted), grouse, woodcock, and snipe. Access to these species for shooting is controlled by law (which enforces a closed season) and by the owners of the land over which they range. Much has been written about the sport of shooting game birds and about the art of cooking them. It's not my plan to add to that here. Of more interest to me at River Cottage are the nongame birds, generally regarded as pests, for which there is no closed season and which may be taken by anyone, at any time, on their own land or, with the permission of the landowner, somebody else's. These are democratic quarry rather than the objects of exclusive and expensive sport, and include wood pigeons and rooks.

Some mammals, too, are available to everyone – at least to everyone who can safely and legally handle a gun. Those hunted for sport and food in this country basically include the deer family (red, roe, sika, muntjac, and fallow); hares, both brown and blue (the Scottish mountain hare); rabbits; and, occasionally (not often enough, I would say) squirrels.

These are the birds and mammals to which I devote the rest of this chapter. To them I add one further source of land-based protein, partly for want of a better place to put it but also in the hope that it may particularly appeal to urban foragers whose access to pigeons, rabbits, and the like may be somewhat limited. I am talking about a beast neither furred nor feathered, but which carries its house on its back: not your pet tortoise (though that, too, might be pretty tasty), but the common garden snail.

owning a shotgun

By far the easiest way to kill a bird or small mammal (though not a snail) is with a shotgun. In the hands of a skilled shot, it is also one of the most humane. But there is no point in owning a shotgun unless you intend to use it fairly regularly and know how to handle it responsibly – and, indeed, unless you can convince your local police station that you can do this, you will not be given a license to keep a gun. Just as important as a license is competence with the gun. Either join a shooting school or seek informal tuition from a gamekeeper or other enthusiast. Buying and keeping a gun is easier in the U.S., so good training is even more crucial.

Having said that, you don't have to own vast tracts of land to exercise a passion for shooting, or even be a paid-up member of a syndicate shoot. I have always preferred shooting alone or with, at most, one other like-minded human companion, to a ten-gun, gin-and-tonic-fueled pheasant massacre. And if the sport you intend to pursue is not the expensive social one of shooting carefully managed game birds but the often more challenging and enjoyable one of setting out alone to reduce the population of edible vermin, you may be able to benefit, as I have here in Dorset, from the goodwill of local farmers and gamekeepers. If you are friendly with such types, and can demonstrate to them that you know how to handle a gun responsibly, they may allow you on their land to flight or decoy pigeons, stalk rabbits, shoot the odd roe deer, and bag a few young birds from the springtime rookery. And if it's rabbits you're after, there are many landowners who would be happy for you to shoot on their land. If such access is granted – for shooting, ferreting, or even gathering snails – be aware that it is a privilege, and observe to the letter any conditions to which your access is made subject.

shooting at home

You are not allowed to use a shotgun in a built-up area, or within fifty yards of a public road. This means that, practically speaking, it is not feasible to use a shotgun on your own land unless you live in the country and have at least three or four acres. However, if you do have a large garden, bordering on farmland, regularly visited by pigeons, rabbits, or squirrels, it may be possible to shoot on and over it in a limited capacity, but it is only sensible to do so with the understanding of your neighbors. Explain what you intend to do and ask them if they mind. Ask permission to recover any birds that may fall on neighboring land.

air rifles

If you have a large garden, in leafy suburbs or a country village, which gives you a certain amount of space and relative privacy from your neighbors, you are quite within your rights to use an air rifle to shoot incoming pigeons and squirrels. (The latter can be as much of a problem for the gardener as for the farmer, owing to their devastating habit of gnawing the bark of young trees. They're also rather partial to young vegetables. But if you are serious about this, you should get a decent gun, pressurized to the maximum legal level, and make sure it is properly sighted.

Since it is a less lethal weapon than a shotgun or a rifle, you don't need a license to own an air rifle, but nevertheless you do need to handle it responsibly. Always use it safely, firing only when the backdrop to the target is either clear sky or solid ground.

cooking wild meat

I have a few general provisos on the subject of cooking wild meat. It is true that much wild meat is very dense and lean – reflecting the energetic lifestyle of the animals from which it comes. From the cook's point of view, however, this means that although the meat is rich and highly flavored, there is always a danger of dryness, and of toughness. Traditionally, marinades have been prescribed as the best means of countering this, and the main ingredient of most marinades for game seems to be wine. This is a mistake. In my experience, marinating game in alcohol is counterproductive. It tends to pickle the meat, drawing the juices out of it, so that when cooked it is, if anything, even dryer. The most important ingredient of any marinade for game is not wine but oil (olive is usually best), followed by flavorings such as herbs, onions, and garlic. The oil lubricates the meat, resulting in a better texture. A little wine – say, a tablespoonful for 2 pounds of meat – can be added for flavoring, but that's it.

More important than marinating is the way that game is subsequently cooked. Almost all game, from a pigeon breast to a haunch of red deer, can be cooked hot and fast and served pink. This keeps the juice, and therefore the flavor, inside the meat. Personally, I would apply this maxim to all roasting, grilling, and flash-frying, whether the meat is in lean cuts or on the bone. Resting the meat properly after cooking helps with the tenderness issue.

Casseroles and stews are, of course, another option – especially for older, tougher animals. Here long, slow cooking will gently tenderize the meat. But again, lack of fat in the meat is a problem. It is a big mistake to think that just because a meat is cooked in a liquid medium it won't be dry. Stewed meat can be the dryest and least appetizing of all. What's needed in a slow-cooked game dish is added fat, and the best way to achieve this is by adding good bacon or pork belly. The flavor of bacon complements most game – and vice versa. I like to use large

(¾-inch-cubed) pieces of bacon in my casseroles, as they give up their fat slowly over a long cooking period but keep their shape. Taking on the flavors of the herbs and the game, the pieces of bacon become delicious morsels in their own right.

Incidentally, I am happy to add wine at the cooking stage – the flavor is good with game, and the alcohol will cook out before it can have any adverse effects on the meat.

the beasts and birds

Unlike most of the wild plants described in this section, most of the wild meat described below (with the notable exceptions of rooks and squirrels) can be bought as well as shot. What follows is a few thoughts on how you might get to pursue these very worthwhile quarry yourself and, failing that, how you might acquire them for the pot in some quantity, for not too much money.[23] Should you end up getting them from a butcher or game dealer, they certainly won't cost you much – and I offer a few tips on making the right choice.

RABBITS There is no shortage of rabbits in Britain, and, provided we do not completely destroy our rural landscape, there probably never will be. The introduction of myxomatosis, a particularly revolting disease, though initially devastating, has had absolutely no significant long-term effect on the population. I hate to see a rabbit suffering from "mixy," and will always try to put it out of its misery if I can. But mixy rabbits are not good eating.

There are other, far more humane methods of controlling rabbits than such grotesque biological warfare, and they have the added bonus of keeping the meat in good condition. When a serious impact on numbers is required, night shooting with a handheld spotlight, and either a shotgun or a .22 rifle, is extremely effective. Ferreting is another option. Some people think it is cruel but it has never struck me as being so: the rabbit, fleeing from a natural predator, hits a net, gets tangled up and, before it realizes what's happening, is dispatched by a swift blow on the back of the neck.

If you want to shoot or ferret for rabbits try, as I suggested above, approaching a local landowner, farmer, or gamekeeper. If you do not already know them personally, you will need to approach gently: perhaps start by asking if they have any to sell or give away; if they ever shoot them themselves (and if so, could you go with them). They may be surprised, they may even be hostile – in which case you're better off well away from their patch anyway – but if you show genuine interest, and some knowledge of your sport, you should get a fair hearing and, with any luck, the access you require.

If you don't wish to hunt rabbits but simply to locate a ready supply, some gamekeepers will let you have them for nothing, especially if you are prepared to drive by the keeper's cottage to pick them up. Others will happily drop them off for you, but the least you can do is offer them a bit of beer money. The going wholesale rate for rabbits in Britain is about 50p ($1) apiece, so you should always be ready to pay at least that. Rabbits obtained at such a bargain rate you will almost certainly have to gut and skin yourself (see below).

When it comes to buying rabbits, any decent country butcher can get them for you, though they may be harder to find in larger cities. Wild rabbits will vary in price depending on where you are, but they should never be expensive. Butchers sell rabbits either whole and unskinned (but usually gutted) or whole and skinned, or skinned, portioned, and wrapped in cellophane. All too often, the liver, kidneys, and heart have already been discarded – a great shame, as all are excellent. If you are ordering rabbits in advance, request that the innards be kept for you (see page 367 for a simple suggestion on how to serve them). It's worth taking the head for stock.

Be aware that many of the rabbits sold in butcher shops and supermarkets are not wild but farmed – and often farmed as intensively as chickens. If the label doesn't specify wild rabbit, or contain a warning that "this produce may contain lead shot," then assume it is farmed.

Rabbits are best for eating when they are not breeding or feeding their young: this means from August to February.

Gutting and skinning Unlike hares, which are hung with the guts in, rabbits should be gutted, or "paunched," as soon as possible after killing, either when you get home or even in the field. It isn't difficult: with a very sharp knife, make an incision, no deeper than is necessary to pierce the skin (you don't want to pierce the intestine, if possible), starting at the urinary tract between the rabbit's legs and working up to the beginning of the breastbone. Pull out the stomach and intestines, carefully separating the membrane that attaches the stomach to the kidneys, so the two kidneys remain attached to the carcass. Leave the liver and heart attached to the lungs inside the chest cavity. At the first opportunity, remove the innards, discard the lungs, but keep the liver,

heart, and kidneys (wrap them in plastic wrap and keep in the fridge) and rinse out the inside of the beast. In this state the rabbit can be hung for three or four days before skinning though this is not advisable in warm weather.

To skin a rabbit, take a pair of pruning shears or strong kitchen scissors, and cut off all four feet above the "knees." Lay the rabbit on the table on its back, tail end toward you. With a very sharp knife, make a crosswise slit, at right angles to and a couple of inches or so below the cavity slit, across the belly and the tops of the thighs. Take the skin that is released and pull it down off the thighs and turn the back legs out of the skin, pulling it inside out like a pair of socks and down over the tail (hard to describe but really quite easy to do).

Then turn the body over so the head is toward you, get a good grip of the skin, and pull down toward the head as far as it will go. Ease out the front legs, one by one. You can either cut through the neck and discard the head with the skin or, to keep the carcass whole and the head on, use the point of the knife to loosen the skin around the head until it can be pulled right off.

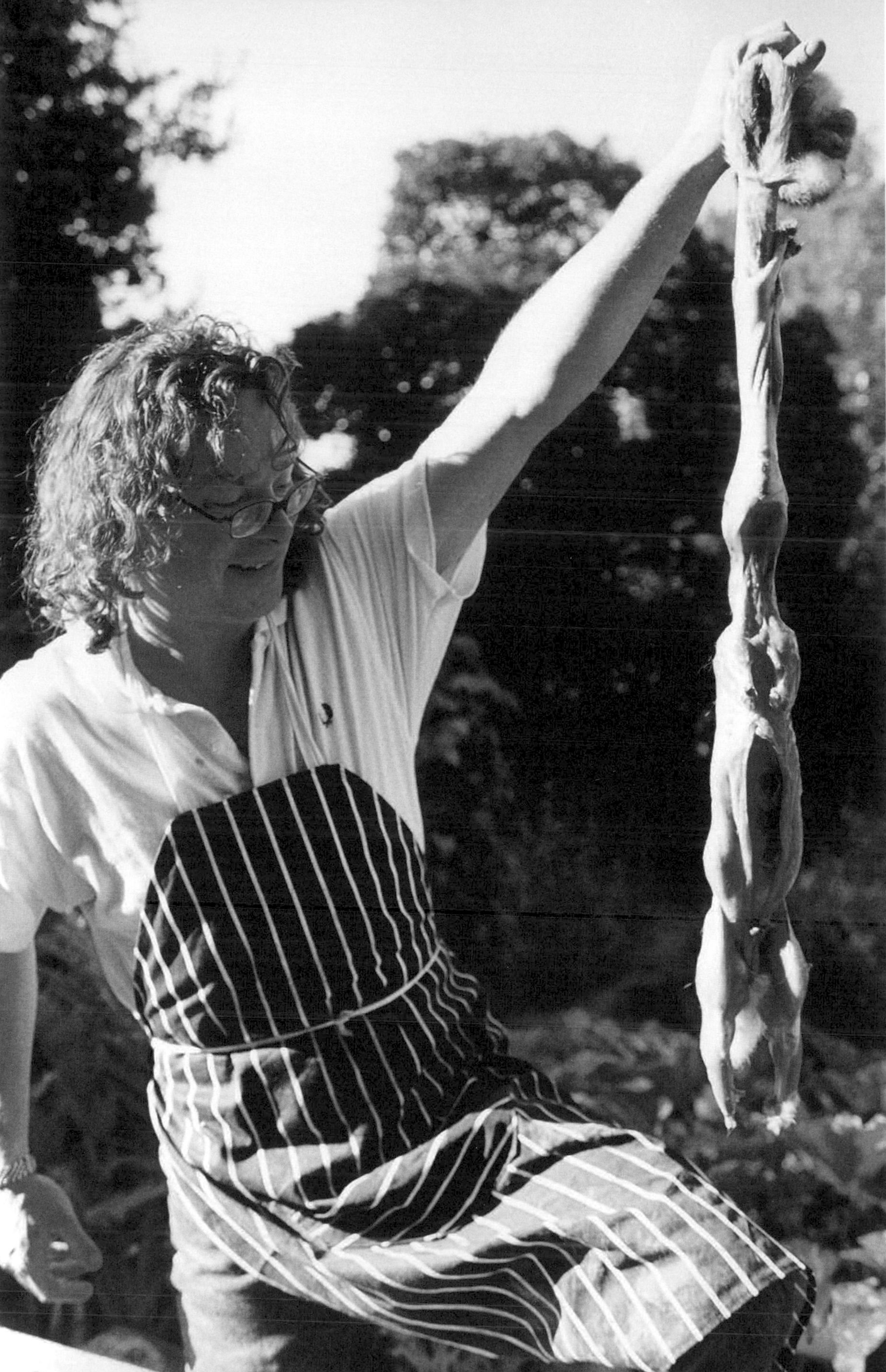

Jointing You can roast a rabbit whole (see below), even with the head on, but almost all other recipes require it to be cut into serving pieces.

First, cut off the legs: use a sharp knife to cut between the muscles that join the legs to the hips and shoulders, then cut through the bone with a heavy knife or cleaver. Cut away the thin flaps of meat that joined the ribs to the belly. These look almost useless, but don't discard them: they contract when cooked and make very tasty little boneless portions. Cut off the neck and head (which can be used for stock, or included in your casserole, then discarded). The remaining back, or "saddle," should be cut with a cleaver into three or four equal pieces.

Cooking Many old recipes call for wild rabbits to be soaked overnight in acidulated saltwater before cooking. The idea of this is to bleach the flesh and remove any "gamy" flavor – a crazy notion, in my view, as rabbit is not a strong-tasting meat at the best of times. The idea that the meat is made more attractive by being bleached white, or more palatable by being robbed of its natural taste, is an outdated piece of dainty nonsense and should be disregarded.

Rabbit is a well-flavored delicate meat, but it does have a tendency to dryness. Stews and casseroles are therefore among the best preparations, and pancetta, bacon, or fresh pork belly are useful additions to help keep the meat lubricated. Brown your rabbit meat and bacon/pork together, tossed in a little flour if you want to thicken the gravy, then put it in a pot with a few sliced vegetables (try carrots, onions, and celery), a bay leaf, a sprig of thyme, and some peppercorns. Water or stock, combined with wine, cider, or beer, can be used as cooking liquids. The cooking time will depend on the age of the beast: a big old buck rabbit is best given a long, slow simmer for an hour and a half, until the meat is flaking off the bone. But a younger animal will be tender and succulent in about half that time. A particularly nice way to finish a rabbit stew is to strain off the cooking liquid, boil it to reduce, then enrich it with a little cream and a spoonful of strong mustard.

Rabbits can be roasted, but again the lack of natural fat means that any attempt to do so will be a battle to preserve some juiciness in the meat. If this battle is won, then a roast rabbit is a very fine dish indeed. It is sensible to remove the front legs and roast only the saddle and rather chunkier thighs. Cover the rabbit in bacon and roast in a preheated 375°F oven for thirty-five to forty-five minutes. Remove the bacon and turn up the heat to brown the rabbit for the last ten minutes, basting every couple of minutes with the fat and juices in the pan.

The trio of fresh rabbit innards – heart, liver, and kidneys – should not be wasted: they are delicious quickly fried and served with a few salad leaves. Rinse all the items well and trim the liver of any discolored (yellowy-brown) parts. Fry a little chopped bacon or pancetta, and when it is nearly ready, throw the innards in the pan and sauté for just a few minutes, until nicely browned. Scatter the meat over a lightly dressed salad of green leaves, such as romaine lettuce, arugula, watercress, and dandelion greens (or chicory).

For two excellent recipes using boned-out rabbit meat – Rabbit Satay with Spicy Peanut Sauce and Rabbit Burgers – see pages 412 and 416.

HARES The hare is a very different beast from the rabbit, which it superficially resembles: cleverer, rarer, more shy, much faster – and even more delicious to eat.

Note that there are two kinds of hares to be found in the British Isles. The brown hare, the larger of the two, is widespread throughout the country, and the only one you are likely to encounter in the south. The blue or mountain hare is common only in Scotland, where it greatly outnumbers the brown hare. The blue hare is smaller than the brown, and sometimes a bit tough, but still reasonable eating. The brown hare is quite one of the most delicious wild creatures you could ever hope to eat.

In Britain, the hunting of hares by almost any method is becoming controversial. Some conservationists maintain that hares are in great decline and should be protected. Many farmers, on the other hand, claim to be overrun with them, and argue that without their annual hare shoots (which can bag several hundred hares at a time) they would have a serious problem. The truth is that both parties probably have a point: the distribution of hares in the U.K. is very uneven. In Dorset, I don't see many at all, but in Gloucestershire and Wiltshire I have sometimes seen upward of fifty in a couple of hours' walk. The Countryside Commission is monitoring the situation but, at present, "is not concerned about overall hare numbers."

Hares are not strictly classed as game, and do not benefit from a closed season as such. But they do enjoy partial protection, in that it is not permitted to offer a hare for sale from the end of March to the beginning of August. This is when they are rearing their young and, given the concern that has been expressed about numbers in some areas, I think it is appropriate that they should be considered off-limits during these months.

The most controversial way to pursue hares is coursing, in which greyhounds, lurchers, or other dogs built for speed are set in pursuit of the animals. Many people regard this as cruel, and it is among the sports due to be banned if the drafted legislation concerning hunting with dogs goes through. Personally, in the right circumstances I don't think coursing is necessarily cruel. One man and one dog (or sometimes two), in pursuit of a hare for the pot, seems to me like a sporting hunt. The hare will often escape, and if it doesn't it will be swiftly killed. Far more questionable is the practice of netting hares, keeping them alive, and transporting them for coursing competitions, where the main object of the exercise is not getting a hare to eat but gambling on the performance of the dogs.

Shooting hares is a more specialized pursuit than shooting rabbits. A brown hare is a large, fast-running creature, and if you don't know what you are doing you are more likely to wound one than kill it. It takes a skilled shot to kill a hare with a shotgun, and the pellet size used for rabbits or pigeons (usually six or seven) is simply not appropriate. These days, if I want to shoot a hare I will set out specifically for that purpose, walking up September stubble or the winter plowed fields equipped with special cartridges (shot size four) to do the job properly.

As I mentioned, many keepers now have an annual hare shoot, usually in January or early February. Traditionally, the hare shoot is for other keepers and local farmers rather than the landowner or syndicate, but if you are very friendly with a keeper, he might let you come along.

The eating qualities of hares have long been celebrated, and there is still a regular market to supply those in the know. Good butchers may keep them in stock, but to be sure of getting one you should order it a few days in advance. The price of a hare may vary considerably according to local availability, but they are rarely expensive. Last season, my local butcher was selling them for £8 to £10 ($16 to $20) apiece – not bad when you consider that a large specimen will feed six greedy people. You may get a better price from a game dealer, and better still from a gamekeeper (you should get them for a knockdown price from a keeper just after a hare shoot).

Many butchers keep hares in the freezer. Like most game, whose meat is always close-textured, it freezes reasonably well, and a defrosted hare would make a good casserole if cooked very slowly. But fresh is preferable, and essential if you are roasting. A good butcher who deals regularly in game should be able to give you a fresh hare, well hung, skinned, and jointed, with the collected blood in a plastic tub.

Preparation Hares should always be hung for at least four days to help develop the flavor and tenderize the meat. In unusually warm weather, try to find a cool place such as a cellar. In cold weather, you can hang a hare for up to ten days if you like it really gamy. They are usually hung head down with the guts still in. This makes the job of gutting them a rather smelly one – and one I prefer to do out of doors. In many hare recipes, you will be wanting to use the blood, both for its flavor and for its useful thickening properties. It collects in the chest cavity while the hare is hanging and can be emptied into a bowl when it is gutted. If your hare is dripping blood from the mouth when you hang it (its lungs may have been punctured by shot), then put a plastic bag over its head, secured with a rubber band, to catch the blood.

Hares are often skinned before being gutted, and this is the method I prefer. The technique is as for rabbits (see page 365) – with the proviso that with your first cut (across the belly of the animal), you should take care to release a flap of skin without piercing the membrane that holds in the stomach contents. When the animal has been skinned, it is then a relatively simple matter to slit this membrane, while holding the hare head down over a lined trash can, and release the intestines and stomach contents into the can. The heart, lungs, and liver will remain in the chest cavity, along with a considerable quantity of blood. It is therefore best to remove them over a bowl or bucket, in which you can collect the blood. Once you have saved as much blood as possible from these organs, they can be discarded – unless you have a young hare that has not been hung too long, in which case the liver will be mild enough to add, finely chopped, to your sauce, or to fry up and eat on toast.

The skinned and gutted hare should not be washed, but picked over for bits of fur sticking to the meat and then wiped with a damp cloth. It can then be jointed (if required for your recipe) as for a rabbit – except that each back leg can be divided into two portions and the saddle into four or five with a meat cleaver. Covered, the meat can then be stored for a day or two in the fridge.

Cooking When roasting a hare, it is customary to roast only the saddle (i.e., body), removing the legs and casseroling them separately (or use them in a game pie). However, if you have many mouths to feed, the back legs, which have plenty of meat on, can be left on for roasting. The saddle alone will serve only four at most. Keep the back legs on and it should serve six.

Providing they have been well hung, all but the most ancient of hares can be roasted. However, like rabbits, they must be well protected from drying out. Six to twelve hours in a marinade (olive oil, a *little* red wine, bay leaf, thyme, and sliced onions) beforehand will help to ensure the meat is tender and moist, especially if you baste it during cooking too. Before roasting, the hare should be thoroughly wiped free of the marinade, then lightly rubbed with more olive oil. Another trick is to line the inside of the hare with a few slices of bacon and place it upside down for the first half of the cooking, then remove the bacon and deglaze the pan with the strained marinade and a little stock or water. Use these juices to baste the hare, now right side up, for the rest of the cooking. Roast hare can be served just a tiny bit pink, which it should be after thirty-five to forty minutes in a preheated 400°F oven.

You can use the blood to thicken the gravy for a roast hare. The juices in the roasting pan should be deglazed with water or stock, then added slowly and by degrees to the blood, which you have warmed just a little in a small saucepan. Stir constantly, over low heat, to emulsify this sauce. Add a little of the excellent red wine that you are proposing to drink with the hare and a teaspoon of red currant jelly. Heat the sauce through, but do not let it boil. Taste and season with salt and pepper if necessary, then pour into a warmed sauceboat and serve.

For slow cooking, see the recipe for Jugged Hare (page 420), one of the finest of English game dishes.

GRAY SQUIRRELS Okay, squirrels have lovely fluffy tails and can perform clever tricks to nick the food off your bird table. But they are a damn nuisance to forestry (and, not infrequently, to the gardener), there are plenty of them, and they happen to be delicious. I say, let's eat them!

The squirrels of interest to the cook are, of course, gray squirrels. Red squirrels are a rare and protected species and, anyway, too small to be worthwhile as food. Unfortunately, so unrecognized is the squirrel as food, that it comes under very little control. And in areas where it has run amok, threatening whole plantations of young trees, people have resorted to poisoning with Warfarin – another slow and unpleasant method of pest control, which, like myxomatosis in rabbits, renders their meat quite inedible.

Clearly, it is no more cruel or uncivilized to kill and eat a squirrel than a rabbit. The plus is that the meat is, if anything, even better than rabbit. I know one chef who occasionally, and mischievously, puts squirrel on the menu of his New Forest restaurant as "flightless partridge," and in gastronomic terms the comparison with that delicious bird is a valid one.

Squirrels can be taken at any time when they are not hibernating but are not really worth eating in spring and early summer, when they are fairly scrawny and busy feeding their young. They get plumper and tastier as they fatten up on fruits, nuts, and berries in high summer and autumn, and are at their best from August to early winter, just before hibernation. The two most effective ways to acquire them are trapping and shooting.

Personally, I'm not too keen on trapping, although it can be very effective and has the advantage of providing meat that is not full of lead shot. Squirrel traps, baited with birdseed or nuts, catch the animals alive without injuring them. But the trapped squirrel may spend many hours in the tiny trap cage before it is found and dispatched by the trapper – and that's the bit I'm not too keen on. If you do use traps, do so conscientiously: they should be checked every morning and evening. Never set or bait a squirrel trap that you cannot check within twelve hours.

Squirrels can scratch and bite something fierce, so taking one out of a trap is something to be done with care. The best method is to hold a coarse sack over the entrance to the trap, release the gate, and shake the squirrel into the sack. Locate the squirrel in the sack, hold it firmly, and dispatch it with a single blow from a stout stick on the back of the head.

Instead of trapping, I prefer to shoot squirrels with a rifle or shotgun. I always aim for the head, or at least the front end. Apart from being the best way to make a clean kill, this helps to minimize the amount of lead shot in the back legs, which is where the worthwhile meat is.

Air rifles can also be effective. You can get fairly close to a gray squirrel, especially if they are not often shot at: they tend to think they are pretty safe once they are up a tree. Always aim for the head or heart, not the belly, where you are likely to wound without killing it.

Gamekeepers are likely to be sympathetic to requests to shoot or trap squirrels on their land, since they are, in the spring, voracious egg eaters, both of song and game birds. But be aware that some people won't like you killing squirrels, and be correspondingly discreet in your pursuit. Anyone taking squirrels should make sure that nobody in the vicinity is using poison.

Buying squirrels is not easy. I have never seen squirrel on sale in any butcher's, which I think is a shame, given its excellent eating quality. If you can't, or don't want to, trap or shoot squirrels yourself but are interested in cooking them, try contacting a local gamekeeper or forest ranger.

Preparation Like rabbits, squirrels should be paunched (gutted) as soon as possible after killing (see page 364). They can then be hung for up to four days in cool weather, though this isn't really necessary, especially with younger animals. Skinning is as for a rabbit (see page 365), except harder! Older, larger squirrels can be particularly tough to skin.

All the good meat on a squirrel is on the back legs, or haunches. There is also a bit of worthwhile meat on the saddle. The best way to joint them therefore is to cut a skinned squirrel in two, just below the front legs. The two haunches, still joined together, with the saddle attached, make a perfect one-person portion. Or they can be separated to make smaller portions for a casserole. The front third – head, neck, shoulders, and forelegs – can be discarded, but is certainly worth keeping for stock. Roast the pieces briefly before putting them in a stockpot with vegetables and herbs.

Cooking First, you need to decide whether your squirrel is young or old. Size is the best indication but, apart from being larger, older squirrels are likely to have harder, more ragged claws and longer, more worn teeth.

Young squirrels (ideally killed in the autumn of their first year) are particularly tender and delicious, and haunches of them can be simply sautéed, broiled, or grilled. Or use them in any good chicken or rabbit recipe (including the Rabbit Satay with Spicy Peanut Sauce on page 412).

Older squirrels could still be given the broiler-or-grill treatment, but will need marinating first and will be a little chewier. They are also ideal for slower cooking and could be substituted for pheasant, partridge, or rabbit in any casserole recipe. One set of haunches approximately equals a partridge (and serves one); two or three can be substituted for a pheasant or a rabbit. And don't forget the bacon, to help keep them juicy.

DEER The species of wild deer that can be found in Britain are, in order of descending size, red, sika, fallow, roe, and muntjac. The distribution of these five species varies hugely around the country, but all are sufficiently prolific in some parts at least to be regarded as pests, in need of control. The roe, in particular, is hugely successful throughout Britain and particularly on the increase here in the southwest. Luckily, all five species are excellent eating, and the roe arguably the best of all. The species found in the U.S. are white-tailed deer, mule deer, caribou, elk, and moose.

The only acceptable way to kill any of the above deer species is with a high-powered rifle, the caliber of which must be suitable for the intended quarry (this is stipulated by law). Nor is this something you should attempt alone until you have been trained, and accompanied several times, by an expert (either a professional stalker or a gamekeeper or farmer who really knows what he is doing). Having issued that proviso, I would emphasize that deer stalking, undertaken in a responsible way, can be a truly thrilling, close-to-nature experience – and the final reward is one of the finest of all wild meats, venison.[24] If you want to learn how to stalk, talk to a local gamekeeper or contact a shooting and conservation organization.

Buying Venison can be found increasingly in butcher's shops and even supermarkets. In such outlets much – perhaps most – of the venison will be farmed. This is not necessarily a bad thing – farmed venison can be excellent, often being grazed entirely naturally. Some is less good, as the deer are fed a supplementary diet of processed feed to speed up their growth. There is no way you can tell from the labeling, so you'll just have to try it and see. You may prefer to insist on wild venison – in which case, order it from a butcher you trust, or go direct to a game dealer, or even a gamekeeper.

Preparation Deer should be eviscerated ("gralloched") as soon as they have been shot. This is like gutting a rabbit on a large scale. Any experienced stalker will show you how to do it the first time you kill a deer. The second time, why not have a go yourself? It is also easier to skin a deer that is still warm, though this is not usually done on the hill but back in a cool game pantry. A skinned, gutted deer can be hung in a game pantry for up to a week – or up to three weeks in a properly refrigerated meat storage locker. A reasonable hanging period such as this is good for both the flavor and texture of the meat.

Smaller deer such as roe and muntjac are usually butchered like a hare: into two shoulders, two haunches (back legs), and a saddle. The saddle is the prime roasting joint, though the haunches and shoulders also roast well. Large beasts, such as mature red deer, are butchered more like lambs: they can be divided into chops, and racks of chops, as well as legs (haunches), shoulders, and saddle. The neck makes excellent stewing venison.

The innards of any deer you shoot should not be disregarded. The liver of all young deer, and roe in particular, is absolutely delicious. Treat it as for calf's liver – i.e., serve just pink – and try the Stalkers' Breakfast on page 416 or include it in my recipe for Game Terrine on page 414. The heart and kidneys can also be used, as fresh as possible, just like lamb's (they're about the same size).

Cooking Venison is delicious, flavorful meat but because it is so lean (there is almost no fat running through it) it has a particular tendency to dryness. Read up on venison cookery and you will find all sorts of elaborate suggestions for combating this: slow roast, pot roast, marinating in advance, barding, larding, basting. I have tried them all. But without doubt the best advice I have ever been given about cooking venison came from the writer A. A. Gill. Venison joints, be they haunches, shoulders, or saddles, should never be marinated or cooked slowly, he told me. For maximum succulence and taste, roast them like a leg or saddle of spring lamb – studded with garlic, rosemary, or thyme if you like, rubbed with butter or olive oil, then roasted hard and fast and served a little pink. He's absolutely right, and this approach works for all venison joints except those taken from a really huge and ancient stag or hind, which is really only good for stewing anyway. A whole tenderloin taken from the saddle of a young red deer, sika, or large roe can be grilled whole and served very pink.

Venison stews need added fat: pork belly or thick-cut bacon or pancetta will do the job. Use wine as a flavoring but don't overdo it – as I have said above, the acidity of wine actually draws the juices out of the meat and makes the texture more dry and fibrous. With venison, this is fatal. The best liquid medium for a venison stew is a good strong stock made in advance from roasted bones. Add plenty of stock vegetables to your stew, especially carrots and onions (or whole shallots), and strong herbs such as thyme, bay, and rosemary. Juniper is also an excellent flavor to combine with venison.

WOOD PIGEONS The wood pigeon population of the U.K. is estimated at about twenty million. As their favorite spring foods are the young crops of peas, wheat, and rapeseed oil, they are hardly the farmer's friend; in fact, they are regarded as the single most devastating agricultural pest. No bad thing, then, that they are absolutely delicious to eat. The only U.S. equivalents are quails and doves.

As with rabbits, your best bet for some good pigeon shooting is to get permission from a friendly landowner to shoot them on his or her land. You can bag a few pigeons by walking up the edge of a wood, or through it, and shooting them as they fly off at your approach. But by far the most effective techniques are decoying – where you wait for pigeons in a blind constructed next to the field in which they are feeding, with decoys to lure them in

– and evening flighting, where you wait inside the edge of a wood for pigeons coming in to roost. Both these techniques require good shooting skills and some understanding of pigeon behavior, flight paths, etc., but professional pigeon controllers can achieve huge bags – I believe the record is over six hundred in a day. Whoever achieved that can't have missed many. If you are interested in developing your skills and understanding of pigeon shooting, it is well worth spending a day in a blind with an expert decoyer.

You may never shoot five hundred, or even fifty, in a day, but if ever you do get a lot more than you want for your own consumption, it's worth bearing in mind that pigeon freezes very well.

Another highly specialized but very effective technique is pigeon sniping with an air rifle (see page 362). You have to get very close (not more than thirty yards away), and you have to shoot very straight. This can also be done from a blind, and the pigeons are left to settle on the field in front of you. Another technique is to climb a tree in a wood and sit on a branch waiting for the pigeons to come in to roost. If you want to do this, don't be reckless and attempt to shin up into the canopy by free climbing, then descend in the dark. Find a good tree in broad daylight and throw up a rope, or better still, a rope ladder, to make your climb a safe one. Go up and find a good comfortable sitting and shooting position. And when you go back in the evening, don't change your mind about which tree to climb and where in it to sit!

If you are shooting pigeons with an air rifle and the bird is facing you front on, aim either for the top of the breast or for the head; if the bird is side on or has its back to you, always go for a head shot. The back and wing feathers are almost impenetrable to an air gun pellet, and you may surprise a few pigeons but you won't kill many. A good head shot will kill the bird instantly, and a miss is likely to be a clean one.

If you can't shoot your own pigeons, you will almost certainly have to pay for them.[25] As far as I know, almost all pigeons on sale in the U.K. are wild. You may be able to buy direct from a gamekeeper or farmer, if you are in touch with one who regularly shoots pigeons. Otherwise, buy from a game dealer or butcher. They will certainly be cheaper if they are still feathered and undrawn rather than oven-ready, and since you will often be using just the breasts, cut off the bone (see below), you should take them feathered when you can. But even oven-ready pigeons should be cheap, and if you are using whole birds in your recipe you will certainly save some plucking aggravation if you buy them in this form.

Preparation If you have shot some pigeons, or acquired freshly killed birds from a keeper or dealer, they can be cooked straight away, and should certainly not be hung for more than four days. If it's hot, don't hang them at all. Either pluck and draw them, put them in the fridge, and use within two days, or just cut out the breasts.

To pluck a pigeon (and any other bird), use your thumb and forefinger to pull out a few feathers at a time (if you grab too many you may tear the skin). Work over the breast and back, the tail, then the legs and wings. Don't worry about the wing tips or the head and neck. Once you've denuded the rest of the bird, these extremities should be cut off, along with the feet – a strong pair of kitchen scissors or poultry shears is best for this. A little care is needed when removing the head: below the neck and above the breast is the crop of the bird (the pouch where they store undigested food). In a pigeon this is likely to be full – of corn, clover, peas, or whatever it has been feeding on. I like to remove the head and neck by cutting right through at the base of the crop, about ½ inch above the breast. It means that some of the contents of the crop may be spilled, or left sticking to the carcass, but they are easily wiped off. The reason I don't cut closer to the breast is because a bird I am plucking is going to be cooked whole (otherwise I would just take the breast off), and I want the breast to be fully covered by its skin.

Once plucked, the bird should be drawn – i.e., gutted. This is a bit messy, but if the bird is fresh it shouldn't be smelly. With the tip of a sharp knife, make a small slit in the skin between the tail of the bird and the point of the breastbone. Push two fingers through this opening back into the cavity of the bird, and pull out all the soft innards. They come out quite easily. If you can identify the heart and liver, these can be kept and used, but the rest should be thrown away. If you really don't like this kind of thing, you could wear rubber gloves.

Unless you have a nice young bird that you want to roast whole, or are planning a casserole of whole birds (which will have more flavor because the bones are included), the easiest way to deal with pigeons is just to remove the breasts. This is simple, but should be done with care so as not to waste meat. Pluck away a few feathers on the bone; then, using a very sharp knife, slit the skin along the breastbone. Slip your fingers between the skin and the breast muscle, and pull back skin and attached feathers to expose the raw meat. Cut the breasts as close as possible to the breastbone by slicing the meat away from the bone with the tip of the knife; cut right back behind the wing, so as to include as much meat as possible. The breasts can then be wrapped in plastic wrap, (or, if you suspect they are old birds, placed in a simple marinade of olive oil and sliced onions) and kept in the fridge until needed, but not for more than a couple of days.

It is a shame to waste the carcasses of debreasted birds, as they make an excellent stock. You don't have to pluck the whole bird, either. Once you have removed the breasts, simply take the flaps of skin and skin the bird, turning it inside out. You can clip off the wings, feet, and neck with a stout pair of kitchen scissors. Then draw the guts and crop contents from the birds, as described above, and roast the carcasses for eight to ten minutes in a hot oven. Put in a stockpot with onions, carrots, celery, leek tops, bay leaf, etc. Cover with water and simmer gently for a couple of hours. This stock can be used as the liquid for a pigeon pie or casserole. Alternatively, strained through cheesecloth or a cotton cloth and supplemented with a good slosh of wine, it can be reduced right down to make a sauce for the panfried breasts. It's almost indistinguishable from good beef stock.

How to age pigeons Before you decide whether or not to debreast your pigeons and how you are going to cook them, it's useful to know whether you have old or young birds on your hands. Young pigeons are more tender and can be roasted whole, or the breasts cooked fast and served pink. Older birds are more suitable for pies and casseroles.

It is not easy to be sure of a pigeon's age unless you encounter the bird before it is plucked and drawn – which of course you will if you have killed it yourself. A flexible beak, a thick neck, and a supple, pliable breastbone are all signs of a young bird. Look for the "flush of youth" in the fine color of its feathers. In the U.S., the only pigeon sold in markets is squab – young (about 4 weeks old) domesticated pigeons that have never flown – so you needn't worry about estimating a store-bought bird's age.

If the bird is oven-ready from a butcher or game dealer, you still have a bit to go on; try pressing gently to see if the breastbone is supple. Does the skin look slightly rosy, as if it is stretched from beneath by a plump and youthful breast? Or is it a whitish gray, slightly wrinkled, contracting over a hard, prominent breastbone and tough, dark meat? Experience will sharpen your response to these factors, and in time you will be able to tell a youngster even, if necessary, through the clinging cellophane of its supermarket wrapping.

Cooking When you have identified a young pigeon, it can be roasted whole, with a strip of bacon over the breast, or, if you like the meat very rare, spatchcocked (cut open down the breastbone, then turned over and flattened with the palm of your hand) and griddled whole on a cast-iron griddle. But to be honest, most pigeons that come my way get the breast-only treatment.

The breasts of all but the oldest pigeons are dense and rich but reasonably tender: they can be cooked fast and served pink, either on a dry cast-iron griddle (in which case, brush them with a little olive oil) or in a lightly oiled frying pan. Cook for five to six minutes, turning frequently, for meat still just pink in the middle. Alternatively, the breasts can be butterflied – slit almost in half with a knife, then opened out and flattened like little minute steaks. Just a minute on either side is then sufficient.

Breasts cooked like this are particularly delicious when served on top of a simple green salad, perhaps dressed with walnut oil, red wine (or balsamic) vinegar, and sprinkled with a few lardons of pancetta or bacon, and toasted walnuts. One breast, still just a little pink and bloody, cut into four or five slices, is a decent first-course portion per person, though it would take two to make a really satisfying main course.

Tough old birds will always be best braised or casseroled. The meat is so rich it can be thought of almost as beef, and recipes for stews and daubes adapted accordingly. Pigeons can be casseroled whole, then cut in half to make two portions, though very hungry pigeon fans might want a whole one each. Alternatively, you can make a breast-only stew, using a stock made from the roast carcasses of the birds (see page 376). Cooking for one and a half hours, in a preheated 325°F oven, with wine and stock vegetables as well as the stock, will do the trick.

See also the recipe section for Pastilla (page 413), Game Terrine (page 414), and Pigeon Pitas with Pea and Peppercorn Purée (page 417).

ROOKS In many areas of rural Britain, particularly Somerset, South Wales, and the northwest, young rooks have long been rated as food. At one time, they were so popular that poor country folk who could not afford a gun would shin up the trees in the rookery to remove the young "branchers" just before they were ready to fly the nest. Hardly anybody climbs rookeries anymore, except professionals who occasionally do it as a means of pest control. But the tradition of culling the young branchers in mid-May, as they start to leave the nest, has not entirely vanished. In Victorian times, this used to be considered a suitable sport for boys and young ladies, who would traditionally gather on May 12, with their specially made rook rifles, for a little genteel sport. Today, it's more likely to be done by a farmer or gamekeeper with a shotgun or .22 rifle.

It's worth doing because the breasts of young rooks are as good, if not better, than pigeons. Young rooks remain worthwhile until midsummer, after which time the meat becomes tough and coarse – but not, as some have suggested, unpleasant tasting. There is no U.S. equivalent.

I can't recommend climbing a rookery without professional guidance, unless you are an expert climber yourself. But if ever you do happen to climb for young rooks, be sure to take a small backpack or drawstring bag with you. You can put the branchers in it alive, and they will stay nice and quiet until you can climb down and dispatch them quickly with a knock on the head.

A more realistic option is to shoot the branchers. If you know anybody with a rookery on their land, then they may be happy for you to attempt to reduce the local rook population somewhat – they may even be grateful for an introduction to the pleasures of rook meat.

Exactly when the young rooks emerge from their nests and wander up a branch to stretch their unused wings (hence the name *branchers*) will depend partly on what kind of a spring it's been. In the north, it usually happens about a week or so later than in the south. But the second week in May is about the right time to start looking out for them, and they have usually all flown by the end of the month.

It's pretty easy to shoot branchers with a shotgun. Apart from the odd practice swoop, they don't fly much – certainly not very fast or far. The downside is that you are likely to have a lot of lead shot in what is a rather small portion of meat. More sporting, and less damaging, is some kind of rifle, though to own anything more powerful than an air rifle you need a license (and they are harder and harder to come by). Young rooks do make a very challenging target for an air rifle, especially since you will probably have to allow for the swaying of the trees in the breeze.

Rooks are not available on the market, and, unless you know a farmer, gamekeeper, or landowner who regularly culls his own May branchers (or can be persuaded to do so), you will have to shoot them yourself.

Preparation and cooking Apart from their tender little breasts, young rooks have very little meat on them, and they are really not worth the trouble of plucking, drawing, and serving whole. However, if you really want to make the most of your rooks, it is worth saving the carcasses for stock, made in the same way as for pigeons (see page 376). This will give you a good stock to add to your rook pie, or it can be strained and reduced right down, with a good slosh of wine, to make a sauce to go with sautéed rook breasts.

Use rook breasts exactly as you would pigeons', including any of the pigeon recipes at the end of this section. They are about 30 percent smaller, and really you will need four breasts per person as a main course.

SNAILS No guns, nets, or traps are required in the pursuit of the final quarry of this chapter – though a flashlight and a garden hose might come in handy. I wanted to mention snails here because they are one of the greatest unsung land-based freebies, available to everyone.

Many gardeners expend a fair amount of energy (and some, sadly, use an unfair amount of chemicals) in an effort to reduce the snail population. This would surely be a more satisfying and less guilt-ridden task if the snails were not poisoned or squashed but put to good use in the kitchen.

All English snails are edible, but there are two species of particular interest to the forager gourmet. Largest, and rarest, is the so-called Roman snail, *Helix pomatia*, which was indeed introduced by the Romans as a food. These are relatively rare, but occasionally locally prolific. Although they are a classic eating snail, I do not like to kill them myself: it is such a rare pleasure to find them, and the alternative, which is just as good, is so commonplace.

My only snail quarry, therefore, is the common (or garden) snail, *Helix aspersa*, which is what the French call *petit-gris*. In case you did not realize, this is the plain old regular snail – the one you squash on your garden path on a rainy night. They are not quite as impressive, size-wise, as the Romans, but the flavor is just as good, or better, and they provide a fine and tasty morsel of meat. They are widely available in the U.S.

Most average-sized suburban gardens that are not mercilessly sprayed with pesticides probably have enough snails in them to make a nice starter for two. And if you take to the hedgerow, you can find enough for a feast.

Snails are easy to find, once you know where to look, and can be gathered at any time of year. From winter until the first decent spells of mild weather in early spring, it is hibernating snails you must look for. This means looking under things – stones, bricks, logs, flowerpots, or anything else that provides them with shelter (untidy gardens are always better for snail hunting). The good thing about a hibernating snail is that its gut is empty, which means it is ready for cooking without purging.

Once the weather is milder and the young shoots that they feed on start to come up, snails will be on the move. The best time to look for them is on a warm or mild day after (or during) rain or at night, with a flashlight.

I used to collect snails regularly as a child (for racing rather than eating), and my proven technique was to go out after a rain and tread down the grass growing against the Cotswold dry-stone walls near where I lived. They can also be found at the base of trees, underneath large leaves (such as hogweed), under stones and, once you get the hang of it, just about anywhere that looks likely. Here at River Cottage, if I want to find a few snails I go out in the early evening and give the whole garden and the walls of the house a good drenching with the hose. A few hours later, after dark, I come out with a flashlight and they are cruising all over the place – especially on the walls of the house.

Except when they are hibernating, snails cannot be eaten as soon as found. They need to be purged, to rid them of any unclean (or unpleasant-tasting) matter in their gut. The best way to do this is to feed them on a one-item purgative diet: sliced carrot, or lettuce, is an easy and effective option. You will need to keep them in a cool, well-ventilated container, with space to move. I use a large plastic washing-up bowl with fine-meshed chicken wire stretched over the top. The best preparation is five days on the purgative diet, then forty-eight hours' total starvation: this final phase clears out the gut and reduces the sliminess of the snails. If, however, you are in a hurry to eat your snails, you could give them three days of the purgative diet and skip the starvation.

Cooking Once they have been purged, there are various traditional ways of preparing snails, before finishing them in the sauce of your choice.

The French usually remove cooked *petits-gris* from their shells and finish them in a sauce, discarding the shells (the snails they serve in the shell are the larger Roman snails). The initial process is therefore simply to shake the snails in a bowl or sieve until they all retract into their shells, then throw them into a pan of well-salted, rapidly boiling water (which may be flavored with a few stock vegetables and a splash of vinegar). After the water comes back to a boil, they are simmered for just ten minutes, then drained. When cool enough to handle, the meat is removed with a pin and a twist of the wrist (there is a knack to getting them out whole and unbroken, but you'll soon pick it up).

The Spanish, on the other hand, like to serve their snails still attached to the shell, but with the body of the snail outside the shell. This is achieved by putting the snails in a pan of unsalted, cold freshwater so that they all come out of their shells. The water is then placed over a gentle heat, so that the snails "drop off," remaining out of their shells. The water is then salted, brought to a boil, and the snails are simmered, again for ten minutes.

Snails can be a bit slimy, and to counteract this, some authorities recommend tossing the live snails in salt to draw out the slime before cooking. I don't really like doing this to live snails (snails are not sophisticated creatures, but if anything could distress them, throwing salt on them would be it), so I cook mine first, the French way, and if they seem a bit slimy once out of their shells I toss them with a bit of salt, leave them for a few minutes, then rinse them off. It seems to do the trick.

Snails prepared in either manner can then be finished in a number of ways – in all cases, allowing at least a dozen snails per person. One of the nicest and simplest preparations is a mussel-style garlic butter: gently fry two finely chopped cloves of garlic in a pan with 3 tablespoons of butter. Add half a glass of wine and bring to a fierce bubble, then throw in the snails (Spanish or French style) and allow to bubble for just a couple of minutes. Add a handful of chopped parsley and serve in warmed bowls with French bread.

To make a snail gratin, proceed as above, without the wine and using French-style, shell-less snails. Then pile the garlicky, buttery snails into ramekins, top with bread crumbs, and brown under the grill.

One of my favorite of all snail dishes is a snail and wild mushroom risotto: add shell-less, French-style snails, sautéed in butter, garlic, and a little wine, to a wild mushroom risotto a couple of minutes before the rice is done. I prefer this risotto without Parmesan.

hedgerow | hedgerow greens

The wait for the first crop of spring vegetables from the garden – it might be radishes, it might be baby spinach – can seem agonizing. Despite my best efforts, and even with the help of some early spring sunshine, cultivated vegetables always seem painfully slow to get under way.

Nature, of course, is a rather better gardener than I am. Her spring greens are always well ahead of mine. The good news is that a fair number of hers are also edible. The obvious, irresistible answer is to pinch a few of hers while waiting for mine to develop. It's hardly a chore. I can think of half a dozen wild greens I now use regularly, all within a five-minute walk of my front door.

It should come as no surprise to anyone interested in food to hear that the countryside is full of exciting edible vegetables growing wild and free. After all, our cultivated vegetables are all descended from wild ancestors – and some of the best hedgerow vegetables are descended from cultivated strains that have fallen out of favor. There are few plants indeed that do not make a feast for some lucky creature. And if you want to be one of those lucky creatures, then this section of the book is for you.

So many wild plants are edible – in the technical sense, at least – that it is not my intention to be in the least comprehensive. What I have chosen for the list that follows are those wild vegetables, herbs, and flowers that are both fairly common and, in my opinion, genuinely worthwhile. Try them once, and my guess is you will want to try them again. But first up, a few thoughts on the best hunting grounds.

where to forage

Those of us who live in the country love to refer to this thing called "the hedgerow" – I've even named this section after it. But to be honest, I'm never quite sure precisely what bits of land we mean by it. Personally, I take it to be all those long lines of trees, bushes, and wild plants that divide up the fields and flank the country lanes and footpaths. If all that is included, along with the little woods, thickets, and groves that cluster at the major axes, then this is certainly a good place to start looking for wild food.

But it's not the only place to look for edible shoots, leaves, and flowers. Wild plants will grow wherever birds, insects, or the wind give them a chance. If conditions are right where the seed falls, and the ground remains undisturbed, the plant will flourish. Foragers should always be ready to look in unlikely places and expect the unexpected.

The best place to start foraging is, literally, your own backyard. I imagine there is hardly a garden in the country so immaculately kept that there is not some edible weed lurking in a neglected corner – and there are certainly millions of gardens where the uninvited greens hold sway! Once you discover what you can do with them, you may decide to adopt the kitchen scissors as your preferred means of control, in place of the weed cutter.

Converts to foraging who have the right combination of laziness and enthusiasm might consider setting aside an area of the garden as an "edible weed patch." Better still, several areas: one light, one shady, one damp, one dry. Let them go, then see what grows. Many plants, such as nettles and sorrel, will grow back fast, and can be treated as a cut-and-come-again provider throughout their season.

When you roam away from home, don't restrict your foraging to the romantic rural notion of the hedgerow. Check out that pile of earthy rubble at the end of the parking lot – it might be teeming with fresh young nettles.

favorite hedgerow greens

By "greens" I mean the leaves, shoots, and stems of edible wild plants that can be used as principal ingredients in recipes or that, when simply cooked, give you a more or less substantial portion of a vegetable that can be an accompaniment to another dish. Some of the more strongly flavored plants, whose leaves or other parts are used in small quantities as flavorings rather than as vegetables, are grouped together under Favorite Hedgerow Herbs (see page 388). The following plants are listed roughly in the order in which they can be harvested, beginning in early spring.

ALEXANDERS *Smyrnium olusatrum* Alexanders are one of the best wild vegetables of spring, especially since the part of prime interest to the wild foodie is not the leaf but the fleshy, succulent stem: so good, it's worth serving on its own, like asparagus. Also known as horse parsley, it is rarely found in the U.S.

The stems can be picked from February in a good year, and are at their best as the first flower buds begin to appear in late March/April. Cut the stems close to the ground and strip away any leaves or side shoots. Cut into 4- to 5-inch lengths and peel away the outer membrane (easily done with a sharp knife). The stems can then be steamed or boiled. Tossed in melted butter and seasoned with freshly ground black pepper, they are worth serving, asparagus style, on their own (with brown bread) as a starter – or as an accompanying vegetable, particularly with oily fish such as mackerel or herring.

The leaves and flowers are also quite edible, both having a mild aniseed flavor with a slightly bitter note. Choose younger, smaller leaves to add to salads.

The flowers, which change from greeny yellow to cream as they develop, can be picked from April to early June. Briefly blanched, they can be served as a pretty garnish for the stems. Or they can be eaten raw in salads or deep-fried in batter – a good treatment, as they are relatively "meaty" flowers, with a strong flavor.

SEA BEET or SEA SPINACH *Beta vulgaris maritima* This is the genetic ancestor of our cultivated forms of beet, from Swiss chard to beets – the mother of all spinach, if you like. It grows in challenging places: poor-quality soils that are stony, sandy, or chalky. It loves a salty sea breeze. No great surprise, then, that there are loads of it here in Dorset, on the cliffs, coastal footpaths, and seawalls. It's common all around the British coast, though less frequent in Scotland. It is not found in the U.S.

The thick, leathery leaves are even more succulent than those of cultivated spinach varieties, and although when raw they taste a little soapy and tannic, they really come into their own when cooked. The leaves can be picked all spring and summer from late March until the first frosts, but good-sized, succulent leaves are harder to find in high summer, when the plant is flowering and can become straggly.

In early spring, the stalks may be tender enough to cook with the leaves, but generally they should be stripped off and discarded. As with all spinach, always wash the leaves well, in at least two changes of fresh water, or the dishes you prepare from them may be gritty.

The gratin on page 343, made with wild mussels and sea beet, is one of the most luxurious wild food dishes I can think of. Fresh sea beet can be substituted for spinach in any recipe.

HOGWEED (COW PARSNIP) *Heracleum sphondylium* One of the first hedgerow greens I ever tried, and still a firm favorite, hogweed is an extremely common biennial herb widely distributed throughout Britain, and is easily found in hedgerows and along towpaths, roadsides, and the edges of woods. It has a most unusual, slightly camphorous taste, which I predict will grow on you even if you don't take to it at once.

The young shoots appear first in a kind of embryonic envelope, actually a closely furled leaf, on the side of the main stem. You can pick them at this stage, or a little later when they have uncurled, but always choose the young, fresh shoots that point upward, rather than stems with open leaves lolling on their side. Most plants will be overgrown by the end of June, but where shoulders of road have been mown down later in the summer you can expect to find a vigorous second crop.

The youngest, most tender shoots do not need peeling or trimming, and can be eaten raw in salads, or steamed or boiled for four or five minutes until tender but still a bit crunchy. Serve them with a ramekin of warm melted butter flavored with lemon zest and black pepper, or again with that very useful anchovy sauce (see page 97). I also like a simple salad of raw hogweed and good crispy bacon, with a squeeze of fresh lemon and a drizzle of olive oil.

Smaller shoots and the curled shoots inside the "envelopes" are delicious deep-fried in batter.

FAT HEN (LAMBSQUARTERS) *Chenopodium album* I keep finding fat hen growing among my spinach, which is foolish of it, as I am more than happy to include it in the same pan. One of the most worthwhile of all the wild leafy greens, and luckily one of the easiest to come by, fat hen is found on wasteland and field edges all over Britain, quite often next to paths or growing against walls. It's often one of the first plants to colonize newly broken ground, on building sites and around roadworks. It was once a staple food, and its seeds were identified in the celebrated stomach contents of Tollund Man, a 1,500-year-old corpse recovered entire from a Denmark bog in the 1950s.

In early spring, young shoots of about 6 inches high can be cut just above the ground and eaten raw in salads, or briefly blanched, tossed in a little melted butter and served as a starter or side vegetable. You can serve these whole sprigs of young fat hen, like curly kale and broccoli, with the anchovy dressing on page 97.

Later in the year, when the plant is more substantial, choose the tender leaves and flower heads from the top of the plant, and pick over to discard any tough stalks before cooking. Wash thoroughly, then cook as for spinach: put in a pan with just the water that is clinging to them, wilt down, turning frequently, and simmer until tender. Drain well in a colander or sieve, pressing excess water out with the back of a spoon. Toss with a little butter or olive oil before serving.

SEA KALE *Crambe maritima* This cabbagelike native perennial grows close to the sea in pebbles or pebbles and sand. It used to be relatively common all around our coasts from southern Scotland downward, especially on the big shingle beaches of the south coast. But commercial demand for it as a fashionable vegetable in the early nineteenth century seriously depleted numbers. It seems to be on the increase again but should not be overpicked: just take a few stems from each plant and let it grow to seed. In the U.S., it is found only in California and Oregon.

Early spring is the best time for picking: the young leaves, stalks, and broccoli-like flower heads are all edible, but become tough and bitter later in the year. It is worth scrabbling into the pebbles with your fingers and cutting the stems as low as possible: the pale shoots growing under the stones are naturally blanched and have the best flavor.

Treat sea kale pretty much like purple sprouting broccoli. Wash well and cut away any tough stalks. Steam, or boil in salted water, for eight to fifteen minutes, until tender (as with broccoli, the cooked vegetable should retain a little bite and not be allowed to become mushy). Toss in butter and season with black pepper and a sprinkling of good sea salt.

DANDELIONS *Taraxacum officinale* Like nettles, dandelions are extremely common and easily identified, so the leaves are one of the wild greens that everyone can find and enjoy. The plant is a rich source of folklore and gossip, but best known perhaps for its diuretic effect, as expressed by traditional names in both French and English: *piss-en-lit* and pissabed.

The bitter flavor of dandelion leaves will not be to everybody's taste, but if you like chicory and endive (to both of which the dandelion is closely related), you will find dandelion leaves an excellent alternative. The outside dark green leaves are likely to be unpalatably bitter, even to enthusiasts, so pick leaves from close to the center. The whiter, lower parts of the leaves will be sweeter, and the greener parts can be broken off.

There are two ways to counteract the bitterness. Cut leaves can be stood with their cut ends in fresh cold water overnight. Alternatively, if you have time to invest in your crop, blanch the plants as they grow, by cutting away all the outer leaves and covering the whole plants with flowerpots or black plastic bags: the new leaves, shaded from sunlight as they grow, will be pale and sweet. By pinching off flower heads as they appear, you can use strong, prolific dandelion plants as a cut-and-come-again source of salad into the winter months.

NETTLES (STINGING) *Urtica dioica* This perennial herb is abundant throughout the British Isles and hardly needs describing: every young child is taught to identify it so they can avoid its vicious sting. We should all be taught to cook it as well, because it really is one of the most worthwhile of all the free greens. It's full of good things: iron, vitamins, and natural histamine. It is therefore an excellent tonic, particularly good for improving blood circulation and purifying the system.

The best thing about nettles is that they are so easy to find: wherever you are now, you're probably within walking distance of a nettle patch. A stout rubber glove or gardening glove is the best way to put an impenetrable barrier between your picking hand and the nettle's sting (I don't advise attempting to "grasp the nettle" barefisted in line with the old proverb: it may work once, but by the time you have enough leaves for a soup your hand will be as red as a raspberry and throbbing like hell).

The best nettles for cooking are the young shoots of early spring (March, usually), no more than a few inches high. They can be cut from just above the ground and used, stalk and all. As the plants get bigger, choose only the crown of new small leaves at the top.

By the time the nettles are in flower (May/June), most plants are usually too tough and straggly for cooking, but later in the summer look to the edges of nettle patches where a second seeding will often produce another crop of younger plants. Wherever nettles have been cut back or mowed you will also find new young shoots coming through, especially after rain. If you have a nettle bed in your garden, instead of weedkilling it, why not mow it every few weeks and reap the benefits of a regular crop throughout the summer?

To serve simply as a green vegetable, pick over the nettles and discard any tough stalks. Wash well (and carefully – they can still sting for some time after picking), and wilt in a pan with just the water that is clinging to them and a sprinkle of salt. Keep turning for a few minutes until they are wilted and tender, then drain off the excess water, add a tablespoon of butter, and season with pepper and a pinch of nutmeg. See also the recipe for Nettle Soup (page 422).

WATERCRESS *Rorippa nasturtium-aquaticum* The distinct, peppery taste of watercress is now familiar to everybody from the cultivated version, but the wild plant is also common, and especially satisfying to harvest. A lowland plant, it is found everywhere in Britain except the highlands of Scotland and central and northern Wales. It grows only in moving water, usually shallow streams and ditches, and is often found in the summer months in great profusion. I've got a fine bunch growing by the river in the long field at River Cottage.

When picking wild watercress, there is a very real danger that it may be infected by liver fluke – a nasty parasite spread by cattle and sheep. If there is any grazing upstream of where you are picking, the watercress is certainly not safe to eat raw. Your best bet is to inquire locally, and any watercress that you do pick should not be eaten until it has been thoroughly washed in fresh clean water (not from the stream). Don't take any chances with raw watercress: the safest option is to cook it, which will kill the parasite.

Despite becoming the 1980s equivalent of the shrimp cocktail on the dinner-party circuit, watercress soup remains one of the great soups – check the recipe on page 423.

SORREL *Rumex acetosa* This perennial herb is common throughout the British Isles and, along with nettles and sea beet, must rank in my top-three wild leafy greens. Various kinds of dock and sheep's sorrel, found in the U.S., are similar. Far from being just another spinach substitute, it has an inimitable gooseberry-lemon tang that can be enjoyed raw in salads or cooked in soups and sauces. A few leaves plucked straight from the hedgerow are a refreshing and restorative snack on a hot summer walk.

Sorrel can be found in the hedgerow and in open meadows and pastures throughout the year, but is at its best in early spring (as early as February after a mild winter), when the thick and succulent shield-shaped leaves are just coming up. Later in the summer when the plant is flowering, the leaves are thinner, drier, and tougher, but younger leaves at the bottom of the plant will still be worthwhile.

Before using sorrel either raw or cooked, pick over the leaves, discarding the stalks, and wash thoroughly. Use stainless-steel pans and utensils when cooking sorrel, as the acid chemicals react with iron and aluminum, and this can affect the flavor. Sorrel always turns a dirty green when cooked, so don't be put off by that.

I think the best way to enjoy raw sorrel leaves in a salad is in a simple mix with two or three times as much good sweet lettuce (romaine or Little Gem) and a plain dressing of olive oil, sea salt, and black pepper.

MARSH SAMPHIRE or GLASSWORT (SEA BEANS) *Salicornia europaea* This succulent plant of the tidal zone looks almost like a miniature cactus. It is one of the most distinctive and worthwhile of all wild vegetables, with its excellent al dente crunch and distinctive sea-fresh, salty flavor.

It has been harvested and used as a vegetable for centuries, and with its seashore origins it has long been a popular accompaniment to fish. Until recently, there was a tradition among many fishmongers of giving away a couple of handfuls of samphire to customers while the plant was in season, but I haven't reaped this benefit for a good few years now. The vegetable has become trendy, and sells for fairly silly prices in upscale produce markets.

The answer is to gather your own: samphire is local, but prolific, on salt marshes and tidal mudflats all around the coast – most famously in Norfolk, and also in southwest Wales. It can be picked at low tide, traditionally from the longest day (June 21) until the end of August when, after flowering, it tends to become fibrous and tough.

Picking samphire is both messy and tough on the back – bending over, shin-deep in mud, to pull the little shoots up by the roots (to cut samphire is a misguided conservation measure, as a plant thus damaged will die anyway). The way to enjoy it is to put on old clothes and make a party of it. If it descends into childish mudslinging, then so be it: both you and the samphire are sure to need a thorough washing when you get home.

Very young and tender samphire can be nibbled raw, but in most cases it will need cooking.

Samphire is worth serving on its own, asparagus style: after rinsing thoroughly in fresh cold water, the samphire sprigs can be cooked, roots and all, in a steamer, or in simmering unsalted water, for six to eight minutes, until tender but still just crunchy. Drain, and serve on warmed plates with warmed ramekins of melted butter. Each little bunch can then be picked up by the slightly woody roots, dipped in the butter, and stripped of the tender green flesh with the teeth (practice makes perfect).

If you want to serve samphire as a side vegetable (for example, with fish) so that all that appears on the plate is edible, then it needs a thorough picking over: after an initial rinsing, remove and discard the slightly woody roots and any stems that are not fresh, crisp, and green. What's left can then be steamed or boiled as above, tossed with a tablespoon of butter, and served.

favorite hedgerow herbs

The following wild plants are also worthwhile, though used more as flavoring herbs than vegetables.

CHIVES *Allium schoenoprasum* This tough little herb is reliably one of the first to show, often pushing its spiky shoots through February snow. Wild chives tend to be common only locally, although they are becoming more frequent, perhaps as escapees from cultivated herb gardens. In some country lanes, in the first warm days of spring, you can smell their oniony savor a long way off.

One of the most versatile of all herbs, chives should be on hand whenever that green, oniony bite is called for. Mixed with sour cream, crème fraîche, or thick yogurt, they can be added to many soups as a garnish, especially chilled summer soups, such as the Nettle Soup on page 422. The same mixture makes a lovely filling for a baked potato. I also like chopped chives on a tomato salad, as a change from basil.

WILD GARLIC *Allium ursinum* The day I first arrived at River Cottage (and, within a few minutes, decided to rent it), the wild garlic was in full swing. From the verdant green spikes of early March until it dies away, yellowish and rather grim, sometime in June, it carpets the path from the cottage to the polytunnel field. Every time I walk through it, a vapor of pungent, garlicky sweetness arrests my senses.

Very common throughout England and Wales, less so in Scotland and Ireland, this native bulb is found in damp woods and shady lanes; you will often smell the plant before you see it. Folklore credits wild garlic with all kinds of beneficial properties, chiefly warding off vampires and evil spirits. The young green leaves, picked before the flowers have died (usually early May), have a strong, garlicky smell but are pleasantly mild in flavor and can be used raw in salads and sandwiches. Finely chopped, they can be used as a more potent alternative to chives.

The leaves become bitter if cooked for more than a minute or two, but the bulbs can be dug up and used as a mild alternative to cloves of garlic. The spiky white flowers are also edible and look amazing in a green salad.

A delicious hedgerow version of garlic bread can be made by beating soft butter with finely chopped wild garlic bulbs. Spread it into cuts made at intervals in a baguette or other stick loaf, wrap it in foil, and bake in a hot oven for twenty minutes. Add a sprinkling of finely sliced wild garlic leaves just before serving.

COW PARSLEY or WILD CHERVIL *Anthriscus sylvestris* An extremely abundant biennial herb, cow parsley is the plant that defines the British roadsides in summer: its white flowering stems, growing up to two yards high, can be seen for mile after mile on country roads and roadsides throughout the British Isles. It is infrequent only in the northernmost highlands of Scotland.

It is, in fact, to cultivated chervil, and not parsley, that this herb is most closely related, and it has a similar spicy, grassy flavor. The leaves are at their most tender and have the best flavor when the plant is still only a few inches tall, in early spring (March), but it remains worthwhile until the stem has become woody and hollow and the leaves tough and hairy (usually May/June). Being biennial, tiny new young plants will appear in the autumn, but they remain hard to find and identify until the following spring.

Young chervil leaves are an excellent all-round herb for salads and garnishes and make a good companion to chives: snip either or both over potato salad, throw them in an omelette, use as a garnish for soups, and add to other wild greens recipes for extra flavor.

WARNING Wild chervil can be confused with several poisonous plants, notably fool's parsley and the deadly hemlock water dropwort. The distinction from hemlock is relatively easy: wild chervil has fine hairs, becoming thicker as the plant gets older, on its ridged stem. The stem of hemlock is smooth, and blotched with faint purple spots. Hemlock water dropwort is always found growing in, or very close to, water. Fool's parsley is a flimsier plant than wild chervil, has darker, cream-colored flowers (as opposed to white), that grow in closer clusters than chervil, and has small drooping green bracts beneath the flower heads. It is not lethal but it is certainly not edible.

HORSERADISH *Armoracia rusticana* Horseradish is found throughout Britain, usually on cultivated or broken ground. This perennial herb is easily recognized by its large, thick leaves, pointing skyward like giant donkey's ears. But it is the thick root beneath them that is of interest to those who like a little heat in the kitchen.

The root can be dug up as soon as the plant can be identified by the leaves (usually April), but will be more substantial later in the summer. It should be washed, peeled, grated, and used sparingly. It is the combination of horseradish with vinegar (or acetic acid) that makes the commercial sauces so inferior. For a real horseradish sauce, see the recipe on page 238.

Fresh horseradish has a clean, aromatic heat that complements many foods. Its famous partnership is, of course, with roast beef, although it also makes a very exciting marriage with smoked fish, especially eel.

WILD FENNEL *Foeniculum vulgare* For me, this highly successful garden escapee is one of the most exciting plants to find growing wild. From the first pungently aromatic aniseed-flavored shoots of early spring, to the vigorous two-yard stems of high summer, the plant is a joy to behold, to smell, and to use. I rarely pass a specimen without, at the very least, plucking off a few green fronds to chew. Happily, fennel is increasingly common and is now widespread in the coastal zone of middle and southern England, often appearing on the coastal path, on cliff tops and on roadsides and empty lots near the coast. The perimeters of seaside parking lots seem to be a particularly happy hunting ground.

As a flavoring herb for fish, fennel is hard to beat. When baking fish in foil, stuff it with fennel fronds and/or seeds and use more chopped fennel to finish a sauce made from the cooking juices and a little cream. Crème fraîche mixed with chopped fennel is a nice thing to serve with blinis and smoked fish. Fennel is also good added to mixed herb salads.

Come the late summer, when the plant is overgrown (sometimes to two yards or more) and has seeded, you can cut down whole plants a foot or so above the ground (don't worry, they will grow back next year) and take them home for drying. Hang them upside down in bunches in a warm, airy place until quite dry. The stalks of fennel dried in this way can be used on next year's grill for cooking fish, particularly sea bass, sea bream, and gray mullet, which will be infused with a smoky, aniseedy flavor – see page 331 for a more detailed recipe. You can also collect the seeds from the flower heads of the dried fennel and use them to flavor soups and stocks, especially when cooking fish.

favorite edible flowers

The shoots and leaves of spring and the fruits and nuts of summer are not the only edible parts of the hedgerow vegetation. In between, plugging the gap nicely, come the flowers. Flowers are not just a novelty garnish: they have flavors ranging from sweet and aromatic to hot and spicy, and are always fun to cook with.

BROOM BUDS *Sarothamnus scoparius* This native shrub is common throughout Britain, on scrubland, in empty lots, and by the side of the road, particularly on sandy soils. The flowers should be picked when still in bud, when they have a wonderful leguminous flavor, reminiscent of runner beans. In an early spring, the first butter-yellow flower buds appear in March, and can be picked sometimes until early June. Scotch broom, a similar plant, has naturalized in the U.S. Pacific Northwest.

I love to throw a handful of broom buds into a salad, and also into a stir-fry of green vegetables for just the last thirty seconds. The freshest, tightest buds can be pickled in spiced vinegar and used like capers.

CRAB APPLE BLOSSOMS *Malus sylvestris* The delicate pink and white blossom of the crab apple tree is seen in the hedgerow in April or May. It is pleasantly scented and makes a particularly good flower fritter (see the recipe for elderflowers, below). See also page 405 for the entry on the fruit of this tree.

ELDERFLOWERS *Sambucus nigra* This deciduous tree shrub is found abundantly everywhere in Britain except the northern tip of Scotland and the Scottish Isles, in woods, on roadsides, and wasteland. It seems like a generous gift from nature that such a common hedgerow plant can have so many, and such delectable, culinary uses.

The creamy-colored sprays of highly scented flowers are the elder's greatest gift to the kitchen. You don't need many, and whatever liquid, syrup, or batter you dip them in will be infused with their delightfully intense Muscaty taste. They can be used in many ways, imparting their flavor to sorbets, ice creams, cordials, jellies, and jams. Their affinity with gooseberries is well known.

The transfer of flavor is easily achieved: pick the flowers on a dry, sunny day, if possible, and choose ones that are well opened but still fresh – the sprays should be full, not yet losing any flowers. The flower heads can simply be dipped into hot syrups or fruit purées and left to infuse for a few minutes before being strained out. For jams, jellies, and ices that are not going to be strained, three or four flower heads can be wrapped in cheesecloth or a square of cotton cloth, dipped into a hot pan, and removed after a few minutes.

In this way, you can experiment widely with the flavor of elderflowers. But some recipes are worth having down pat: Elderflower Cordial (see page 427), Elderflower and Gooseberry Fool (also page 427), and this simple sorbet: dissolve 1 cup superfine sugar in 2 cups water, then bring to a boil, and boil hard for seven minutes to get a light syrup. Off the heat, add eight elderflower sprays, and the juice and grated zest of three or four lemons. Leave the flowers to infuse until the syrup is cool, then strain and pour into an ice cream machine. Or freeze until slushy, whisk thoroughly to disperse the ice crystals, part-freeze again and whisk again, then freeze until firm, in the traditional fashion.

Delicious fritters can be made by dipping whole elderflower heads in a good batter (such as the tempura batter on page 340) and deep-frying them. Serve hot, sprinkled with superfine sugar, with a squeeze of lemon and perhaps a trickle of elderflower cordial. For uses of the fruit, elderberries, see pages 405–406.

PRIMROSE *Primula vulgaris* The lovely primrose, which is a common perennial growing in Great Britain in shady lowland woods, on chalk banks, and often railway cuttings, gets its name from the Latin *prima rosa*: the first flower of spring. Though it may appear as early as late March, it is more often found in April and early May.

Like the cowslip, primroses were traditionally used to make a country wine. But given the fate of the cowslip (which is now so rare in the wild that it has become a protected species), it is hard to justify picking primroses in the kind of quantities that are needed for wine making.

The flowers are pleasant tasting, and have a little pool of nectar inside, which makes them a refreshing mouthful on a walk. They can be used to decorate a salad in which the young leaves can also be included.

Primroses, like violets, can also be crystallized in sugar and used for decorating cakes and mousses; carefully paint the leaves with lightly beaten egg white and sprinkle with superfine sugar until completely coated. Leave in a warm, dry place until hard.

WILD ROSE or DOG ROSE *Rosa canina* The wild rose is a common plant in the hedgerow and on the edge of woods. Its white or pink flowers appear in June or July, lasting sometimes into August.

Wild rose petals have long been used in both the boudoir and the kitchen, to give their scent to potpourris and flower waters (in the former), and to syrups, jams, and jellies (in the latter).

Rosewater can be used as both a scent and a flavoring. It is easily made by pouring boiling water over a few handfuls of petals in a bowl. Cover and let steep for half a day. Strain the rosewater first through a sieve, pressing through the petal juices to maximize the flavor, then through cheesecloth or a cotton cloth. Bottle and keep in a cool place. Try adding a teaspoon of this homemade rosewater to a strawberry sorbet or a rice pudding. It is also one of the best flavorings for Turkish delight. See also Rose Hips on page 406.

And finally, one rather tasty root:

PIGNUTS *Conopodium majus* Many wild roots and rhizomes are technically edible, but the only one I have ever eaten that afforded me any real pleasure is the pignut. And that pleasure was considerable. Pignuts grow best (sometimes in huge profusion) on untreated pasture, and are recognizable by their pretty white flowers (see the photograph opposite). Trace these down the stem to the ground, and a few inches beneath you will find a little irregular-shaped tuber, which may vary in size from a pea to a golf ball. Scrape off the brown papery husk and you have an instant snack. Raw pignuts have a crisp texture like a very fresh hazelnut, and a similar nutty flavor, but with a surprising peppery aftertaste, not unlike the tang of a very good extra-virgin olive oil. They are not found in the U.S.

They can also be cooked – just simmered for a few minutes in lightly salted water – after which they become more tender and mealy, losing some of their pepperiness but gaining some sweetness: the flavor of a cooked pignut is somewhere between a sweet potato and a roast chestnut (not a bad place to be, I think you'll agree).

hedgerow | wild mushrooms

I have to credit wild mushrooms with heavily influencing my career choice. I'm not referring to the notoriously inspirational properties of certain species of fungi. But it was an encounter with a mushroom while on holiday in Scotland that sparked a chain of events that eventually led to the first television series I presented, *A Cook on the Wild Side*. I was seventeen at the time, and the mushroom, which I nearly trod on while walking up to a loch to fish for brown trout, was quite simply the biggest I had ever seen. Its dark brown cap was the color of an overbaked loaf of bread and the size and shape of a slightly deflated football cut in half. Underneath the cap was a mass of cream-colored spongiform pores. Overall, the mushroom seemed in prime condition: firm, hard, and cool to the touch. Part of me wanted to take it, and part of me wanted to hide behind a tree and wait for the gnome who obviously lived in it to come home from his afternoon walk. In the end I left it where it was.

The next day, I went into Inverness in search of a mushroom field guide and eventually found a copy of *Mushrooms* by Roger Phillips (still the best taxonomic guide there is). I was pretty sure I could identify the specimen as something rather charmingly called a penny bun (or cep, from the French *cèpe* – known in the U.S. as porcini). And I was amazed to read that it was in fact fairly common, especially in the Highlands. But what surprised me even more was the bold typeface at the end of the entry that pronounced judgment on the mushroom's status with regard to the risk of poisoning. It said, "Edible. Excellent." That afternoon I returned to my mushroom and, without any further consideration for the resident gnome, filched it.

Not having an elaborate repertoire of mushroom recipes at my disposal, I decided to treat my prize catch much as I would a regular field mushroom: sliced and fried gently in butter with a little garlic, then served on toast. It was quite delicious. But more than that, it was exciting, adventurous, and new. Like a first kiss, or a first beer, I somehow knew it was a turning point. Life was never going to be quite the same again.

At that time, nearly twenty years ago, we were, as a nation, collectively ignorant about the edibility of our native fungi. We just about knew what a field mushroom was, and if we lived in the country we may even have had the confidence to pick and eat it. But pretty much everything else was a toadstool, pregnant with the risks that this ancient pejorative implies.

That's all changed now. Wild mushrooms are no longer fiendishly dangerous, they are fiendishly trendy. "Are the ceps fresh?" you will hear besuited yuppies loudly asking the waiters in expensive London restaurants from August onward. But there's still something maybe even they don't know: the secret, solitary pleasure of creeping through bosky woods in early autumn, the smell of leaf mold rising from the warm, damp floor, the feeling that something rather weird may be happening not very far away.

Now, as then, I still find there is something intense and even spooky about mushroom collecting. Focused, often solitary, it is less casual, and more committed, than other forms of food foraging. It often seems to me more like hunting than gathering: in fact, it may well be the perfect way to satisfy the sublimated blood lust of those reluctant to kill for food!

safety

But whatever the thrills of the hunt, safety first: there are some three thousand species of large-bodied fungi growing in Britain, of which most are quite harmless, about a hundred are both edible and worthwhile, and about twenty may be seriously harmful, even fatal. The priority of all mushroom gatherers must be to home in on the happy hundred, and avoid at all costs the terrible twenty.

The first thing to say on that score is that nothing on the pages that follow, neither the text nor the pictures, is intended to be a foolproof guide to the identification, and therefore absolute safety, of edible mushrooms. I have been selective in the mushrooms I am writing about, and selectivity always rules out absolute certainty. At the end of the day, it is more important to be able to identify a poisonous mushroom than an edible one, and I'm afraid that's not something this book is going to help you with. The only foolproof field guide, therefore, is a comprehensive, fully illustrated one, as it allows you to make direct comparisons between the edible target mushrooms and similar-looking fungi that may be inedible or poisonous.

favorite fungi

It would be a mistake to dash into a wood armed with a field guide and attempt to identify every fungus you see, and pick all the edible ones you can lay your hands on. Better to start with a few species and slowly build up a repertoire as you gain confidence and expertise. What follows is a clutch of my favorites, all of which are fairly common, and fairly easy to identify.

For each species I offer a few simple cooking suggestions. Bear in mind that these are often little more than conceits (as opposed to receipts). All are subject to variation according to your personal whim, and many may be appropriate for species other than those for which they are specified.

FIELD MUSHROOM *Agaricus campestris* and others. The term *field mushroom* is a loose one, used to refer to several members of the Agaricus family. Perhaps the defining characteristics of the fungi that go by this name are that they grow mainly on pasture and grassland, and look much like the ordinary cultivated mushrooms that you see in the shops, which are basically the same species.

They are among the most common wild mushrooms, and among the easiest to find, since they grow on pastureland and are about as well camouflaged as a golf ball on a well-watered fairway in May (speaking of which, golf courses can be happy hunting grounds for mushrooms). The cap is generally white or off-white, sometimes buff or gray-brown. The gills can be pale pink when the mushroom is young and fresh, changing to pale brown as it first opens, and darkening almost to black when the mushroom has opened and been standing for a few days.

Besides the *campestris*, there are two other notable and fairly common species of Agaricus: the large (sometimes plate-sized) horse mushroom (*Agaricus arvensis*) with its buff-colored cap and aniseedy smell; and *Agaricus bisporus*, father of the cultivated mushroom, with its slightly flaking cap, beloved of compost and fallow fields – I have even found it pushing through cracked tarmac in a London parking lot.

It is sometimes hard to be sure exactly which species of Agaricus one has encountered, but there is only one that will do you any harm: the aptly named yellow stainer, which superficially resembles the ordinary field mushroom but whose cap has yellow streaks, deepening when handled or bruised. When cut, it smells distinctly of carbolic acid. It is not lethal, but could cause a stomach upset.

Gathering field mushrooms is widely thought of as an autumnal pursuit, but the mushrooms can appear as early as July, if the right combination of damp weather followed by sunshine occurs. While mowing and grazing seem to encourage their growth, the greatest enemy of all field mushrooms is chemical farming. You are far more likely to find a good crop on organic pastureland and untreated hay meadows – sadly fewer than they once were.

Like all mushrooms, field mushrooms should be checked for maggots and other parasites, but good fresh specimens rarely need washing or peeling: simply wipe off any dirt, grit, or leaf matter with a cloth.

Freshly gathered field mushrooms can be used in any recipe that calls for cultivated mushrooms – to which they will always be superior. Although field mushrooms complement many other ingredients – especially shellfish – generally speaking, I like those I have gathered simply cooked and served, so that they taste as much as possible of themselves.

PENNY BUN (PORCINI) *Boletus edulis* and other boletus. The French call it *cèpe*, the Italians (and Americans) call it *porcini* ("little pigs"), but our name – sadly, rarely used – is surely the most charming of all. These days this bun will cost you rather more than a penny – though it's still free to those who take the time to hunt it down.

Whatever you call it, this mushroom is widely considered the greatest culinary prize of the fungus hunter. So much so that any known habitats to which the public has easy access (such as the New Forest) are literally becoming overrun by mushroom collectors, both amateur and professional. The result is that in some places you'd have to get up a lot earlier than I would be prepared to, just to stand a chance of finding a penny bun.

I don't, however, condemn those who pick mushrooms and sell them commercially. They have as much right to profit from their own special expertise as a scallop diver or lobster potter. But I don't like to compete with them either, as it's a competition I (and other amateurs) can hardly win. Luckily, for the time being at least, I have a few stamping grounds that are not yet main roads on the mushroom map. I wish you luck in finding the same.

The whole boletus family is distinguished by its round-capped, classic toadstool shape, but more precisely by the lack of gills, of the kind that field mushrooms have. Instead, you will find under the cap a mass of tiny tubes, which make the underside look like a fine sponge. In the case of the penny bun, the cap is dark brown and the pores creamy white, turning yellowish in older specimens. They grow near trees, often in grassy clearings and along the edges of woods. They can be huge – sometimes as much as 12 inches across and weighing over 1 pound.

Other species of boletus are just as worthwhile: the summer cep (*Boletus aereus*) with its toast brown stem, is found near beech and oak; the bay bolete (*Boletus badius*) has a thinner stem and a chestnut-brown cap; and the orange birch bolete (*Leccinum versipelle*) is found near birch and has an unusually long stem. All are good eating and make a worthwhile contribution to a mixed bag of boletus.

There are many other types of boletus, some good to eat, some indifferent. The only really nasty member of the tribe is the devil's bolete (*Boletus satanus*), distinctive for its white-gray cap with red-orange pores underneath and the flush of red veining on the stem. It is not thought to be deadly but can certainly cause severe gastric upsets. If in any doubt you should (as with all mushrooms) consult a comprehensive field guide.

Where possible, pick boletus mushrooms on a dry day as, once picked, wet mushrooms lose condition rapidly. The Boletus family, and particularly the penny bun, are sadly prone to larval infestation. Check carefully in the base of the stem and the centre of the cap before cooking. Clean off any dirt with a mushroom brush. (You don't have a mushroom brush?! Neither do I, but a pastry brush does the job.)

My initial preparation for penny buns and other boletus is always the same; they can then be used in a number of ways. Heat a generous tablespoon of olive oil in a large frying pan and throw in a crushed clove (or two) of garlic. Add the sliced ceps before the garlic takes color and a light sprinkling of salt to help release their juices. Cook fairly gently, tossing and turning the mushrooms until the water they release has evaporated (if there is a lot of it, which there will be if the mushrooms were very wet, turn up the heat to boil it off, then turn it down again). Cook until the mushrooms are tender and tasty and any liquid left in the pan is sufficiently reduced to be a sauce rather than a nuisance. Season to taste with salt and freshly ground black pepper, and stir in a tablespoon of butter. Boletus cooked like this can be served on toast or, better still, on a mound of creamy mashed potatoes.

CHANTERELLE (GIROLLE Fr.) *Cantharellus cibarius* Happening on a patch of chanterelles is a joyous affair. One of the prettiest and best flavored of all wild mushrooms, they look shockingly cheeky when you first encounter them – like little orange piglets hiding in the mossy grass. They are to be found in all kinds of woodland but are especially associated with pine, beech, and birch. I have had my best successes in Scotland and Ireland, where chanterelles can be locally prolific in the mossy banks and grassy patches of damp woods. They can be found as early as July in wet summers and as late as December in mild winters.

The egg-yellow, trumpet-shaped mushrooms have forked veins that are almost continuous with the stem. The caps of larger and older specimens can be ragged at the edges. They are widely, and rightly, said to smell of apricots – appropriately enough, given their color.

Chanterelles are firm fleshed and robust – one of the few mushrooms that can stand washing (not that they need it, if picked carefully). I rarely combine them with other ingredients in composite dishes, preferring to prepare them to their own greater glory, and enjoy them on their own. They are good simply sautéed in butter with a little garlic and chopped wild chervil (or parsley), but my favorite preparation is to cook them gently in milk with a little salt, garlic, and pepper until the liquid has reduced to a creamy, glossy coating sauce.

CHICKEN OF THE WOODS or SULPHUR POLYPORE *Laetiporus sulphureus* Chicken of the woods is one of the fungi that make it worthwhile looking up as well as down when you are out mushrooming in the U.K. It's one of only two bracket fungi that are really worth eating – the other is called beefsteak fungus. It's not that common, but when you do find one, its many layers of sulphur-yellow meat may sometimes provide you with well over 2 pounds of excellent fungal flesh.

Chickens grow on old trees, favoring oak and yew, though they are occasionally found on willow and sweet chestnut. They may appear anytime from the onset of mild weather in April until the first frosts of late autumn. Only fresh young specimens are really good for the pot – the yellower, the better. Older, woody specimens fade to dull, pale yellow and eventually to white, by which time they have a cardboard texture and an insipid, musty flavor. The last time I found a chicken in good shape was with fellow Dorset fungus enthusiasts Paddy Rudd and Nick Cadwell. I had to shin up an old oak to get it, but it was worth the trouble, as it added wonderful flavor and texture to our Stuffed Puffball (see page 425).

For general culinary purposes, first wipe the fungus clean and cut it into slices or cubes according to your recipe, trimming away any damaged, tough, or woody pieces as you go. Chicken of the woods can then be treated pretty much like meat. Why not chicken? Slices or chunks can be simmered in a little stock or cooked gently in butter until tender, then rolled in seasoned flour, dipped in beaten egg, tossed in bread crumbs, and deep-fried. The result will be better than any chicken nugget you'll get from a fast-food place, with or without a "Mc" in front of it.

They also complement real chicken (the feathered kind) as well as pork and beef, and can be added in cubes or thick slices to stews and casseroles made from any of these meats. Always add to a simmering pot just about half an hour before serving.

ST. GEORGE'S MUSHROOM *Calocybe gambosa* The St. George's mushroom is supposed to appear every year on the day of its eponymous saint (April 23). In reality, it will usually be early May before the first specimens appear, but it's nonetheless welcome for that, being one of the very few worthwhile fungi that can be found before high summer (others are the tree ear, morel, and chicken of the woods). It likes pastures, meadows, grassy wood edges, and road shoulders, and is usually found in small clusters or rings. The creamy white-brown color of the cap makes the unpicked mushroom look like an unfeasibly premature field mushroom, but the color of the gills (the same creamy white) makes identification at this time of the year fairly foolproof. It is not found in the U.S.

St. George's mushrooms are usually very clean, and barely need a wipe. Smaller ones can be kept whole and used like button mushrooms. Larger ones should be sliced. Generally speaking, they can be prepared like field mushrooms, though they are less palatable raw. They have a particularly good texture, so I never purée them into a soup, though I sometimes add them, lightly sautéed, to a creamy soup made from other mushrooms.

GIANT PUFFBALL *Langermannia gigantea* A good-sized giant puffball in decent condition is one of the great fungal finds – all the better because it usually comes as a complete surprise. Although they are not uncommon in grassy fields, hedgerows, and wood edges, the effort of actively looking for them is rarely rewarded. They are more likely to be encountered while searching for other species, and most likely of all on a long, late-summer walk when fungi are far from the mind.

Puffballs have been found well over a yard in circumference, but the more usual size is somewhere between your fist and your head. I found some near River Cottage with my friends Paddy and Nick when we were filming the television series. There were nine in all, in a circle about twenty yards in diameter, and they were all pretty much head sized. It was one of the most exciting mushroom-hunting moments I have had, and the fact that the cameras were there to record it was pretty amazing: a television first, I think?

To be worthwhile, a specimen must be a clean, milky-white color and largely unblemished, both on the outside and throughout. Older specimens will start to wrinkle and darken until they are a gray-brown, dried-out shadow of their former selves, puffing out their spores (some seven billion of them) into the autumn winds. In a good fresh specimen, little cleaning is needed. Simply wipe the puffball clean and cut a thickish slice off the base to check that the inside is white all the way through.

The texture and flavor of the giant puffball is like that of a firm young field mushroom, with no gills. Thin slices of puffball can be used like sliced field mushrooms, sautéed and served on toast, or made into risottos, sauces, and soups. They are also good cooked in milk (like chanterelles – see above). But the great joy of the giant puffball is its size, and I prefer to serve it in a way that preserves the spectacle: stuffed. For the full recipe, see page 425.

PARASOL and SHAGGY PARASOL *Lepiota procera* and *Lepiota rhacodes* This excellent mushroom is fairly common and easy to identify. As the name suggests, it really does look like an umbrella. The stem is often impressively tall (up to 12 inches) and the cup impressively wide (up to 10 inches in diameter), with a distinctive nipple in the center. Both stem and cap are slightly scaly, and there is a ring on the stem where the cap was attached before the mushroom opened. The shaggy parasol looks similar, but the pale brown scales on the cap are rougher and more substantial, giving it a very distinctive flaky appearance. Both species are often found growing in dramatic rings – rarely more dramatic than in the photograph on pages 354–355.

Parasols and shaggy parasols make excellent eating – firm fleshed and highly flavored, almost chickeny – provided you get to them in time. Ideally, they should be picked just before or just after the cap has opened away from the stem. Once they have been fully open for a while they become dry and unpalatable.

Young specimens can be sliced and used like field mushrooms. When just opened and still fleshy, the caps make great fritters. Dip them in batter (as for zucchini flowers on page 99) and deep-fry until crisp and golden.

OYSTER MUSHROOMS (PLEUROTTES Fr.) *Pleurotus ostreatus* A good find of oyster mushrooms can be spectacular, but, like the chicken of the woods, you are unlikely to make one unless you remember to look up as well as down when you are tramping the woods. Oyster mushrooms grow on the trunks or branches of dead or dying deciduous wood, especially beech. They grow in layered shelves, rather like a bracket fungus, but they have the veins to indicate that they are a true mushroom. The color varies from silvery gray ("the color of a Weimaraner dog," as a friend of mine once observed) to a fawny beige. Oyster mushrooms are now being cultivated on a large scale, and can be bought relatively cheaply in the supermarket. But the cultivated variety does not have the strength of flavor of the truly wild mushroom.

Since they grow off the ground, oyster mushrooms are usually very clean, needing barely a wipe. Even in wild oyster mushrooms, the flavor is not strong, though it's certainly pleasant enough, and the texture is good. I like to fry them up in olive oil, whole or in large slices, with plenty of garlic. They are also particularly good in

Asian-style clear soups, where the distinctive texture contrasts nicely with the softness of noodles and the crunch of green onions.

MORELS *Morchella esculenta* Morels are among the most sought after, and therefore the most expensive, of all wild mushrooms. I suspect that this is due rather more to their rarity, and their very distinctive shape, which looks so good on a plate (chefs in expensive restaurants love to use them as a garnish), than their taste. Not that they don't have a good flavor: they are pleasantly musty and distinctive. But £150 a pound ($300)? Give me a break. On the other hand, if you can get them for free . . .

Knowing the common wind line in a forest is useful when collecting many kinds of mushrooms, but particularly morels, as they start to release spores almost as soon as they emerge from the ground. Mark the first morel you find with a stick and then walk away from it in the direction of the usually prevailing wind. If you don't know the wind line, you can walk around the stick in an ever-increasing spiral. When you find a second mushroom, mark that too, and walk in the line indicated by joining the two sticks.

Morels are distinctive in a number of ways, besides their price. They are strictly spring mushrooms, occurring from March to May in open woodland and other shady places, mainly on chalky and sandy soil. They are sometimes found on burnt ground in coniferous forests. The cap is wrinkled and pitted like a sea sponge, 3/4 to 3 inches across, and the white stem is hollow inside. Beware of the superficially similar and mildly poisonous (it won't kill you, but may make you sick) false morel. It is of similar size and coloring, but close examination reveals that instead of pitted sponge, the cap comprises tubular lobes, like a brain.

The deep pits in the cap of the morel are a favorite hiding place for tiny insects, and the priority of preparation is to remove them. A good flick and shake will get rid of some of them, but there may be persistent lurkers. Morels can therefore be dropped into well-salted water and left until the insects crawl out. They are then usually cut in half – the cap and stem are both hollow – to expose the final hiding place for debris, be it animal, vegetable, or mineral.

The spongy cap of the morel makes it a good absorber of sauces – another reason why these mushrooms are often used to garnish expensive dishes in top restaurants. Meat and game are served with an intense reduction of juices, which the morel can nicely mop up. But if you haven't paid a fortune for your morels, you can feel liberated to use them in ways – and quantities – that a Michelin-starred chef would consider criminally extravagant: they make a particularly beautiful risotto.

Morels dry well. Thread whole ones on a string and leave them in a warm, dry place or very low oven until completely desiccated.

TREE EAR *Auricularia auricula-judae* This highly distinctive mushroom grows exclusively on dead or dying wood, usually elder, and varies in color from pale reddish brown to dark. It is strangely gelatinous and fleshy in texture, and does indeed look very like a dismembered ear, or collection of ears, stuck on the side of a tree. Hard and cold when young, it eventually dries out to a crisp. In mild weather it can be found at any time of year.

It's the young specimens that make good eating, and though the flavor is mild the texture is intriguing: pleasantly resistant to the bite. I like to cut them into fine slivers and add them to creamy sauces, especially for fish. They should first be gently cooked in butter, or simmered in a little stock, to tenderize.

hedgerow fruit and nuts

If spring is the season for green things, then late summer/autumn at River Cottage is definitely the season for sweet things: fruit and nuts. After all, the sun has spent months doing what it does best – turning starch into sugar. All around me, birds, mammals, even fish (chub and grayling love elderberries) are taking advantage of those energy packets, fueling up furiously, making fat to help them through the winter months ahead. Under the circumstances, it seems a pity that just about the only wild fruit that is well known and widely appreciated by us humans is the good old blackberry. Not that I have anything against the blackberry – a marvelous fruit. But I think it's time we started getting our fair share of the other delights on offer. There are plenty of them.

In September and October, when most of the harvest described below comes into its own, I find there's also a little more time. The days may be getting shorter, but the minutes and hours seem to get longer. Midsummer madness is taking a retreat. The vegetable garden is finally on the wane and can do without too much attention for a month or so. The livestock is hardly demanding. It's now that I finally get around to doing the things I have been promising myself all summer: a little bit of fishing on the beach; a good walk to remind myself of some favorite places I haven't visited for a while, with a basket in hand, to take advantage of any goodies encountered along the way.

"Summer, what summer?" you hear people say in Britain. "It's over before it's begun." But a few good days around now can put things right.

favorite wild fruits

As the birds will tell you, the number of wild fruits and berries that are technically edible (i.e., not poisonous) runs into the hundreds. Only a few of them are tried, tested, and enjoyed by us humans, and I sometimes wonder if we may be missing out on some goodies. I can't advise random experimentation, but can certainly vouch for all of the following.

BILBERRIES or BLAEBERRIES *Vaccinium myrtillus* Probably the wild ancestor of the cultivated blueberry, the blaeberry (the Scottish name for this berry) is a smashing little fruit and, to those encountering it for the first time, a lovely surprise. But even when the season is in full swing the berries are rather sparsely distributed on the parent bush. This makes it somewhat laborious in the picking: I defy any individual working alone to pick 2 pounds of blaeberries in less than an hour and a half.

The leafy green bushes cling low to the ground on scrubland, moors, and in sparse conifer woods with acid soil. The plants flower from May to June and sometimes bear fruit as early as the beginning of July, particularly in the South, though August and September are the best months. I have done most of my blaeberry picking in Scotland, and although they are occasionally found on moors in Devon, Dorset, Cornwall, and Wales, they are definitely more common in the north. Their U.S. equivalent is the huckleberry.

Blaeberries have a good enough flavor to eat raw, and make a refreshing wayside snack on long Highland walks. But they definitely improve with cooking, and it is well worth investing the (considerable) time to gather enough to take back to the kitchen.

Before cooking, the berries should be lightly rinsed. Then put them in a heavy pan, still wet, with just a sprinkling of sugar (3 or 4 tablespoons per 1 pound fruit). Heat gently for just a few minutes, until the juices start to run. Stir very gently to dissolve the sugar without breaking up the fruit. These very lightly stewed berries can be eaten on their own with thick yogurt, cream, or ice cream, or incorporated into the classic Scottish pudding, cranachan (see my version on page 123), or mixed with other fruits for a summer pudding.

But whenever I have a decent quantity of blaeberries, the first thing I make is a blaeberry crumble tart, a variation of the Blackberry and Apple Crumble Tart on page 430. The blaeberry version is, if anything, even better – perhaps my very favorite of all wild food desserts.

BLACKBERRIES *Rubus fruticosus* The blackberry, or bramble, is perhaps the best-known fruit of the wild harvest. It might be a romantic notion, but I'd like to think that at least half the population of Britain has, at least once in their lives, picked and eaten a wild blackberry. This (completely made-up) statistic gives me hope that out there somewhere are millions of potential converts – not just to the joys of the hedgerow harvest but to the whole notion of more natural, unprocessed foods.

Blackberries are abundant and widespread, growing in hedgerows, at forest edges, and in empty lots throughout Britain, though they are less common in the highlands of Scotland. One of the curiosities of this easily gathered fruit is the vast number of microspecies (possibly as many as four hundred), often highly localized, and each with subtle differences in size of berry, flavor, and time of fruiting. Sometimes, brambles growing within a few yards of each other will produce fruit of noticeably different flavor, and regular pickers will soon make a note of their favorite bushes. Here at River Cottage, there is one particular patch in the field by the river where the plump berries taste distinctly of strawberries.

As a general rule, the sweetest, best-flavored fruits are those that ripen first – usually in August here in Dorset but later the farther north you go. There is a local tradition that blackberries should not be gathered after the end of September, because "the devil has pissed on them." I've never seen him at it, but it is certainly true that whatever fruit remains by then tends to be either moldy, or small and slightly insipid.

In a good year, blackberries can be had in such abundance that it is a pity not to lay by a few good things made from them that can be enjoyed for weeks and months to come. They freeze well and also make an excellent sorbet: put 2 pounds of fresh ripe blackberries in a pan with the juice of half a lemon, a little water, and about 1 cup sugar. Heat gently until the juices run, stirring to dissolve the sugar. Do not boil hard, as this spoils the fresh blackberry taste. Rub the fruit through a nylon sieve to extract the juice and pulp. Discard the seeds and skin. Taste for sweetness and tartness and adjust, if you like, with more sugar or a squeeze of lemon juice. Let the mixture cool, then pour into an ice cream maker. Or do it the old-fashioned way, freezing the mixture until half frozen, then whisking it to a slush, refreezing it, whisking again, etc.

The blackberry crop can also be enjoyed in summer puddings and all kinds of pies and tarts, including the Blackberry and Apple Crumble Tart on page 430.

CRAB APPLES *Malus sylvestris* There are more crab apple trees around than you might think. Where my parents live in Gloucestershire, we encounter one or more on almost every dog-walking route, and here at River Cottage I know of at least three within walking distance. Look and you will find. Its delicate blossom, white with a hint of pink (as a paint company might put it), is a good way to identify a tree in May, to which you can return in the autumn in the expectation of fruit.

The true wild crab apple (*sylvestris*) has a small round fruit, rarely much larger than a golf ball, which becomes a golden yellow when ripe – usually late September or early October. But there are other varieties to be found, larger and less perfectly shaped, which are probably the descendants of cultivated apples that have reverted to the wild. The distinction is not that important, as the fruit from any wild apple tree can be put to good use.

The sour sharp taste of crab apples means that they're barely palatable raw. Cooked with added sugar, though, they reveal a flavor that is both deeply appley and pleasantly fragrant. They can be added to tarts and pies made from cultivated apples for a tarter flavor. Their excellent acidity and high level of pectin mean that they combine well with other wild fruits for making jellies and jams (see recipe on page 432). Preserves made from blackberries, rowan berries, and rose hips can all be improved by the addition of crab apples: try two parts berry fruit to one part crab apples. See also Crab Apple Blossoms on page 391.

ELDERBERRIES *Sambucus nigra* In August and September, the heavy sprays of dark purple elderberries sometimes seem to weigh down the whole hedgerow. If any wild fruit is more prolific than the blackberry, it must be this. It is a pity that it is not quite so tasty.

Even so, such an amazing annual glut can be put to good use. The bitter taste of raw elderberries is much improved by cooking them with sugar. Even though cooked elderberries do not (in my opinion) have a good enough flavor to stand on their own, they can be very pleasant combined with other fruits. They can certainly be added to a summer pudding, and work well combined with tart crab apples or cooking apples in crumbles and pies, as well as jellies and preserves. But their real redemption comes in the making of cordials and wines: see the recipe on page 433.

WILD GOOSEBERRIES *Ribes uva-crispa* Near the village where I grew up in Gloucestershire, we used to pick great basketloads of "goosegogs" from a long line of bushes growing by the side of a leafy lane, and also on the embankment of a disused railway. I have never seen them in such profusion since, though odd bushes and groups of bushes do occur in woods and hedgerows throughout lowland Britain – particularly in Yorkshire and Lancashire. They ripen from July onward, and are sometimes found as late as September.

In a very good summer, some plants will occasionally produce fruits sweet enough to eat raw, but the fine flavor of wild gooseberries, like most cultivated kinds, is best brought out by gentle cooking with a little sugar and just enough water to keep them from sticking to the pan.

ROSE HIPS, from the WILD ROSE or DOG ROSE *Rosa canina* When my family moved from London to Gloucestershire, my mum tried her hand at various traditional country recipes. One of the most successful was the classic preparation for rose hips, the well-known syrup. Although it was once thought of as a health cordial for sickly children (justifiably, in view of its very high vitamin C content), we preferred to look on it as a greedy treat to pour on pancakes, waffles, and ice creams. Rose hips served another amusing purpose in my youth: if the hips are broken open they reveal a tightly packed bunch of hairy seeds, which make a lethal itching powder.

The wild rose is common throughout the British Isles in the woods and hedgerows, and from late August to November its glossy red, ovoid berries can be found in profusion. The timing of the harvest of rose hips is important, since they will have much more flavor, and yield a more vitamin-rich syrup, when they have been softened by the first frost. On the other hand, by early November they are often too withered to be of any use.

My mum's syrup is made as follows: bring 2 quarts of water to a boil and coarsely chop 2 pounds ripe rose hips. Throw them into the boiling water, bring back to a boil, then remove from the heat, cover, and let infuse for half an hour. Strain through a jelly bag, then return the pulp from the bag to the pan and add another quart of boiling water. Reboil, infuse again, and strain as before. Combine the two liquids in a clean pan and boil hard until reduced by half. Off the heat, add 4 cups superfine sugar and stir to dissolve. Bring back to a boil and boil hard for five minutes. Pour into warmed sterilized bottles or jars (as for jam), then let cool. Store in a cool place.
Note Some garden varieties of rose also produce cookable hips – notably *Rosa rugosa.*

ROWAN or MOUNTAIN ASH *Sorbus aucuparia* This small, deciduous tree is common throughout Britain, in hedgerows and scrubland, and often grows on high ground near water (hence mountain ash). But rowan is also increasingly popular as a garden tree and among designers of municipal landscapes. So you may not have to climb a mountain to get your fruit. The waxy red berries appear from August, but are best gathered in late September and October when they are ripe but not yet mushy.

The berries are not edible when raw and not palatable when cooked until made into some kind of preserve. Rowan jelly (see page 432) is a lovely tart preserve, good to serve with venison or duck, or just on toast. It can be made either entirely with rowan berries or by combining the berries with crab apples or cooking apples.

SLOES, WILD DAMSONS, and BULLACES *Various subspecies of Prunus domestica* Sloes are the hard, purple fruits of the blackthorn bush, which are ready to pick between mid-September and October. Damson plums are usually cultivated, but wild escapees are often found in the hedgerow – smaller, harder, and more bitter than their tame cousins. The word *bullace* covers various species of the cultivated plum that have reverted to the wild.

All of these fruits are usually too bitter to eat raw, but some bullaces and wild damsons may be redeemed by gentle cooking with sugar and can then be used in crumbles, tarts, pies, etc. (or sieved to make a delicious tart sauce for vanilla ice cream). They all come into their own when combined with strong alcohol and sugar and left to macerate into a delicious liqueur. See page 431 for full instructions. Beach plums are the U.S. equivalent.

WILD STRAWBERRIES *Fragaria vesca* Though fairly common in theory, a decent crop of wild strawberries is a pretty exciting find. The best place to look is in deciduous woodland and shady scrub on chalky soil. Occasionally, small woods will be quite dominated by this perennial herb, but unless such caches remain well-kept secrets, overpicking and the taking of plants for transplanting into gardens can quickly decimate stocks.

It is very rare to be able to pick more than a small bowlful of wild strawberries. Their subtle, scented flavor doesn't in the least benefit from cooking, and I prefer to eat them on their own, with a light sprinkling of superfine sugar and perhaps just a smidgen of cream.

Wild strawberries are far more powerfully scented than the cultivated kind, and one or two can be used to aromatize other desserts. The first time I went for lunch at the Connaught, I chose an old favorite of mine, crème brûlée, for dessert. The whole delicious thing was deeply aromatized with the scent of strawberry: at the bottom of my ramekin was a single wild fruit.

favorite wild nuts

At River Cottage, I'm spoiled for wild nuts. The path up to the cottage is bordered by a prolific hazel thicket – a boon for pea stake in the spring, and loaded with delicious nuts in late summer. On top of that, there's a sweet chestnut just a few hundred yards up the hedge. I also have a beech tree, which this year is absolutely loaded with mast. I won't be using it myself (though you can make a useful flour from it). But as soon as it starts to fall, I will be collecting it by the wheelbarrow-load – the pigs will enjoy it, and, if I can collect enough of it, it should affect the flavor of their meat: I can't wait to see if it does.

The timing of the nut harvest is sweet, too. Just as the summer vegetables are over in the garden, and the blackberries in the hedge are on the wane, the nuts ripen. Though usually smaller than the cultivated equivalents you'll find in the store, wild nuts often have a superior taste and, because they can be eaten straight from the tree, a higher sugar content. (When nuts are stored for a long time, some of the sugar content reverts to starch.)

As far as us British humans are concerned, the three most worthwhile nut species you will find in the wild are the following:

HAZEL *Corylus avellana* If you want to find a hazel tree, follow a squirrel. And if you want to get a decent crop of nuts off it, shoot the squirrel (see page 370). One of the problems with wild hazelnuts is that the squirrels and birds (particularly jays) decimate the crop before the nuts are really well developed. Luckily, I don't mind my hazelnuts a bit on the green side – even as an accompaniment to fried squirrel.

The hazel is a common tree in woods and hedgerows throughout Britain, and it bears its crop of nuts (also called cobnuts and filberts) from late August, though they are not usually harvestable before mid-September. It is not found wild in the U.S. I like to eat my first crop of the year au naturel, cracking them with my teeth like a squirrel and munching a decent pile at a sitting. I also like to add shelled raw nuts to a crunchy green salad. But when the novelty of new-season's cobnuts in the raw state eventually wears off, the oven can be deployed to bring out the deep, nutty flavor that lurks within them. Shell a good pile of nuts and spread the kernels on a baking tray. Place at the top of a preheated 375°F oven for just ten minutes, then remove. When they are cool enough to handle, the papery skin can be rubbed off. Roasted cobnuts are delicious as a snack straight from the oven, either just as they are, or tossed in a little salt or, better still, light soy sauce. When cool, they can also be stored in a glass jar for weeks.

Home-roasted cobnuts always seem to have a much better flavor than anything you can buy, and can be used in all kinds of recipes, savory and sweet. Ground into a powder in a food processor, they are especially good in cookies, cakes, meringues, and crumbles. For the best flavor, store the nuts whole, then reroast for just a couple of minutes and process just before including in your recipe.

SWEET CHESTNUT *Castanea sativa* Probably introduced by the Romans as a crop tree, the sweet chestnut is widespread in woods and parks in England, less common in Scotland. It is not found in the U.S. The broad-trunked tree with its spreading branches has pointed, dark green leaves and produces its spiny, nut-containing fruit in August. The nuts will not be ready until October, and can be collected as windfalls among the tree's yellow-brown leaf litter, sometimes until mid-November if the squirrels haven't gotten there first.

The sweet chestnut tree at River Cottage is prolific, producing a bumper crop of small but perfectly formed nuts every autumn. They are a great treat, and though the nuts are on the small side, the flavor is superb. Every year I find something new to do with them: a current favorite is incorporating pieces of roasted chestnut into a rice pudding.

Most people have enjoyed chestnuts on an open fire, either at home or from a street vendor in the city, cooking them on an open brazier. There is great comfort and pleasure to be had from this autumnal tradition (as Nat King Cole will happily testify, year after year). As with so many wild foods, the pleasure lies as much in the ritual of preparation as in the eating. Before roasting, the chestnuts should be slit down one side from top to tail with the point of a sharp knife, otherwise they may explode. I then usually put them on a coal shovel, which I place on top of hot coals scraped to the edge of the fire. Turn occasionally, and they should be ready in ten or fifteen minutes.

Despite, or perhaps because of, the popularity of roast chestnuts, few people in this country realize just how versatile this nut really is. On the Continent, and in Italy in particular, chestnuts are processed and used in all kinds of ways – dried, ground into flour, or canned both whole and as a sweetened purée. They are then used to make breads, cakes, and cookies, as well as many savory dishes. If you have access to a large crop of chestnuts, it may well be worth trying some of these processes.

When chestnuts are required for almost any recipe, sweet or savory, they must be peeled first. This is most easily done by slitting the shells and covering the chestnuts in boiling water in a pan. Bring back to a boil, simmer for five minutes, then take off the heat. Shell, with fingernails (or a sharp knife if you have no fingernails), while still hot but cool enough to handle. Then peel off the inner skin. They are still crunchy like this, and need further cooking in most recipes.

Peeled chestnuts can be gently braised in a little stock until tender, then served as a side vegetable, particularly with game. Coarsely chopped, they can be added to braised celery, steamed cabbage, or creamed Brussels sprouts.

An excellent way to preserve a good quantity of chestnuts for use in desserts and sweet recipes is to make a sweet chestnut purée: dissolve 2 cups sugar in 2 cups water and boil hard for five minutes to get a light syrup. Add 2 pounds peeled chestnuts and simmer gently in the syrup until they are very tender. Remove them from the syrup and purée in a food processor, adding enough of the syrup to get a thick but almost pourable consistency. Pot in sterilized jars and keep in the fridge. This purée will last for months and can be used to fill cakes and meringues, as a sauce for pancakes and ice cream, or like a jam, on toast, with a sprinkling of cinnamon.

WALNUT *Juglans regia* The walnut tree, introduced from Asia about five hundred years ago, does not spread very successfully when left to its own devices. Most specimens have been deliberately planted by man. But they are not uncommon in woods and parkland, and indeed in people's gardens, and it seems a shame not to use them when you find them. Indeed, the knowledge that any walnut you find is sadly not destined to spawn a future tree is the best possible motive for arranging a different fate for it, in the kitchen.

Walnuts do not always ripen fully in Britain, and it is best to allow them the benefit of any autumn sunshine and pick them as late as possible: late October or even early November. Ideally, the fruit surrounding the nut should be split and the shell of the nut showing through. Peel away this fleshy case and, if you are not ready to use the walnuts straight away, or want to keep them for your nut bowl, let them dry in a warm, dry place for twenty-four hours, then transfer them to a cool, dry place. This should ensure they don't go moldy.

Wild walnuts can be used instead of the imported cultivated kind in any recipe, but because they have a particularly strong flavor I prefer to use them in savory ones. They make a lovely pasta sauce: coarsely chop about 1¼ cups walnut kernels, then cook in a pan with a little olive oil and crushed garlic. Add two tablespoons of thick cream, then bubble to reduce, stir in a handful of freshly grated Parmesan, season with freshly ground pepper, and serve with tagliatelle or pasta quills. Walnuts also make great pesto, in place of pine nuts.

One thing British walnuts are always good for, when green and unripe, is pickling. Pick young green walnuts in July, wash them well, and prick them all over with a needle. Put them in a bowl and cover with brine (½ cup salt per quart of water, boiled and cooled). Let pickle for a week, changing the brine every two days. Rinse with fresh water, then let dry on a rack for two or three days. Then pack them in jars and cover with a hot, strong pickling vinegar, made by combining a quart of white wine vinegar or cider vinegar with a tablespoon each of cloves, allspice berries, and white peppercorns, plus three bay leaves and two cinnamon sticks, all heated together gently for one hour without boiling. Seal the jars and leave in a dark place for one month at the very least, and preferably three.

hedgerow recipes

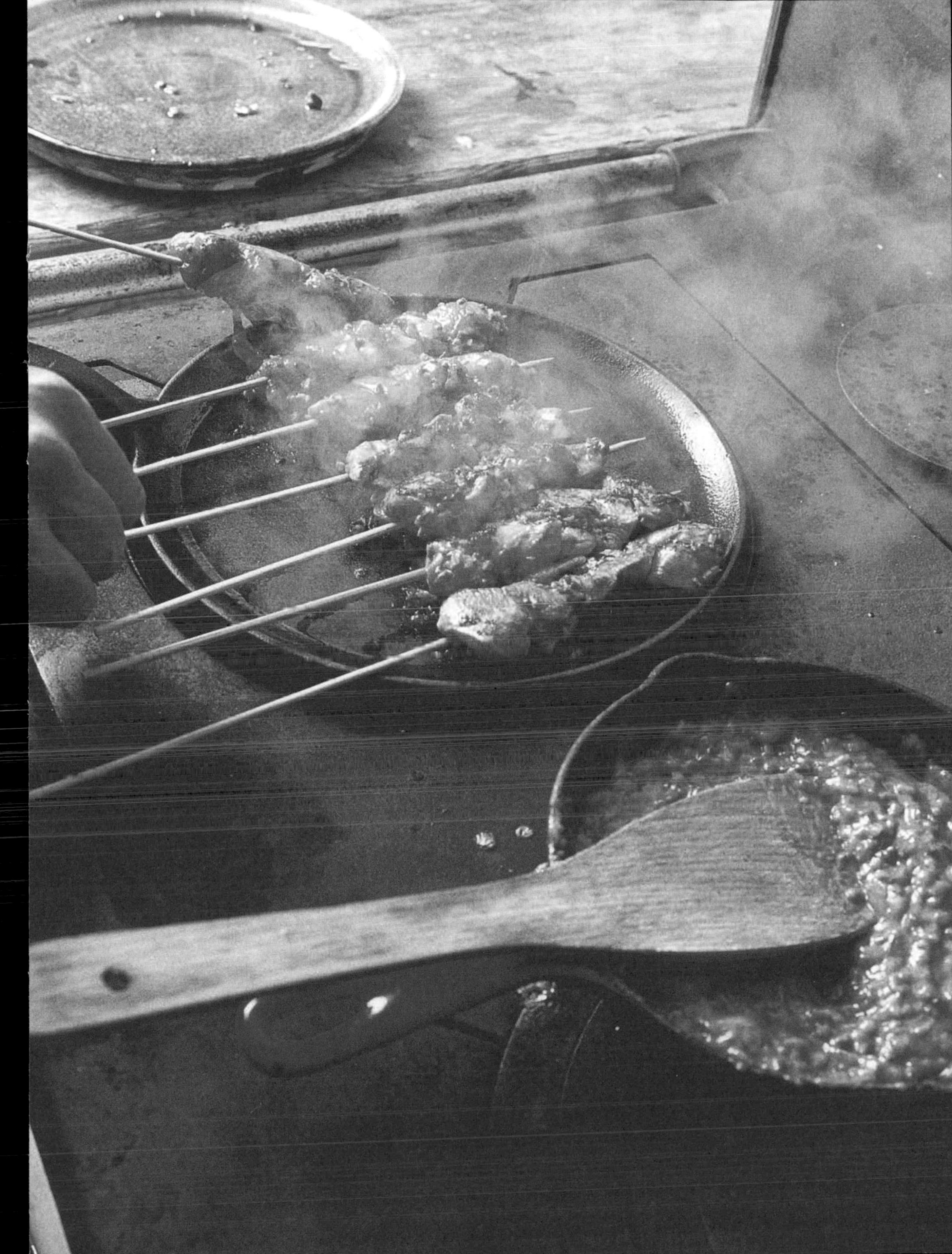

rabbit satay with spicy peanut sauce

makes 10 to 12 skewers

After a spotlit foray around neighbors' fields one summer evening with a local gamekeeper, I had 30-odd rabbits on my hands. I saved the saddles to make this recipe, while the rest of the meat went for burgers (see page 416). You could also use the meat from the back legs, cut into cubes, for the satay.

You probably won't have 30 rabbits at your disposal, so I've adapted this recipe for 1 to 1½ pounds meat (or the meat from a couple of good-sized rabbits).

1 to 1½ pounds lean rabbit meat, cubed

FOR THE MARINADE
A walnut-sized piece of fresh ginger, finely grated
1 to 3 fresh chiles (to taste), finely chopped
2 garlic cloves, crushed
½ small onion, grated
2 teaspoons coriander seeds, crushed
2 tablespoons dark soy sauce
1 tablespoon brown sugar
Juice of ½ lime

FOR THE SPICY PEANUT SAUCE
1 onion, finely chopped
2 garlic cloves, crushed
1 tablespoon peanut or sunflower oil
½ to 1 fresh red or green chile (to taste and according to heat), finely chopped (or use chile sauce from a bottle)
2 to 3 tablespoons dark soy sauce
1 tablespoon brown sugar
⅓ cup crunchy peanut butter
Juice of ½ to 1 lime

Mix all the ingredients for the marinade together in a large bowl, add the rabbit meat, and leave in the fridge for at least 2 hours. Soak the bamboo skewers in cold water for at least half an hour.

For the spicy peanut sauce, gently cook the onion and garlic in the oil until soft and lightly browned. Add the rest of the ingredients and mix well, then let it bubble and thicken in the pan. Taste and adjust the flavor by adding more lime juice, chile, or soy, according to your preference (personally, I like plenty of lime). Add a little water to get a nice, "pourable-but-only-just" consistency. This sauce will keep for a week in a sealed jar in the fridge. If reheating it, you may need to add a little more water.

Thread 5 or 6 pieces of marinated meat on each skewer. Cook on a grill or on a lightly oiled heavy grill pan, turning regularly, until nicely browned (about 10 minutes). Serve with the peanut sauce – and with a fresh green salad if entertaining at home, or in a hot dog bun if picnicking.

variation speedy stir-fry version

This is such a great marinade that I often make it up specially for lean cuts of pork, beef, or chicken from the freezer. If you're after a quick but delicious supper rather than convenient finger food, then there's really no need to make up satay sticks. Just prepare the marinade in the morning, throw in your chosen meat, cut into cubes, and let marinate for the rest of the day. Come suppertime, heat up a little oil in a wok or heavy frying pan and add the meat, along with any leftover marinade. Stir-fry for about 10 minutes, then serve with plain steamed rice or noodles.

b'steeya

serves 6

This is a really extraordinary dish that takes a little bit of time and care but isn't very difficult to make. It's North African in origin – hence the combination of sugar, nuts, and cinnamon with meat.

Free-range chicken, duck, or pheasant is a viable alternative to pigeon. Using whole birds means you can make a well-flavored stock from the carcasses, but for a fast-track version you could buy lean meat for the pie and either use a ready-made stock or leave it out altogether.

6 pigeons (including, optionally, hearts and livers)
2 onions, 2 leeks, and 2 carrots, all coarsely chopped
4 cinnamon sticks
A large glass of red wine
Oil for frying
⅔ cup butter
6 eggs, beaten
A good bunch of parsley, finely chopped
A good bunch of cilantro, finely chopped
3 tablespoons superfine sugar, plus extra to decorate
2 teaspoons ground cinnamon, plus extra to decorate
¼ cup sliced almonds, toasted
About ½ package of filo pastry
Salt and freshly ground black pepper

If the birds are not oven-ready, pluck and draw them (see pages 373–376), reserving the hearts and livers if you wish to use them. Then cut off the breasts, running the blade of the knife as close as possible to the bone. Put the carcasses in a roasting pan and roast for 10 minutes in a preheated 400°F oven, then transfer them to a large saucepan with the onions, leeks, carrots, and cinnamon sticks, packing everything in tightly. Add just enough water to cover, then bring to a boil. Skim off any scum from the surface and simmer gently, uncovered, for at least 2 hours. Strain the stock into a clean pan, ideally through cheesecloth or cotton. Add the red wine and boil hard until the stock is reduced to an almost syrupy consistency. You should be left with about 6 tablespoons. Set aside.

Cut each pigeon breast into 4 or 5 pieces and throw them, with the liver and hearts if you are using them, into a lightly oiled hot pan to brown for a couple of minutes. Season and set aside.

Melt half the butter in a pan, add the eggs, and scramble gently. Take off the heat while still pourable. Mix in the parsley, cilantro, and some black pepper.

Thoroughly mix together the sugar, ground cinnamon, and toasted almonds. Melt the rest of the butter and brush some over the surface of a pan. Line the pan with 1 or 2 sheets of filo, letting it overhang the edges, and brush with more melted butter. Make 2 or 3 more layers of butter brushed filo, then arrange the pigeon pieces on top and pour half the reduced stock over them. Add the scrambled eggs, then the rest of the reduced stock. Spread the cinnamon, almond, and sugar mixture over in an even layer. Put 2 more layers of filo, brushed with butter, over the top of the pie, then tuck in all the overlapping edges and brush with yet more butter.

Place the pie in a preheated 425°F oven until the top is crisp and golden – about 10 minutes. Take the pie out and turn it out, upside down, onto a baking sheet. Put it back in the oven for another 5 to 10 minutes, until it is crisp and golden brown top and bottom. Turn right side up again onto a serving plate.

Dust the finished pie with more confectioners' sugar and decorate with thin lines of ground cinnamon in a criss-cross diamond-shaped pattern. Serve at once.

game terrine

serves 10

These days, terrines seem to be regarded as something for professional chefs in restaurant kitchens. In fact, they are an old-fashioned staple of the farmhouse kitchen and not nearly as difficult as people think. I find them immensely satisfying to make, and to eat.

The way I see it, making a terrine is like building a wall: it's a matter of bricks and mortar. The mortar is a stuffing, in this case made from pork, bread crumbs, and the livers of the game; the bricks are whole pieces of game fillets from the leg and breast. When cut, the finished terrine has a lovely marbled cross section. It is delicious served with Cumberland sauce or homemade chutney.

FOR THE PÂTÉ

1 pound sausage meat
Livers from all the game (if they're not available, use about 6 ounces chicken livers), finely chopped
2 handfuls fresh white bread crumbs
1 egg
3 tablespoons finely chopped parsley
Leaves from a few sprigs of thyme, chopped
5 to 6 juniper berries, crushed in a mortar
2 garlic cloves, finely chopped
A splash of red wine
A splash of brandy
Salt and freshly ground black pepper

A selection of lean game meat, about 2 pounds in all, which could include:
- Pheasant breasts (hung about 5 days)
- Pigeon breasts
- Duck or other wild fowl breasts
- Saddle and hindquarters of 1 rabbit, boned
- Saddle and hindquarters of hare, boned
- Lean strips of venison (from the leg or fillet)

PLUS

Oil or fat for frying
10 ounces bacon to line the dish

First of all, make the "mortar" that will hold the "bricks" of the terrine together. In a large mixing bowl, combine the sausage meat and the chopped livers. Next add the bread crumbs, egg, parsley, thyme, juniper berries, and garlic. Add the wine and brandy, season with salt and pepper, and mix everything together thoroughly, preferably with your hands.

Cut the game meat into strips of roughly the same size, about 2 fingers thick. Heat some oil or fat in a heavy frying pan and fry the game pieces, in batches, for about 2 minutes, until nicely browned.

Remove the rind from the bacon and run the back of a knife along each slice to stretch it. Line a loaf pan or ceramic terrine dish with the stretched slices of bacon, overlapping them slightly and leaving the ends hanging over the edges of the dish. Arrange a layer of pâté in the terrine, followed by a layer of game meat, then another layer of pâté followed by another layer of game meat, seasoning with salt and pepper between each layer. If you like, you can put the same kind of meat in each layer – i.e., a layer of rabbit, then pigeon, and then pheasant). However many layers you end up making (I usually go for 3), be sure to finish with a layer of the pâté.

Fold the exposed strips of bacon over the top of the terrine and cover tightly with aluminum foil. If your terrine dish has a lid on it, so much the better. Place the terrine dish in a roasting pan half-filled with hot water and cook in a preheated 350°F oven for approximately $1\frac{1}{2}$ to 2 hours. Test with a skewer to see if it is cooked – if the skewer does not come out of the terrine piping hot, then it is not ready.

For the best possible texture and easy slicing, your terrine should be pressed as it cools. Find a piece of wood or plastic that fits snugly inside the terrine dish and weight it down with a brick or two. (Another similar-size dish or loaf pan with a brick inside often does the trick, but wrap it in plastic wrap if you're using a pan.) Leave the terrine until completely cold – for several hours or overnight.

To serve the terrine, slice it thickly with a very sharp knife and put it on serving plates with a small salad of lightly dressed green leaves and a blob of good fruit chutney (for example, the River Cottage Chutney on page 117). Bring toast to the table.

rabbit burgers

makes about 10 "quarter pounders"

If you ever shoot, or otherwise acquire, a large number of rabbits, these burgers are very worthwhile. The minced pork adds a little bit of essential fat to keep them juicy.

1 onion, finely chopped
A little oil
2 pounds ground minced lean rabbit meat
8 ounces sausage meat or minced pork belly
Leaves from a good sprig each of marjoram, thyme, sage, and rosemary, all finely chopped

Gently cook the onion in the oil for a few minutes until softened, then let cool completely.

Mix the meats, chopped herbs, and onion together thoroughly by hand. Then shape into "quarter pounder" patties – ideally not more than ¾ inch thick, so they cook through fairly fast. Wrap in plastic wrap and chill until ready to cook.

Cook the burgers on a grill or in a lightly oiled heavy frying pan for 3 to 4 minutes on each side.

Serve in a split bun with a choice of Fresh Tomato Salsa (see page 104), homemade Tomato Ketchup (see page 105), or mustard mayonnaise (ideally made with good homemade mayonnaise mixed 5 to 1 with English mustard).

stalkers' breakfast (roe liver and mushrooms)

serves 4

A roe deer liver, the fresher the better, is one of the great delicacies of the wild pantry. It is, of course, not that easy to come by, though it may not be quite as hard as you might think. If you know anyone who stalks regularly, ask them to let you have a few slices when they shoot a roe. Alternatively, try contacting a local game dealer, or ask your butcher if he can track one down. You can use calf's or lamb's liver for this recipe instead, but it won't taste quite the same.

1 pound roe deer liver
3 tablespoons unsalted butter
6 ounces large field mushrooms, sliced (2 cups)
A few sage leaves, chopped
Salt and freshly ground black pepper
Toast or fried bread, to serve

Prepare the liver by removing any outer membrane and large tubes, then cutting it into thin strips. Melt half the butter in a heavy frying pan until it starts to foam (do not allow it to burn). Add the mushrooms and fry until they are nicely colored and the water coming out of them has evaporated. Move the mushrooms to one side of the pan, add the remaining butter, and fry the strips of liver for about 3 minutes, turning from time to time. Throw the chopped sage in for the last minute of cooking. Season with salt and pepper to taste, then pile the liver and mushrooms onto toast and serve at once.

pigeon pitas with pea and peppercorn purée

serves 4

This is a way of serving up pigeon, kebab style. Apart from being wonderfully alliterative, it's very tasty. Incidentally, if you take the breasts off pigeons you have shot yourself, or bought whole, never throw away the carcasses. Roasted, they make excellent stock.

8 wood pigeon breasts
A little oil

FOR THE MARINADE
½ glass of red wine
2 tablespoons olive oil
Generous sprigs of thyme
1 to 2 garlic cloves, crushed
2 bay leaves, crushed
10 juniper berries, crushed
A few twists of fresh black pepper

TO SERVE
4 large pita breads
About 2 cups shredded romaine or Little Gem lettuce
½ onion, finely sliced
Split Pea and Green Peppercorn Purée (see page 119)
Spicy fruit chutney, sieved to make a sauce

Slice each pigeon breast into 3 or 4 pieces and place in a nonmetallic bowl. Add all the ingredients for the marinade and mix well. Cover with a plate and leave in the fridge for at least 4 hours or overnight.

Remove the meat from the marinade and wipe off any bits of herb sticking to it. Put the pitas into a toaster, or on a dry griddle, just before you start to cook the pigeon.

Heat a griddle or a heavy frying pan without any oil, then add a small drizzle of oil to the surface. Throw on all the sliced pigeon breasts and flash-fry, turning occasionally with a metal spatula, for just 3 to 4 minutes. Remove them from the heat while you prepare the pitas.

Split the toasted pitas open with a knife and gently push apart the sides to open them up like a pocket. Put some lettuce and onion in the bottom of each, then pile in the hot pigeon pieces. Top it off with a generous smothering of the split pea purée and sieved fruit chutney.

jugged hare

serves 6 to 8

This is perhaps the ultimate dish for game-lovers, and an excellent excuse to get out your very best claret. I try to cook it at least once a year.

The season for hares is from September to the end of February, and during this time any good butcher can get you a hare if you give him a bit of notice. When you order it, mention that you intend to jug it and ask him to save the blood for you. The hare should be hung for 4 or 5 days – longer only if you like a very gamy flavor.

If you are pressed for time, you can omit the marinating, in which case just add all the marinade ingredients to your pot along with the browned hare pieces.

1 large brown hare, skinned, plus its blood (liver optional)
A bottle of good red wine
3 ounces good bacon or pork belly, cut into ¾-inch pieces
2 tablespoons olive oil
1 onion or 3 shallots, sliced
1 large carrot, sliced
2 tablespoons butter
1 heaping tablespoon flour
6 tablespoons brandy
2 squares of baking chocolate, grated
Salt and freshly ground black pepper

FOR THE MARINADE
2 tablespoons olive oil
3 garlic cloves, crushed
5 to 6 shallots, sliced
A few sprigs of thyme
A few sprigs of parsley
2 bay leaves
8 black peppercorns

Section the hare with a heavy knife or meat cleaver, cutting off its legs and dividing the saddle into 5 or 6 pieces (or you can ask your butcher to do this). In a deep dish, combine all the marinade ingredients with a glass of the red wine, then add the hare and mix well. Cover and leave in a cool place overnight.

After the hare has marinated overnight, start to prepare the dish at least 3 hours before you intend to eat it, or even the day before. Remove the pieces of hare from the marinade and wipe dry with a clean cloth. Cook the bacon or pork belly for a few minutes in the oil in a large frying pan. Add the onion or shallots and the carrot and cook for a few minutes, then transfer the bacon and vegetables to a large, heavy, flameproof casserole (in which the hare will also be cooked).

Put the frying pan back on the heat and add the butter. Coat the pieces of hare in the flour, then add to the pan and cook, turning occasionally, until nicely browned. Transfer the meat to the casserole and add the herbs from the marinade. Pour over all the remaining wine, the brandy, and the liquid from the marinade, then add just enough water to barely cover the meat. Season with salt and pepper and bring to a very gentle simmer. Cover and cook over low heat, or in a preheated 300°F oven for 2 to 3 hours. The hare is done when the meat is quite tender and begins to come away from the bone.

The next stage is to make a liaison of the blood and the cooking liquid. This has to be done carefully if the sauce is not to separate, but even if it does it is only the appearance, not the flavor, that will be affected.

Remove the pieces of hare from the pot and put them in a warmed dish. Strain the stock through a sieve to remove the vegetables and herbs, then return it to the pan over a very low heat. Have the blood ready in a small basin. Spoon a little of the cooking liquid into the blood to both warm and thin it and stir well. Add the grated chocolate to the pan. Then ladle in the warmed blood, a little at a time, stirring as you go. When the liaison is smooth and well blended, bring back to a boil. Return the pieces of hare to the pot and bring back to a gentle simmer before serving.

Give each person a couple of good pieces of hare on a nice warm plate, and plenty of sauce from the pot. I always serve jugged hare with Creamy Mashed Potatoes (see page 114) and not much else. It's too rich and interesting to need any further accompaniment – except that top-notch claret.

variation lepre con pappardelle

In this classic Italian version of the dish, the meat is taken off the bone and the sauce is much reduced, then combined with the meat again and served with the wide noodles called pappardelle. Follow the recipe above, omitting the flour and browning the hare pieces without it. Don't add any salt until the end, as the heavy reduction of liquid could make it very salty.

When the hare is cooked (you may leave it for rather longer than 2 hours – it should come easily off the bone), remove it from the sauce. Before performing the liaison with the blood, strain the sauce first through a sieve, then through cheesecloth or a cotton cloth, so you have a very clean stock. Boil this hard to reduce it to about ¾ cup. Then add the chocolate and perform the liaison with the blood, as above. Check the seasoning and adjust as necessary. The idea is to produce a rich, dark, intense sauce. Set this finished sauce aside.

When the meat is cool enough to handle, take it off the bones, picking off and discarding bits of membrane and gristle and breaking the good clean bits of meat into small, neat pieces. Add the cleaned meat to the sauce and heat through until just bubbling. Serve with squares of fresh pasta (ideally homemade) cut into wide pasta ribbons. Strictly no Parmesan on this one.

nettle soup

serves 6

This is my basic recipe for nettle and other "wild greens" soups, including fat hen and chickweed. I still think nettle is the best. A well-made nettle soup is no mere emergency fodder but a truly luxurious dish. It's worth noting that nettle and other green soups freeze extremely well.

An excellent variation is to mix the nettle leaves with watercress or romaine lettuce. The carrot and celery are optional but do make for a more robust, full-flavored soup. I sometimes add a few fresh or frozen peas as well, to give sweetness and improve the texture.

I normally use a chicken stock, but I have been known to use fish stock. This gives the soup an unusual (though not unpleasant) taste. If you do use a stock cube, the best ones are monosodium glutamate–free.

I used to thicken my soups with potato, but some varieties have a tendency to impart a slight stickiness when blended. Now, I generally use cooked rice or even rice cakes: these can be put straight into the blender and produce a smooth, creamy texture. But you can easily use a medium potato to thicken this soup, if you prefer: peel and dice it fairly small and add it just before the stock.

½ shopping bag full of nettles, tops or young leaves (see pages 386–387)
4 tablespoons butter
1 large or 2 medium onions, finely sliced
1 large carrot, chopped (optional)
2 celery stalks, chopped (optional)
1 large garlic clove, crushed (optional)
4 cups good chicken, fish, or vegetable stock
A pinch of freshly grated nutmeg (optional)
3 tablespoons cooked rice or 3 rice cakes
2 tablespoons heavy cream or crème fraîche
Salt and freshly ground black pepper

TO GARNISH
A little extra cream or crème fraîche
A small bunch of chives, chopped
Leaves from a few sprigs of wild chervil or parsley, chopped

Pick over the nettles and wash them thoroughly. Discard only the tougher stalks, as the soup will be blended.

Melt the butter in a large pan and cook the onion, plus the carrot, celery, and garlic if using, until soft but not brown. Add the stock and pile in the nettles. Bring to a boil and simmer for 5 to 10 minutes, until the nettles are tender. Season with salt and pepper and with nutmeg if you wish.

Purée the soup in a blender with the cooked rice or rice cakes (you will probably have to do this in 2 batches).

Return to a clean pan, stir in the cream, and reheat, but do not let it boil. Check the seasoning, then serve, garnishing each bowl with a swirl of cream and a generous sprinkling of chopped herbs.

To serve cold On warm spring or early summer days, I love to serve this soup cold. After blending and adding the cream, pour the soup into a bowl and let cool, then transfer to the fridge for a couple of hours before serving. For accelerated cooling, fill a large basin or saucepan with ice cubes and water and place the bowl of soup in the iced water. Stir to chill, adding more ice cubes if the first batch melts. Stir well just before serving and ladle the soup out into bowls. Garnish each with a swirl of cream and a sprinkling of chopped chives and wild chervil.

watercress soup with poached egg

serves 2

I'm lucky enough to have a ready supply of wild watercress growing in a stream in a nearby field. It has an even more intensely peppery flavor than the cultivated variety. You shouldn't really eat wild watercress raw, especially if livestock have access to the water upstream, as there is a small risk of catching a nasty parasite called liver fluke. But cook it thoroughly, and the risk is removed. The poached egg finish is optional, but it does turn a soup into a supper.

2 tablespoons butter
A dozen wild garlic roots (or 1 small onion or shallot), finely chopped
2 cups fresh vegetable or chicken stock
2 good fistfuls of watercress, trimmed and well washed
2 tablespoons cooked rice or 2 rice cakes
Freshly grated nutmeg
2 eggs, at room temperature
A little heavy cream, to serve
Chopped wild garlic leaves (or chives), to garnish
Salt and freshly ground black pepper

Melt the butter in a large pan over a low heat, add the wild garlic or onion, and cook until soft – do not allow it to color. Add the stock and bring to a boil, then add the watercress, bring back to a boil, and simmer for just a minute. Place in a blender with the cooked rice or rice cakes and process until smooth. Return the soup to the pan, reheat thoroughly without boiling, and season to taste with nutmeg, salt, and pepper.

The perfect poached egg: Poach the eggs one at a time. Break each egg into a cup, being careful not to break the yolk. Bring a small pan of water to a boil. When it is boiling rapidly, stir fast with a large spoon to create a vortex. Pour the egg into the center of the vortex, place the lid on the pan, and turn off the heat under it. Leave for exactly 2 minutes ("the time it takes to toast and butter a thick slice of bread" – Delia Smith, egg guru).

Serve the soup in warmed bowls, with a drained poached egg in the center of each one and a blob of cream next to it, topped with a sprinkling of chopped wild garlic leaves or chives. And, of course, your toast.

poached egg on toast with sorrel

serves 1

A poached egg on toast becomes a rather glamorous supper dish with the addition of a sauce of wilted sorrel. This simple sauce is also excellent with pork and veal (hot or cold) and fish.

A good fistful of wild or cultivated sorrel
3 tablespoons butter
1 tablespoon crème fraîche (optional)
1 large fresh-laid egg
A thick slice of brown bread
Salt and freshly ground black pepper

Pick over the sorrel, tearing out any coarse stalks, then wash it well and shred finely. Melt half the butter in a pan and throw in the sorrel. Stir it and it will quickly wilt to a purée. If it is very wet, transfer briefly to a sieve to drain off any excess water, then put it back in the pan. Season to taste with salt and pepper, then stir in the crème fraîche if you like. Turn off the heat, but leave the sauce in the pan to keep warm.

Then poach your egg and make your toast (see page 423). To finish the dish, drain the egg carefully with a slotted spoon, then place it on the toast and pour over the sorrel sauce. Eat at once.

stuffed puffball

serves 2 to 10 (depending on foraging success)

This is one of the most spectacular and satisfying wild food recipes I have ever cooked. The fungal flavors in the finished dish are intense, to say the least; it's not for the faint-hearted. But true fungophiles will appreciate it.

The stuffing was based simply on the "catch of the day" when I went out foraging with my Bridport friends Nick and Paddy. It's a flexible affair, and you could use whatever combination of wild meat and wild mushrooms comes your way. Buttered steamed young comfrey leaves make a good accompaniment.

1 large puffball (8 to 16 inches in diameter)
Oil for frying
About a dozen wild garlic roots (or 1 small onion or shallot), finely chopped
Breast meat from 1 pigeon (or more, as available), chopped
About 1 pound chicken of the woods mushrooms (discard any woody bits, then chop coarsely)
A slosh of wine
A few horse or field mushrooms, chopped
Parsley, sage, thyme, finely chopped
A few potatoes, parboiled and coarsely chopped
1 tablespoon soft butter
Salt and freshly ground black pepper

Cut the top off the puffball and remove carefully; this is going to be your lid. Hollow out the interior of the puffball, leaving the sides and base at least 2 inches thick (any thinner and they may collapse during baking). Coarsely chop the flesh that you have removed from the puffball.

Heat some oil in a large pan, add the wild garlic, and cook for a couple of minutes, then add the pigeon meat. Cook for a couple of minutes, until browned, then add the chicken of the woods. Add a sprinkling of salt at this stage to help draw the water from this fungus. If the mixture begins to look dry and is sticking to the bottom of the pan, add a little water and a slosh of wine. Simmer gently until the liquid is nearly absorbed, then transfer to a large mixing bowl.

Return the empty pan to the heat and add a little more oil. Throw in the chopped puffball flesh, along with any other mushrooms you have gathered, and stir-fry for a few minutes, until much reduced in volume. Add to the rest of the mixture, along with the herbs and chopped potatoes. Mix everything together well and season to taste with salt and pepper.

Fill the puffball with the mixture and replace the lid. Smear the top and sides of the puffball with the soft butter and wrap completely in foil. Bake in a preheated 375°F oven for 2 hours.

To serve, unwrap the puffball, remove the lid, and spoon out the filling. Serve with pieces of the lid, sliced; further slices of puffball can be taken horizontally, as the level of the filling descends.

porcini lasagne

serves 6

This recipe comes from my friend Mauro Bregoli, chef at the excellent Old Manor House restaurant in Romsey, Hampshire. Mauro cooked this dish for a bunch of hungry fishermen after a great day's trout fishing on the River Test one October. It is quite the best mushroom/pasta combination I have ever had. He is reluctant to give quantities: "Make sure you have plenty of everything, and then there will be enough" is his sound philosophy.

I have inserted some quantities of my own, but they are no more than a rough guide. The dish can be made with reconstituted dried porcini, but it will not be quite as good.

FOR THE BÉCHAMEL SAUCE
3 tablespoons butter
¼ cup plain flour
2 cups hot milk
A pinch of freshly grated nutmeg
Salt and freshly ground black pepper

At least 8 ounces Parmesan cheese
At least 1 pound fresh porcini or other boletus (ideally, twice that quantity), cleaned (see page 397)
Lasagne sheets (preferably fresh, but dried can be used) – enough to make at least 3 layers in an 8 x 10-inch baking dish
About 8 ounces Parma ham, sliced very fine
Truffle oil (optional)
Butter

Make the béchamel sauce in the usual way: melt the butter in a pan, stir in the flour, and cook for a few minutes, then add the hot milk by degrees, stirring to thicken. Bring carefully to a boil, reduce the heat, and simmer for just a minute.

Season with nutmeg, salt, and pepper. Grate half the Parmesan and stir it into the béchamel. The finished sauce should be a thick pouring consistency; add a little more hot milk if necessary.

Prepare the rest of the ingredients: slice whole boletus into large but very thin slices. If you are using dried lasagne that requires precooking, cook it according to the instructions on the package. Scrape the rest of the Parmesan into shavings with a large knife or a potato peeler.

Pour a small amount of the béchamel over the bottom of an ovenproof dish. Put a layer of lasagne on top, followed by a layer of thinly sliced porcini, a layer of Parma ham, and a layer of Parmesan slivers. Season with a few drops of truffle oil, if using Then pour over a layer of béchamel and repeat the layers. You can make as many layers as you have ingredients or space for, but finish with a layer of sauce, some grated Parmesan, and a few tablespoons of butter. Bake for 20 to 30 minutes in a preheated 375°F oven, until nicely browned on top.

elderflower and gooseberry fool

serves 6

The heady, muscat scent of elderflowers combines beautifully with the sharp tang of the first early-summer gooseberries.

10 freshly picked heads of elderflower, plus a few sprigs to decorate
4 cups gooseberries
2 to 4 tablespoons superfine sugar
A strip of lemon zest
1¼ cups heavy cream

Gently shake any insects off the elderflowers. Place the gooseberries, elderflower heads, 2 tablespoons of sugar, lemon zest, and a splash of water in a pan and stir over a low heat until the sugar has dissolved. Bring to a gentle simmer and cook for 10 to 15 minutes, until the gooseberries are soft and mostly broken up. Rub the mixture through a sieve into a bowl, then taste and add more sugar if necessary.

Whip the cream to soft peaks and then fold into the gooseberry purée. Divide between large wine-glasses and chill for at least 2 hours. Serve with a little sprig of elderflower in each glass.

elderflower cordial

This cordial – lemony sharp yet highly aromatic – makes one of the most refreshing drinks known to man! If you don't use tartaric acid, the cordial will keep for several weeks in the fridge, but if you wish to keep it for much longer, you will need to add the acid and sterilize the bottles (see page 131) to make sure there are no yeasts or bacteria that could cause fermentation. This version should keep for a year.

20 to 30 freshly picked heads of elderflower
Zest of 2 lemons and 1 orange
Up to 3 pounds sugar
Up to ⅞ cup freshly squeezed lemon juice (3 to 5 lemons, depending on juiciness)
Tartaric acid (optional)

Shake any insects off the elderflowers, then place the flowers in a large bowl with the lemon and orange zest and pour over enough just-boiled water to cover them completely (6 to 8 cups). Cover and leave for at least 4 hours, or overnight, until cold.

Strain the liquid through cheesecloth, a clean cotton cloth, or a jelly bag, gently squeezing it to extract all the juice. Measure the amount of liquid and pour it into a saucepan. To every 2 cups liquid, add 1⅓ cups sugar, 3 tablespoons lemon juice, and a heaping teaspoon of tartaric acid if you are using it. Heat gently to dissolve the sugar, stirring occasionally. Bring to a gentle simmer and skim off any scum. Let the cordial cool, then strain once again through cheesecloth, cotton, or a jelly bag.

Pour the cordial through a funnel into clean bottles, filling them to within about ¾ to 1 inch of the top. Seal the bottles with screw tops or corks. (Alternatively, you can freeze it in small plastic containers.)

To serve, dilute to taste with ice cold water – at least 5 to 1 water to cordial.

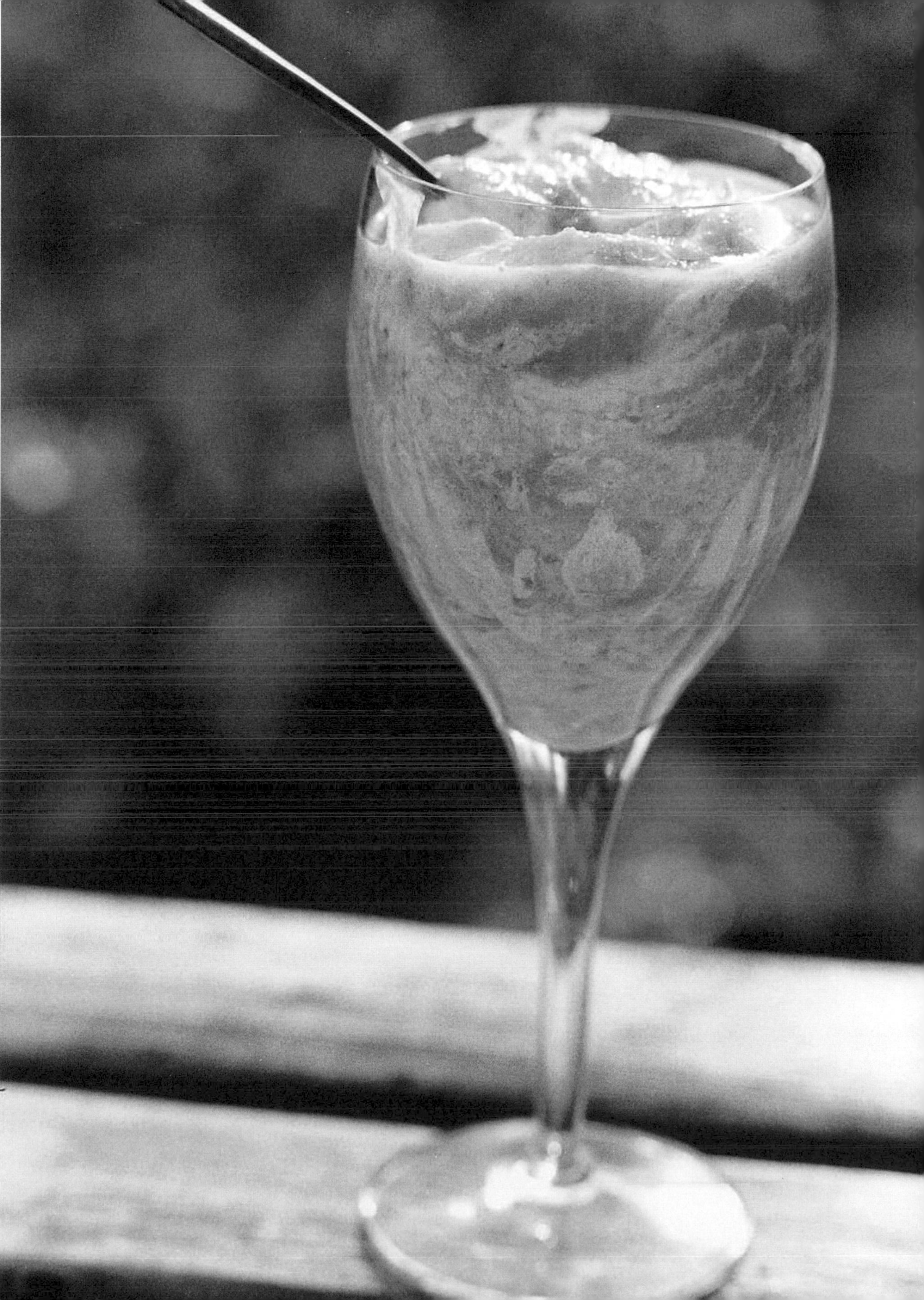

blackberry and apple crumble tart

serves 8

This is a winning combination of tart and crumble – a simple fruit tart with a light crumble topping. Blackberry and apple is a classic late-summer filling, but it can easily be adapted for all kinds of fruits – gooseberries or rhubarb are particularly good. The first time I ever made it was in Scotland, with wild blaeberries – a rare and delectable treat that would also work with wild huckleberries.

The precooking of the fruit filling is not essential, but it does make for a more compact tart with a more even fruit layer. I would always do it with large, lumpy fruits like rhubarb and plums.

4 cups blackberries, gently washed
1 pound Granny Smith apples, peeled, cored, and cut into small pieces
3 tablespoons superfine sugar
½ tablespoon lemon juice

FOR THE CRUMBLE
⅔ cup all-purpose flour
5 tablespoons unsalted butter
3 tablespoons light brown sugar
6 tablespoons ground hazelnuts (or almonds)

FOR THE SWEET SHORTCRUST PASTRY
1¼ cups all-purpose flour
7 tablespoons unsalted butter, diced
1½ tablespoons superfine sugar
1 egg yolk

First, make the pastry: sift the flour into a bowl and rub in the butter with your fingertips (or process it in a food processor), then stir in the sugar. Mix in the egg yolk and add just enough cold water to bring the mixture together into a dough. Wrap in waxed paper or foil and chill for at least 30 minutes.

Put the blackberries and apples in a pan with the sugar, lemon juice, and a tablespoon of water and place over low heat. Cook until the apple is completely soft and the juices have run from the blackberries. Strain off some of the juice (reserve this), so you have a thick, pulpy compote that is not too wet.

Roll out the pastry to ⅛ inch thick and use to line a 10-inch tart pan, then chill in the fridge for 30 minutes or in the freezer for 10 minutes. Line with parchment paper or foil, fill with dried beans or pie weights, and bake blind in a preheated 375°F oven for 15 to 20 minutes. Remove the paper and beans and return the pastry shell to the oven for a few more minutes, until firm and lightly colored.

To prepare the crumble, sift the flour into a bowl and rub in the butter, then mix in the sugar and ground hazelnuts or almonds.

Spread the fruit in the cooked pastry case and sprinkle over the crumble in an even layer. Bake in a preheated 375°F oven for about 30 minutes, until the crumble top is nicely browned. Serve the tart hot or cold, with the reserved juices as a sauce, and with custard or ice cream if you like.

sloe, bullace, or damson vodka

With the exception of the best (usually cultivated) damsons, which make excellent jam and a fine ice cream, these three fruits are usually far too tart or bitter to use in cooking, even with lots of added sugar. However, combined with alcohol and sugar they make a wonderful fruity liqueur. It could also be made in the States with beach plums. I prefer using vodka to gin as it is more neutral, and you therefore get the pure flavor of the fruit without the overriding taste of juniper that gin gives.

4 pounds sloes, bullaces, or damsons
8 cups sugar
3 bottles of cheap vodka

Prick each fruit several times with a pin, then transfer to a large glass container with a stopper or tight-fitting lid. Add the sugar and pour in the vodka. Seal and leave in a cool place away from direct sunlight. Every week or two, turn the jar upside down, then back again. After 6 months, strain the liquid through several layers of cheesecloth or a clean cotton cloth, then bottle and seal tightly. Leave for at least another 6 months. It will be even better after 2 years, if you have the patience.

rowan and/or crab apple (and other fruit) jellies

The wild fruit jellies I make most often are rowan or crab apple – or a combination of the two. Pure rowan berries give the jelly a distinctive woody flavor and a beautiful amber color, but it can be on the syrupy side. It will set firmer, and have a slightly tarter flavor, if combined in a 2-to-1 ratio with crab apples.

The same procedure can also be followed for rose hips and sloes, again adding half as many crab apples or cooking apples by weight if you want a jelly that sets well. Jellies made from crab apples only, or from blackberries and elderberries, need much less water (just enough to start the juices running), as they will give out plenty of liquid of their own. The basic principle of measuring the liquid and then adding the appropriate amount of sugar works for all wild fruit jellies.

At least 2 pounds rowan berries
Crab apples
Sugar

Remove the berries from their stems and wash well. Peel and coarsely chop the crab apples, but leave in the cores; they help keep the pectin level up, and any seeds or coarse fibers will be strained out anyway.

Place the fruit in a large, heavy pan with enough water almost to cover it. Bring to a boil and simmer, stirring occasionally and crushing the fruit with a spoon against the side of the pan, until the berries are very soft and pulpy. Strain through a cotton cloth or jelly bag. If you want a clear jelly, let it drip through, but if you want to maximize your returns, squeeze it through. Your jelly will cloud a little but will taste none the worse – although you won't win any prizes at the county fair.

Measure the juice, then transfer to a clean pan with 3 cups sugar for every 4 cups of juice. Stir over a low heat until the sugar has dissolved, then boil rapidly, skimming if necessary, until you reach the setting point for jelly. This can be measured at 221°F on a sugar thermometer or tested by dropping $1/2$ teaspoon of the mixture onto a cold plate. Wait for a few seconds, then give it a prod with your finger. If the jelly is ready, the top of the blob should crinkle, and if you separate the blob with the end of a spoon, the two halves should not run together.

As soon as setting point is reached, remove the pan from the heat and pour the jelly into hot sterilized jars (see page 131). Seal. Leave for a few weeks to mature before eating. The jelly should keep for up to a year.

blackberry/elderberry wine

This is one of the simplest and most successful country wines. Do not expect it to taste like Château Margaux, but enjoy it for its direct, distinctive fruity flavor. The sugar content of the fruit itself varies considerably, so no two batches will be quite the same. It can end up rather alcoholic and concentrated – in which case use it like cassis, for making delicious hedgerow kirs. For more on country wine making, see under Hedgerow in the Bibliography on page 440.

4 pounds blackberries or elderberries, or a combination of the two
8 cups superfine sugar
Juice and zest of 1 orange
Juice and zest of 1 lemon
1 package active dry yeast

Tidy up the fruit but do not wash it, then put it in a sterilized crock. Bring 8 cups of water to a boil, pour it over the fruit, and mash it up coarsely to help release the juice. Cover the crock and let stand at warm room temperature for a couple of days, stirring twice daily with a sterilized implement. Strain the liquid through a jelly bag or a clean cotton cloth.

Put $2^1/_2$ quarts of water in a pan. Add the sugar and heat gently until dissolved. Bring to boiling, then immediately remove from the heat. Add the orange and lemon juice and zest to the sugar syrup and let cool. Then add this flavored syrup to the fruit juice.

Mix the yeast with a little warm water and leave in a warm place until it starts fermenting. Add to the fruit mixture. All the ingredients for your wine are now blended, so pour the wine into a demijohn (fermentation jar) with an airlock. Leave at room temperature (65° to 70°F) until it stops fermenting. This may take 2 to 6 months. You can tell when it has stopped fermenting because there will be no more bubbles in the airlock. Then "rack off" the wine into another demijohn. *Racking off* means siphoning carefully so as to leave behind any sediment in the bottom of the first demijohn.

Let mature for at least 6 months, then rack again, this time into bottles, and seal. This wine usually keeps well, and benefits from being aged for several years.

notes to the U.S. edition

In editing this book for an American audience, we sought to do two things: (1) to make it as much a treasure trove of information, inspiration, and solid cooking guidance for Americans as it is for its original British audience; and (2) to retain Hugh Fearnley-Whittingstall's engaging style and amiable yet impassioned arguments about the proper ways to choose, prepare, and store food grown in the garden, butchered from prize animals, or foraged or caught locally, as well as his opinions on supporting the environment, vibrant local economies, and resourceful use of plants and animals.

To that end, the recipes and cooking instructions, as well as the information about cuts of meat and their storage and preparation, have been Americanized, so that the ingredients, terminology, and measurements are familiar to U.S. readers. The first sections of each chapter, which contain many of Fearnley-Whittingstall's observations and conclusions about how the provenance and production of our food affects animals, humans, and our environment, translate to the U.S., so they remain as they were written. However, sometimes important specifics differ, such as how the word organic is applied in the U.S. as opposed to the U.K. We've made our best attempt to address these particulars. Any errors or omissions are that of the American publisher, Ten Speed Press.

1. [26] In the U.S., cities, counties, and states establish the rules for official farmers' markets in their jurisdiction, and these rules may or may not address who can do the selling or whether the produce or meat being sold must be produced by the seller. For a directory of U.S. farmers' markets, check the Agricultural Marketing Service (AMS) website at www.ams.usda.gov. States, counties, and cities also often have searchable listings for farmers' markets and farm stands. Two other websites, www.eatwild.com and www.localharvest.com, provide detailed information on pasture-raised animals and where to buy meat, eggs, and dairy, and more farmers' markets listings. Some nonprofits and producers' associations also have member listings (see note 8).

2. [136] To prevent the possible spread of BSE, at this writing, the USDA prohibits the introduction of the "skull, brain, trigeminal ganglia, eyes, vertebral column, spinal cord and dorsal root ganglia of cattle over 30 months of age and the small intestine of cattle of all ages" into the human food supply.

3. [137] According to a 2006 study, over 90 percent of U.S. shoppers purchase their meats at supermarkets, supercenters, or warehouse clubs. The same (industry-sponsored) study identified consumers' top reasons for selecting meats (in descending order): price, product appearance, nutrition, package size, convenience, and time available for preparation. Other studies have shown that the majority of Americans also want their meat animals to be humanely treated.

4. [140] The organic label in the U.S. doesn't guarantee an animal was raised extensively or treated humanely. It only means the animal ate organic food and didn't receive antibiotics, growth promotants, or animal by-products in its feed (see note 8). Nor do the terms natural and free-range ensure "good pork from a high welfare system." Aside from personal contact with a producer or butcher who can and will answer all your questions about a pig's life and death, your best bet is one of the comprehensive private or nonprofit assurance schemes (see notes 7 and 16).

Since heritage breeds do better when raised extensively, buying Berkshire, Red Wattle, Yorkshire, Tamworth, Large Black, and other heritage pork is another way to put humanely raised, good-tasting pork on your table. Heritage Foods USA, the marketing arm of Slow Food USA, keeps a list of members who raise heritage pork according to strict standards. Also check www.localharvest.org and ww.eatwild.com for heritage producers.

5. [173] The situation in the U.S. regarding dairy-cross beef is similar to that in the U.K, with the majority of meat sold probably originating with dairy-cross calves that have been finished for market with the help of hormones, antibiotics, and intensive feeding and with little or no regard for the animals' welfare.

6. [173] Mandatory country of origin labeling for beef, lamb, and pork (among other agricultural commodities) was passed into law in the U.S. Farm Bill of 2002. Implementation has been delayed twice. At this writing, the labeling for red meats will go into effect in September 2008.

7. [173] In the U.S., meat, especially beef, marked with an establishment's premium label, is increasingly available at supermarket and supercenter chains like Safeway, Food Lion, and Super-Target. The promise of premium beef is usually based on a trio of claims: it comes from a certain breed (typically Angus), it's aged, and certain quality-control systems are in place to ensure tenderness and good marbling. The labels make no pledges about animal welfare. Other supermarket chains are beginning to market the products of certain producers who raise beef extensively. At this writing, Whole Foods, which already has a set of production and welfare standards for any meat products it sells (e.g., no antibiotics, no animal by-products in feed, annual inspection by Whole Foods of each producer's operation), is developing a more comprehensive Animal Compassionate label with some specific welfare standards for the production of chickens, beef cattle, ducks, pigs, and sheep.

8. [174] Meat labelling in the U.S. is fraught with problems. Organic certification for foods sold in the U.S. is handled by no fewer than 95 domestic and foreign agencies, all accredited by the USDA. All of these agencies comply with USDA-formulated standards for production and processing – and some go above and beyond the national standards. Unfortunately, there is no agency with standards comparable to those of the U.K. Soil Association. USDA standards do speak to the provenance of animals and what they are fed (100 percent organically produced feed) and prohibit the use of hormones or antibiotics (vaccines are permitted). Organically raised animals sold in the U.S. also must have access to the outdoors, which could be, and often is, a small area. The national standards don't concern themselves explicitly with housing densities, environmental considerations, or provisions for animals to exercise normal behavior patterns.

A proliferation of labels is beginning to show up on meat packages in the U.S., many of which seem to promise some higher measure of quality, safety, or wholesomeness. Here's what the USDA-approved labels mean:

- Free range/free roaming: The animal has been allowed access to the outside.
- Fresh: The meat's internal temperature has never gone below 26°F.
- Grain fed/corn fed: The animal has been fed a grain-based diet that may also contain other ingredients and supplements. Industrially raised animals are typically fed a grain-based diet, because it's highly caloric and helps them get to market weight quickly.
- Halal: Prepared according to Islamic law and under Islamic authority.
- Kosher: Prepared under rabbinical supervision.
- Natural: Produced with no artificial colors or artificial ingredients and/or minimally processed.
- No hormones/antibiotics/animal by-products: The animal was raised without being fed or injected with any of these substances. (Hormones are not allowed at all in the raising of pigs and poultry, so the hormone-free label on pork and poultry is redundant.)

The following are the main features of USDA-approved organically raised meat:

1. All feeds are 100 percent organically produced. (Certain vitamin and mineral supplements are allowed.) Refeeding with animal parts or manure is not permitted, nor are feeds containing plastic pellets or urea.
2. No hormones, antibiotics, or growth promoters are allowed. If an animal becomes sick and is treated with an antibiotic, the meat from that animal may not carry the term organic on its label. Vaccines are allowed.
3. Meat animals must be raised under organic management from birth or from the second day of life for poultry.
4. Animals must have access to the outdoors; ruminants must have access to pasture.
5. Temporary confinement is permitted for reasons of health, safety, to protect soil or water quality, or because it's appropriate to the animal's stage of production.
6. There is a complete audit trail documenting the animal's path from birth through slaughter, processing, and distribution.

At this writing, the USDA is working on a set of labeling standards for grass-fed animals.

The USDA's system of labeling and standards stops short of addressing many aspects of husbandry that conscientious producers and consumers care about. A number of nonprofit agencies and industry associations have stepped into the breach, establishing labels that signify standards the USDA does not address fully or address at all, such as humane treatment of animals, pest management, and manure management. Among these institutions are Humane Farm Animal Care (see note 16), the American Humane Association (see note 16), the Food Alliance, the Animal Welfare Institute, the Wild Farm Alliance, the Husbandry Institute, and the American Grassfed Association. Some retailers, including Whole Foods (see note 7) and Niman Ranch, have also developed standards that exceed those of the government.

9. [174] Free-range or pink veal, mostly raised by small producers, is beginning to gain market share in the U.S. It faces some resistance from the larger veal industry, which feels this product shouldn't be called veal at all. Two websites, www.eatwild.com and www.localharvest.org, will lead you to producers in your area.

10. [175] Defra is the British Department of Environment, Farming, and Rural Affairs, and its mandate is roughly analogous to that of the USDA and EPA combined. The USDA has no welfare recommendations or rules that are equivalent to the Five Freedoms, however. (See note 8 for an explanation of USDA-approved labels for meats.)

11. [181] Small producers in the U.S. are faced with a constantly dwindling number of slaughterhouses available to them. Smaller plants are disappearing in the face of the growth of large-scale corporate slaughterhouses unwilling to deal with anyone except big clients. This has meant that many small producers must drive long distances, often across state lines, to a slaughterhouse that will handle their herds.

12. [189] Per capita lamb consumption in the U.S. is so low (about 1 pound per person per year) that the domestic lamb and mutton industry is a small one: 7 or 8 million animals are farmed for meat per year, down from a peak of 56 million in the mid-1940s. But immigration from Latin American, Middle Eastern, and European countries where lamb is popular has stimulated demand, so that the U.S. now imports almost as much lamb and mutton from Australia and New Zealand as it produces. Intensive farming is the norm in the U.S., with over 95 percent of the lambs marketed raised in large feedlots.

13. [190] Technically, baby lamb is slaughtered at about 8 weeks, spring lamb at about 5 months, and regular lamb at under 1 year. Most of the lamb sold in the U.S. falls into the latter category. Organic and free-range lamb can be ordered from small producers who market directly to the public. Look for them on www.localharvest.org and www.eatwild.com and at local farmers' markets.

14. [190] Mutton is much more difficult to find than lamb. (Most U.S. mutton is exported to Mexico.) A careful search of the websites will yield a few sources.

15. [210] Egg shoppers in the U.S. are faced with a dizzying array of labels and an equally dizzying lack of standards. Among the labels is "free-range," though the USDA has no guidelines for the category. Nor do government or industry sources closely track the percentage of the market held by the various labels, among which are also "cage-free," "vegetarian-fed," "organic," and others (see the www.ushs.org, for a guide to the most commonly encountered labels). However, some sources estimate that cage-free eggs total 2 to 5 percent of the national market and up to 10 percent of the California market. The USDA has reported that organic eggs made up only about 1 percent of the market in 2004, with an estimated average annual growth rate of 8 to 13 percent for the remainder of the decade.

16. [210] Humane Farm Animal Care, a nonprofit organization, has developed a Certified Humane Raised and Handled sticker for use in U.S. stores. It parallels the Red Tractor logo and the RSPCA Freedom Food label, on which it was partially based. The American Humane Association (AHA) has put together the Free Farmed Certification Program, which also closely echoes the rules set down by the RSPCA, and its label can be found on qualifying products. Many higher-end and specialty grocers carry the certified meats of these organizations.

17. [210] Again, the organic label in the U.S. doesn't guarantee an animal was raised extensively or treated humanely. It only means the animal ate organic food and didn't receive antibiotics, growth promotants, or animal by-products in its feed (see note 8).

18. [211] An organic chicken will eat better-quality, additive-free food and will have fewer shots than its conventionally raised cousin, but it is still likely to live out a short, beakless life in a barn with forty thousand similarly raised birds. (See note 8 for the more limited scope of the organic label in the U.S.) Nonetheless, a label bearing the term organic is, as always, a good start. But other, better indications that a bird has been extensively raised and/or might be tastier than a supermarket chicken exist, including:

- It's a heritage breed, such as a Dark Cornish or Barred Plymouth Rock.
- It's labeled "grass fed" or "pastured," and you can ascertain that the claim has merit. In other words, you find out from your butcher, or the farmer if buying directly, that the chicken actually spent much of its time outdoors eating grass and bugs, rather than being allowed only theoretical "access" to the outdoors.
- It bears a label, such as "Free Farmed" or "Certified Humane," that signifies a more rigorous set of welfare and husbandry standards than those outlined in the USDA's organic, free range, and natural programs.
- You (or your butcher) buy your birds direct from a farmer who can tell you all about how the bird was raised and slaughtered.

19. [211] The U.S. broiler industry dwarfs that of the U.K., raising nearly 9 billion birds per year and slaughtering about 1 million every hour. Almost all of these birds are raised intensively, in vertically integrated farming systems owned or controlled by a handful of giant agri-business companies like Tyson and ConAgra. The farmers who raise the birds are typically under contract to one of these huge processors, and the pressure on them to cram as many birds as possible through the system is enormous.

20. [289] In the U.S., shellfish harvesting is regulated at the state level, with each state's agency reporting to the U.S. Fish and Wildlife service. Visit www.fws.gov/offices/statelinks.html for a list of state agencies.

21. [359] Hunting in the U.S. has a different social and political history than it does in the U.K., and it is regulated on the state, rather than federal, level, making generalizations difficult. An important difference is that certain game birds, such as pheasants and partridge, are typically (intensively) farmed for release for managed hunts (or for selling directly to game-meat wholesalers). Some states, such as Montana and Idaho, also permit game farming of large mammals, such as deer and elk, while others, including California and Wyoming, do not. However, the hunting of wild animals, from waterfowl to caribou, is a popular sport across the socioeconomic spectrum. Indeed, hunting still functions to feed hunters and their families in the U.S., rather than merely serving as a trophy-bagging diversion for the elite (though it certainly can be that, too).

22. [360] About 37 million quail are farmed annually in the U.S., most of them intensively, for sale to restaurants, specialty meat markets, and game preserves. D'Artagnan, a large mail-order operation based in New Jersey, sells organic quails, but free-range farmed quail are difficult to find. Check with your local farmers' market or CSA.

23. [363] Game, both wild and farmed, is available to the non-hunting U.S. consumer through well-stocked butcher shops, specialty meat stores, or online from sources like Broken Arrow Ranch in Texas or Nicky's in Oregon. The distinction between wild and farmed can be murky, however: venison and elk and game birds like pheasant, partridge, mallard duck, quail, and wild turkey are widely farmed and "field harvested" (shot in the field rather than slaughtered), then marketed as wild or free range. Larger mammals are raised fairly extensively throughout their lives. Birds, in contrast, may well spend a substantial part of their lives indoors in intensive conditions.

24. [371] In the U.S., the term venison can be used for the meat from deer, elk, moose, and similar large animals. Sellers must label their meat with its source. Again, hunting regulations in the U.S. vary from state to state (see note 21).

25. [373] Domesticated young pigeons are marketed as squab in the U.S. The birds are slaughtered at about four weeks old and have never flown, which yields particularly tender meat.

bibliography

Cooking the Books, "The Glen," St Brides Netherwent, Caldicot NP26 3AT; tel/fax: 01633 400150; e-mail: cooking_the_books@msn.com

An invaluable source of used and antiquarian cookbooks, Cooking the Books may be able to help you track down out-of-print titles.

food/sourcing ingredients

The Authentic Food Finder, The Write Angle Press, 1998.

Blythman, Joanna. *The Food Our Children Eat*. Fourth Estate, 1999.

———. *The Food We Eat*. Michael Joseph, 1996.

Brown, Lynda. *The Shopper's Guide to Organic Food*. Fourth Estate, 1998.

Davidson, Alan. *The Oxford Companion to Food*. Oxford University Press, 1999.

Eyton, Audrey. *The Kind Food Guide*. Penguin Books, 1991 out of print.

Henrietta Green's Food Lovers' Guide to Britain. BBC Books, 1995 out of print.

West Dorset Food Links Local Food Directory (free brochure giving information on local farmers, food processors, and small retailers; for similar publications in your area, inquire at your local reference library)

gardening

Baker, Harry/The Royal Horticultural Society. *Growing Fruit*. Mitchell Beazley, 1999.

Baker, Harry. *The Vegetable Garden Displayed*. Cassell, 1989.

Culpepper, Nicholas. *Culpeper's Complete Herbal*. Wordsworth Editions, 1995.

Don, Monty and Sarah. *Fork to Fork*. Conran Octopus, 1999.

Fearnley-Whittingstall, Jane. *Gardening Made Easy*. Phoenix Press, 1997.

Hessayon, D.G. *The Fruit Expert*. Expert Books, 1990.

Larkcom, Joy. *The Fruit Garden Displayed*. Batsford, 1998.

Morgan, Joan and Alison Richards. *The Book of Apples*. Ebury Press, 1993.

Salt, Bernard. *Gardening Under Plastic*. Batsford, 1998.

farming/livestock

Case, Andy. *Starting with Pigs*. Broad Leys Publishing Company, 2000.

Castell, Mary. *Starting with Sheep*. Broad Leys Publishing Company, 1999.

Heiney, Paul. *Home Farm: A Practical Guide to the Good Life*. Dorling Kindersley, 1998.

Hunt, J. Small-scale Sheepkeeping. Faber & Faber, 1997.

Lampkin, Nicolas. *Organic Farming*. Farming Press, 1990.

Lyon, Russell. *Pig Rearing and Health*. Smallholder Publications Ltd, 1991.

Newton, Jon. *Organic Grassland*. Chalcombe Publications, 1993.

Seymour, John. *The Complete Book of Self-Sufficiency*. Dorling Kindersley, 1996.

Straiton, Eddie. *Calving the Cow and Care of the Calf*. Farming Press, 1994.

Thear, Katie. *Starting with Chickens*. Broad Leys Publishing Company, 1999.

Upton, Jane and Dennis Soden. *An Introduction to Keeping Sheep*. Farming Press, 1996.

hedgerow

Berry, Cyril. *First Steps in Winemaking*. Nexus, 1996.

Drapeau, Pierre. *Encyclopaedia of Country Winemaking*. Nexus, 1999.

Gillmor, Robert, et al. *How to Identify Edible Mushrooms*. HarperCollins, 1996.

Mabey, Richard. *Food for Free*. HarperCollins, 1983.

Phillips, Roger. *Mushrooms and Other Fungi of Great Britain and Europe*. Pan Books, 1981.

———. *Wild Food*. Pan Books, 1983.

Spooner, Brian. *Mushrooms and Toadstools of Britain and Europe*. HarperCollins, 1996.

cooking

Bareham, Lindsey. *The Big Red Book of Tomatoes*. Penguin Books, 2000.

———. *A Celebration of Soup*. Michael Joseph, 1993.

Carluccio, Antonio. *A Passion for Mushrooms*. Pavilion Books, 1990.

Coates, Prue. *The Poacher's Cookbook*. White Lion, 1993.

David, Elizabeth. French *Provincial Cooking*. Michael Joseph, 1960.

Davidson, Alan. *Mediterranean Seafood*. Penguin Books, 1972.

———. *North Atlantic Seafood*. Penguin Books, 1979.

Fearnley-Whittingstall, Hugh. *A Cook on the Wild Side*. Boxtree, 1997.

———. *Cuisine Bon Marché*. Macmillan, 1994.

The Good Cook Series (Pork and Offal). TimeLife Books, 1980.

Good Housekeeping Complete Book of Preserving. Ebury Press, 1991.

Grigson, Jane. *Charcuterie and French Pork Cookery*. Michael Joseph, 1967.

———. *The Constance Spry Cookery Book*. J. M. Dent & Sons Ltd, 1956.

———. *Jane Grigson's Fruit Book*. Michael Joseph, 1982.

———. *Jane Grigson's Vegetable Book*. Michael Joseph, 1978.

———. *The Mushroom Feast*. Michael Joseph, 1975.

Henderson, Fergus. *Nose to Tail Eating*. Macmillan, 1999.

Larousse Gastronomique. Hamlyn, 1988.

McFadden, Christine, and Michael Michaud. *Cool Green Leaves and Red Hot Peppers*. Frances Lincoln, 1998.

McGee, Harold. *On Food and Cooking: The Science and Lore of the Kitchen*. HarperCollins, 1991.

Mrs Beeton's Book of Household Management. Ed. Nicola Humble, Oxford University Press, 2000.

Schwartz, Oded. *Preserving*. Dorling Kindersley, 1996.

Stein, Rick. *English Seafood Cookery*. Penguin Books, 1988.

———. *Rick Stein's Taste of the Sea*. BBC Books, 1995.

Style, Sue. *Fruits of the Forest*. Pavilion Books, 1997.

index

E

F

G

H